ISBN: 9781314551280

Published by:
HardPress Publishing
8345 NW 66TH ST #2561
MIAMI FL 33166-2626

Email: info@hardpress.net
Web: http://www.hardpress.net

HISTORY

OF THE

UNITED STATES

SANITARY COMMISSION

BEING

THE GENERAL REPORT OF ITS WORK DURING
THE WAR OF THE REBELLION.

BY

CHARLES J. STILLÉ.

PHILADELPHIA
J. B. LIPPINCOTT & CO.
1866.

E 631
.58

PREFACE.

THE Sanitary Commission at its session in July, 1865, adopted the following resolution:

"*Resolved,* That the Standing Committee be instructed to employ such literary and clerical assistance as it may deem necessary in preparing a final History of the United States Sanitary Commission, at any expense which may be required in order to make a useful and dignified record of the work which the American people have done through its Agency."

In pursuance of this resolution the Standing Committee decided, after careful deliberation, that the report of the Commission's work during the war should be presented to the public in three distinct parts, as follows:

First: A General History of the Commission's origin, purposes, and methods of operation.

Second: A Narrative of its Special Relief service.

Third: An Account of the organization and practical working of its Supply System.

I was assigned by the Committee to the task of preparing the General History, and the present volume is the result of my labors. It is now published by the Commission as the official Report of its operations during the war. With the view of rendering this final record complete and accurate, the Archives of the Commission, and those of nearly all its Branches, com-

5001

prising many thousand documents have been placed at my disposal, and much time and labor have been expended in examining, and classifying for historical purposes, the material contained in them. The principal difficulty has been so to employ the riches found in this great storehouse as to illustrate fully the subject, without encumbering its discussion with details which would prove wearisome to the general reader.

I have been kindly assisted in my work by several of my friends and colleagues, whose position as officers of the Commission rendered them specially qualified to treat of certain important portions of its history. Thus the chapter on " CONTRIBUTIONS FROM CALIFORNIA AND THE PACIFIC COAST" in this volume has been prepared by Rev. Dr. Bellows, President of the Commission; that on its " FINANCIAL SYSTEM AND HISTORY," by Mr. George T. Strong, its Treasurer; and that on the operations of its " BUREAU OF VITAL STATISTICS," by Dr. B. A. Gould, its Actuary.

The object of the Commission in publishing an official Report of its work is two-fold. It feels that the share of those who contributed in any way to sustain it should be commemorated by a lasting memorial, and it is moved by an imperative sense of its duty to posterity, to place on record for its example and guidance an account of the practical working of the most successful method of mitigating the horrors of war known in history. With this design, and in this spirit, this volume has been prepared. It has been found impossible in a general history such as this, to do that full justice to individuals which gratitude, and a sense of the value of their services, would dictate. In the other volumes, now in course of preparation, and which are confined to the exploration of a limited and special field, this omission will in some measure be supplied.

But the Commission feels, that while an expression of its grateful appreciation of the services and self-sacrificing efforts of its Constituents should not be withheld in any history of its work, the story it has to tell has a far deeper import and significance. If it can succeed by presenting a faithful record of its experience, in showing how grand a work of beneficence was done by the American people for their Armies through its agency,—if it can impress upon the minds of those who may read its Report a belief in the truth of its theory, and the practical success of its methods,—if it can teach those who come after us, when the misfortune of war befalls them, as it has done us, how much may be done to relieve its misery by a wise system of organized voluntary effort,—if it can explain even imperfectly, how a voluntary system can work efficiently in harmony with Government agencies,—if, in fine, it can make clear how much there is in the necessary relations between such a system and the Government, to strengthen and encourage the action of popular sympathy, as well as to embarrass and weaken its efforts, then, the principal objects which the Commission has in view in publishing this record will be accomplished.

The Commission is perfectly aware that in presenting a history of events of such recent occurrence, in which it has been necessary to speak of the acts of many persons still living, it has undertaken a task both difficult and perilous. While it has avoided in its Report the discussion of questions the importance of which ceased with the war, it has not hesitated to criticise with the utmost freedom the policy and measures of the Government, where they seemed radically defective in providing for the care and comfort of the sick and suffering of the Army. This has been done in no spirit of mere fault-finding, but with the higher object of teaching future generations to avoid the errors of the present. He who, at the termination of a successful war, bestows indiscriminate eulogy on all the measures adopted by the Government for its prosecution, is not the best friend of his country, but rather he, who, having clearly seen its short-comings, does not hesitate to expose the evils which have flowed from them, and raises a voice of warning against their recurrence.

C. J. S.

PHILADELPHIA, *June*, 1866.

CONTENTS.

CHAPTER I.

THE NATURE AND OBJECT OF ARMY RELIEF.

CHAPTER II.

DEVELOPMENT OF THE THEORY OF A PREVENTIVE SERVICE.

CONTENTS.

CHAPTER III.

ORGANIZATION OF THE UNITED STATES SANITARY COMMISSION.

CHAPTER IV.

INSPECTION OF CAMPS AND HOSPITALS.

CHAPTER V.

RE-ORGANIZATION OF THE MEDICAL BUREAU AND APPOINTMENT OF A NEW SURGEON-GENERAL.

B

CHAPTER VI.

HOSPITAL TRANSPORT SERVICE IN THE WEST AND IN THE PENINSULAR CAMPAIGN. HOSPITAL CARS.

CHAPTER VII.

SUPPLEMENTAL HOSPITAL SUPPLIES.

CHAPTER VIII.

CONTRIBUTIONS FROM CALIFORNIA AND THE PACIFIC COAST.

CHAPTER XII.

CHATTANOOGA.

CHAPTER XIII.

FREDERICKSBURG—GETTYSBURG—THE WILDERNESS.

CHAPTER XIV.

MORRIS ISLAND—OLUSTEE—NEWBERNE.

CHAPTER XV.

DEPARTMENT OF THE GULF.

CHAPTER XVI.

SPECIAL INSPECTION OF HOSPITALS.

CHAPTER XVII.

THE COMMISSION'S BUREAU OF VITAL STATISTICS.

CHAPTER XVIII.

FINANCIAL HISTORY OF THE COMMISSION.

C ,

CHAPTER XIX.

INTERNAL ORGANIZATION—RELATIONS WITH THE GOVERNMENT.

THE UNITED STATES

SANITARY COMMISSION.

CHAPTER I.

THE NATURE AND OBJECT OF ARMY RELIEF.

THE History of the great Rebellion, probably to a greater extent than that of any war, is fruitful in lessons which concern man as a citizen of a state founded upon the ideas of modern *The Office and Teachings of History.* civilization. The highest office of all history, as is now universally recognized, is instruction, in order that from its teachings future generations may learn to avoid the errors of the past. When written with this intention, it has comparatively little to do with the details of mere military operations, or the intrigues of courts or cabinets, or even with the heroic achievements which have shed lustre on the national character. These are topics which have engaged almost wholly the attention of those who have related the story of former wars; and certainly there is enough in the annals of the war which subdued the Rebellion, when fittingly told, to serve the great purpose of keeping alive the national gratitude and per-

3

petuating the national glory.   Still it is impossible to
gain a complete and harmonious view of the lessons
taught by the war, unless we embrace in it all the
great agencies, many of them wholly novel in history,
which combined to bring it to a successful termination.

The American war was a popular one in the widest
sense, not only a war the prosecution of which was
Characteristics maintained by unprecedented popular en-
of the Late War. thusiasm, but a war the origin, progress, and
methods of which were all peculiar in this, that they
were modified and controlled by the great popular
ideas which lie at the basis of American civilization.
If we wish, then, to gain any true view of the principles involved in the struggle, and to understand
fully the novel and striking lessons which it developed,
it is essential to study the nature of these popular
ideas and their influence upon the modes adopted by
the government in prosecuting the war.   The power
of the public opinion of a free people in controlling
the military policy of a country has been remarked in
other nations and in former wars.   Never has there
been an instance in History such as that presented
in this country during the late war, in which everything which was accomplished, good or bad, was due
to the impulse of popular ideas.

Thus its history presents far more than that
of any other war a true picture of the civilization of
The popular ele- the people who conducted it.   It is not
ment in the war. merely to the indirect influence of this popular element upon the policy of the government, powerful as it was, that the student of our recent history
must direct his attention, but also to those organiza-

tions of popular enthusiasm, sympathy and benevolence wholly outside of the government, but all undertaken to strengthen its hands, without whose potent influence manifested in a thousand ways, the result of the war might have been disastrous. It would be indeed a matter of curious and interesting speculation to inquire how long and how effectively the government could have carried on the war without the aid of this organized popular sympathy. It is proposed in the following pages to give the history of one of these extra-governmental organizations, and to claim for it whatever may be due to the intelligence, humanity and patriotism of the American people acting through its agency with the design of promoting the health, comfort and efficiency of the vast armies called into the field to subdue the rebellion.

The very first popular impulse which succeeded the grand burst of enthusiasm by which seventy-five thousand citizens were suddenly transformed at *Organization of popular benevolence.* the call of their country into soldiers, was directed to some rude and imperfect means of ministering to them such aid and comfort as was suggested by the anxious and tender solicitude of their friends, rather than by considerations of the necessities of a military organization. This impulse was as earnest, and as spontaneous, and as general, on the part of those who staid at home, as that which rallied round the flag of the country the very flower of its youth. Throughout the length and breadth of the land, men who were unable to bear arms, and women, true sisters of mercy, whose record of deeds of charity in this war forms perhaps the brightest chapter in its whole history, were inspired with a zeal and enthusiasm in behalf of those who went forth in their stead, which in its depth and earnestness, and at last, as experience was gained, in its practical efficiency, was wholly unparalleled in the annals of other nations. In other countries and in former wars, particularly in grand revolutionary uprisings, which have stirred the popular heart from its lowest depths, evidence is not wanting to prove the existence of a spirit of lofty sacrifice for the welfare of those who defended the cause with their lives. In most cases, however, this enthusiasm was not of long duration, and produced but a feeble impression upon the general progress of the war ; in all it lacked that peculiar element of organization so characteristic of our American system, which, when guided and directed by zealous patriotism, and practical good sense and benevolent feeling, has made the history of this war quite as remarkable in those aspects which concern the progress of humanity, as in the many lessons which it teaches of the successful determination of a free people to maintain its nationality.

There were many reasons aside from zeal for the cause in which they were engaged, both in the character Nature of the of the volunteers raised immediately after sympathy felt for the volun- the fall of Sumter, and the circumstances by teers. which they had been suddenly transformed into soldiers, which made them from the beginning peculiarly the objects of tender popular care and solicitude. The *nuclei* of all the first regiments raised were the militia or volunteer companies existing in the various towns and cities throughout the country.

These companies represented all the available military organization of the country at that time outside of the regular army, and although they were composed wholly of young men of character, intelligence and courage, such as had never before made up the rank and file of any army, they were on many accounts those likely to suffer most seriously from the fatigues and privations of a soldier's life.   Most of them had had no experience whatever of campaigning, and their knowledge of a soldier's duties was confined to the requirements of a holiday parade.   Being generally residents in populous towns or cities, their habits were those acquired by the indoor-life of students, artizans, and tradesmen of different sorts.   Their officers were as ignorant as they, selected as they had been for their position in organizations which had existed before the war by their comrades rather on the score of good fellowship, than because they were supposed to possess any military qualification whatever for actual service.   In short, for any real efficiency, the military organization as it existed before the war, or as it was hastily improvised by regiments raised in a few days immediately afterward, and then hurried on to the "front," was almost valueless.

To the calm observer who knew anything of history, the view of this mass of enthusiastic and undisciplined men, calling themselves soldiers suggested some sad forebodings.   It constituted a precious element of the vital force of the population, and was composed precisely of that class of men who from their previous habits and modes of life were not only least likely to bear well exposure and priva-

Peculiar dangers to which new troops are exposed.

tion, but also certain to become victims of diseases which have always proved the scourge of armies. Nothing but the unreflecting enthusiasm which was then the characteristic of the popular mind, or utter ignorance of the perils which encompass the soldier in the hospital or the camp, and which exceed ten-fold those of the battle-field, can explain the recklessness with which our best and bravest young men were then hurried into active service.

The two great difficulties which threatened to make our military operations unsuccessful, were the ignorance Ignorance and of the officers in regard to the most elemen-inexperience of their officers. tary duties of their position, the absence, consequently, of all real military organization and discipline, and the self-reliant, independent habits of the private soldiers, who, willing and anxious to be instructed in their new duties, were not inclined to show much deference to mere official rank unsupported by a corresponding knowledge of the duties devolving on him who held it. Both of these difficulties were traceable to one source—inexperience. Other nations, upon sudden emergencies, have been compelled to form an army in the face of the enemy, but they have had at least the skeleton of a military organization in long-tried officers, well versed in the details of the service. We were forced to try the novel experiment of improvising the most artificial and complicated of human organizations—an effective and disciplined army, under what had been hitherto esteemed insurmountable obstacles. It is not to be wondered at that those who judged the American people by foreign precedents felt their hearts sink within them at the prospect. How this apparently impossible task was finally and successfully accomplished, with what fearful waste of life and energy, and at what cost and sacrifice, the American armies became at last thoroughly trained and perfectly efficient bodies, capable of the highest military achievements, how in certain departments, such as the Quartermaster's and Commissariat bureaus, a success was gained beyond that recorded of any similar service in military history, it is not our province to dwell upon. We are concerned now with the dangers which threatened to impair the health, and therefore to destroy the efficiency of the soldier, dangers all the more serious because neither the public, who looked on with so much delighted enthusiasm as regiment after regiment was equipped and sent to the seat of war, nor the officers, who were entrusted with the responsibility of their precious lives, seemed to have any adequate conception of the absolute necessity of preventive measures to maintain this buoyant energy of our young men ever fresh and active. Indeed it seemed as if the whole affair was in the eyes of the multitude the gorgeous pageant of a summer's holiday, and the object in view one to be accomplished by a pleasant excursion of sixty or ninety days,—absurd self-conceit shivered into atoms by the first actual shock of real war.

In the early history of the war the troops were raised by companies under authority of the Governor of each state, and were not transferred to the military authorities of the United States until a sufficient number of companies were gathered together to form a regiment. In the interval between

Characteristics of the first volunteers.

their enlistment, and their transfer to the General
Government, the men·were collected in camps within
the state, under its authority and became the recipients of its peculiar care.   Each State had a
Hospital Department, the main business of which was
the selection of regimental surgeons, but which incidentally concerned itself about the health of the soldiers while at recruiting depots within the State.   As
was to be expected, the degree of care bestowed upon
the troops by these State Hospital Departments varied
in almost every State.   In some, an attempt was made
to enforce a proper sanitary police, in others, almost
every article which could be needed by the Surgeon in
the performance of his duties was liberally supplied
by the State authorities, while in most, in consequence
of the short period which elapsed between the time of
recruiting and that of the transfer of the regiment to
the General Government, those precautions which
were essential to the health of the soldier, and which,
to be really available, should have been taken as soon
as he began his military life, were almost wholly
neglected.   In one important State, where, in addition to the constant concentration in camps of men
enlisted for the general service, a reserve force of
fifteen thousand men was raised by the authority of
the State for its own defense, which was to be retained
within its own borders, no provision whatever was made
in the law creating this force, that the Hospital Department should control in any way measures tending to
the sanitary condition of the troops, the character
of their clothing, the location of camps, or the erection
of quarters.   The condition of things in this respect

in Pennsylvania had its parallel in nearly every State. A loose impression prevailed that volunteers should not be controlled by the ordinary methods of military discipline. No regular, normal, steady sanitary system was practicable, where in some respects it was most needed. Gross neglect prevailed, therefore, in the recruiting camps, partly owing to a total ignorance of sanitary laws, partly to the feebleness and defectiveness of the military organization, and partly to the incompetency of the officers, without whose intelligent and zealous co-operation nothing could be done.

Thus the obstacles in the way of raising for an emergency a tolerably efficient army, formidable as they are to all governments, became ten-fold more so to the Government of the United States, which was forced in the hour of the greatest peril to adopt and make useful such rude military organizations as the different states chose to send them,—organizations differing in some respects, but all alike in this, that a large portion of the troops, owing to imperfect inspection, were unfit for any military duty whatever, and that their officers, and especially the staff-officers, were almost universally without any knowledge of their new duties.

While many watched with anxiety the utter neglect of every lesson taught by experience or common sense in the formation of that army on whose efficiency the national life depended, and were General neglect of precautionary measures. filled with the gloomiest anticipations of the future, there was a strange blind confidence, a sort of careless *insouciance* in regard to the whole matter among the mass of the population. There was unbounded en-

4

thusiasm for the cause, and a perfect faith in the pluck and endurance of the volunteers, who were vaguely regarded as competent for any task that might be assigned them. If some skeptic, whose fears had been quickened by reading history, faintly whispered the necessity of discipline in the ranks, and of sanitary measures in the camps, in order to insure permanent success, he was told that the volunteer, from his very condition and previous habits, could not be trained in the same severe discipline as that found essential in a regular army, and that, after all, the American was a thoroughly self-reliant being, whose native qualities would insure his exemption from those evils which had demoralized armies made up of different material in former wars.

This strange infatuation pervaded all ranks of the people, and as it seemed a foregone conclu-
Apprehensions felt for the re-sult.
sion that discipline, such as that which existed in other armies, could not be enforced in ours, of course little effort was made to introduce it among the volunteers. The effect of this absurd theory soon became apparent. The ignorance of the officers concerning their duties was manifest at the very first test. The injury to the health of the troops, and therefore to their *morale* and efficiency, mainly due to the ignorance, incompetency, and carelessness of their officers on their arrival at Washington, is now known to have been absolutely disastrous. Experienced military officers looked with dismay on the prospect of making an active campaign with such troops, while those who were more sanguine, only because they were more ignorant, could not fail to be oppressed with

an anxious fear lest the best strength of the nation should be uselessly sacrificed. But before the actual shock of arms took place, leading minds throughout the country, who saw most clearly the deep-seated cause of the evil, were thoroughly studying the whole subject, and anxiously searching for a remedy.

At that time the experience of the Crimean war was fresh in the memory of all. That experience was a complete chapter by itself on sanitary sci-ence. It taught the great truth that the "cause of humanity was identified with the strength of armies." We were left to no vague conjecture as to the causes which produced the fearful mortality among the allied troops before Sebastopol,—a mortality, which as has been truly said, has never been equalled since the hosts of Sennacherib fell in a single night. Public opinion in England, indignant and horror-stricken at this frightful result, long before the war closed, called loudly for investigation and remedy. The result has been a contribution of inestimable value to our knowledge of every thing which concerns the vital questions of the health, comfort, and efficiency of armies. The results of these investigations, both in regard to the causes of the evil, and the wonderful efficiency of the remedies which were applied for its removal, had been recently given to the world in parliamentary reports, in the works of professional men, and especially in the invaluable testimony of Miss Nightingale, so that all the conditions of the problem were perfectly known, and its solution could be arrived at with the exactness and certainty of a scientific demonstration. The description of the causes which had produced a mortality in the

British army so fearful, that had it continued at the rate which was maintained in January, 1855, it would in ten months have destroyed every man in it, was so accurate, and bore so wonderful a resemblance to evils already known to exist in our condition, that the lesson seemed prepared specially for our warning and benefit. Earnest men who loved their country, and who had some humane consideration for the health and lives of those who were defending it, determined that something should be done to avoid a similar catastrophe here.   They knew that the British people had been able only to investigate and deplore the causes which had led to so direful a result.   They felt that here a wise, thorough, and persistent effort should be made at the outset of the war, guided by the Crimean experience, to forestal the insidious march of those diseases, which, if unchecked, would inevitably overwhelm our army and with it our country in ruin.

The experience of the Crimean war taught those who consulted it the nature of the terrible dangers What was taught by that experience. which encompass all armies outside of the battle-field, the possibility of mitigating them, and the sanitary measures, which in strict accordance with the general laws of health should be adopted to provide for the safety of an army.   But it taught many other things, which were far from encouraging to the zeal of those who suppose that the ease of applying a remedy has in actual practice any due relation to the undisputed magnitude of the evil to be abated.   They found, in the first place, a certain inflexible military routine in the management of everything connected with the administration of the Medical

Department of an army, the preservation of which in all its integrity was considered as essential to the very existence of the troops who might be perishing through its adherence to regulation and precedent, as any part of the military system. They found, too, that the medical staff, however much it might deplore the evil, was helpless to effect a remedy, for under the existing system it had no power to initiate, order and execute sanitary works. While the evidence was overwhelming that the plainest teachings of modern science had been neglected, not only in the construction of hospitals, but in the adoption of suitable precautionary measures to insure the health and comfort of the soldier in camp, it was also evident that the natural jealousy which is the result of a certain *esprit de corps* in any thoroughly organized administrative body, always manifests itself with a most determined spirit against any plans which seek to infuse new life into that body even through the regular channels, and especially against any extra official effort to render its machinery less cumbrous and more efficient. While the experience of the Crimea, therefore, clearly proved the cause of the evil and the nature of the remedy, it no less clearly proved the practical difficulty of applying that remedy outside and independent of government agencies, and the almost insurmountable obstacles of transferring to such agencies a portion of that zeal and enthusiasm for the welfare of the soldier which in modern times, at least, to the credit of the civilization of the age let it be said, is the strongest and most characteristic impulse of the people towards an army which is fighting its battles. Still the success of Miss Nightingale's efforts in the hospitals at Scutari, and the astonishing results which were produced in the improvement of the health of the troops, by the adoption of the measures recommended and enforced by the Government Sanitary Commission which was sent out to the Crimea in April, 1855, led those to persevere who clearly saw the nature of the difficult task before them. Thus encouraged they sought to initiate some methods which should anticipate and guard against, and not follow, as in the Crimea, the fearful havoc caused by the neglect of sanitary laws.

The importance, therefore, of rousing public opinion to the absolute necessity of forcing upon the government the adoption of precautionary measures to insure the lives and safety of our troops in camps, in barracks and in hospitals, was the practical lesson which was taught by the Crimean experience to those who had studied it with a view of rendering it applicable to our needs. Some of these earnest-minded men became afterwards active members of the United States Sanitary Commission, but that organization bore no resemblance whatever, except in name, to the body which was sent out by the British Government in April, 1855. The latter was invested with plenary powers to do anything and everything which could improve the sanitary condition of the troops, whether in the camps or the hospitals. It will appear hereafter that our Sanitary Commission in its organization, methods, operations and results was wholly original, and peculiarly American in its characteristics. The occasion of its existence was un-

The influence of such teachings in favor of similar measures here.

questionably an emergency which might prove and did prove in many respects similar to that which occurred in the Crimean war, but that war only taught the necessity of precautionary measures, and shed no light whatever upon the practical question how far it was possible to adapt those measures to our American system.   Indeed, it will be seen as we proceed, how our peculiar condition and circumstances embarrassed the action of those among us, who sought to base the care of our army upon a system deduced from the positive results of experience.   It will perhaps be found that it was almost as difficult to make our Government believe in the necessity of taking such precautionary measures, as it became afterwards to convince those whose immediate duty it was to enforce them, that supplemental aid, and the advice of an unofficial organization might be so given as not to impair military efficiency and discipline.

The powers conferred on the British Sanitary Commission were wholly unexampled in the history of the administrative system of Great Britain.   The results of its labors have been on the whole, perhaps, the grandest contribution ever made by science to the practical art of preserving health among men required to live together in large masses.   Its existence was due, as we have said, to the horror which was inspired by the accounts of the perishing army before Sebastopol, and to the wide-spread conviction that this result was attributable to causes which might be removed by wise sanitary measures. Three gentlemen, each distinguished for his practical acquaintance with the laws of hygiene and the principles of sanitary science, Dr. Sutherland, Dr. Milroy, and Mr. Rawlinson, were appointed in February, 1855, by the Minister of War, Lord Panmure, Commissioners, to proceed at once to the Crimea, and there, on the spot, to reform the abuses to which the evil was due. They were told expressly in the letter which announced their appointment and defined their duties, that in the prosecution of their labors they were not to be content with merely issuing an order, but that "they should see instantly that the work they ordered was commenced, and superintend it day by day until it was finished. They were further directed to use all diligence in ascertaining whether any and what removable causes of disease connected with the camps and hospitals existed, to represent such defects to the military and naval authorities, to issue instructions for their removal, and to *see that their instructions were complied with.*" Thus it will be seen, that in all matters within the scope of their instructions, they were supreme, over-riding all considerations of rank, and introducing for the first time into the English system the practical heresy of breaking through all the solemn formalities of regulation, precedent, and red tape, upon the strict observance of which the safety of the country, to the mind trained in official habits, absolutely depends. The result justified this extraordinary, almost revolutionary, departure from the ordinary methods of administration; the rescue of thousands from impending death will be its justification in history, while perhaps the stoutest defender of routine and precedent will now admit that this was one of the emergencies of that necessity which knows no law. No such extraordinary powers as were conferred upon these Commissioners, and fully exercised by them when it was necessary to accomplish their object, were ever granted by the Government of the United States to any body of men outside of the regular military organization; but, perhaps, many will recall periods during the war when such a despotic authority wisely exercised by such a Commission as that sent to the Crimea, would have saved thousands of lives to the country and millions of dollars to its treasury.

During the months of May and June, 1861, regiment after regiment arrived at the National Capital in a most unsatisfactory condition, so far as concerned their real efficiency as soldiers. These regiments had made their journey in cattle cars, as crowded and as ill-provided as if they were carrying beasts to the shambles; while most of them were utterly unprovided with any means of relief for those of their number who had become ill or exhausted from their long exposure. On arriving, no preparations had been made for their reception. Men stood for hours in the broiling sun or drenching rain, waiting in vain for rations and shelter, while their ignorant and inexperienced Commissaries and Quartermasters were slowly and painfully learning the duties of their positions. At last, utterly worn out and disgusted, they reached their camps, where they received rations as unwholesome as distasteful to them, and endeavored to recruit their wasted energies while lying upon rotten straw, wrapped in a shoddy blanket. The reality of all this fearful misery in such striking contrast with the gay and cheerful scenes which they had just left, soon

Condition of the Regiments on their arrival at Washington.

5

taught the soldier, who was in earnest, that true military discipline was not only essential to his efficiency but to his safety, and indeed to his very existence, as part of this vast human machine. With the more reflecting in many regiments, who were the smaller portion, an attempt was made to uphold it, while with the many, the irritation and annoyance constantly suffered, through the incapacity of their officers, engendered a dangerous spirit of mutiny. On all hands there was utter distrust in the organization, which not only cooled perceptibly their early enthusiasm for the National cause, but which soon showed itself in the alarming prevalence of certain diseases, well-known in camps, which led officers of experience in the regular army to predict that fifty per cent. of the volunteers, before the end of the summer, would fall victims to diseases entirely preventible by wise measures of precaution rigidly enforced.

We shall recur again, more in detail, to the actual sanitary condition of the army before its advance into American method of remedying great public evils. Virginia. We refer to it now merely to show what a just cause of alarm for its safety existed at that time. No lover of his country, and no friend of humanity could fail to appreciate the reality of the danger. It is one of the fortunate peculiarities in our American life that when great evils force themselves upon the public attention as requiring immediate and practical remedy, earnest and thoughtful men are to be found who generally, by means of some formal organization, determine, with more or less force, to grapple with them. These attempts are often very crude and unsatisfactory in their origin, but they gain in strength and practical value as experience is acquired, and although many blunders are made, yet to such organizations is undoubtedly due nearly all that is grand, comprehensive, and far-reaching in conception, and successful in practice, in our American life. The nature of the crisis was so serious, and the principle by which any remedy could be applied by a scheme of voluntary organization so difficult of determination, that those who felt the evils most deeply, hesitated longest, for fear of making confusion worse confounded by any interference with government measures, however defective they might be. But at last the fearful risks to the health and safety of the army, and the importance of the vast interests dependent upon its efficiency, gave rise to earnest, energetic measures. The evils themselves were so glaring, the danger from them to the health and efficiency of the army so imminent, and the Government apparently so helpless to provide an adequate remedy, that it was determined by some enlightened men, most of whom had been taught by their profession the value of preventive hygienic measures, to try the experiment of infusing some of the popular enthusiasm and popular sympathy into the cumbrous machinery of Government. This was to be done not irregularly or in the way of embarrassing intervention but strictly in aid of the Government plans, as far as possible, through Government means, and wholly in subordination to the great objects which the Government had in view in prosecuting the war. This was the germ, the original conception of the functions of a Sanitary Commission, but we are yet far removed from the fully developed maturity and power which this idea acquired.

It is, of course, not intended to assert that this was the first attempt made by means of a voluntary Preventive mea- organization, to aid the acknowledged help-sures suggested. lessness of the Government in bestowing that care upon the army which public opinion demanded. As we have said, the desire to aid and comfort the soldier was coeval with his entry into the Government service, and this desire was manifested in providing for him such extra comforts as the anxious care of his wife, or mother, or sister could suggest. But while giving full credit of praise to these spontaneous and self-sacrificing efforts to pour the riches of home comforts into the camps of the soldiers, those who examined the subject more closely were satisfied that the object all had in view was not to be gained by measures such as these. They thought they had discovered the root of the evil in the want of an effective organization of nearly all the measures of the Government concerning the health and comfort of the soldier. They were not disposed to supplant the Government as the proper and most efficient care-taker of the army, but simply so to mould the popular will that it should aid, encourage, and uphold what-ever was undertaken by the Government in the direc-tion of humane and careful guardianship of the soldier. The whole history of the Sanitary Commission, which, from the beginning, has had for its main design a pre-ventive service, has been completely intertwined with that of relief afforded to the soldier; but at the outset the intention was not to concern itself with supplying other wants of the soldier than those which, on inquiry, should turn out to be real, and then to urge upon the Government, acting through its appropriate channels, the adoption of a suitable remedy. To those who had made a careful survey of the whole field, guided by the light which the experience of other countries afforded them, a general system of relief, based upon some such theory as this, seemed the only one which could be of practical value to the vast armies which it soon became evident would be called into actual service.

This idea or theory was as yet, however, in *embryo* only, in the minds of certain thinking men. Into the untried future, with all its fearful dangers, they hesitated to cast what might prove in practice, an additional element of confusion and embarassment to an already sorely-pressed Government. With a perfect conviction of the scientific truth of their theory they waited until the way seemed clear for its successful application. The principle of outside interference was already recognized, indeed its influence seemed inevitable in a war conducted in modern times, in which, perhaps, the most striking characteristic is the increased respect professed for humanity. It being therefore settled that in some way in this war, popular extra-governmental measures for the relief of the needs, real or supposed, of the soldier were certain to be adopted, one great difficulty was removed from the minds of those who, from their very zeal for the success of the cause, had hesitated to interfere in any way with the Government measures, defective and

Dangers of extra-official intervention.

imperfect as they seemed. Such men now thought it their duty to attempt to direct, control, and organize the excited benevolence of the country towards the army, upon some principle which would promise success in solving the very difficult problem which was now before it.

CHAPTER II.

DEVELOPMENT OF THE THEORY OF A PREVENTIVE SERVICE.

THE earliest movement that was made for army relief was begun, as it is hardly necessary to say, by the women of the country. It was most natural that their tender care and anxiety for friends who had gone forth to scenes of danger should manifest itself by an attempt to provide them with home comforts, and, as far as possible, to maintain a home influence upon them. On the 15th of April, 1861, the day on which the President's call for troops appeared, the women of Bridgeport, in Connecticut, organized a society with the somewhat vague idea of affording relief and comfort to the volunteers. In Charlestown on the same day, and at Lowell a few days afterwards, the women of those cities formed societies, having the same general object in view. It is worth while to look at the end proposed by the women at the last named place, in order to show what strange notions prevailed at that time in the most enlightened communities, as to the character of the measures which might be adopted outside the Government for the benefit of the soldier. They proposed to supply nurses for the sick and wounded, and to bring them home when practicable, to purchase

The first relief movement made by the women of the country.

39

clothing, provisions, and matters of comfort not supplied by Government regulations, to send books and newspapers to the camps, to preserve a record of the services of each soldier, and to hold constant communication with the officers of the regiments, in order that they might be kept informed of the condition of their friends. This is, indeed, a formidable list of objects to be attained, and it is now obvious that it was put forth rather as a mode of supplying the supposed immediate wants of men, who had gone forth from a particular locality, than as a part of a general system applicable to the whole army. On the 19th of April, the ladies of Cleveland organized a society, the object of which was the care of the families of volunteers. Here, as the ground of benevolent action was an old and very well-trodden one, and as the objects of their care were wholly within their own oversight, it is only necessary to speak of it now as the commencement of an organization which some time afterwards adopted the system and methods of the Sanitary Commission, and became one of its most efficient auxiliaries.

The history of the Women's Central Relief Association, of New York, as the first body in which the Women's Central Relief Association, of New York. principles, which were afterwards fully developed in the Sanitary Commission, took form and shape, is on that account well worth study.

In one of the last days of April, 1861, two men accidentally met in the street in New York, the one the Rev. Dr. Bellows, afterwards the honored President of the Sanitary Commission, the early founder of its policy, and its successful champion and guide through all the difficulties which beset its operations during the war; the other, Dr. Elisha Harris, afterwards one of its most laborious, intelligent, and zealous members. Their minds were pre-occupied, as were those of all thoughtful men at that time, with the alarming condition of the country, and with the necessity of making some great exertion to prevent the spread of those evils which threatened to impair the health and efficiency of the army which was then gathering in all quarters. They were induced to attend a meeting, which had been called at the " Infirmary for Women," with the view of devising some means of contributing to that object. They found there a number of ladies, full of zeal and enthusiasm in the cause, most desirous of information as to the best mode of making themselves useful, but very much divided in opinion as to the best means which they should adopt, and with a very imperfect idea of organization. It was suggested, after some consultation, that an association, upon a wider basis, embracing the churches, schools, and all societies of women in the city, already engaged in any way in the work of relief to the army, should be attempted, and it was decided to call a general meeting, to be held at the Cooper Institute, to perfect this plan. The invitation or call for this meeting, which was prepared by Dr. Bellows, and which is somewhat remarkable as containing the first public announcement of principles of relief which afterwards became familiar from their practical application by the Sanitary Commission, was signed by ninety-two of the best known and most influential ladies in New York.*

On the appointed day, the great Hall of the Institute was crowded with an earnest, enthusiastic, and patriotic First public assembly of women.   MR. D. D. FIELD pre-
meeting for sided at the meeting, and addresses, filled
army relief in
New York.   with practical suggestions as to the duty of women in the emergency, and as to the modes by which they might contribute to the comfort and health of the army, were made by the late venerable Doctor Mott, Doctor Alex. H. Stevens, the late Rev. Dr. Be-thune, and others.   The light which we have now gained from the experience of the war, could not, of course, then guide the counsels of those who were thus earnestly striving to do their whole duty in this matter, but it is not a little remarkable that the con-stitution adopted by the Society, then organized, in the earliest days of the war, embodied many of the principles, the practical value of which that experience has only confirmed and established.   This constitution had been prepared by Doctor Bellows; it was adopted by the meeting, and the "Women's Central Associa-tion of Relief," which afterwards occupied so con-spicuous a position as one of the great feeding tribu-taries of the Sanitary Commission, was organized under it.   After announcing that the women of New York had associated themselves together with the view of furnishing comforts, stores, and nurses in aid of the Medical Staff, and that they were desirous of organizing for such purpose the scattered efforts of the women of the country, it declares that in accom-

* Appendix, No. 1.

plishing this object "they will collect and disseminate information upon the actual and prospective wants of the army; establish recognized relations with the Medical Staff, and act as auxiliary to it; that they will maintain a central depôt of stores, and open a bureau for the examination and registration of nurses."

The Society thus organized, the first step, of course, was to obtain information as to such actual and probable future wants of the army as could be in any way met by the modes proposed. Application was at once made by Dr. Bellows, on behalf of the As- *Dr. Bellows' in-* sociation, at the head-quarters of the Medi- *terview with Dr.* *Satterlee, Medi-* cal Department of the army in New York, *cal Purveyor.* at that time in charge of an old and experienced officer, Surgeon Satterlee, as Medical Purveyor. It soon became apparent that this scheme of outside and supplemental aid to the troops was not likely to be looked upon with much favor in official quarters. Whether it was due to that uniform jealousy which is perhaps naturally excited by an attempt to interfere with the performance of official duty by irresponsible methods, even where those methods claim only a very subordinate share of control, or even where they are humbly offered in aid of the work, without the slightest intention of unkind criticism,—whether this general motive had a controlling influence, or whether the whole project was looked upon as a wild scheme, due to the influence of the general excitement that was then pervading all classes in regard to the war, certain it is, that in the opinion of the representative of the Medical Bureau, the plans proposed by the women could prove of no practical value whatever to the army.

The delegate of the Association had prepared certain queries and suggestions concerning the possible wants of the troops, which the Government either might not, or would not meet. These he submitted to Dr. Satterlee in order to show the earnestness of purpose, and the definiteness of the aim of those who sent him. He found that there was little prospect of that sort of co-operation which he had thought possible or desirable. Indeed, in this first interview between the representative of the organized voluntary benevolence of the country, and that of the official authority, it was manifest that the officers of the Medical Staff thought the zeal of the women and the activity of the men assisting them, superfluous, obtrusive, and likely to grow troublesome, and that the sphere of the public in the work of aiding and relieving the army was predestined to be a very small one. "To *humor* a temporary excitement was about all the interest the officials in New York exhibited in the movement; to render it harmless by guiding it into a speedy nothingness was their apparent policy."

At the same time, the statements made by Surgeon Satterlee to Dr. Bellows, in regard to the nature of the preparation made by the Medical Department to meet the emergency, and his evidently wholly sincere convictions of the uselessness and folly of outside interference with its operations, could not fail to make a deep impression upon a mind like his, trained to regard with much respect the opinions of those who spoke of their own specialty with the authority of a long tried experience. He felt it his duty to state, publicly, the results of his

<small>Effect of statements made by Dr. Satterlee.</small>

interview with Dr. Satterlee, and to express his conviction that the efforts being made by the women
were ill-advised and uncalled for. The zeal of his
constituents was not cooled by this result. They were
disposed to attribute the rebuff which they had received to the bureaucratic spirit of the Medical Department, and at any rate to seek fuller and more
satisfactory information upon the general subject at
Washington.

Meanwhile "the Physicians and Surgeons of the
Hospitals of New York," and "the New York Medical Association for furnishing Hospital Sup- Movement of
plies," had held various meetings, and the certain Medical
Associations in
last named body had opened a depôt for lint, New York.
bandages, etc. The great "Lint Question" was then
exercising the public mind, and was actively discussed.
Nothing can better illustrate the utter vagueness and
confusion of ideas which then prevailed as to what
was · necessary to be done for the army, than the
strange interest which was excited even among professional men, in regard to what the war has proved
was one of the most insignificant items of relief.
Still at that time it was the absorbing topic. What
is the best material for lint? how is it best scraped
and prepared? by what means can it be best gathered
in the largest quantities? These were the questions
which, for a time, engaged the attention of those who
aspired to the high office of doing something to
preserve the lives, and promote the health of those who
had gone into the field. Another question, much discussed at that time, both by the "Women's Central,"
and by the "Association of Physicians and Surgeons,"

was the selection and training of suitable nurses for Military Hospitals. Extensive arrangements were made to provide a corps of specially qualified persons who should perform those duties to the sick and wounded, which army regulation and usage had heretofore assigned to soldiers detailed for that purpose. For some reason, not very apparent, this branch of volunteer relief occupied a very subordinate place in the medical history of the war.

It soon became evident that the real difficulty lay far deeper than the settlement of the "Lint Question," or the employment of suitable nurses, could reach, and it was determined by the various Associations, of which we have spoken, to send delegates to Wash-
Delegation sent ington in order to learn definitively, at head-
to Washington. quarters, in what way, if at all, the voluntary offerings of the people could be best made available for the relief of the army. Accordingly, Dr. Van Buren, representing "the Physicians and Surgeons," Dr. Jacob Harsen, since deceased, (an excellent and public-spirited man,) "the Lint and Bandage Association," and Dr. Bellows and Dr. Harris the "Women's Central," went to Washington on this errand of investigation. They reached there on the 16th of May. They found everything in the greatest confusion. Direct communication between the capital and the North had been re-established only on that day, since the 19th of April. Troops were slowly gathering, but it was evident that no adequate preparations had been made for their reception, or suitable care. The Departments were overworked, new duties and new labors, tasked to the utmost, the

strength and capacity of all in official employ. The Government, as far as could be seen at the first glance, was pursuing that "tentative policy" which was so long its characteristic during the war, not only in regard to matters of general concern, but in regard to measures of reform, which the new condition of things called for in almost every detail of administration. There was no end to the advice and suggestion which it was receiving from all quarters, and upon all subjects, recommending the most radical and even revolutionary changes of the whole system, in order to meet the emergency.

Amidst this motley crowd of well-meaning but troublesome counsellors, the New York delegation was forced to make its way, supported only by Condition of the earnest conviction that the business things at Washington. which had brought it to Washington was one of the most important which could then engage the attention of the Government. Its members were, from the beginning, regarded as theorists, possibly with very good, but certainly with very impracticable ideas, which, if adopted, would tend to derange the whole Government machinery. The kind and courteous hearing accorded to them by the military authorities was due, probably, far more to their personal character, and the position they held in the community they represented, than to the smallest confidence in the schemes they had to propose.

Their first visit was to General Scott, on whom they desired to impress the importance of a thorough re-inspection of the army, in order to eliminate Interview with from it those diseased men and mere boys, General Scott. Re-inspection of wholly unfit for military service, who had, troops.

through the carelessness of the original mustering officers, been enrolled in the ranks. This measure seemed indispensably necessary, for without it the army would have been encumbered, before it had marched ten miles, with a mass of helpless men, who would have wholly interfered with its movements. The order was issued at once, and its necessity was fully justified by the result of the inspection. It had not proceeded far, however, when it became evident that if the army was reduced in number to the point which a rigid system of inspection would warrant, the large proportion disbanded would produce the utmost consternation and alarm in the country. As this was a result to be avoided at all hazards, much of the bad material was retained, and contributed, doubtless, to the demoralization of the army some time afterwards. By this order, the first of a series of preventive measures, which were adopted by what afterwards became the Sanitary Commission, was inaugurated.

The next interview of the delegation was with the head of the Medical Bureau, at that time Acting Surgeon-General Wood. As the very fact of their mission implied a belief on their part, and upon that of those they represented, of the existence of grave defects in the organization and administration of the Medical Department of the army, they felt it necessary to exercise the utmost tact, prudence, and skill in their efforts to convince the Chief of the Bureau that a system which had worked well hitherto in a small army would necessarily require great modification to enable it to meet the wants of the vast masses which would now

Interview with the Acting Surgeon-General.

be thrown upon its care. They found Dr. Wood very courteous, and very willing to listen to practical suggestions. Some of these were made by Dr. Van Buren, one of the delegates, who spoke with the authority of a great professional reputation, and. who referred to the experience he had gained during a service of five years on the Medical Staff. Still they found the Acting Surgeon-General indisposed to take those large and generous views of the necessities of the case which the situation in their opinion demanded. It was clear that the present war, in his view, as far as the demands on the Bureau were concerned, was only the Florida or the Mexican war on a large scale, and that the existing machinery was capable of such expansion as fully to provide for every possible contingency. The Bureau was a well-organized, thoroughly-tried, and hitherto wholly successful Department of the Government, and any attempt from the outside to interfere with its methods, could produce only confusion, embarrassment, and all those evils which destroy an army by introducing into it loose notions of military discipline and responsibility.

None could feel more deeply than the enlightened gentlemen, to whom he was then speaking, the value of thorough and exact discipline in every department of the army. It was their earnest desire then, as it has been the constant policy of their successors, the Sanitary Commission, ever since, to urge, upon the Government the strictest ideas of official responsibility. As will be seen hereafter, respect for official rights

Views of the Delegation in regard to discipline.

7

and official authority has been sedulously maintained by them towards every department of the
Government, and especially towards that very department whose legitimate functions they were desirous of
aiding. They recognised not only the value, but the
indispensable necessity of a thoroughly organized
Medical Department, acting with absolute authority
within its proper sphere; but at the time of the conversation with Dr. Wood they knew that it was wholly
unequal to the work in hand, and they proposed, in
the interests of humanity and patriotism, to supply its
practical deficiencies through its own channels and by
its own methods, until such changes were effected by
legislation as would enable it to perform thoroughly
every duty which could be required of it.

During this interview it soon became apparent
that the effort to induce the Medical Department
Preventive to acknowledge that it needed the support
scheme pro-
posed. of the people, and would accept it in some
intelligent and methodical way would prove hope-
less, because it was contrary to the whole antecedents
of the Bureau, and inherently troublesome. The
delegation · then made an attempt to accomplish its
object in a way which might seem more consistent
with the bureaucratic spirit of the Medical Staff.
It proposed a scheme of preventive, service in the
army, looking to measures which would insure
the investigation, by suitable persons, of the causes
of all preventible disease in camps and hospitals,
who should have authority to secure their removal.
This service was to be intrusted to a mixed Commission of civilians, of medical men, and of military

officers, who should be appointed by the Government, and charged with everything relating to the hygienic and sanitary needs of the army. This Commission was intended to co-operate with the regular Medical Bureau, and according to the original intention of those who proposed it, was to possess authority to enforce its recommendations.

The conviction that the only true way to guard effectively against diseases affecting the health and lives of men living in masses, was, by Comparative adopting preventive measures of a hygienic value of preventive measures. and sanitary kind, was, as we have said, not a new one to any member of the delegation. The wonderful results of such measures as applied to the over-crowded portions of manufacturing towns in England were familiar to all, and the fresh experience of the Crimea proved that these same measures were just as essential to the preservation of the health of armies. On the journey to Washington, in an earnest discussion as to the plans which should be adopted to rouse the Government to undertake some measures by which the health of the volunteers would be assured, Dr. Harris had strongly urged that the only true system which would cover the whole ground, and reach the seat of the evil, was the preventive system, founded upon the same principles, and administered by a Commission similar to that whose labors had produced such happy results in the Crimea. Dr. Bellows was much impressed with these views. They revived his recollections of the wonderful results of sanitary measures in large towns with which his former studies in Social Science had rendered him familiar. The

subject was maturely considered and canvassed from
every point of view; the possibility of introducing so
novel and extraneous an element as an independent
Sanitary Commission, with real powers, into our system, its desirableness at the present crisis, the proper
sphere of its functions, the qualifications of those who
were to compose it,—all these matters were thoroughly
discussed, and the result was a unanimous determination that should the state of affairs at Washington
prove such as they feared, they would urge upon the
Government the appointment of a Commission with
full powers, whose business it should be, either through
the Medical Bureau or independent of it, as might
appear best on examination, to establish a preventive
hygienic and sanitary service for the benefit of the
army.

Their interview with Dr. Wood not only served to
convince them more thoroughly of the absolute neces-
Objections to a sity for some such measure, but it also re-
merely advisory
system. vealed to them the serious obstacles in the
way of accomplishing any reform whatever, and especially one of so sweeping a nature as they proposed.
It should be distinctly borne in mind that the
merely advisory position towards the Medical Bureau,
which the Sanitary Commission consented afterwards to occupy was not one of its own choosing,
nor was any such diluted scheme proposed to the
Acting Surgeon-General by the delegation from New
York. Its members were far too earnest in their
anxiety to secure the adoption of true sanitary measures for the care of the troops, and they had had too
much experience in the perfect uselessness of giving

advice and issuing recommendations without the power to enforce their adoption, to suppose that any real good could be effected in this way. It was thought important, however, to secure at the outset, a foothold by establishing at least friendly relations with the Medical Bureau. Something might be done in this way at any rate to methodize, and render of some practical value the scattered benevolence of the country. The delegation was perfectly satisfied that no system except one which should clothe its officers with power not merely to investigate the causes of preventible disease in the army and recommend their removal, but also with power to carry their recommendations into effect, would cure the difficulty. But its members were also perfectly convinced, from their interview with the Acting Surgeon-General, that the adoption, by the Government, of any such system, at present at least, was impracticable. They were therefore obliged to accept the modified plan upon which the Sanitary Commission was afterwards based, because it was the only one for which they could hope for the slightest possible co-operation from the Medical Department.

This plan is detailed in a letter addressed by the delegation to the Secretary of War, under date of May 18, 1861, and in a letter from the Acting Surgeon-General to the Secretary, of the twenty-second of the same month.* The first of these letters, after alluding to the incessant and irresistible motions of the zeal of the people in the offer of medical aid, the applications of nurses, and the contributions of supplies, the importance of bringing

Letter to the Secretary of War.

* See Appendix No. 2.

into system and practical shape the general zeal and benevolent activity of the women of the land in behalf of the army, and the desirableness of regulating the relations of volunteer associations to the War Department, and especially to the Medical Bureau, asked that a "mixed Commission of civilians distinguished for their philanthropic experience and acquaintance with sanitary matters, of medical men, and of military officers, be appointed by the Government, who shall be charged with the duty of investigating the best means of methodizing and reducing to practical service the already active but undirected benevolence of the people towards the army, who shall consider the general subject of the prevention of sickness and suffering among the troops, and suggest the wisest methods, which the people at large can use, to manifest their good-will towards the comfort, security, and health of the army." The other letter, that of the Acting Surgeon-General to the Secretary of War, shows

Letter of the Acting Surgeon-General to the Secretary of War, asking for the appointment of a Sanitary Commission. clearly how far his conference with the New York delegation had impressed him with the necessity of creating a Sanitary Commission, and what limited powers he was willing to accord to it. He says: "The Medical Bureau would, in my judgment, derive important and useful aid from the counsels and well-directed efforts of an intelligent and scientific Commission to be styled a 'Commission of Inquiry and Advice in respect of the Sanitary Interests of the United States Forces,' acting in co-operation with this Bureau in elaborating and applying such facts as might be elicited from the experience and more extensive obser-

vations of those connected with armies, with reference
to the diet and hygiene of the troops, and the organization of military hospitals, etc." He goes on to say
that this Commission is not intended to interfere with,
but to strengthen the present organization, and hints
very clearly that it is expected to confine its operations
to the volunteers. How far such a scheme accords
with that of the Crimean Commission, with its plenary
powers not only to investigate the causes of disease,
but order when possible their removal, and especially
to insist that the orders given were duly carried out,
and with the original plan of the New York gentlemen based upon the successful experience of that
system, the most cursory examination will render
apparent. Such as it was, however, it was deemed
expedient to accept it, simply because it was the only
sort of semi-official recognition which the Government was then willing to extend to what it ignorantly
supposed to be the result of a transient popular excitement, but which afterwards proved itself, as the agent
of the benevolence of the country directed towards
the care and comfort of the army, one of the most
potent causes of its efficiency.

The Acting Surgeon-General suggested, in his letter, the names of five eminent gentlemen whom
he proposed as Commissioners under the *Names of Commissioners sug-*
new organization, two of whom were *gested by the*
members of the delegation which had in- *Acting Surgeon-General.*
duced him to ask for it. So far as these two gentlemen, and indeed all the members of the delegation,
were concerned they were not only undesirous, but in
their opinion from the absorbing nature of their pro-

fessional occupations, wholly unable to give that time and attention to the duties of such a position which their importance seemed imperatively to demand. The magnitude of the work, and the special qualifications which it seemed to them to require for its proper fulfillment, pointed in their opinion, to the necessity of selecting experts only as members of the Commission, or at least the creation of a body in which the largest share of the work, as well as the influence, should devolve upon experts. But it soon became evident that if the Commission was to have any measure of practical success, those who had been the fathers of the idea, must also stand as its sponsors during its growth and development, guiding it with their fostering care, and nurturing it with their constant counsel and encouragement. It was, therefore, by an unexpected turn of events, settled that Dr. Bellows and Dr. Van Buren, two of the most overworked men in the country, in their respective callings, should be called upon to give shape and practical direction to the theory which they had proposed for the care of the sanitary interests of the army. How this was to be done when that theory was shorn of all the power which they deemed essential to its successful and effective working, and especially how they, deeply immersed in their ordinary duties and wholly untrained in systems of administration, were to suggest such measures as would render the experiment successful, were very perplexing questions. But the necessities of the situation, and particularly the vast importance of establishing a strong bond of sympathy between the proposed Commission and the

people, by connecting with it the names of well-
known men in whom the public would repose confidence, and who in turn would rouse that public
to a thorough appreciation of its scope and aim,
finally induced these gentlemen to accept the position into which they had been so unwillingly forced.
They, perhaps, supposed that their functions would
be confined to superintendence and direction, and
they certainly could have formed no idea of the
engrossing nature of the duties they were obliged to
assume during the four years of the war, a period
rendered by their connection with the Commission,
the most laborious and harassing of their whole
lives.

But the task of the New York gentlemen, now
grown so wholly beyond the limits which they had
proposed to themselves on going to Wash-   Opposition in
the War De-
ington, was not yet completed. They had   partment.
asked, as we have seen, in an official communication
to the Secretary of War, that a Commission should be
appointed, and their application was enforced by the
approval of the Chief of the Medical Bureau. To
complete their task, they were of course forced to
procure the sanction of the highest officers of Government. Here a new class of difficulties met them. In
the Medical Bureau the objection to their scheme was
its alleged interference with a thoroughly organized
and long tried Government machine, but as they as-
cended into the higher regions of official authority it
was found that the lofty motives which had been fully
recognized in the office of the Surgeon-General, were
little appreciated by his official superiors. It was more

8

than insinuated that their scheme was a cunning
device to gain power for selfish ends. The perfect
disinterestedness of their motives was a quality so
rare in the moral atmosphere of Washington, as to
suggest to those who had lived longest in it grave
doubts as to its reality and genuineness. One Secretary, utterly incapable of comprehending the scope
and aim of the grand scheme of reform they were
urging with such unselfish zeal, begged its advocates
to state frankly, precisely what they wanted, as it was
evident to him that they could not want only what
they seemed to be asking for. Another thought it
one of those many visionary schemes of reform which
the great intellectual activity of the country, excited
by the new condition of things, was forcing upon the
attention of the Government. The President himself
with all his humane instincts could not understand it,
)and regarded its establishment, to use his own expressive language, as adding a "fifth wheel to the coach."
The highest officers of the Government were unanimous in thinking the whole plan impracticable, and
there can, it is feared, be little doubt that the appointment of the Commission was at last consented to as
if it had been a "tub thrown to the popular whale."
The Government was apparently satisfied that it could
do no good, but also that it could do no great harm,
and that after a short trial it would be abandoned as
practically worthless, and remembered only as a
monument of the folly of weak enthusiasts, and of
well-meaning but silly women.

Meanwhile, during those days of painful anxiety
which preceded the birth of the Sanitary Commis-

sion, the unusual spectacle was presented of men who would have scorned to ask at such a time any personal favor of the Govern- ment, patiently waiting in the ante-chambers of high officials, seeking an opportunity to prove to their puzzled comprehension that the being they were asked to usher into the world was no monster, but the legiti- mate offspring of the purest and holiest impulses of the American people.   At length the hour for a safe deliverance seemed approaching, when just at this juncture an unlooked-for event occurred which, for a time, dashed all their hopes.   DR. LAWSON, the Sur- geon-General, who had long been prevented by disease from performing the duties of his office, died, and DR. FINLEY, as the next in rank, was at once appointed his successor.   No sooner had he entered upon his office than he informed the Secretary of War that he disapproved entirely of the proposed Sanitary Com- mission, and that he could not concur in the recom- mendation of Dr. Wood who, as Acting Surgeon- General had asked for its appointment.   Then fol- lowed a scene, into the details of which we do not propose to enter, between the Surgeon-General and those who having toiled so painfully to induce the Government to permit the inauguration of this great work of mercy, suddenly found themselves checked in their humane endeavor.   After much explanation and negotiation, it was agreed that the operations of the Commission should be confined to the volunteers, and in that shape the project received at last the reluctant approval of the Surgeon-General.   The significance of the distinction thus made between the supposed

Dr. Finley appointed Sur- geon-General. His opposition.

wants of regular and volunteer troops is very painful and suggestive, and it was one unfortunately which influenced the opinions, and controlled the action of almost all officers of rank in the regular army at the outset of the war. That volunteers could ever make good soldiers, and especially that their officers could ever be fitted for high commands, or learn how to take care of their men, was long esteemed rank heresy according to the creed of professional soldiers.

It is humiliating to record the utter inability on the part of our highest American officials to appreciate the best-considered and most widely-extended system of mitigating the horrors of war known in history, and especially at a time when the existence of the Government was dependent upon the health and efficiency of that army, which the appointment of a Sanitary Commission was designed to promote. Much may be said in explanation of this indifference as to the want of familiarity with such subjects by the prominent officials, more as to the engrossing nature of questions the decision of which seemed to be of more pressing and instant importance. Still the fact remains not only to instruct us as to the obstacles which all projects of reform, however praiseworthy, must always meet from the *vis inertiæ* of the Government, but also as an encouragement to those who, sustained by their deep convictions of the wisdom and propriety of change, persevere manfully until success crowns their efforts.

In striking contrast with the want of sympathy which was shown by our Government to popular

efforts to extend relief to the army outside
the regular channels is the course pursued
by the English Officials during the war in
the Crimea. If there be any system of administration more completely tied to precedent, formalism, and routine, than another, it is that of the English
Government. Yet the memorable letter of Mr. Sid-
ney Herbert to Miss Nightingale begging her to
organize a corps of nurses and proceed at once to the
hospitals at Scutari, and adopt such measures as she in
her discretion might think best to mitigate the horrors with which it was evident the Medical Staff there
could not successfully cope, shows, that when the necessity is made apparent, the most enlightened English
statesman, with a full knowledge of his official responsibility, does not hesitate to cut at once the "red tape"
in which the cause of humanity may be otherwise
strangled. No deputation of influential men representing the deep feeling of popular sympathy, be it
remembered, dictated these instructions. The letter
was a private one, but its inspiration and the authority it conferred came alike unprompted from an
official source. In this letter Miss Nightingale was
told "You will of course have plenary authority over
all the nurses, and I think I can secure you the fullest
assistance and co-operation from the Medical Staff,
and you will have an unlimited power of drawing on
the Government for whatever you think requisite for
the success of your mission. Deriving your authority
from the Government, your position will insure the
respect and consideration of every one, especially in a
service where official rank carries so much weight.

*Contrast be-
tween the action
of our govern-
ment and that of
Great Britain in
the Crimea.*

This will secure you any attention or comfort on your way out there, together with a complete submission to your orders. Your own personal qualities, your knowledge, and your power of administration, and among greater things, your rank and position in society, give you advantages in such a work which no other person possesses. If this succeeds, an enormous amount of good will be done now, and to persons deserving everything at our hands, and which will multiply the good to all time." Can we be blamed for regretting that words of encouragement, such as these which were addressed to Miss Nightingale to induce her to enter upon her arduous duties, words which might have been so fittingly spoken to the eminent philanthropists who urged our Government to adopt a similar system at the outset of the war, were withheld from them until their task was finished, and their success assured in the grateful appreciation of a whole people.

CHAPTER III.

ORGANIZATION OF THE UNITED STATES SANITARY COMMISSION.

AFTER much negotiation, involving tedious delay, on the 9th of June, 1861, the Secretary of War issued an order* appointing Henry W. Bellows, D. D., <small>Names of the</small> Prof. A. D. Bache, LL.D., Prof. Jeffries Wy- <small>Commissioners.</small> man, M. D., W. H. Van Buren, M. D., Wolcott Gibbs, M. D., Samuel G. Howe, M. D., R. C. Wood, Surgeon U. S. A., G. W. Cullum, U. S. A., Alexander E. Shiras, U. S. A., in connection with such others as they might choose to associate with them, "A Commission of Inquiry and Advice in respect of the Sanitary interests of the United States Forces." They were to serve without remuneration from the Government, and were to be provided with a room for their use in the City of Washington. They were to direct their inquiries to the principles and practice connected with the inspection of recruits and enlisted men, the sanitary condition of volunteers, to the means of preserving and restoring the health and of securing the general comfort and efficiency of the troops, to the proper provision of cooks, nurses, and hospitals, and to other subjects of a like nature. The mode by which they proposed to conduct these inquiries was detailed

* See Appendix No. 3.

in the letter of the New York delegation to the Secretary of War of the 22d of May. The order appointing them directed that they should correspond freely with the Department and with the Medical Bureau concerning these subjects, and on this footing and within these limits, their relations with the official authorities were established. To enable them to carry out fully the purposes of their appointment the Surgeon-General issued a circular, announcing the creation of the Commission, and directing all the officers in his department to grant its Agents every facility in the prosecution of their duties.

On the 12th of June the gentlemen named as Commissioners in the order of the Secretary of War of the First meeting of 9th, (with the exception of Professor Wy- the Commission. man who had declined his appointment,) assembled at Washington. They proceeded to organize the Board by the selection of the Rev. Dr. BELLOWS as President. Their first care was to secure the services of certain gentlemen as colleagues, who were supposed to possess special qualifications, but whose names had not been included in the original warrant. Accordingly Dr. Elisha Harris and Dr. Cornelius R. Agnew were unanimously chosen Commissioners at the first meeting, and George T. Strong, Esq., and Dr. J. S. Newberry, in like manner, at the one next succeeding.* At the first session "a Plan of

---

* The following named gentlemen were elected by the Board, Members of the Commission at different periods during the war; Rt. Rev. Bishop Clark, Hon. R. W. Burnett, Hon. Mark Skinner, Hon. Joseph Holt, Horace Binney, Jr., Rev. J. H. Heywood, Prof. Fairman Rogers, J. Huntington Wolcott, Charles J. Stillé, E. B. M'Cagg, F. Law Olmsted.

Organization," prepared by the President, was presented, discussed, and finally adopted.*

On the 13th the Commission, in a body, waited on the President and Secretary of War, who gave their formal sanction to this "Plan of Organization" by affixing to it their signatures. This Plan forms the Constitution of the Sanitary Commission. Plan of Organization. It deserves careful study, not merely as a statement of the methods by which it was proposed that the great truths of sanitary science should be practically applied to secure the health and efficiency of the soldier, but also as an evidence of the sagacity, foresight, and definiteness of aim of those who devised it. The experience of the war suggested but little alteration even in its outline, while to a strict adherence to the general principles it embodies, the Sanitary Commission owes all the wonderful success it has achieved. This plan reduces to a practical system and method the principles laid down in the letters of the New York gentlemen to the Government authorities, and endeavors to apply them to the actual existing condition of the army. Confining its proposed operations within the limited sphere of "inquiry" and "advice," which had been assigned to it by the Government, it declares what it proposes to do, and by what methods, in each of these departments of duty. In order that its work might be carried on systematically and thoroughly, two general committees were created, one respecting "Inquiry" the other "Advice." The object of the first was to determine by all the light which could be derived from experience, what must

---

* See Appendix No. 4.

9

necessarily be the wants and condition of troops brought together as ours had been, to ascertain exactly how far evils which had proved the scourge of other armies had already invaded our own, and to decide concerning the best measures to be adopted to remove all causes of removable and preventible disease. Each branch of "Inquiry," under this head, was referred to a distinct sub-committee. From the first was expected suggestions of such preventive measures as experience in former wars proved to be absolutely essential, to the second was entrusted the actual inspection, by its own members or their agents, of the camps and hospitals, so that the real condition of the army in a sanitary point of view, concerning which there were then many conflicting rumors, could be definitely known; to the third was referred all questions concerning the improvement of the health and efficiency of the army in respect of diet, clothing, quarters, and matters of a similar nature.

In regard to the other branch of the duty assigned to the Commission under its appointment,—that of "ADVICE," the Board took the same wide and comprehensive views as had guided them in regard to the needful subjects of inquiry. Their scheme of organization declares that the general object of this branch of their service shall be "to get the opinions and conclusions of the Commission approved by the Medical Bureau, *ordered* by the War Department, and *carried out* by the officers and men." It will be seen by this enumeration of the functions with which the Commission considered itself invested as an adviser of the Government, that it had no intention of wasting its time in the barren and thankless task of merely counselling lazy, ignorant, or worthless subordinate officials. If it urged them to undertake some much needed reform requiring possibly hard work, it was to be understood that it controlled the power which could enforce compliance with its suggestions. It cannot be denied that the term "advice," as referring to the performance of a duty like this with which the Sanitary Commission considered itself charged, does not seem very appropriate. We must look, however, for its practical meaning and significance to all the features of the "plan," as defined by its projectors, and deliberately adopted by the Government. It is important that a clear conception of the true functions of the Commission in this matter of advice should be had, for thus only can its practical relations with the Government officials during the war be understood.

So far it will be observed all the details of the plan pointed to a strictly preventive service, consisting in a thorough investigation of the causes of pre- System of relief. ventible diseases, and to advice to be given in a somewhat peremptory form, perhaps, to the Government as to the proper remedies to be employed for their removal. All this was in strict accordance, no doubt, with the original conception of the Commission, and the space occupied by it in the "plan," is an evidence of the paramount importance attached to it as part of the general scheme, still the necessity of devising some general system by which the contributions of the country for the relief and comfort of the army, then diverted into many channels and often failing to reach their destination, could be rendered more practically

useful, and reach the soldier in a way more in harmony
with the discipline and usages of the army, was not
lost sight of in the organization of the Commission.
It was proposed, in order to accomplish this object,
that a Convention composed of delegates from Societies
throughout the country working in aid of the soldier,
should meet at an early day in New York, where the
subject could be fully considered, and some wise general system of carrying out their plans agreed upon.
This Convention was never held, and although the relief system occupied comparatively so unimportant a
place in the proposed work of the Commission at the
outset, still the wise counsels which it afterwards gave
as to the organization of Aid Societies, and the wise
methods it pursued in the distribution of the bounty
of the country, at last made it the main channel by
which that bounty was directed to the army. Indeed
the interest excited in thousands of homes throughout
the land whose inmates were members of these Aid
Societies in favor of the Sanitary Commission, and who
looked upon it only as the almoner of their vast offerings
for the relief of the army, led to the popular error that
it was only a relief association upon a grand scale,
and quite overshadowed in popular estimation its
original purpose, if not the exclusive and peculiar
work which it proposed to engage in. The Commission itself, however, never departed from the true
scientific idea and conception of a preventive system,
and always regarded the relief system, vast as was the
place occupied by it in the war, as inferior in the importance of its results to those due to well-considered
and thoroughly executed preventive measures.

Before proceeding to describe the measures which were adopted by the Commission to carry into practical effect the object of its organization, it Sketch of the Commissioners. Rev.Dr.Bellows. may be well to glance at some of the more striking characteristics of those who had undertaken this hazardous experiment of Sanitary Reform in the army. The REV. DR. BELLOWS, to whom much of the credit of the original conception of a Sanitary Commission at all suited to the peculiar circumstances of this country was due, and who was with entire unanimity selected as its President, possessed many remarkable qualifications for so responsible a position. Perhaps no man in the country exerted a wider or more powerful influence over those who were earnestly seeking the best means of defending our threatened nationality, and certainly never was a moral power of this kind founded upon juster and truer grounds. This influence was not confined to his home, the city of New York, although there it was incontestably very great, but it extended over many other portions of the country, and particularly throughout New England, where circumstances had made his name and, his reputation for zeal and ability, familiar to those most likely to aid in the furtherance of the new scheme. This power was due, partly of course, to the very eminent position which he occupied as a clergyman, partly to the persistent efforts and enlightened zeal with which he had long advocated all wise measures of social reform, partly, perhaps, to his widely extended reputation as an orator, but principally, and above all, to that rare combination of wide comprehensive views of great questions of public policy with extraordinary practical sagacity and wisdom, which enabled him so to organize popular intelligence and sympathy that the best practical results were attained while the life-giving principle was preserved. He had the credit of not being what so many of his profession are, an *idéologue;* he had the clearest perception of what could and what could not be done, and he never hesitated to regard actual experience as the best practical test of the value of his plans and theories. These qualities, so precious and so exceptional in their nature, appeared conspicuously in the efforts made by him to secure the appointment of the Commission by the Government, and it will be found that every page of its history bears the strong impress of his peculiar and characteristic views. The first fruit which the Commission received from his labors was the "Plan of Organization," and in order to show how soon a grand idea was developed to its full maturity in his fertile mind, it is only necessary to say that this fundamental law which, by a strange prescience, seemed perfectly fitted to meet all the emergencies which arose in a service hitherto untried and unknown, assumed the shape and form it now bears, during the labors of a single morning.

With Dr. Bellows were associated several men of great public reputation, each possessing some peculiar qualifications by which the general success of the Professor Alexander Dallas Bache. work was assured. PROFESSOR ALEXANDER DALLAS BACHE, the Vice-President, occupied, with peculiar fitness, the position to which he had been called. He was the head of a great national work, that of the Coast Survey; he was a man of eminent scientific reputation at home and abroad, and his judgment on all subjects, remarkably clear and true, was invaluable in the Council of an organization, which, if it effected the good it contemplated must constantly maintain cordial relations with the Government, and yet from the very nature of the case the utmost skill and delicacy were required to maintain those relations in all their integrity. The high official rank of Professor Bache, and his long experience as an officer of the Government were scarcely less serviceable to the Commission at the outset, than the unwearied zeal, stimulated by perfect faith in the idea it embodied, which distinguished him in his efforts to give practical effect to its methods during the whole period of its history.

DR. VAN BUREN was one of the members of the Commission to whom it was indebted for services in the early period of its history, which when Dr. Van Buren. viewed by the light of experience it would seem impossible to have dispensed with. To his eminent professional reputation which had done so much to secure a respectful hearing of the claims of the Commission at the outset, he joined a calm and sober judgment, not only of what ought to be done, but of what, with proper efforts, could be done. His former connection with the Medical Staff giving him a thorough knowledge of the defects of the system, gave also a practical value to his suggestions of remedy which it is impossible to over-estimate. The Commission did not hesitate to follow implicitly his counsel in all its suggestions of reform measures, and the following pages will show that the wisdom and propriety of his advice has been fully confirmed by the experience of its whole history.

PROFESSOR GIBBS was one of the members of the Commission from whose earnestness, wisely tempered Professor Gibbs. judgment, and great scientific ability much assistance was expected by his colleagues. Perfectly convinced of the truth of the principle upon which the Commission was based, he devoted himself with untiring zeal to a special investigation of all the scientific questions (non-medical) which were brought before the Commission at the commencement of its work. This duty, as will be seen hereafter, became a most serious and responsible one, but the Commission was always satisfied that its reputation as a quasi-scientific body was safe in his hands. But his services were by no means confined to this special field of inquiry. His zeal and earnestness, his comprehensive and practical views upon all questions of general policy were always conspicuous, and while he commanded the respect and confidence of his colleagues, he exerted a most important influence upon the whole work of the Commission.

DR. ELISHA HARRIS, another of the Commissioners, had had greater opportunities for observing the prac-Dr. Elisha Har- tical working of purely Sanitary measures ris. than any of his colleagues. His position as Physician of the Great Quarantine Hospital at New York had led him to a thorough study of Sanitary laws. He had become familiar with all the methods adopted by the English Government to restore to health its shattered army in the Crimea, and his suggestions therefore as to the practical measures to be followed here, founded upon that experience, were, of course, of the very highest value.

DR. AGNEW brought to the service of the Commission the valuable experience he had gained while performing the duties of a Medical Director of Dr. C. R. Agnew. the troops then being raised in New York. He soon exhibited a practical skill, executive ability, and at all times a perfect generosity of personal toil and trouble in carrying on the Commission's work which gave him, during its whole progress, a commanding influence in its councils. Oppressed by serious and responsible professional cares he nevertheless watched over with keenest interest the details of the Commission's service, and he set an example of self-sacrifice and disregard of personal interest when the succor of the soldier claimed his attention, or required his presence. It is not too much to say that the life-saving work of the Commission at Antietam, the relief which it afforded on so vast a scale after the battles of the Wilderness, and the succor which it was able to minister to thousands of our soldiers returning to us from rebel prisons diseased, naked, and famishing, owed much of their efficiency and success to plans arranged by Dr. Agnew, and carried out at personal risk and inconvenience under his immediate superintendence.

The arduous and responsible post of Treasurer fell to the lot of Mr. GEORGE T. STRONG, and the exactness and fidelity with which he discharged Mr. George T. its duties during its whole history, were Strong. scarcely less conspicuous than the unwearied zeal with

10

which he strove to direct aright its general policy by his wise and judicious counsel.

DR. NEWBERRY was recommended as a man of broad views, of enlarged experience, and of high scientific reputation. The peculiar sphere in which his great abilities shone forth most conspicuously during the war was the Western Department, where he was charged with the superintendence of the Commission's work as Associate Secretary. Still his advice and general views founded upon personal observation of the wants of that great field, made him a most valuable member at the Council Board of the Commission. His suggestions in regard to everything concerning the armies operating in the West, exerted so controlling an influence as to shape wholly the policy of the Commission in carrying on its special work among them.

Dr. John S. Newberry.

These eight gentlemen were the true founders of the Sanitary Commission. By them the earliest development of its policy was shaped and guided, to them, and to the General Secretary whom they appointed, the merit of whatever was wise in its conception, or practical, efficient, and life-saving in its plan and method during its whole history, is justly due. On this account it has seemed best to sketch some of the modes by which the peculiar qualifications of each were made to advance the general design. The other members of the Commission, Dr. Howe of Boston, Dr. Wood, Acting Surgeon-General, Colonel Cullum of General Scott's Staff, and Major Shiras of the Subsistence Department, all rendered valuable aid at the commencement, but other pressing duties of a public nature soon absorbed their attention, and thus the Commission was deprived of the benefit of their counsel and experience.

It will be observed on referring to the Plan of Organization that it was designed that the office of Resident Secretary should be one of the highest im- Resident or General Secretary. portance. He was to be charged with the chief executive duties of the Commission, to correspond constantly with its President, and to reside in Washington, where he was expected to maintain intimate personal relations with high Government officials. By him were to be appointed the agents of the Commission, charged with the inspection of camps and hospitals, and with the duty of giving the "advice" of the Commission where the case needed advice. They were to receive their instructions from him, and their reports were to be made to him. It was made his business also to see that the recommendations of these Inspectors received the attention of the proper Government authorities, and were duly enforced. In short, he was to be the General Manager of the Commission, responsible for the faithful performance of all the work which it had undertaken, even in its minutest details. It was of course not easy to find a man wholly qualified for such a position. It was necessary that he should possess perhaps the rarest combination of qualities found in human experience. He must unite great administrative capacity with unswerving faith and reliance upon great fundamental principles of policy, and his capacity was to be tested in a field of labor perfectly new, and hitherto wholly unexplored, at least in this country. The Commission, after a good deal of deliberation, decided that Mr. FREDERICK LAW OLMSTED, at that time Architect in Chief and Superintendent of Appointment of the Central Park in New York, possessed the Frederick Law Olmsted. essential qualities requisite for this position, and he was induced to accept it. How he performed the duties of the office, how much the Commission is indebted to his earnestness of purpose and his extraordinary power of organizing labor in a new field, it will be the business of the historian to tell in almost every page of this work. It is only necessary to say here that by the public, to whom the name of Mr. OLMSTED was familiar as the author of the most complete and philosophical account ever published of the condition of the Southern country before the war, and as the Director of a great public work, the successful management of which had been marked by incorruptible integrity, and the rarest administrative ability, his appointment was universally regarded as a sure guarantee of the success of the Commission's plans.

The original qualities of Mr. OLMSTED's mind as well as his peculiar training gave him, in truth, some very great advantages in the novel and extraordinary position to which he had been called. The theory of the Commission in regard to its relations ·with the Theory of the Government had been from the first, that it relation between the Government would carefully avoid doing any thing to and the Commission. impair the responsibilities of Government officials, or undertake in any way to perform duties which rightly belonged to them. In its view the Government machinery was the true and proper agency for performing the Government work. If that machinery was found defective or unable to accomplish what the novel circumstances of the times demanded, then its business was to urge in the proper quarter that the machinery might be so enlarged or modified as to suit the emergency. But the Commission always scrupulously avoided interfering with Government farther than to proffer its aid. In other words, it sought to do its work through Government channels, and by means of existing Government agencies. Its whole system of Inspection, of Relief, General and Special, and of the distribution of Hospital supplies, and indeed its whole organization, was based on this theory. Its object was to *supplement* Government deficiencies, not in any way to substitute itself for the Government organization; but on the contrary to endeavor to secure from every Government official the full measure of his responsibility. The delicate and difficult task of determining exactly where the Government responsibility ended, and that of the Commission began, devolved practically upon its General Secretary, who was charged with the administration of its executive service. Any mistake in this matter at the outset would have been fatal to all hope of success; nothing but constant collision, resulting at last in the withdrawal of the Commission from the field, would have marked any unwise interference with the details of the recognized usages and regulations of the army. Fortunately, the matter was in the hands of one whose studies and experience had thoroughly trained him in a science little understood in this country,—that of administration. The foundation of that science is the principle that each agent of any organization shall have his share of responsibility for the work exactly defined, and that he shall then be accountable to his superior officer for the thorough and faithful performance of that particular portion of the work, and nothing more. Pursuing this plan, and insisting upon its constant observance by his subordinates, the General Secretary soon placed their relations with the officers of the army upon the most friendly and cordial footing. Thoroughly understanding the distinct field occupied by the Government and the Commission, he insisted that each should maintain a proper recognition of the other's work. The remarkable fact, that during the whole war, there was scarcely a single instance of discourtesy or official insolence towards men occupying the anomalous position held by the Agents of the Commission in the army, is due perhaps quite as much to the constant observance of this rule, as to the personal character or personal services of the Agents themselves.

The position which the General Secretary occupied towards the Government was a very delicate one in Confidential na- another respect. It was designed that he ture of those re- lations. should be on a confidential footing with the War Department, and this, of course, involved a communication to him of so much of the plans of campaigns as might be necessary to enable the Commission to make due preparation for the performance of its appropriate duties. It also increased his responsibility in the selection of Agents who must necessarily be with the army without any recognized military *status*, but who nevertheless must know much of the plans of the General, and the movements of the troops. It was essential, therefore, that those men, in addition to their special qualifications, should possess great discretion, and be of undoubted loyalty. Besides, the plan of operations in the various branches of the service proposed by him must receive the approval of the War Department, and he was to be responsible for their execution in the spirit in which they were conceived. It was natural, therefore, that he should deem it essential for the satisfactory execution of the Commission's work, that he should control its Agents and operations throughout the whole field. Feeling deeply the responsibility of his own position, he knew that he could only properly discharge it by insisting that every one in the executive service of the Commission should receive instructions only through him, and faithfully report to him the execution of his orders.

The machinery composing the internal organization of the Commission being thus complete, no time was lost in setting resolutely to work to perform Camp and Hospital Inspection. the duties which had been devolved upon it. The two great wants at that time, in the opinion of the Commission were an exact knowledge of the condition of the troops, so as to ascertain what sanitary measures were most essential, and some definite plan of raising money to sustain its work. It was thought best that both these objects should be prosecuted simultaneously, as it was evident that an application to the public for money would be greatly aided by a truthful statement of the actual needs of the army as observed in the camps and the hospitals by competent and trustworthy men. The President and Dr. Newberry proceeded on a tour of inspection of the camps at the West, while the other members of the Commission undertook to

visit those at Fortress Monroe, and in the vicinity of
Washington and New York.   Before separating however, they signed two papers, one addressed to the
people of the country at large, the other specially to
the Managers of Life Insurance Companies, stating
their plans, and asking for contributions to enable
them to carry them into execution.

The whole policy of the Sanitary Commission in
regard to raising the funds necessary to a proper sup-
Financial policy port of its work, was so peculiarly Ameri-
of the Commis-
sion.   can in its character, and exerted so marked
an influence upon every step of its progress during
the war, and it resulted in such immense contributions
to its treasury, that the reasons which dictated it
deserve careful consideration.   It might be supposed
that an organization called into official existence at
the request of the Medical Bureau, having no other
end or object than to aid the operations of that
Bureau, making use of Government channels only to
convey the stream of popular bounty for the relief
of the Government service, might naturally claim to
be supported, as are the other branches of Government
work by Government pay.   But from the very first,
the design of the founders of the Commission was
settled, that it should do its work only on the principle
of that voluntary system of organization, which is one
of the most striking characteristics of our American
civilization, and which, with its free and untrammelled
spirit has done such marvellous things for the country
in every department of labor.   All it asked, therefore,
from the Government was permission to work; the
inspiration which led its members to hope for success

came from the people themselves, and to that public opinion, which is the true sovereign in this country, they held themselves alone, but always responsible. They felt that they could here undertake a task which would have been impossible in any other country, not merely because this was a peoples' war, as it has sometimes been called, but because experience had taught them that their task, so far as enlisting the sympathy and support of their countrymen was concerned, was comparatively easy. It was not necessary to create any interest or enthusiasm in the cause, but simply to win confidence in the system which was proposed, by instructing the public as to the necessity of its adoption, as the best means of meeting the emergency.

Besides these motives for adhering persistently to the voluntary system—motives which have been so long operative in the American mind, that their action seems almost instinctive when any great organized effort is to be made—there were other reasons for an unwillingness to apply to the Government for pecuniary aid. Among others, it was deemed essential that the Commission should be wholly free from that sort of control which would have been the inevitable accompaniment of dependence on the Government for means to execute its work. The mere suspicion that in any way it could be made an instrument of Government patronage would have wholly destroyed its usefulness. Above all things it was important that it should be entirely out of the reach of unscrupulous politicians, who, if they gained a foothold, would strive in some way to

11

degrade it from its high position, and make it subserve their own selfish ends.

The Commission, therefore, full of faith in the sympathy and intelligence of the people, appointed its Modes of raising Secretary and other officers, and prepared to money. go to work without a dollar in its Treasury. It was satisfied that all that was necessary to secure contributions was, not to convince the public that something must be done for the army outside the Government agencies, but that the preventive and precautionary measures which it advocated were best suited to promote the true interests of the soldier. It was idle to tell people then, and it has proved equally idle to tell them at any period of the war, that the Government could do, and was doing all that was possible or desirable. The countless forms of popular sympathy growing more clamorous and persistent in their offers of relief as the war went on, and after experience had improved the efficiency of the Government agencies, all bore unmistakable evidence of the irrepressible determination of the American people to manifest in some way their direct personal interest in the soldier. However defective some of the schemes which grew out of this state of popular feeling may have proved as to the true mode of affording relief, they all betokened the existence of a spirit in the highest degree creditable to the humanity and civilization of the country,—a spirit prompted by the universal instinct, that it was impossible for any Government, with its utmost zeal and efforts, to bestow that tender care upon the soldier which the American people desired he should receive. The task then of the Commission was limited to proving that preventive means were the best adapted to accomplish this general desire.

The difficulty was at the start only, for no doubt was felt that the experience of a few months of the neglect of sanitary measures among the troops would afford the saddest and most conclusive evidence of the truth of the Commission theory. *Educating the public mind in regard to the value of a preventive system.* But it was very undesirable that lessons of wisdom should be learned at so fearful a cost. The Commission endeavored to popularize the general elementary truths of sanitary science, and to enforce their application by a picture of the terrible results which had followed the violation of sanitary laws in the British army during the Crimean and Indian campaigns. There was much in the experience of other countries in relation to this subject to discourage them in their attempt. History shows that there are no measures upon which it is more difficult to fix public attention, and thereby assure efficient action than those of a strictly preventive nature. While the pestilence is far off we sit still, idly hugging to ourselves the delusion that in some way we shall escape its visitation. The general principles of sanitary science, particularly as applied to armies are so obvious and simple, that more than a hundred years ago they were advocated in England upon the same grounds, and almost in the same terms, as have been employed in our own day. Yet neither the elaborate works of Sir John Pringle, on Diseases in the Army, nor that of Dr. Lind on the modes of preserving the health of seamen, nor the immortal work of John Howard, on Prisons and Hospitals, had succeeded in gaining a proper recognition of sanitary laws, and their due administration in the public service. Information on the subject there was in abundance; never indeed was a scientific truth more plainly demonstrated; what was needed was to urge its practical application to the cure of existing evils.

The Commission wisely addressed itself in the first instance to the Managers of Life Insurance Companies, as to men of more than ordinary intelligence and influence, whose direct interest lay in fostering every well-considered scheme of a life-saving kind. The first contributions in large amounts came from these institutions. The New England Life Insurance Company gave one thousand dollars. This example was soon followed by the various Life Insurance Companies in New York, one of them, the Mutual, having given in all, nine thousand dollars in aid of the Commission's Treasury. In order to stimulate contributions, and to organize the financial affairs of the Commission upon a sure basis, certain prominent gentlemen in New York were invited to act as a Central Auxiliary Finance Committee.* Through the exertions of these gentlemen large sums were contributed by public institutions and private individuals throughout the country, and sufficient money was obtained to enable the Commission to give its experiment a fair trial.

Appeal to Life Insurance Companies.

* The following named gentlemen composed this Committee:—Hon. Samuel B. Ruggles, Christopher R. Roberts, Robert B. Minturn, George Opdyke, Jonathan Sturges, Morris Ketchum, David Hoadley, J. P. Giraud Forster, and Charles E. Strong.

CHAPTER IV.

INSPECTION OF CAMPS AND HOSPITALS.

In addition to the work of inspection undertaken by different members of the Commission in various parts of the country two competent gentlemen, Dr. Tomes and Mr. Dunning, were employed to make certain specific inquiries in relation to the condition of the camps at Fortress Monroe. Their reports did not cover the whole ground which was afterwards explored by the gentlemen engaged in the great inspectorial work of the Commission, still they formed the basis of that work, and they contained information as to the actual condition of the army which confirmed the worst fears of those who had sent them forth.

Organization of the System of Inspection.

Mr. Olmsted, assisted by Dr. Harris, investigated the condition of twenty camps of volunteers in the neighborhood of Washington, in the early days of July, and his report of that examination embodies an exceedingly interesting account of the condition of the newly-raised troops as observed before they had received the actual shock of battle. In this report Mr. Olmsted points out specifically some of the more obvious evils which attracted his attention. He says "that a complete system of drains, so essential to the health of the men, did not

Inspection of the Camps near Washington.

exist in any of the camps, that the tents were so crowded at night that the men were poisoned by the vitiated atmosphere, that the sinks were unnecessarily and disgustingly offensive, that personal cleanliness among the men was wholly unattended to, that the clothing was of bad material and almost always filthy to the last degree, and that there was scarcely a pretence of performing the ordinary police duties of a military camp." There seemed to be an abundance of such food—beef and pork—as the Subsistence Department was permitted by law to furnish, but under the regulations no green vegetables could be issued, and of course none were provided. The consequence was that the army was generally believed to be in great danger of decimation by scurvy or dysentery. The cooking was said to be, of all the subjects, that on which the army most needed instruction. While this ignorance continued serious results must ensue to the troops from eating ill-prepared food. Mr. Olmsted traces in his report all these difficulties of the service to their true source—the inexperience of the officers, and the consequent want of discipline among the men. He says (p. 14) "that he is compelled to believe that it is now hardly possible to place the volunteer army in a good defensive condition against the pestilential influences by which it must soon be surrounded. No general orders, calculated to guard against their approach, can be immediately enforced with the necessary rigor. The Captains especially have, in general, not the faintest comprehension of their proper responsibility, and if they could be made to understand they could not be made to perform the part which properly belongs to them in any purely military effort to this end."

The report of Dr. Bellows and Dr. Newberry of the condition of the various camps at the West, visited by them, told substantially the same story. *Inspection of Camps at the West.* Everywhere were conspicuous those frightful evils which are inseparable from a bad military organization, and defective administration. The result was a perfectly shiftless condition of things which betokened the early demoralization, if not actual mutiny of the army.

The alarming state of affairs revealed by these reports made a profound impression upon the members of the Commission, and at a session held early in July, it sought by every *Action of Commission on the Reports of the Inspectors.* means at its command, to induce the Government to adopt measures to avert some of the more obvious dangers to the National cause which those Reports had indicated. It strongly urged that means should be taken 'at once to provide accommodations near the railroad station at Washington for the use of troops arriving and departing, that some system should be adopted by which the soldier could transmit to his family a part or the whole of his pay, that a rigid system of camp police should be enforced, that competent cooks should be employed, that a stricter discipline, which should keep the men out of the dram-shops in Washington, should be maintained, and that a liberal supply of fresh vegetables should be issued. Of these recommendations, though urged upon the Government with anxious pertinacity, very few were then adopted. The extraordinary laxity of discipline which at that time prevailed in the army seemed to have invaded every branch of the Government, and it was not until the terrible events of the next few weeks had demonstrated the necessity of discipline that it was willingly submitted to, and thoroughly enforced, and formed the basis of the system by which the army under General McClellan was re-organized.

It may be supposed that with the thorough knowledge of the real condition of the army which the The Battle of Commission had thus acquired, the result of Bull's Run. the battle of Bull's Run could not much surprise its members. The battle itself proved the existence of some of the highest qualities of the soldier among the volunteers, but the disgraceful rout and confusion with which it ended, caused by a panic and a delusion, and the utter demoralization which followed it, showed plainly that the most brilliant courage in battle may be rendered wholly useless by radical defects in organization and discipline. The Commission, as was its duty, had reiterated its warning to the Government in regard to these defects, but the advice which it had given, and which it had striven so hard to enforce, had been wholly unheeded.

In order to ascertain accurately the causes which produced the fearful condition of things after the Inquiry into the battle of Bull's Run, so far as they were Causes of the Defeat. dependent upon the condition, physical and moral, of the men, and to determine how far the result was due to causes which a proper foresight could have guarded against, the Commission instituted, immediately after the battle, a minute inquiry into the whole subject. The nature and extent of this inquiry may be inferred when it is stated that it consisted of seventy-five questions, embracing almost every conceivable subject connected with the history of the battle. These questions were placed in the hands of seven Inspectors of the Commission, and answers were obtained from very many officers and men who had taken part in the battle, and these answers comprised nearly two thousand items of information. The questions referred to such points, among others, as these: the strength of the Regiments, their last meal, the first movement on the 21st, (the day of the battle,) the degree of vigor of the troops at the commencement of the battle, and the causes of exhaustion before it began; the Commissariat service; the extent of the exhaustion during the battle and its causes; the desertion of their commands by the officers; the causes of the retreat; the distance passed over in accomplishing it; the physical and moral condition of the troops during its continuance; and the extent and degree of demoralization and its causes. The answers were carefully collated and tabulated by Mr. E. B. Elliott, the accomplished Actuary of the Commission, and it is believed that there is no instance in history in which the causes of the loss of any considerable battle have been so thoroughly sifted and examined, on the spot, and within a week after the disaster, and in which the minutest details, affecting the result, have been so carefully preserved and their influence so accurately noted. The facts developed by this inquiry have of course a general interest wholly independent of any

12

question affecting the sanitary condition of the army. They proved so clearly the inefficiency of the Government measures in regard to the care and discipline of the volunteers, that it was deemed prudent to withhold it from general circulation at the time.* It was adopted, however, by the Commission as its guide in the renewed efforts it proposed to make to induce the Government to adopt the only true means of avoiding similar disasters hereafter. It clearly proved the value of the recommendations made by the Commission previous to the opening of the campaign. In certain Regiments, the Second Rhode Island for instance, whose sanitary condition, in the largest sense, had been reported satisfactory before it left its camp for the battle-field, no taint of demoralization was visible. But in regard to the mass of the troops, and especially such portions of them as had been notoriously neglected by their officers ever since they had arrived in Washington, it was very evident that their utter demoralization could be clearly traced to this neglect. For in such Regiments the depressing effect of long abstinence from food, exhaustion before the battle, an over-tasking of their physical powers in it, and the horrors of the retreat were wholly unchecked by the force of discipline. The men who had never been taught their duty as soldiers, now became a hungry and ferocious mob. The streets of Washington presented a strange aspect for some days after the battle, and no where has the painful scene been better described than in this report of Mr. Olmsted. "The

---

* It now forms Document No. 28 of the Commission and is accessible to the public.

appearance of the streets," he says, "was in the strongest possible contrast to that which could be imagined of a city placed by a strong necessity under the severe control of an effective military discipline. Groups of men wearing parts of military uniforms and some of them with muskets were indeed to be seen; but upon second sight they did not appear to be soldiers. Rather they were a most woe-begone rabble, which had perhaps clothed itself with the garments of dead soldiers left on a hard-fought battle-field. No two were dressed completely alike; some were without caps, others without coats, others without shoes. All were alike excessively dirty, unshaven, unkempt, and dank with dew. The groups were formed around fires made in the streets, of boards wrenched from citizens' fences. Some were still asleep, at full length in the gutters and on door steps, or sitting on the curbstone resting their heads against the lamp-posts. Others were evidently begging for food at house-doors. Some appeared ferocious, others only sick and dejected, all excessively weak, hungry, and selfish. There was no apparent organization: no officers were seen among them, seldom even a non-commissioned officer. At Willard's Hotel, however, officers swarmed. They, too, were dirty and in ill-condition; but appeared indifferent, reckless, and shameless, rather than dejected and morose."

In this alarming condition of things the Government utterly paralyzed and helpless, sent for General McClellan, and being taught at last by the near prospect of the enemy's advance to Washington the real danger of its position, it invoked

Reform in the Discipline of the Army.

for its salvation that spirit of discipline which it had previously so lightly valued. It had been said that it was impossible to enforce discipline among volunteers. General McClellan, with the cordial co-operation of the Government, now determined to try the experiment. The result was, what might have been expected from the uncommon power of organizing possessed by the General, and the intelligence of the troops. Writing in September, Mr. Olmsted says;—"Ten times the rigor of enforcement in regard to the regulations, that had been previously used with volunteers, has made the best of an ineffective system, and shown what might have been done with volunteers before July. Even the demoralized Regiments, with but very few exceptions, are now in better condition, better spirit, in better health, than they were when they received the order for the advance to Bull Run. The very measures which the Commission urged, which it was said could not be enforced, would not be submitted to, and would be useless with volunteers, are now rigidly enforced, are submitted to with manifest satisfaction by volunteers and are obviously producing the most beneficent results, and this equally in the new and in the older Regiments. The most exact disciplinarians are the favorites of the volunteers; the best disciplined Regiments are the most contented Regiments."

The lesson taught by the battle of Bull's Run was unquestionably the most wholesome lesson learned by the people of the North during the whole war—but in our gratitude, when we remember that its stern teachings first settled the real duties

Lessons taught by the defeat.

and position of the soldier, and placed the relations of the Government towards him on a juster and more rational basis, and forever scattered to the winds the poisonous doctrines with which the public mind and conscience had been drugged, we should not forget the fearful cost of blood and national humiliation at which that lesson had been learned.

While the army was being re-organized under General McClellan, several subjects more immediately connected with the health of troops de- Condition of the manded the attention of the Commission. Military Hospitals. In no Department of the Government were its preparations less suited to meet the emergency than in that of the Military Hospitals. At the outset, from the necessity of the case, buildings constructed for totally different purposes were converted into Hospitals, and in the important matters of location, ventilation, accommodation for the patients in the wards, and conveniences outside of them, these buildings combined those conditions which have been recognized by modern science as most unfavorable to the recovery of the sick. The attendants, the nurses, and the administrative staff generally, of those at least in the vicinity of Washington, were so unqualified for their positions, that any civil hospital under such a management, would have been considered a disgrace to the science and humanity of the country. This condition was made so apparent from an investigation made by Dr. Van Buren and Dr. Agnew, two of the most competent observers in the country, in the latter part of July, that the Commission thought it its duty to protest against its continuance, and to advise the Government to erect Hospitals specially adapted for the proper accommodation of the sick and wounded. It was recommended that arrangements should be made in them for the reception of fifteen thousand patients. These Hospitals were to be built according to what is known as the "Pavilion System," each ward forming one of a series of detached wooden buildings, capable of accommodating forty or fifty patients, and provided with all the appropriate conveniences needed by them. The report stated that this was the best modern system of Hospital construction, and if adopted would save both lives and money. The subject was thoroughly discussed during the September and October sessions of the Commission. In their efforts to secure reform in this important matter the Members of the Board had the hearty co-operation of those Government officials to whose special Department, the execution of the plans for these Hospitals when approved by the Secretary of War, would be assigned. General Meigs, Quartermaster-General, General Van Vliet, Quartermaster of the Army of the Potomac, and Dr. Tripler, the Medical Director of that army, were all present during these discussions. They exhibited the greatest interest in the subject and requested the Commission to submit drawings and plans of buildings such as it would approve for Plans for Hospital buildings prepared by the Commission. Hospital purposes. On the 26th of September, these plans, prepared under the direction of a Committee consisting of Dr. Gibbs, Dr. Van Buren, and Dr. Agnew, were sent to the Government authorities. The subject was again further discussed during the October session, and by the close of that month, the Commission had the satisfaction of learning that the plans submitted by it had been finally adopted by the Secretary of War with some slight modifications. The Government seemed disposed in this instance to invoke the direct aid and counsel of the Commission in a greater degree than it had ever done before. The War Department not only adopted the Commission's plans as a whole, but they requested certain of its members, supposed to possess special qualifications, to aid its own officers in the selection of sites for five model Hospitals which were afterwards erected in accordance with these plans. For once, the suggestions of the Commission were met with a frank, cordial, and generous spirit on the part of the Government.

Thus was inaugurated that great Hospital system, one of the noblest triumphs of the war, making slow progress indeed until after the re-organization of the Medical Bureau, but afterwards, when fully developed, resulting in the erection of build- Result of the New System. ings upon substantially the same plans as those first adopted, at all points where General Military Hospitals were located. The arrangements thus made for the care of the vast number of sick and wounded of the army were on a scale unprecedented in history, not only in their vastness, but in their fulfillment of all the requirements of humanity and science. The result has been, as is well known, a far lower rate of mortality here during the war than has ever been observed in the Military Hospitals of other countries, and it is well worthy of consideration how far this result, so gratifying to our National pride and to our instincts of humanity, is due to the early, persistent, and at last successful efforts of the Sanitary Commission to induce the Government to make suitable arrangements for the reception and care of the sick and wounded of the army.

The Commission, while striving to settle upon a proper basis this momentous question, had not ne- Plans of Inspection, Enlarged and Systematized. glected measures looking to the gradual development of that part of their plan from the faithful execution of which they anticipated the most permanent and satisfactory results—the Inspection of Camps and Hospitals. The preliminary surveys which had been made, and which have been already referred to, although far from exhaustive in their character, had revealed so much of the real condition of the army, that they confirmed its estimate of the importance of maintaining constant and minute inquiries extending over all the various armies. The Commission watched with the greatest anxiety the slow progress of improvement in the health and *morale* of the army under the new system of discipline inaugurated and enforced by General McClellan, and it sought to discover in what way it could aid him, as well as the Generals in command in other parts of the country, in their efforts to promote the efficiency of the troops.

The state of its Treasury having somewhat improved after the battle of Bull's Run, it was determined to employ six competent gentlemen Six permanent Inspectors appointed. Their instructions. as Inspectors of Camps. Of these Dr. Buell was assigned to the Camps in Missouri, Dr.

Aigner to Cairo, Ill., Dr. Douglas to General Banks' Column in Northern Virginia, Mr. Dunning to Fortress Monroe, and Dr. Tomes and Mr. Knapp to the Department of the Potomac. It was of course foreseen that the first difficulty would be to establish harmonious relations with the officers of the Regiments in the performance of a duty which was certainly inquisitorial, and might be deemed meddlesome. The gentlemen selected as Inspectors were chosen with special reference to their power of rendering the faithful performance of this duty as little unpleasant as possible. They were minutely instructed to observe, with the greatest care, all the requirements of military etiquette, to advocate the most exalted ideas of military discipline, and above all things, and by every means in their power, to magnify and make honorable the arduous and responsible offices of the Surgeon. They were furnished with a list of questions, one hundred and eighty in number, prepared and arranged with the greatest care by the Secretary, assisted by those members of the Commission whose scientific knowledge suggested certain special topics of inquiry.* These questions were intended to elicit information of the most exact and minute kind in regard to the actual condition of the men. They embraced such subjects as the site and general condition of the camps, the ventilation and condition of the tents, the bedding and clothing of the men, the source and quality of the water, the character of the rations and cooking, the general discipline of the camp, the character of the Medical Officers, the

* See Documents of the Commission, Nos. 19, 19a.

13

sickness and mortality among the troops and its causes, and the nature of the Hospital accommodation. These inspections were thoroughly and carefully made, and the study of the facts brought to light by them convinced the Board that by this means alone could it gain light to guide them in the performance of the duty which had been confided to it.

But such was not the only nor perhaps the most important object had in view by the Commission in Influence of the instituting this system of Inspection. It work of Inspec- tion in the was hoped that the Agent, while pursuing Army. his inquiries in the camps, would be listened to as an adviser also. The result did not disappoint this confident expectation. It would appear, at first sight, that the Commission was attaching undue importance to this portion of its work. To send a body of men, however respectable in personal character and attainments, and however inoffensive in their bearing towards those in authority, but without the slightest power to order the removal of evils which they might observe,—to send such men into a Military Camp to inquire into matters which involved the competency of the officers for the proper performance of their duties, would seem at first sight a plan likely only to excite contempt, if not provoke insult from that class of officers, who really most needed advice and instruction. But no such result attended the experiment. The Inspectors were almost universally received with courtesy by the officers, and their suggestions were listened to with the greatest interest and attention. The specific evils in the camps which were pointed out by them might not always be cured, but this was due in almost all cases to the same ignorance of the proper mode of remedying them, as that which had permitted their existence. The want of information on the part of some of the officers as to the nature and scope of their duties was very extraordinary, but the prevalent disposition was an anxiety to learn, as the prevalent feeling was a sense of their responsibility. When some of these men were told that their duties were not confined to mere routine drill and parade, and that the same army regulations which required a Captain to instruct his men in the manual, also enjoined upon him a daily inspection of the pots and kettles, bedding and clothing of his Company, their surprise was almost ludicrous. The suggestion that a Captain of Volunteers was to be expected to perform such duties was often indignantly repelled; he had not come into the army to keep a boarding-house, or act the chamber-maid. But with the great mass of the officers, suggestions like these led to serious reflection, and a determination to perform all the duties of their position, however unexpected or irksome they might prove. Thus it happened, all through the war, that the system of Inspection, although without the shadow of a military authority to enforce its recommendations, proved of the greatest benefit to the soldier, for if it did nothing else it taught the officers that they were to be the fathers of their men, as well as their leaders, and by timely suggestions of their duty it helped them to help themselves.

This system of Inspection was maintained during the whole war as a distinguishing feature of the Com-

General results of systematic Inspection. mission's work. As every day's experience afforded new evidence of the value of this mode of prosecuting inquiry, it was gradually extended to other fields of labor connected with the army organization, and always with the most favorable results. It will be seen hereafter in what various ways through its agency vast good was accomplished. It is not, perhaps, too much to say, looking back now to the full development of its capacity as a measure of prevention, that by its means many lives were saved, and some of the more obvious causes of disease either forestalled or removed. But before the war had lasted six months the Commission was satisfied that as an aid to the Government in ascertaining exactly the nature of the evils which impaired the efficiency of the army, by teaching the officers the importance of certain special duties towards their men, and in maintaining, as the representative of the people in the army a perpetual stimulus to the performance of those duties faithfully, it had proved an Agency of inestimable value.

It soon became clear that the Commission, in its disinterested labors could not reckon upon the aid and Relations with the Head of the Medical Bureau. co-operation of the Medical Bureau. It soon appeared that the Surgeon-General had no admiration for the Commission, and no sympathy whatever with its methods of accomplishing the objects of its appointment, to which, as we have said, he had reluctantly consented. At the same time it was equally clear that all the old traditions of the army conceived in a spirit which never looked beyond the wants of ten or fifteen thousand men, and for that reason, if for no other, wholly inapplicable to the existing emergency were to be maintained in all their vigor. It was hardly to be wondered at that a gentleman grown gray in the service, full of that *esprit de corps* so natural, so honorable, and in its place so useful among military men, who had spent long years in perfecting the details of a service which he conscientiously believed to constitute a well ordered system fully adapted to the wants of the army, should dislike suggestions of radical change, or that he should especially resent the interference of so anomalous and unprecedented an Agency as the Sanitary Commission. With due respect for the personal character and former services of the Head of the Bureau, the Commission plainly perceived that his devotion to routine and his undisguised hostility to their body would render all their plans for promoting the health and efficiency of the army practically worthless. The evidence of a daily growing want of harmony between the views of the Surgeon-General and themselves was furnished by the reports of all their Inspectors, and by their own observation. After some hesitation the grave step of requesting the Government either to remove the Surgeon-General from his post, or place him in honorable retirement was resolved upon. This measure was adopted by the Commission on the 12th of September. The Commission acted in this matter under the conscientious conviction that it would be impossible to execute the task confided to it by the Government unless such a change were made, and its relations with the Medical Bureau placed upon a more friendly and cordial footing. No such change was then made, and the evils which were deplored by the Commission, the far-reaching results of which were clearly foreseen, produced their natural fruit in the total inadequacy of the Medical Department to meet the claims upon it, a state of things which lasted until a thorough re-organization of the Bureau was effected principally by the agency of the Sanitary Commission.

At the same time the Commission made some other important recommendations with a view of improving the efficiency of the service, and looking specially to securing the careful and humane treatment of the sick and wounded. In these recommendations they had the cordial aid and co-operation of General McClellan, but even his power, vast as it was at that time, could not pierce the hardened mass of routine and precedent which then impeded the efficient action of so many of the Government agencies. It was asked in the first place, that the General commanding the Army of the Potomac should select his own Medical Director, who should be responsible to him, and not to the Medical Bureau. This was rendered necessary in the opinion both of the Commission and the General, by the defective organization of that Bureau, and its apparent utter inability to appreciate in any true spirit the responsibilities of its position. Although the application was enforced by the statement that the most "insufficient provision had as yet been made for the wants of the sick and wounded of that army, and that it was now too late to embarrass the hand that would seek to supply the crying deficiencies with any other responsibility than such as was due to the General commanding,"—yet it

[Marginal note:] Various recommendations to secure greater efficiency in the service.

was of course contrary to all precedent, and was therefore denied.

The Commission also asked that an "Ambulance Regiment" should be created under General McClellan's direction, with the utmost promptness, and that, in view of the utter want of experience, the neglect, and even the positive inhumanity of the soldiers detailed as nurses, as well as in order to secure the services of all enlisted men in the discharge of their ordinary military duties a corps of nurses, men, and women also, if deemed expedient, should be engaged for the special care of the sick and wounded. This application met the same fate as that concerning the position of the Medical Director. The neglect of these recommendations vastly increased the horrors of the Peninsular Campaign. The want of proper arrangements for the transportation of the sick and wounded, and the character of the nurses provided by the Government during that campaign were such as to be in the highest degree disgraceful to the reputation of the country for administrative capacity, and for humanity. It is not, of course, intended to assert that this sad condition of things arose from any wilful neglect of duty on the part of the subordinate officers of the Bureau. It was due to that utter inadequacy of means to the end in view which its chiefs were unable to comprehend, and to the blind guidance which they afforded to a Government which with equal blindness was willing to follow it.

Finally the Commission asked that in view of the unreasonable, and indeed illegal, attitude assumed by the Medical Bureau toward a body specially appointed by the President to advise and assist it in its labors, its relations with that Bureau should be placed on a basis of entire confidence and co-operation, its disinterested counsel should be received without jealousy, and its requests when made in writing should be granted, or reasons given in writing why they were denied. No answer was vouchsafed to this application, and the Commission with heavy heart, but undiminished courage, was left to pursue its thankless task in the cold shade of Government neglect and indifference. The truth was that the Commission had already made itself too much felt as a power in the army to gratify those in official authority, but it was also too deeply set in the affections of the people to render an open attack upon it prudent. It was disposed to rip up too many old abuses, to disturb too profoundly the self-complacency of those who thought that the most difficult problems of the time could be solved by some easy process of routine and precedent; it was far too inquisitive, earnest and persistent to invite the sympathy of those who had so long borne rule in the offices at Washington. Not a word was whispered against the purity and disinterestedness of the motives of its members, or the wisdom of its counsel, or the extreme delicacy with which its Agents respected the acknowledged rights of official authority, but it was meddlesome, because it seemed determined to get at the root of the evil, and very troublesome because it suggested methods of reform hitherto unknown to the bureaucracy of the Government. Its members were, doubtless, it was said, good men, but they were sentimentalists, not because they recommended measures wholly unwise, but because it was impossible for any one, however able, not thoroughly versed in the details of the service, to suggest any reform, however apparently judicious or necessary, which could have any practical value. But the members of the Commission did not look to Government for encouragement; all they asked, as has been said before, was permission to work. They found their reward in their own consciences, and although humiliated by the evident want of sympathy with their arduous labors manifested by the authorities, they looked with the utmost confidence to being sustained by that High Court of Errors and Appeals called in this country Public Opinion,—a tribunal which does not hesitate to reverse very often the judgment of Presidents, of Secretaries, and even of Chiefs of Bureaus, and force them all at last to submit to decrees based not on considerations of prescription and usage, but upon the eternal laws of right and justice and humanity.

The Commission was busily engaged during the latter portion of the year in introducing into every division of the army its system of Inspection. The important questions concerning voluntary contributions of hospital supplies, the extent and character of the relief which should be given to soldiers in "irregular circumstances," and the collection, arrangement, and preservation of the vital statistics of the army were also carefully studied. Having been thoroughly considered in all their aspects, and the exact nature of the duty to the Commission in relation to them being clearly defined and settled,

Various departments of the Commission's work organized.

14

separate departments were created under the general organization of the Commission, which should have these subjects in special charge. The operations of these departments form, in popular estimation at least, the most conspicuous feature of the Commission's work, and it will be necessary therefore hereafter to present a somewhat detailed account of their true scope, and the methods by which their designs were accomplished. We need say here only that their early establishment in the history of the Commission is an evidence of the thorough and conscientious spirit with which the work was entered upon, and of the broad foundation upon which all its plans for improving the health and effi- ciency of the army were based. The vast increase of the army during the first six months of the war, seventy-five thousand men having been called out early in May, and eight hundred thousand during the month of July, only made clearer to its members their percep- tions of their duty, and stimulated them to renewed activity and vigor.

Towards the close of the year the Commission pre- sented to the Secretary of War an elaborate report of The Commis- the result of its labors.* This report, pre- sion's Report to the Secretary of pared by the General Secretary, Mr. Olm- War. sted, was as remarkable for the wide and comprehensive survey it presented of the peculiar needs of the newly raised volunteers, as for the clear and definite statements it made of what the Commis- sion had done, and what it proposed to do in aiding to supply those needs. The report attracted universal attention at home, and inspired the public with confi-

* See Doc. No. 40.

dence both in the Commission's plans, and in the sound judgment of the men who had devised them, while it extorted unwilling praise even from foreign and unfriendly journals. It exhibited a picture of the actual condition of the army made up from the results of nearly four hundred inspections. The returns from these inspections embraced every column of the army, and they were carefully tabulated by the Actuary of the Commission. The Secretary was thus enabled to survey the whole field, and to speak with positive certainty as to the real condition of things. The important question of " encamping," with its manifold ramifications, was thoroughly examined by the light of the experience thus gained. Camp sites and drainage, the tents with their poor material and want of ventilation, and the defectiveness of the camp police were treated upon at large, and the necessity of measures to improve their condition pointed out and enforced. The clothing of the men, their want of personal cleanliness, the defectiveness of the cooking arrangements, and the general absence of strict discipline in the army and its causes, were topics that furnished a most instructive and interesting chapter of the Report. The vastly important questions of the prevailing diseases in the army with their tendencies, the hospital accommodations, and the qualifications of the surgeons were discussed at great length, and with much force, and the grave defects of the military administration in these respects fearlessly exposed. Many other subjects affecting the condition of the troops were brought to the notice of the Government, and the whole Report must be considered as the most exhaustive and authoritative *exposé* of the various causes which affect the true efficiency of an army that has ever been made public. While the dangers of the condition were thus boldly presented, the remedies for existing evils were clearly indicated. Not the least characteristic feature of this Report is the tone of perfect sincerity, earnestness, and ardent love of country which pervades it throughout. The Commission felt the responsibility of its position, and while not unmindful of the delicacy of its relations with the Government, it was determined that no false spirit of compromise with evils which were poisoning the very life-blood of the Republic should degrade its policy. Perfectly convinced of the enormity of these evils, and the possibility of the removal of most of them by timely and judicious measures, and determined to urge constantly upon the Government the absolute necessity of the performance of its duty, the Commission did not hesitate to define thus the position it occupied :

"The one point which controls the Commission is just this: A simple desire and resolute determination to secure for the men who have enlisted in this war that care which it is the duty and the will of the nation to give them. That care is their right, and in the Government or out of it, it must be given them, let who will stand in the way."

CHAPTER V.

RE-ORGANIZATION OF THE MEDICAL BUREAU AND APPOINT-MENT OF A NEW SURGEON-GENERAL.

THE early months of the year 1862, it will be remembered, were not marked by military operations which resulted in great battles, at least on land. The period was one rather of preparation and expectancy, than of actual conflict. The expeditions of General Burnside to Roanoke Island, that of General Sherman to Port Royal, and that of General Butler to New Orleans, were each accompanied by Agents of the Commission, Inspectors and Relief Officers, who, as far as the limited means at their disposal permitted, endeavored to apply its methods to the care of the health, and to the improvement of the efficiency of the men in these several armies. In each of these expeditions, the troops suffered much from ignorance on the part of their officers, as to the best mode of caring for them while on shipboard, and when they were transferred to their new quarters on land. A judicious distribution of suitable "Sanitary" stores was made, and many practical suggestions offered by the Agents of the Commission looking to the improvement of the

Military Expeditions in the early part of 1862.

109

condition of the men, were adopted by the military authorities.

While the Commission did not neglect its duty of providing for the wants of these distant expeditions, Preparation and distribution of Medical and Surgical Mono- graphy. its chief attention was fixed upon plans for the general improvement of the military administration, so far as it related to the hygienic and sanitary interests of the army. Among the practical inconveniences which had been observed by its Inspectors in the prosecution of their work, was the want of familiarity on the part of many of the Surgeons with those latest teachings of medical science, which would enable them to treat skilfully and successfully the sick and wounded under their charge. The low standard of professional ability in the army at that time, was perhaps unavoidable, for the Surgeons had been selected from civil life, in many cases, with hardly greater care than had been shown in the choice of the other officers of the Regiments. Besides, they were called upon to treat diseases in the Military Hospitals, with which they had been little familiar in private practice, and under circumstances in which they were necessarily unable to consult books which might have enlightened their ignorance. In view of this condition of things, the Commission requested certain of its Associate Members, men of eminent professional reputation in various parts of the country, to prepare a number of concise treatises, recording the latest results of medical investigation, concerning those diseases which experience has proved always prevail in large armies. The gentlemen applied to performed their task with remarkable skill and fidelity, and the result was that these treatises or monographs, embracing a compendious system of instruction on many important medical and surgical questions arising in military practice, formed for the Army Surgeons a portable medical library, of great value. These monographs, nineteen in number, were prepared at intervals, and distributed by the Commission to all the Medical Officers of the army. The mode thus adopted for increasing the efficiency of the service is another illustration of the wide and comprehensive views taken by the Commission of the nature of the duty confided to it. These little manuals were gladly welcomed by the Surgeons, and perhaps nothing contributed more to maintain cordial relations between them and the Agents of the Commission, than this practical proof of the enlightened and liberal policy adopted by it, a policy which was prompted by an earnest desire to help them to help themselves. [See Appendix, No. 8.]

But the great work of the Commission, without the accomplishment of which it was felt, that all else it might do, would prove but of partial and temporary benefit, was the RE-ORGANIZATION OF THE MEDICAL DEPARTMENT OF THE ARMY. Its members were convinced, that while the existing system continued with its utter inadequacy of means to the end, and especially with the positive indisposition shown on all occasions by its higher officers so to modify its arrangements as properly to provide for all the needs of the new condition, there could be no permanent improvement in the care of the sick and wounded. They determined, therefore, to strike at the root of the evil, and to insist upon a thorough reform, to be effected through the legislation of Congress. There were many considerations which induced them to undertake the task of urging Congress to pass such a bill,—a task always arduous and distasteful in its nature, even when the dearest interests of humanity are involved in the success of such an effort.

Aside from their convictions of the absolute necessity of the measure itself, perhaps one of the strongest Motives for this motives which influenced them, was a hope action. that they might be thus relieved from their own painful and thankless functions. They felt that their work would be in a great measure completed as soon as the needed reform was accomplished by legislation, and when some portion of that life and energy and effectiveness which was then beginning to be observed in some of the other important branches of the military service had been infused into the Medical Bureau. Experience had taught them the folly of attacking evils in detail, while the principle of the evil still existed in full force in the system itself. If the particular evil was abated by their agency, yet other evils not before conspicuous soon forced themselves, hydra-headed, upon their observation, until they seemed to be engaged in a task not only wearisome and endless, but utterly barren of results at all commensurate with the labor required for the radical reform of abuses. They hoped then to embody in a measure to be sanctioned by Congress, provisions which would force the Medical Department to do through its regular official channels the work which the Commission had hitherto done so partially and so unsatisfactorily. If they could succeed in this way in securing the appointment of a Surgeon-General who should have some adequate conception of the real wants of the Army, and capacity and energy enough to carry into execution such a liberal system of providing for those wants as Congress might be induced to prescribe, and particularly if a thorough system of inspection could be established and enforced by official authority, they felt that vast progress would have been made in accomplishing the very purposes which it was the object of their appointment to secure. Their struggles with the War Department and the Medical Bureau had been unceasing; their suggestions of reform were often unheeded; their warnings of certain impending danger had induced no proper precautions; they had tired out everybody in authority with their importunity for the remedy of abuses, and they now determined to make an effort to give that practical effect to their plans by force of law, which they had tried so long, and in vain to do by argument and persuasion. If they could succeed in this object they would gladly return to the Government the imperfect and inadequate powers which had been conferred upon them, and with entire confidence retire from the field, placing the responsibility for the humane and proper care of the sick and wounded upon that department of the Government, where they had always contended it rightfully belonged.

It will be observed that at this period the Sanitary Commission could have formed a very imperfect idea of the labors which the future had in store for it. At that time its system of Hospital and Battle-field relief, and many other branches of its work had just been

15

The full scope of
the Commission's
work not then
understood.
commenced. It was impossible to foresee the grand developement of its plans which was caused by subsequent events. At that time every part of its system was subordinate to the preventive service, its treasury was low, its Hospital supplies which during the war amounted to over fifteen millions of dollars in value, were comparatively limited, and a general impression prevailed that the war would not be of long duration. Hence the thoughts and energy of its officers were concentrated upon an effort to render this preventive service thorough and practical, and as the best means to that end they endeavored to secure a re-organization of the Medical Department.

It should be remarked, that there was nothing unusual or offensive in thus directing the attention of Congress specially to the defects of the Medical Bureau. These defects were conspicuous, simply, because it was inevitable, that an administration which had performed its work creditably during the time of peace, should be unsuited to the emergencies of a war of colossal proportions. The necessity of finding new means to accomplish different ends, was just as apparent in all the branches of the Government service in direct relation with the Army, as it was in the Medical Bureau. No popular outcry was needed to procure a complete re-organization of the Quartermaster's and Subsistence departments, or of the Corps of Engineers. In each of these important branches of the service, and in the selection of officers to command the different armies, the time-honored principle of promotion by seniority

Defects in certain Government Bureaus at the commencement of the war.

had been ignored. The evidence was constant and irresistible, that without some such changes the Army could not be kept together as an organized force. The Government did not hesitate therefore one moment to sacrifice routine, usage, and precedent, to what was clearly the law of absolute necessity. The reason why the defects of the Medical Bureau were not at once in like manner recognized and remedied, was undoubtedly, because the evils arising from those defects, were to persons unfamiliar with the subject not as obvious and as immediate in their results, at the outset of the war at least, as those existing in the other Bureaus.

The mass of mankind, and particularly of those called upon to govern in an emergency such as that of the Rebellion, concern themselves only *Difficulty in securing Government action.* with practical difficulties. They have perhaps too much to do with the troubles of the present, to incline them to take precautions against evils which they think uncertain, or which at any rate can bear their fruit only in the future. It became therefore the imperative duty of those, who had studied the causes of the inefficiency of armies, to urge upon the Government the adoption of wise measures of precaution in everything which related to the vital question of the health of the troops. Their business was to instruct those who seemed profoundly ignorant of the elementary principles of the subject, that it was just as essential to success, that the health and comfort of the soldiers should be carefully looked after, as that arrangements for their food and shelter, and for selecting the most competent officers to command them, should be thoroughly organized and carried out in practice.

The history of the Medical Department previous to the war, is that of a Bureau whose operations were Sketch of the confined to the wants of fifteen thousand History of the Medical Bureau. men on a peace establishment. Its *personnel* consisted at the outbreak of the Rebellion of a Surgeon-General, twenty-six Surgeons, and eighty Assistant Surgeons. Of the Surgeons many were incapacitated for all duty, and one-half were unfitted for service in the field. The average length of service of the first thirteen on the list was thirty-two years, and that of the remaining, twenty-three years. By an act passed in 1834 a rigid examination of candidates for the post of Assistant-Surgeon in the Army was made necessary, and many young men of promise were thus introduced into the medical staff. These officers were scattered at isolated points on the frontier, without access to books, having no contact with their professional brethren in civil life, and with very little opportunity while their duties confined them to the medical care of a single company of soldiers, of improving themselves in a knowledge of that science which is perhaps of all others the most progressive. At these remote garrisons they were kept for at least five years, and the consequence was, that unless, in rare and exceptional cases, their professional ambition became deadened from the simple want of a stimulus to preserve it in proper activity. Zeal for professional advancement indeed too often became subordinate to the interest which was felt in questions of military rank and precedence,—petty subjects, the discussion of which in the absence of loftier topics enlivened the dull routine of garrison life.   The progress of the war proved that many of these Surgeons, particularly the younger among them, removed to a wider sphere of action, and permitted to carry out a more liberal system, recovered from the pressure, by which their energies during years of the mechanical performance of mere routine duties had become impaired.   Some of them indeed during the war gained great and deserved distinction by the executive ability which they displayed in the administration of some of the higher offices of the medical staff.   Still the tendency of the condition of things by which the Surgeons of the army were surrounded before the war, was necessarily towards complete stagnation in respect of everything which could stimulate a true professional zeal.   Brilliant indeed must have been the powers, and strong the thirst for professional knowledge which could long have resisted the deadening influence of a long exile from the great centres of science and civilization.

The operations of the Bureau before the war, were on a scale, and conducted upon a system, which may be inferred from the limited number of the members of the staff, and the dispersion of the Army in small detachments, in garrisons along our extensive frontier. *Limited scale of its operations before the war.* The arrangements existing in European armies for the care of the sick and wounded, which had improved with the increasing knowledge of medical science, and the more general diffusion of humane principles, were considered inapplicable to our limited establishment.   Our Medical authorities therefore, as they had no occasion to imitate them, concerned themselves little about such improvements. It seems incredible, upon any other supposition, that deficiencies, such as were supplied during the war, could have existed at its commencement. It is perhaps still more extraordinary that any one who was at all familiar with the subject, could have supposed it possible that the old machinery, however modified, could have been made to perform the new work demanded of it.

Before the war no such establishment as a General Hospital existed in the army; the military hospitals Hospital system before the war. were all Post Hospitals, that at Fort Leavenworth, the largest, containing but forty beds. It was necessary, therefore, to create in the midst of the crisis the entire system by which these establishments, so indispensable to the operations of a large army in the field, are governed. There were at that time no suitable buildings, no trained, efficient and numerous medical staff; no well-instructed nurses, no regulations or arrangements for a suitable diet for the sick, or provision for their clothing; no properly understood relations between General Hospitals and Regimental Hospitals; no means for supplying promptly proper medicines, and no arrangements for the humane and careful transportation of the sick and wounded. As we have before said, patients were crowded in the early part of the war into buildings wholly unsuited for their successful treatment. The agony and suffering which were endured by them during the first nine months of its continuance, owing to the delay in the construction of proper General Hospitals, can never be accurately known, but it is not easy to over-estimate it. The vivid recollection of the horrors of these miscalled Hospitals, which were apparent at that time to the most careless observer, is all that is necessary now to justify the strenuous efforts which were made by humane men throughout the country, to effect a radical change in the whole system.

Previous to the war, there was no organized system of Inspection of Camps and Hospitals, as a means of enabling the Medical Department to perform its duties intelligently and thoroughly; No Inspection of Camps and Hospitals. indeed no officer, bearing the name of Inspector, or invested with functions, such as have been for many years considered indispensable in foreign armies, could be found in ours. The greatest improvement in all modern administrative service, has been the adoption of a system looking to the prevention of evils. The true principle has been ascertained to be, not to wait until the evil is developed, but to anticipate it, hence of all services in an army, that of the Medical Staff whose business it should be, not merely to take care of sick men, but also to make provision, that those in health should not become sick, requires the constant vigilance and intelligent inquiry of a thorough system of Inspection. By such means alone, can the causes, which threaten the health of the troops, be ascertained and their consequences guarded against. Inspectors, with such functions, would seem to be the eyes of the Head of the department, and in any intelligent administration of its affairs, their reports would be relied upon, to enable him to determine the general policy to be pursued in the performance of his duties. In no respect perhaps was the old Medical Bureau in its attempt to apply its methods to the vastly increased needs of its new position, more obviously deficient, than in this essential particular.

The practical administration of the affairs of the Bureau was also much impeded, by its strangely complicated relations with the Quartermaster's and Subsistence Departments of the Army. To the first of these belonged by law, exclusively the construction of Hospitals and their equipment, the vital matter of the transportation of the sick and wounded, and the performance of a number of other duties, seriously affecting the sanitary condition of the troops. To the other, the supply of their food, which in any large view of the question, as affecting their suitable alimentation, was a medical or at least a hygienic matter of the very first practical importance. The Medical Bureau was wholly powerless to control the action of either of these Departments and so to shape their policy, towards those who were sick, or towards those who being well, were in danger from neglect of proper precaution of becoming sick, that they might receive the benefit of the vast modern improvements, which have been made, in this direction. Before the war, while the army was small, and the number of the officers of the Medical Staff so inconsiderable, that the Surgeon-General was able to detect the non-accounting by any one of them, of the most trifling article issued, the evils arising from so clumsy a system, were not very serious. There were no General Hospitals, and therefore it was unnecessary for the officers of the Quartermaster's Department, to provide any but the rudest form of accommodation, for a small number of men. There were no large depôts,

[Marginal note: Relations with the Quartermaster and Subsistence Departments.]

filled with thousands of recruits, drawn from a class, who lived comfortably in their own homes, and hence the ordinary ration had produced no inconvenience to those who enlisted in the regular army. But when the war began, the whole scene changed. Almost immediately came the demand for properly constructed General Hospitals, and a suitable alimentation, for the newly raised volunteers. The Medical Department was in popular estimation responsible for the whole difficulty, whereas, even had it then been able to see clearly the evil, it would have been powerless to provide a remedy. By law, and by regulation, the Quartermaster's Department was charged, as we have seen, with the duty of erecting and equipping the military hospitals. Its officers naturally hesitated to construct them on the vast scale, and with all the appliances, which were called for by those outside the Government, who claimed to have thoroughly investigated the subject. The proper construction of Hospital buildings is of course, a purely scientific question, understood only by Medical men, who have had practical experience in the needs of such institutions. It was not to be expected, that a matter so foreign to the ordinary duties of the officers of the Quartermaster's Department, could be properly studied by them, particularly at the time, when their strength was overtasked by the immense labor required for the performance of duties more in the line of their ordinary service. To bring about a harmonious combination between these two Departments, to get the Medical Bureau in the first place, to see the absolute necessity for the erection of suitable buildings upon a large scale, without delay,

16

and then to convince the Quartermaster's Department of the propriety of executing the plans, on the requisition of the Medical Bureau, was a matter, which involved in the condition of things at that time, serious difficulties, and required most patient and persistent effort, to accomplish.

The utter absence of any control by the Medical Bureau, direct or indirect, over the quantity or component parts of the army ration was also a defect, the result of which was clearly visible in the sickness which occurred in the early part of the war, among the new recruits, in consequence of the food provided for them being unsuited in its character, and not composed of a sufficient variety of articles.

These were some of the more obvious evils of the system, which existed at the commencement of the Rebellion, evils which soon made themselves felt, in the confusion, embarrassment, and inefficiency of the whole service of caring for the sick and wounded. These evils were apparent to any one who took the trouble to examine into the practical workings of the system. They became more and more painfully impressed upon the Sanitary Commission every day, for scarcely a day passed in which some shocking instance of inhumanity and neglect was not brought to its notice, which was fairly attributable to them. It was determined that its duty could only be properly performed, not by attempting to fix the responsibility of this condition of things on the officials who had been trained under the existing system, but by an effort to uproot the system itself, as wholly worthless for the purpose in view. It was proposed to substitute a new organization founded upon some proper appreciation of the real wants of the case. Representing the popular benevolence of the country towards the Army, and with a full view of all the facts, the Sanitary Commission was satisfied that nothing less than such a complete re-organization would cure the difficulty. It commenced, therefore, a movement to effect it, as we have said, by Congressional legislation.

It asked for certain specific objects in the proposed change. It desired, in the first place, that the principle of promotion by seniority, among the higher officers of the staff, should be abandoned. It wished to see at the head of the Bureau a young man of active and vigorous habits, and decided character, with professional ability and practical experience, which would enable him to grapple with the difficulties of the situation, who, while introducing all the improvements of modern science, in the humane and skilful care of the sick and wounded, would have energy enough to enforce their universal adoption in practice. It urged also that a complete and thorough system of Inspection should be established, and that a special corps of Inspectors should be appointed, through whose agency the reform of evils should be faithfully carried out. It asked that General Hospitals should be erected, wherever needed, upon plans recognized as best by universal European experience, and that the construction of these Hospitals should be superintended by officers who had some knowledge of the requirements of such buildings, and who would exhibit some zeal and energy in executing the plans.

Objects proposed by the Re-organization.

It wished that the transportation service of the sick and wounded should be transferred from the Quartermaster's to the Medical Department, and that an enlarged Ambulance system, under the special control of that Department, should be created. It was anxious that a large accumulation of medicines and Hospital supplies should be constantly maintained in the depôts of the Medical Purveyors, so that the evil consequences, which had arisen from the long delays in furnishing such supplies, should not again occur. It wished also that some arrangements should be made, by which men who were languishing in Hospitals from diseases which rendered them incapable of further military service, should be discharged and sent home, and that those who remained under treatment should be provided with Hospital clothing and a proper diet.

In bringing this subject before Congress, in order to secure the proper legislation by which the objects we The subject have enumerated should be accomplished, brought before Congress. the Sanitary Commission was, as we have said, only the exponent of the anxious desire of the American people, who demanded the best possible care for the suffering of the Army. Its efforts were aided, of course, by the influence of many professional and benevolent men throughout the country, and no less effectually, though perhaps more quietly, by some of the junior members of the Medical Staff itself, who were perfectly aware of the deficiencies of the system, and welcomed gladly the prospect of the enactment of any law likely to add to the reputation of the corps' for efficiency. Reforms as radical as those proposed by the Commission make slow progress, even where their necessity is most obvious. Class interests and vested rights are always respectable things, particularly when they are represented in the persons of those excellent men,—excellent in their purity of character and motive, whom the proposed reorganization would displace. It became therefore necessary to enlighten the Military Committees of both Houses of Congress upon the absolute necessity of a change, and to base the proposed action upon the broad ground that it was essential to the preservation of the Army.

It was difficult to make Congress understand, in the midst of all its preoccupations, the importance of the subject. Considerations of mere humanity Obstacles to its due consideration. seemed to have but little influence. It was generally admitted, that the evils complained of existed, but it was said that their importance and their consequences were exaggerated. To correct these false impressions, the Commission resolutely set itself to work. After all the usual means of influence with members of Congress had been resorted to, consisting in personal appeals, the earnest recommendation of the project by persons of position throughout the country, visits of influential deputations to Washington, discussions in the newspapers, and the like, the Commission was at last rewarded on the 18th of April, 1862, by the passage of a bill entitled, " An Act to reorganize and increase the efficiency of the Medical Department of the Army."

This Bill, although omitting some important features which had been proposed, still substantially created a system for the future operations of the Medi-

cal Department, which the Commission had
striven so long to secure.   By this most
important law, the appointment of the Surgeon-General and of the higher officers of the staff, was to be
made from the most competent officers of the whole
corps, thus ignoring the usage of promotion by seniority.   This was a most important step in the right
direction, for if the Surgeon-General could be really
appointed on the ground of qualification only, as the
Bill directed, an efficient head of the whole system was
secured, and vast progress towards a satisfactory result was made.   Eight Medical Inspectors were also
provided for by the Bill, and it may be here said in
passing, that far larger powers of remedying evils
were supposed to have been conferred upon them by it
than they ever actually exercised in practice.   Provisions were embodied in the Bill in reference to the
transportation of the sick and wounded, and to the
General Hospital administration, which experience had
shown to be so much needed, and which those who were
interested in the subject had striven so long and so
wholly in vain to introduce under the old system.
The law, of course, presented a mere outline or general
sketch of the principles of the re-organization of a
Medical Bureau such as Congress desired to establish,
for in an administrative service of this kind, it is impossible, in a general measure, to provide for all the
details which clothe the skeleton, and give life and
vigor to the whole body.   These details based upon
the general principle of the law, must be the work of
him who administers the service, so that on him de-
volves a task for any practical purpose quite as im-

portant as that of the Legislature itself. Hence the vast importance of selecting a man as Surgeon-General to set the machinery in motion, who was thoroughly imbued with a sense of the value of the principles established by the law, and who would be wholly in earnest in his desire to reduce them to practical application.

The post was one of singular difficulty and embarrassment, and yet of such peculiar honor and distinction, that its attainment naturally became an object of the ambition of some of the ablest men of the Medical Staff of the Army. The Sanitary Commission which had watched with so much care and anxiety the progress of the measure which it had proposed to Congress, and could at last congratulate the country on its adoption, felt that its task was only half done, until a competent man was selected for the post of Surgeon-General. The qualities essential to an officer occupying such a position had long been the subject of careful inquiry and study, upon which much light had been shed by the daily intercourse of the members of the Commission with some of the officials of the old Bureau. As has been stated, the removal of the incumbent, had been urged upon the Government in September 1861, upon the ground, that he lacked the essential requisites, for the successful administration of the Bureau, even as then organized. Under the re-organization, it was necessary to seek for a man, who would thoroughly develop in practice, its salutary provisions.

Among the officers of the Medical Staff, whose zeal, intelligence, and successful administration of his duties, had commanded most thoroughly the confidence and

Efforts to secure the appointment of the Surgeon-General.

admiration of the Inspectors of the Commission, was Dr. William A. DR. WILLIAM A. HAMMOND, at that time, Hammond. an Assistant Surgeon in the regular Army. He had been employed since the outbreak of the Rebellion in organizing General Hospitals at Chambersburg, Hagerstown, Baltimore and Wheeling, and his appreciation of the wants of such establishments, and the enlarged and liberal spirit with which he attempted to supply their deficiencies were so conspicuous, that they could not fail to attract the attention of the Inspectors of the Commission. These Inspectors, who were Medical men, and fully competent to form a correct judgment on the subject, entertained a very high opinion of Dr. Hammond's administrative capacity. In the reports made by them to the Commission, they spoke in unqualified terms of praise of the reforms introduced by him into the Hospitals at some of these places, and of the rapidly improving condition of the patients in them, as due to the measures adopted by him. In this way, Dr. Hammond's name first became known to the members of the Commission. He was not only a stranger to all of them, save one, but with that exception his existence even, was previously unknown to any one of them. As they were searching in vain, among the officers of the Medical Staff, with whom they had made acquaintance in Washington, for some one, whom they could recommend for the post of Surgeon-General, their attention had been thus directed to Dr. Hammond. Upon further inquiry it appeared, that Dr. Hammond was comparatively a young man, who had served more than eleven years previous to the war, as an Assistant Surgeon in the army. He had acquired, while in the service, a very high reputation among his professional brethren in civil life, as a man of science, and of great powers of original observation. A reputation of this kind in an officer of the Medical Corps, the period of whose service had been mostly passed, in garrisons on the remote frontier, was so unusual, that it at once suggested the possession on his part of great force and vitality of intellect, and a capacity for broad and comprehensive views of policy, which the long continued influence of narrow routine and formalism tends to crush out of less gifted minds. It appeared also, that Dr. Hammond's reputation was not merely, that of a man of science and professional skill, but that his career in the Army had been marked by the faithful and successful performance of his special duties as a Medical Officer, within the limited sphere in which those duties permitted him to work. He had given to the subject of Hospital construction and administration,—the great need of the time,—more thought and study probably, than any member of the Medical Staff. His opinions on this all-important matter, had been in a great part formed, or modified by a thorough examination of the great military hospitals in different countries of Europe. He was perfectly familiar with foreign military systems, so far as the administration of their medical service was concerned, and such an experience at a time when it was easy to see the defects in the existing system here, but not so easy to suggest the best practical remedy, would prove of course, of immense value, in settling the details of the new organization. In addition to these essential requisites for the position, he had exhibited a zeal and interest, in

17

the reputation of the Medical Staff of the Army, which was esteemed a very important element in forming an estimate of his pretensions as a candidate. At the outbreak of the Rebellion he held the office of Professor of Physiology and Anatomy in the University of Maryland, and was besides engaged in lucrative practice as a Physician in Baltimore. Scarcely a year before, he had resigned his position as Assistant Surgeon to enter upon a wider field of duty, and to prosecute his favorite studies under more congenial auspices. When the war broke out he did not hesitate at once to abandon his Professorship, and to re-enter the Army at the foot of the list of Assistant Surgeons. He had been constantly and actively employed ever since, and his great merit had been recognized as we have said at a very early period, by the Inspectors of the Commission. He was besides, thoroughly impressed with the deficiencies of the existing system, and he cordially agreed with the officers of the Commission, and other humane men, both as to the nature of the abuses, and the necessity of making strenuous efforts to remove them. In the autumn of 1861, the Commission had been thoroughly convinced by the information it had gathered from every quarter, that he was the best man for the place. At that time it urged the removal of the existing Head of the Bureau, and the appointment of Dr. Hammond as his successor. Insurmountable difficulties arose however, not only from the difficulty of displacing the actual incumbent, but also from a strong personal dislike, entertained by Mr. Cameron, then Secretary of War, toward Dr. Hammond, a dislike which had its origin, it was said, in an old family quarrel. It is pitiable to record, that there were great reasons to fear, lest the inefficiency of the Medical Bureau, involving the precious lives and health of so many thousands of our countrymen, would be perpetuated on grounds like these. The failure to secure his appointment at that time however, gave further opportunity for inquiry, and the evidence became more and more clear, that the first impressions as to his peculiar fitness, were well founded. These impressions were strongly confirmed, by an event, which occurred about this time. In their efforts to procure the appointment of a suitable Surgeon-General, the Commission did not neglect, as may be supposed, to invoke the intervention of General McClellan, all-powerful at that time. No one knew better than he, the defects of the system, and no one was more anxious for reform, and especially for the appointment of a competent officer, as Head of the Bureau. In a conversation with the President of the Commission, in which the General expressed his great desire to accomplish so important an object, he took up an Army list, and going over the names of all the members of the Medical Staff in rotation, discussed with remarkable intelligence the peculiar qualifications of each. To each one, subjected to such a scrutiny, some objection existed in his opinion, which would render his appointment injudicious, until towards the foot of the list, he came to the name of Dr. Hammond. He said at once, " He is our man. He is the only one of the whole corps, who has any just conception of the duties of such a position, and sufficient energy, faithfully to perform them." When therefore the Bill for the reorganization of the Medical Department became a law, the Commission felt itself justified on every account, in urging upon the President of the United States the appointment of Dr. Hammond, as the one fit to be made, if the provisions of the law directing, that that officer should be selected on the ground of qualification only, were to be regarded. Strange to say, they were met by an influence, which sought the appointment of one of the senior Surgeons of the staff, a gentleman, eminent for his long service in the Corps, and well known as a model of kindness and courtesy, not only by the officers of the Commission, but by all, who had been brought in contact with him, in social and official intercourse, during his long residence in Washington. But in this matter, the interests involved were too grave, to allow the members of the Commission to heed considerations like these. The law, which they themselves had framed, as well as every humane consideration, prescribed, that the only test of a candidate, should be his peculiar qualifications for the office.

Mr. Stanton, who had been recently appointed Secretary of War, in order to enlighten his conscience Interview of Dr. fully upon the pretensions of the respective Van Buren with candidates, and recognizing the part which the Secretary of War. the Commission had taken in establishing the new system, sent to New York for Dr. Van Buren, one of its most active members, and desired him to come to Washington, in order that he might consult him on the subject. In his interview with the Secretary, in pursuance of this invitation, Dr. Van Buren declined to advise him, in his individual capacity, in regard to the appointment. He told him that the Bill just approved was the creation of the Sanitary Commission, which had given the whole subject careful study and attention, and had also thoroughly investigated the claims of all the candidates for the position of Surgeon-General, and could therefore speak with a full knowledge of the subject, that the result of their inquiries pointed to Dr. Hammond as the best man for the place, and that its members therefore urged his appointment, and that his own opinion coincided with theirs.

The Commission was much encouraged by this evidence of a disposition on the part of the Secretary to execute the law in its true spirit, so far as the appointment of a Surgeon-General was concerned. Amidst the clamor which then prevailed at Washington, urging the selection of different persons, from considerations of personal friendship or partizan influence, it was most grateful to observe that the functionary, with whom the decision in the main rested, was seeking to perform his duty conscientiously by ascertaining the real value of the pretensions of the candidates. This favorable augury, urged the Commission to renewed efforts to secure Dr. Hammond's appointment. The result was that numerous petitions were presented to the President of the United States signed by the most eminent Medical men in the country, bearing exalted testimony to Dr. Hammond's fitness, and urging his appointment. These petitions no doubt settled the question, for, as the President remarked, it was impossible to resist the weight of evidence in his favor, given by the Medical profession of the whole country. The

Appointment of Dr. Hammond as Surgeon-General.

Commission of Surgeon-General of the Army was accordingly bestowed upon him on the 25th of April, 1862.

No one probably ever succeeded to a more arduous and embarrassing position. A young man, taken *Difficulties of his position.* from near the foot of the list, and promoted over the heads of those who numbered almost as many years of service as he did of life, could not expect to find many warm friends or cordial supporters among his former official superiors. This natural result was aggravated by personal controversies which had arisen among the different candidates, and their supporters during the canvass for the office. But this was a small matter compared with the work which was to be done. The whole Department was to be re-organized on true principles, the capacity of the new incumbent for such a work was to be tested to the utmost, and he was to prove, that the extraordinary confidence which had been placed in him by his friends was not ill-founded. The first thing necessary to give efficiency and practical value to his plans, was that he should be surrounded by fit Agents, who appreciating his views, would earnestly strive to shape the new policy by them. The Bill had provided as a most essential feature of the plan for the appointment of an Inspector-General, and eight Medical Inspectors, whose business it should be, not only to enlighten the Head of the Bureau as to the actual condition of camps and hospitals, but who should have also power to enforce the adoption of measures ordered for the remedy of abuses. It was provided that these officers should be appointed immediately after the passage of the Bill, so that the whole machinery could be put in working order at once. The appointment of these officers was unaccountably delayed. A list of such persons as the Surgeon-General deemed competent for these positions, selected from the regular and volunteer staff, had been presented by him to the Secretary of War. Still no action was taken. Many of the active friends of the measure, apprehensive that it would be shorn of all its efficiency if incompetent men were selected for these most responsible posts, were unceasing in their efforts to cause them to be suitably and speedily filled. The nominations were withheld until a resolution passed the House of Representatives, inquiring why they had not been made in accordance with the provisions of the Bill. Meanwhile a rumor became prevalent in Washington, that some of these Inspectorships were to be given to personal friends and connections of prominent party-leaders in Congress. It seemed after all, to the sorrow and dismay of those who had worked hardest for reform, that the poison of political corruption was to be introduced into a body where it was likely to produce its deadliest effect. At last the nominations were made; many of them were of men wholly untrained for this special work, while that of the Inspector-General, was one which experience proved, was eminently unwise. Of those suggested by the Surgeon-General as proper persons for Inspectors, only four were appointed. Thus he was obliged to go to work, surrounded by a set of men as confidential advisers in whose selection he had had almost no share. At the very outset therefore were the plans of the Surgeon-General for the improvement of the service crippled by a refusal to provide him with the means which he deemed necessary to carry them into execution.

This controversy unfortunately was the cause, or at least the beginning, of a want of cordiality be-
tween the Secretary of War and the Head of the Medical Bureau, the effect of which is clearly traceable in every part of the his- tory of Dr. Hammond's administration. Into the merits of this personal controversy it is not the business of the Sanitary Commission to inquire, farther than it may be necessary to show the bad effect which it produced upon the interests of the sick and wounded. It will be our duty to point out, as we advance in the history, the manner in which those for whom the nation had demanded the tenderest care, suffered from a want of co-operation between the War Department and the Surgeon-Gene- ral. The interest of the Sanitary Commission in this controversy rests wholly upon public grounds. As a Commission, whatever may have been the opinion and action of its individual members, it has refrained from defending Dr. Hammond, when his personal integrity, or the technical offence of exceeding his authority, were in question. But it does feel itself called upon to vindicate his administration upon the highest grounds, those which rest upon a belief that it was so conducted by him, that those who suffered through the casualties of war, received a skillful and humane treatment unexampled in military history. This is its duty, not merely because the Medical Bill

was its creation, and Dr. Hammond its candidate for the post of Surgeon-General, but because it is convinced, that so far as he was permitted to act freely, he did a work while in that position, which will always be regarded by men of science and the friends of humanity as one of the proudest monuments of the civilization of our age and our country.

18

CHAPTER VI.

HOSPITAL TRANSPORT SERVICE IN THE WEST AND IN THE PENINSULAR CAMPAIGN—HOSPITAL CARS.

WHILE the Commission was thus striving to secure the re-organization of the Medical Bureau as the best method of advancing the cause of sanitary reform in the Army, its plans for a complete and systematic development of its work in the Valley of the Mississippi had been laid upon a broad and sure foundation. Its affairs, in that region, were confided to the superintendence of Dr. J. S. Newberry of Cleveland, Ohio, its Secretary for the Western Department. The methods adopted by him for turning the great tide of patriotic sympathy at the West into the channels of the Commission, were characterized not only by true administrative capacity, but also by a wonderful knowledge of the peculiar temper of the people whose co-operation he desired to gain. The result was a most remarkable degree of practical efficiency and success in the organization he established. In commencing his work, Dr. Newberry's ambition was a great and noble one. His mind, trained by habits of scientific investigation, had been from the beginning deeply impressed with the value of the Commission's

Development of the work at the West. Dr. Newberry.

138

theory as the true method of Army relief, and with that generous ardor, characteristic of the higher order of minds when the full significance of a great truth is revealed to them, he determined that all within his influence should share his enthusiasm. That sphere afterwards became a wide one, since it embraced the whole Northwest, and he lost no time in employing every means of enlisting the leading men in that region in favor of a National and Catholic system of relief as opposed to one founded upon local and *Stateish* ideas. His plan was to establish Branches of the Commission in each of the great centres of population and influence. These Branches were to be composed of the Associate members residing in the different localities. To them was to be confided the task of instructing the public in regard to the Commission's plans and methods, of founding in every town and village tributary organizations, and of so arranging their work that their contributions should be sent regularly to the Branch Depôts, and thence to a general depôt for distribution in the camps and in the Hospitals. With this object in view, hoping to concentrate all the energies of the Western people in the execution of this great work under the same system and by the same methods, Dr. Newberry went, in September, 1861, to St. Louis, where an association which had taken the name of the " Western Sanitary Commission," had been established under the auspices of General Fremont. It was found impossible to induce the gentlemen composing this association to abandon their independent organization, although they professed a willingness not to interfere with the work of the United States Sanitary Commission east of the Mississippi, provided that the field was fully occupied by the Agents of the National body. Not discouraged by the failure to secure at St. Louis a complete co-operation with his plans, Dr. Newberry proceeded to Chicago, where he met a very different reception. He had a conference with some of the leading men in that city, explained to them the nature and purposes of the Commission, and soon received from them promises of hearty support and complete sympathy. "The Chicago and Northwestern Branch" of the Commission was accordingly formed, and entered upon the work with an earnestness, and prosecuted it with a vigor and success during the war, which was certainly not surpassed by any of its sister branches. The most important practical result, however, of this movement was the gaining, at this great centre of influence, of an assured position early in the war, from which radiated, during its whole progress, not merely the warmth which kept sympathy for the soldier constantly active, but light also, which pointed out the best way to manifest that sympathy. From Chicago Dr. Newberry returned to Cleveland, and established there a Branch, which had for its ablest and most efficient auxiliary the "Soldiers' Aid Society of Northern Ohio," one of the earliest of the relief societies brought into existence by the war. Thence he proceeded to Columbus, to Cincinnati, and to Louisville, where he was met by the same cordial spirit of sympathy which had greeted him at Chicago, and organized branches composed of the Associate Members resident at each of those places. Branches at Indianapolis and at Detroit were organized about the same time. At Pittsburg also, one of the most important contributing depôts under the control of the Commission during the war was soon after established.

The labor, skill, and judgment necessary to accomplish this great work of organization are very inadequately represented by the mere statement of what was done. The Associate Members at the West, like the rest of the public, needed instruction as to the nature and value of the novel and peculiar methods proposed by the Sanitary Commission, and the merit of Dr. Newberry's success is to be tested not merely by the capacity of the instructor, but also by the ignorance of those who came to him to learn. Personal conferences with leading men, the wide distribution of explanatory documents, appeals in the newspapers, public meetings, and various other means of enlightening opinion on the subject were unceasingly resorted to. The result was, that before the end of the year the Western mind had been educated into a firm belief of the superior value of a preventive system, and of a National method of organized supplemental aid as the true means of Army relief. The continuous stream of supplies which the Western people poured into the depôts of the Commission during the war is the best evidence of the earnestness and intelligence of that belief. The confidence of that people in the methods of the Sanitary Commission during the war never wavered. It is very clear that this result was attributable in a great degree to the personal influence of Dr. Newberry,

Results of Dr. Newberry's labors in organizing the West.

and to the skillful and judicious policy pursued by him.

Having thus organized the home field, Dr. Newberry proceeded to Louisville, at that time the Head Quar-
He establishes his Head Quarters at Louisville. ters of the Army, which was to drive the rebels out of Kentucky. He established there the central office of the Western Department. The first point to be settled was the precise nature of the work to be done in that military district. Dr. A. N. Read and Dr. Prentice were appointed Inspectors, and were instructed to make a thorough investigation of the condition of the troops under General Thomas and General Nelson. During the autumn and winter these gentlemen inspected nearly all the regiments in Kentucky, and distributed among them a very large amount of stores. The conduct of these Inspectors in the discharge of their novel and delicate duties, made a most favorable impression in the Army. They received from the Medical Director a public acknowledgement of their services, and what was more important, laid the foundation of that cordial co-operation, and entire harmony between the Medical authorities and the Agents of the Commission, which contributed so greatly during the war to its usefulness and influence in the armies of the West.

In the meantime, on the first of February, 1862, a Soldiers' Home was established by the Kentucky
Organization of Soldiers' Homes. Branch at Louisville, and shortly afterwards another at Cairo, under the special auspices of the Chicago Branch. These were the first of those great resting-places for the feeble and weary soldier created by the Sanitary Commission at the

West, and they afforded on a vast scale, a peculiar and grateful relief not surpassed in its value by that bestowed by any of its numerous agencies.*

Military operations on a large scale, calling for a full development of all the methods of relief organized by the Commission, began in the Western States in the early part of the year 1862. On the 12th of February Fort Donelson, on the Cumberland River, was invested by a large force under General Grant, and a most obstinate struggle for its possession continued for several days. The loss of life on both sides was very great, and many wounded were left on the field. As soon as the news of the victory became known throughout the West, there was manifested in all its large towns and cities an earnest and general desire to aid in some way in providing for the immediate relief of the sufferers. The Army which had achieved the victory had been hastily moved from its base to the battle-field, and it was well understood, that suitable arrangements for the care of the large number of wounded, thus suddenly thrown upon the resources of the Medical Department, were impracticable. To the ordinary difficulties which at that time embarrassed the administration of the Medical service at every step, difficulties due to want of experience, defective organization, limited supplies, and the absence of a forecasting preparation, there were added those arising from the impossibility of establishing General Hospitals near the scene of

Military operations at the West. Capture of Fort Donelson.

---

* During the war thirteen of these homes were in full operation in the West, where more than six hundred thousand soldiers were lodged, and two million, five hundred thousand meals were given.

conflict, which should unite the conditions essential to the proper treatment of the patients. The surrounding country was utterly destitute of all that was essential to such establishments, and it was too far from the base of military operations to render it desirable on other accounts to establish them there.

It was determined then, by the Medical authorities, that all the sick and wounded of the army, who could be removed, should be transported by steamers to the Hospitals on the Ohio River. At first sight it would appear, that such a plan was not only a wise and safe one, but that it was one comparatively easy of execution. To move a large number of suffering and helpless men, upon the large rivers of the West, in commodious steamers, properly fitted up with all the needed conveniences, to well organized Hospitals, under skillful and careful superintendence, would not appear to be a very difficult undertaking, and at any rate, it would seem, of all the modes of providing for those who had been wounded, that, which would produce the least discomfort to the sufferers. The theory was simple enough, but to reduce it to practical effect, required foresight, and preparation, and means of execution, which were not then possessed by the Medical Department. A service of Hospital Transports in the special charge of the Medical Director of the Army, should have been organized before the expedition sailed, and these Transports should have formed just as essential a part of it, as the boats which conveyed the ammunition or food of the Army. The Medical officers were not to be blamed, for they had

Marginal note: Transportation of the wounded in steamers.

no control whatever of the means of transporting the wounded ; that was the business of the Quartermaster's Department, which overwhelmed with its own special duties, could hardly be expected, to give due attention to the organization of an entirely novel mode of accomplishing the work. This was one of the countless practical illustrations of the consequences of a rigid adherence to routine in the early part of the war. The Hospital Transport project was then a novel one, and the official authorities were not disposed to try experiments. Voluntary sympathy and the organized benevolence of the country, taught the Government at Fort Donelson a lesson upon the value of this service on the Western waters, and the best mode of conducting it, which proved of inestimable value to the suffering soldier, in all the subsequent military operations in that part of the country.

Let us look at the manner, in which this great scheme of beneficence was inaugurated, by the Sanitary Commission and others, outside the Govern- Organization of ment Agencies. On the receipt of the news, Hospital Steamers by the Commission. of the surrender of the Fort, the Branch mission. Commission at Cincinnati procured with some difficulty a steamer and loading it with stores, gathered in two days, suitable for the relief of wounded, proceeded without delay down the Ohio. The Boat was accompanied by a large number of the members of the Commission at Cincinnati, and by some of the most eminent surgeons of that city. At Louisville they received on board Dr. Newberry, the Associate Secretary, a number of the agents of the Commission, and a further supply of stores for the wounded. On

19

their arrival at the Fort, they found affairs in a most deplorable condition. There were two boats in the employ of the Government, the "City of Memphis" and the "Fanny Bullitt," misnamed Hospital Boats, for they were Hospitals only as any unfurnished receptacle for vast numbers of suffering men, is a Hospital. The first named boat had been sent from Cairo on the news of the battle. It brought a limited supply of such hospital stores, as could be spared from the Commission's Depot at that place, and was accompanied by Dr. Aigner, the Inspector on duty there. Dr. Douglas also, had hastened down from St. Louis, and arrived about the same time with additional stores. Most of these supplies had been already appropriated by the ill-provided Regimental Surgeons, to eke out the deficiencies in the land Hospitals, so that the Government boats became mere places of deposit for the severely wounded, and were destitute of everything, which could contribute to their comfort, or facilitate their recovery. Their condition is thus described by an eye-witness :

"Some were just as they had been left by the fortune of war (four days before); their wounds, as yet, undressed, smeared with filth and blood, and all their wants unsupplied. Others had had their wounds dressed one, two, or three days before. Others, still, were under the surgeon's hands, receiving such care as could be given them by men overburdened by the number of their patients, worn out by excessive and long-continued labor, without an article of clothing to give to any for a change, or an extra blanket, without bandages or dressings, with but two ounces of cerate to three hundred men, with few medicines and no stimulants, and with nothing but corn meal gruel, hard bread, and bacon, to dispense as food."

The Agents of the Commission, not without considerable resistance on the part of the Medical Director, succeeded in obtaining access to these boats, and several days and nights were passed by them, in relieving the pressing wants of the sufferers by means of the stores, which had been brought from the depôts of the Commission at Cincinnati, Chicago and other places in the West. They succeeded with some difficulty in obtaining permission to transport, on their return to Cincinnati, such of the wounded as they were able to accommodate on the steamer which had conveyed them to the Fort. More than eighty were thus brought by them to a Military Hospital at Cincinnati under all the favorable circumstances which a properly furnished boat, and the most careful nursing could provide. *Relief afforded by the Agents of the Commission.*

Again, after the battle of Shiloh, which took place in the early part of April, the officers of the Commission at the West, enlightened by their experience as to the proper mode of transporting the wounded in Hospital Boats, became actively engaged in the same humane service. The extent and character of this service, and its inestimable value to those, who were its objects, are well set forth in the following extracts from the Report of Dr. Newberry on the operations of the Commission after that battle. *Similar service after the battle of Shiloh.*

"For the space of a mile or more the bank of the river was lined with steamers, closely packed together, loaded with troops, stores and munitions of war. Each of these steamers was discharging its cargo, living or inanimate, upon the steep and muddy bank, and soldiers, forage, provisions, clothing, artillery, army wagons and ambulances—the reinforcements and supplies of the great army which covered the hills for miles around—poured on to the shore in a noisy, turbulent, chaotic flood.

"Immediately on hearing of the battle, the Chicago Branch Commission, with its accustomed promptness, despatched a special train to Cairo, taking large quantities of supplies, and a corps of surgeons and nurses, all under the care of Rev. Dr. Patton and Dr. Isham. These reached the scene of action on the Louisiana— government hospital boat—on Friday evening. The good which they accomplished by their services and much needed stores, can hardly be estimated.

"The Cincinnati Branch Commission was also most creditably represented at Pittsburgh. Two first-class steamers, the Tycoon and Monarch, were fitted out as hospital boats by the Commission, furnished with every comfort and even luxury for the wounded, and manned by a large and efficient corps of surgeons and nurses. These boats were under the care, respectively, of Drs. Mendenhall and Comegys. After dispensing with liberal hand of their stores to the sufferers at the Landing, they both returned, carrying loads of wounded, all thoroughly and tenderly cared for, to the hospitals on the Ohio."

Dr. Newberry, with Dr. Prentice and Dr. Douglas, Inspectors of the Commission, were present, striving to direct the zealous labors of so many workers, with that order, regularity, and system which would render them most efficient, and most extensively useful.

Thus it will be perceived, that at Shiloh the Agents of the Commission held the foremost rank as active laborers. The greater number Various difficulties in the Hospital transport service. of the steamers which had been sent to that battle-field, had been equipped as Hospitals, and furnished with the necessary supplies from the depôts of the Commission, while the *personnel* was composed largely of its officers and members throughout the West. There were also, as has been said, many boats not under the control of the Commission. The Government had sent as many as five or six from St. Louis, which had been almost wholly equipped and supplied by the Western Sanitary Commission. The truth is, the wonderful success which had attended the Commission's experiment of transporting the wounded in Hospital Boats after the surrender of Fort Donelson, had stimulated a great variety of organizations, and even the State Governments, to provide similar means of relief, designed to be made use of in the event of another battle, and the occurrence of that of Shiloh, on the banks of so large a river as the Tennessee, caused the assembling of a large fleet, employed on the same errand of mercy. Those in charge of these boats, had only this in common, that they were acting wholly outside of Government agencies, and that they all hoped in some way to relieve suffering. Still the efficiency of the means at their disposal was much impaired by a defective organization, and by that absence of a due sense of responsibility and subordination which are essential to the success of all associated effort.   Owing to this inherent defect, a vast amount of energy, which had been expended in sending boats to the battle-field provided with a large amount of supplies, and numerous attendants, was comparatively wasted.

It seems ungracious to criticise the work of any body of men engaged in an effort to relieve the suffer-

Hospital trans-ing, even if their methods are not wholly in
ports in charge
of State agents. accordance with true principles, but there was one feature in the mode adopted by those who had charge of the steamers sent by the State Governments of Ohio, Indiana, and Illinois, which was so obviously wrong in principle, and so entirely in contrast with the National and Catholic spirit which characterized the operations of the Commission at all times, that it deserves notice.   These boats were intended solely for the reception of wounded men belonging to each of these States respectively, and all others were rigidly excluded from them.   When it is remembered that the army which fought at Shiloh was composed of men coming not only from all the States of the West, but from other portions of the country also, that they had defended with equal valor the same flag, and had suffered from the same cause, when it is further considered, that from the nature of the case it was impossible that each State represented in that Army could provide specially for the care of the wounded among its own citizens, the indiscreet zeal, which was willing to recognize State lines even in its ministrations of mercy on the battle-field, can hardly be too strongly condemned.   It was only another developement of that obnoxious heresy of State-sove-

reignty, against which the whole war was directed, and its practical injury to the national cause in creating disaffection among the troops who were not recipients of its peculiar care, was scarcely less great, than its violation of those sacred laws of humanity, which make no distinction in the relief bestowed upon the suffering, except to seek first for those who most need succor. Against this *State-ish* spirit the Sanitary Commission resolutely set its face at all times, and in every form, as hostile alike to the dictates of humanity and true patriotism. It recognized in the Union army, wherever serving, Union soldiers only. It always refused to receive benefactions intended for the use of particular regiments, and the money in its treasury, and the supplies accumulated in its depôts, were regarded as a common stock to be used for the general benefit. It was an organization wholly National in its design, and in its objects and methods it was inspired by a thorough devotion to the National cause in its widest sense. Its influence, therefore, extended far beyond that which was due to the mere bestowal of relief on the battle-field, and the constant efforts it made to inculcate a National spirit in the care of the soldier, produced an effect, both in the Army and the country at large, which powerfully contributed to the success of the National arms.

The general policy pursued by the Governors of States, and the permanent agents appointed by most of them in reference to the supposed needs of such of their citizens as were enrolled in the Army, was a fruitful source of embarrassment to the Government during the whole war. Injurious effect of anti-national methods of relief.

If the action of the State authorities had been confined to efforts to improve the general administration of the service, and thus to benefit all alike, its influence would have been irresistible, and its effect most salutary. But while convinced of the defectiveness of the Government methods, the Governors of the various States seemed anxious only to remove their own citizens from suffering the evils resulting from them. The consequence was, of course, an entire want of harmony in opinion and action between the Federal authorities and these zealous State officials, as to the proper relations of the Government to the soldier. The War Department was constantly besieged by applications on behalf of the different State authorities, demanding that the sick and wounded should be removed from the General Military Hospitals, and sent to the States from which they had come, to be there cared for. It was proposed that these men should be treated in Hospitals organized by the State authorities, or in United States Hospitals located within the limits of the State. It will be readily perceived, that if applications of this kind had been listened to, the Government might as well have abandoned at once not only all control over the sick and wounded of the Army, but also all hope of maintaining an effective discipline over those who remained in the ranks. To such an extent had the evil reached at one time, that General Grant found it necessary, during his great expedition against Vicksburg, to prohibit the transportation of men in his Army disabled by wounds or sickness to any point north of Memphis. Thus only could he hope to retain the services of those who might regain their health and strength during their treatment in Hospitals. If half the energy wasted by the Governors of various States in the vain attempt to supplant the Federal authorities in the work they were doing so imperfectly, had been concentrated in a determined effort to force them to do it more thoroughly, we should not now have to tell that the horrors of Shiloh and other bloody battle-fields were mitigated only by the voluntary, and partial efforts of humane and zealous, but irresponsible persons. It would have been our grateful duty rather to have related that these horrors were prevented by that regular, steady, forecasting action of the proper Government agencies, belonging to a perfectly organized system, directed by officers thoroughly trained in a knowledge of their duties.

Notwithstanding all the objections which experience has proved to be inherent in the volunteer system of Hospital Transports organized by the Commission in the West, there were reasons founded upon the prospects of the campaign on the Peninsula, for which the Army of the Potomac was then preparing, which induced the Commission to place at the disposal of the Government its limited capacity of performing the same humane service towards that Army, which it had undertaken on the Cumberland and Tennessee rivers. On the 18th of April 1862 the Acting Surgeon-General approved of the proposition of the Sanitary Commission to assist in transporting by steamers to Hospitals at the North, such of the sick and wounded, as the Medical Director

Transport service in the Peninsular Campaign.

20

of the Army of the Potomac should confide to its care. The Secretary of War immediately directed a steamer, then in the employment of the Quartermaster's Department to be transferred to the Commission to be fitted up and' properly supplied by it for this purpose. Accordingly the " Daniel Webster " a vessel capable of transporting with proper arrangements two hundred and fifty patients was assigned to it, and a volunteer force, composed of several of the higher officers of the Central Staff, a large number of male nurses, and a few ladies accompanied it to York River. During the voyage from Alexandria the steamer was thoroughly refitted, and properly equipped with beds and bedding and other conveniences, required for the patients, and the force on board was organized and instructed in the duties, which would devolve upon them.

The steamer arrived in the river during the siege of Yorktown. The Commission had already dispatched The Sanitary thither in anticipation of events, a large transport Daniel Webster. amount of supplies for the use of the Army, and was provided with two large boats, used as storehouses, besides a well-filled depôt on shore. A glance at the condition of things on their arrival, revealed to its Agents, the same deplorable deficiency in adequate preparation for the reception of the sick and wounded, which had so often before been observed. The first sick men whom they saw, were found crowded in a number of log huts, which had been previously used by the rebels as barracks. · The place was a most pestilential one, surrounded by swamps, and there, the unfortunate soldiers who had been attacked by sickness, were dying by scores, of fever, still clothed in their uniforms, and even wearing their caps. It would hardly be correct to call such a place a Hospital. There were few attendants, no clothing, no medicines, and the surgeons in charge seemed bewildered in their helplessness. Permission was readily obtained from the Medical Director, that these wretched men should be looked after by the Agents of the Commission who had arrived in the Webster, and that the sick, who were in a condition to be moved, should be with the least possible delay, placed on board of that vessel, and transferred to a Northern Hospital. In the course of the day, nearly two hundred and fifty men were removed by the Agents of the Commission, were carefully nursed, were provided with clean clothing and suitable food, and soon found themselves surrounded with all the comforts and conveniences of a well regulated hospital. The change in their condition was most remarkable. No sooner had the vessel left the sickly shores of the Peninsula, than nearly all the patients became convalescent, and not a single man died on the voyage to New York. The Commission was cheered by this first result of its experiment, and encouraged to persevere in this life-saving service.

In the meantime Yorktown was evacuated, and the Army advanced. This of course rendered necessary the removal of the Regimental Hospitals, and Peculiar diffi-culties of the service. their inmates were sent down to Yorktown in order that they should be at once embarked in Transports and sent north. But no adequate prepara-tions had been made by the authorities to meet such an emergency. The "Ocean Queen," a steamer of vast size and capacity, had that very morning been placed in the hands of the officers of the Commission, to be fitted up as a Hospital Transport in the place of the Webster, just sent to sea. Of course nothing was yet ready on the "Queen," but the officers in charge of the sick from the Hospitals, insisted upon depositing them upon the decks of that vessel. No time was lost in useless complaint, and in a few hours, those in charge of her, by the most unremitting labor, and by drawing upon the supplies of the Commission which had been placed on their storeboats, were enabled to provide tolerably for the comfort of those who had thus been thrown upon their care. This event, occurring at the very outset of their operations in this new field of labor, will serve to illustrate some of the difficulties and embarrassments, by which the efforts of the Agents of the Commission to aid the Government in the transportation of the sick and wounded were surrounded.

In order to understand more fully the practical nature of these difficulties it will be necessary to Relations with Government officers while performing this service. consider the exact relations of the Commission to the Government in this business. Its position from a variety of causes was a most trying one, and the service was performed under all the conditions of a presumed authority without command, and of rights without powers. The Commission never undertook to perform the whole service of Hospital Transports on the Peninsula; it proposed to aid the Government in the work by equipping as many vessels as the limited means at its disposal would permit. It was supposed of course, that the number of the boats under its charge would bear but a small proportion to those in the employment and under the direct management of the Medical Director. It had nothing to do with the transportation of the wounded from the field of battle or the hospitals to the boats; its duty in theory began on the boats themselves. In practice, it was responsible for the care of all those who were hurried, without the slightest attention to their first wants, from "the front" to the base on the river. By an agreement between the Commission and the Medical Director, certain boats were to be reserved for a certain description of cases only, and their points of destination were to be regulated by the nature of the disability of the patients thus selected. All these wise provisions were wholly neglected in practice. Owing to the absence of some proper representative of the Medical authorities, no such selection of patients was made, and day after day, a vast crowd of sufferers, differing in every respect, except in a desire to escape from the horrors they had endured, were forced upon the boats in charge of the Commission.

By virtue of the same agreement, these boats were to have been placed under military discipline. But this provision also was neglected, and in addition to their proper duties in the care of the sick, the Agents were obliged to Embarrassments of a volunteer service of this kind. manage and pacify disorderly and insubordinate crews. The exigencies of the Quartermaster's Department also, interfered with their well-arranged plans for the orderly and regular disposal of the sick and wounded. More than once it happened, that after undergoing all the labor and expense of fitting up a steamer which had been assigned to them, for hospital purposes, they were suddenly ordered to return it to the officers of that Department, as it was required for other needs of the military service. Thus it was impossible to foresee, not only for a week, but even for a single day, how many boats would be at their disposal, or the number of patients they would be called upon to provide for. Add to this the utter absence of all control of the crews, the impossibility of calculating upon the continuous and effective services of volunteer Surgeons and nurses, who might and often did forsake their duties at an hour's notice, and the uncertainty of the whole matter of the relations of the Commission to the Government, arising from a want of harmony between the action of the Surgeon-General and that of the Medical Director, and it will be readily perceived, that the officers of the Commission, who were fully imbued with that spirit which taught them to do everything they attempted with thoroughness and system, soon found themselves in a most painful and harassing position. It was with the greatest difficulty that these officers were able to do a tithe of what they hoped to do, for the relief of the vast masses, who suffered from the casualties of war during the Peninsular campaign. Nothing but the patient and untiring zeal and energy, and great administrative capacity of Mr. Olmsted who directed the service, and the unwearied toil and devotion of a portion of his Volunteer Corps with Mr. Knapp at its head, saved the experiment from proving a total failure. Notwithstanding the formidable obstacles thus encountered at every step, the Commission succeeded in transporting from the Peninsula in a comparatively comfortable condition, more than eight thousand sick and wounded men. This result fell far short of its expectations, and was hardly commensurate with the immense labor it called for. But it is a great satisfaction to remember that the most arduous and harassing duty performed by the Commission during the war, was in some degree instrumental in mitigating the horrors of its most disastrous campaign.

This transportation service occurred, it should be stated, at a time when the machinery of the re-organized Medical Bureau was being put in order, and just after the appointment of the new Surgeon-General. The arrangements for the whole Medical service of the army of course absorbed at that time the attention of that officer, and he was probably not fully aware of the mismanagement of the affairs of his Department, by his representative in the Army of the Potomac. Towards the close of the month of May, in consequence of representations made by the Commission to him of the state of things in the Peninsula, a plan for properly systematizing the Commission's work in the transport service, and of defining more accurately its relations to the Government, was agreed upon. This plan consisted chiefly in substituting hired surgeons and nurses for volunteers, and in the introduction of strict military discipline and subordination in the control of the steamers and their crews. The Commission agreed to assist the Surgeon-General by examining at New York into the fitness of all candidates for surgeons and nurses. This plan, however admirable, and based upon the sad experience of the failure of that which had already been tried, was never put in operation. Indeed the necessity for the transportation service in that quarter, soon ceased. Until the Medical Director of the Army of the Potomac was relieved, however, and a wise and humane system under an efficient officer introduced, the utterly inadequate provision made to relieve the agonies and the sufferings of the victims of the Peninsular campaign, still continued to be a disgrace to the civilization of the country. It is satisfactory, however, to know, that the experience gained in that campaign concerning the mode of transporting the sick and wounded, was of great value in creating a proper system, under Government officers, for the performance of this service in other parts of the country during the remainder of the war.

Although this was the last attempt made by the Commission to convey those who had suffered from the Hospital cars. casualties of war to proper Hospitals by water, it was not discouraged by its comparative want of success from making an effort to provide suitable transportation for the same class of sufferers by land. Its failure to induce the Government to organize an Ambulance Regiment, has been already noticed, but every battle-field bore testimony to the absolute necessity of such a provision. The armies as they advanced into the enemy's territory, operated, as is well-known, on long lines of Railways, which connected them with their base of supplies. As the disabled men accumulated at "the front," it became of course necessary, that many of them should be removed on these Railways to points where large General Hospitals had been established. This involved usually a long journey, and it was essential to the humane treatment and recovery of the patients, that their removal should be made with the utmost tenderness and care. In the Peninsula and at the West, those who had been wounded in battle, and the inmates of Regimental Hospitals, whom it was thought desirable to get rid of, were placed in common burden cars, where, like so many sheep, jarred and jolted by every movement, without any of the comforts and conveniences which their condition demanded, and without proper food, clothing, or attention, they often passed hours and even days in indescribable agony. There was scarcely a practical abuse in the whole administration of the Medical service which called more loudly for remedy.

The ingenuity of Dr. Harris, a member of the Commission, who had observed the fearful sufferings produced by this mode of transportation in the Peninsula, solved satisfactorily the problem of conveying sick and wounded men on Railways, with as much ease and comfort to themselves as if they had been making the voyage by water, in properly equipped steamers.

In the attainment of the desired results, the following were some of the more essential objects to be considered: 1. Specially adapted appliances and furniture for the comfort and security of the patients in railway cars, and the special preparation and exclusive use of a sufficient number of easy-running cars for the conveyance of the more serious cases. 2. The perfect ventilation and care of the cars occupied by the patients. 3. The means of preparing and serving food in them, and a suitable provision of surgical and medical supplies. 4. The employment of surgeons

Objects to be attained by them.

21

and nurses exclusively devoted to the business of rail-way Hospital Transportation. 5. The running of special Hospital trains. 6. Such care in the loading, unloading, and movement of the patients as would best insure them from needless change of posture and suffering.

Believing it possible to accomplish these most im-portant objects by means of railway ambulances pro-perly constructed, Dr. Harris laid the plans and drawings of his proposed Hospital car before the Quartermaster-General, General Meigs. That enlightened officer was at once struck with its adaptation to the humane purpose for which it was designed. He directed that certain of the cars at that time in the Government establishment at Alexandria should be placed at the disposal of Dr. Harris, to be fitted up in accordance with his plans. The co-operation of the three railway companies owning the line between Washington and New York was soon after secured. Cars were at once arranged by them for the service of the transportation of the wounded, a portion of the expense of the equipment only being borne by the Sanitary Commission. One of these corporations, that of the Camden and Amboy Rail Road Company, pre-sented to the Commission a Hospital Car thoroughly furnished, as its contribution towards helping forward this great work of mercy. In the West, where all the rail roads leading to "the front" were wholly under the control of the Government, this improved system of railway ambulances was soon afterwards introduced principally through the influence of Dr. Newberry, the Western Secretary.

Plan approved by the Quarter-master-General.

The earnestness of his recognition of their value, and the anxious solicitude with which he watched over the regularity of the service, may be inferred from the fact that at his suggestion the Sanitary Commission purchased a locomotive engine which was used exclusively in moving the Hospital train, thus insuring the rapid conveyance of the patients by means which could not be withdrawn for the other exigencies of the military service.

A very slight description of these Hospital cars will give some idea of the increased comfort provided for the patients conveyed in them. The ordi- Description of nary field and hospital litter or stretcher the Hospital cars. was used in loading, unloading, and carrying the patients. These simple litter-beds, with pillows, mattresses, and comforts attached, were then ingeniously and securely swung in tiers—three high, and end to end —upon light stanchions, and there suspended by stout tugs of India rubber, which gave sufficient elasticity to obviate all jar to the bed and its patient. Thirty of these beds were thus swung along the side of each Hospital car. A number of invalid chairs and a broad couch filled the remainder of the available space. A pantry furnished with medicines, utensils, beverages, and substantial food, ready for serving to the patients hot or cold, made up the sum of creature comforts, while nurses, abundantly provided with towels, socks, blankets, sponges, etc., kept every man clean and warm, however long the trip or stormy the weather. All the usual appliances and skill of a well regulated Hospital were at hand.

The expense of fitting up these cars was borne in a

great measure, as we have stated, by the Commission, and the officers in charge of them were appointed by it. In the autumn of 1862, the transportation service between Washington and New York was begun, and was continued daily with the utmost regularity, and growing efficiency till the close of the war. In the West the system had a rapid developement, and during Developement of the progress of the war more than thirty of the system. these ambulances were in constant use. The Hospital train from Atlanta to Louisville made the journey of more than five hundred miles according to an established time-table, and reached its destination with the exactness and speed of trains on well-managed rail roads in time of peace. Between New York and Boston also, there were cars arranged for the conveyance of the sick and wounded similar in all respects to those which we have described. The service on this line was under the immediate supervision of the Boston Associates of the Commission, and all its details were most carefully and successfully managed by their Secretary, Mr. JOHN S. BLATCHFORD, who in this, as in all other forms of Army relief undertaken by the Commission in Boston during the war, was most conspicuous for his zeal and capacity. The whole number of sick and wounded soldiers conveyed by these Hospital cars during the war was in the East about 100,000, and in the West about 125,000.

It will be observed that the introduction and general adoption of this system of railway ambulances had been Transfer of the secured without the direct intervention of the cars to the Med- ical Bureau. Medical Bureau. The whole subject of transportation, as we have said, was within the jurisdiction, and governed pretty much by the arbitrary discretion of the Quartermaster's Department. The proper business of the Medical officers was to look after the patients during their transportation, not to provide them with the means of conveyance. When the experiment proved a success, the Commission, faithful to its policy of non-interference with Government officials in their appropriate sphere, desired to transfer to the Medical Bureau that portion of the work which had been confided to it by the Quartermaster's Department. The management of the Hospital cars, therefore, was placed in charge of the officers of the Medical Bureau. The Commission, however, never lost its deep interest in maintaining the service in the utmost efficiency, and until the close of the war many of the agents employed in it were paid from its treasury, and nearly all the suitable food provided for the patients came from its storehouses.

To Dr. Solomon Andrews, Jr., the Chief Surgeon of Hospital Trains in the East; to Dr. Henry Janes, the Medical Director of Camp Letterman at Gettysburg; and to Drs. Barnum and Myers, in charge of the service in the West, unbounded praise is due for the zeal and faithfulness with which for nearly three years they conducted all the work of the railway Hospital Trains.

CHAPTER VII.

SUPPLEMENTAL HOSPITAL SUPPLIES.

THE chief business of the Sanitary Commission during the war in the opinion of those who had not
Popular error in regard to the work of the Sanitary Commission. studied its system, as a whole, was the collection and distribution of voluntary supplies, for the relief of the soldier on the battle-field and in Hospitals. It was natural perhaps, that this should be the general impression, for the needs of that portion of its work, were brought more constantly before the public attention than those of any other ; by far the larger portion of its funds was expended in maintaining it in proper efficiency, and its operations resembled more nearly those undertaken by other voluntary associations, engaged in the work of Army relief. Still, as has been said, a system of relief, based on such methods, occupied at the outset, in the plan of the Commission, a very subordinate, although still important place. The vast proportions it afterwards assumed, during the progress of the war, were due to circumstances, which it was impossible to have foreseen from the beginning. It was true, that from the very first, the want of adequate supplies for the sick and wounded in the Hospitals, seemed to forebode almost

as great danger to the efficiency of the army, as the neglect of proper precautionary measures. Still, it was thought, in judging of the comparative importance of urging upon the Government, and the public, the adoption of some means of providing for these two classes of needs, that it was more essential to insist upon those of prevention, than upon those of cure. There were many reasons for this opinion; among others, may be mentioned, the necessity of educating the public mind in regard to the true value of preventive measures. It was supposed also that an imperious, ever pressing necessity forcing the Government to make the same adequate provision for those who were in the Hospitals, as for furnishing food and arms to those who were in the ranks, would soon prove a stern teacher, whose lessons could not in the nature of things remain long unheeded.

The Commission was disappointed in a great measure in this expectation, and after a short experience of those great and pressing wants *Organization of the Supply Department.* of patients in Hospitals, which were unrelieved by the ordinary and proper Government agencies, it determined to organize that department of its work, which embraced the collection and distribution of voluntary supplemental supplies. In the first letter addressed by the New York delegation to the Secretary of War, asking the appointment of a Sanitary Commission, one of the objects which it was urged, might be gained by the services of such a body, was the determination of the best methods, of aiding the Medical Bureau with such supplies, as the spontaneous benevolence of the people was eager to furnish.

The desire was also expressed, that such volunteer action might be harmonized with that of the regular authorities, in a way, as efficient, and as little embarrassing, as extra-official co-operation could be. This statement of the design of the Commission, to aid the Government with the least possible interference with its ordinary methods, embodies the fundamental principle, which underlaid all its work, especially in that department of relief, technically so called, where its Agents were brought into constant and often very delicate relations with the Government officials. In its Constitution or Plan of Organization one of its objects is stated to be, " to secure contributions from patriotic and benevolent individuals and associations, and to organize, methodize and reduce to serviceableness, the vague and haphazard benevolence of the people towards the Army." Immediately after the Commission was appointed, and its plans became known, it began to receive from individuals and associations throughout the country, a great variety of articles intended for the Hospitals, while extra Hospital clothing, and such additional comforts as seemed most needed, had been purchased by its funds.

On the 5th of September, 1861, the General Secretary enlightened by the experience of the results of the distribution in the Camps and Hospitals of more than sixty thousand such articles which had been confided to the Commission, reported to the Board, that depôts for the reception of such extra governmental supplies should be established by it in some of the large cities. It was estimated that unless the Government system could be

Supply depots established.

speedily and greatly improved, a capital of fifty thousand dollars and an income of five thousand dollars a month, at least, in addition, would be needed to establish and carry out a proper national method of supplemental and extra governmental Hospital supplies. This project was approved by the Board, and depôts of supplies were accordingly established at New York, Boston, Philadelphia, Washington, Cincinnati and Wheeling. On the 5th of October, this arrangement was anounced to the public in a circular which was widely distributed, addressed "to the Loyal Women of America." In this circular it was stated, that "the labors of the Commission had been hitherto directed chiefly to induce precaution against certain diseases, which had scourged almost every modern European army, but that, as experience was gained, it became evident, that here as elsewhere, Government alone could not completely provide for the humane treatment of those, for whom the duty of providing as well as possible was acknowledged." The task of aiding the Government in this matter, seemed to devolve peculiarly on the women of the country. This duty was pointed out and enforced, and the advantages to be derived from the well considered system organized by the Commission, enabling it to bestow that aid, systematically and in perfect subordination to the general plans of the Government, were dwelt upon. The women were therefore urged to form societies in every neighborhood, and to devote themselves for a time to the sacred service of their country. It was suggested that energetic committees should be appointed by these societies, who should call from house

22

to house, and from store to store, and obtain contributions in materials suitable to be made up, or money
for the purchase of such material, and that the loyal
women, composing these societies should meet on fixed
days to make garments from the material so procured.

Thus it will be seen that the Commission, with a
wise foresight and a perfect comprehension of some of
The sympathy the most novel and striking characteristics
and aid of the
women of the of our American civilization, sought to
country organ-
ized. make the women of the country its agents
in the vast work of supplying, the most palpable and
obvious of all the deficiencies of the Government in
its care of the Army. Much has been said and written
upon the part taken by American women in supporting the National cause during the war, but the full
extent of the influence they exerted, can hardly be
understood, without adverting to the peculiar position
which they occupy in a democratic society like ours.
Women, in history, have often been the inspirers of
men, rarely their fellow-workers. The power which
they wielded in the late war, was due to the exercise of
those gentler, domestic virtues, which find their birth-
place, and ordinarily their only sphere of action,
within the narrow limits of home. The influence of
these qualities has been little observed in other wars;
here, exceptional circumstances, arising from the peculiar structure of our society, first gave an opportunity
for a developement on a vast scale, of that same
tender, generous spirit of devotion on the part of
woman to those who were suffering in the cause of their
country, as was excited by the needs of her own kindred.
Of course, this spirit of zeal and devotion was not

created by the war, for it had long manifested itself in an organized form, in every part of the country, where any of the countless forms of human suffering required succor. But the peculiarity is, that here, organizations for such benevolent purposes, had been for a long time under the control and management almost exclusively of women. The admirable plans arranged by them for conducting such societies, and the wonderful success, which had attended these schemes, both in their organization and practical result, first suggested the employment of their extraordinary zeal for kindred purposes on a much larger scale, and in a novel field of labor. The Commission was convinced that in the intelligent zeal and devotion of these women, in their habit of prosecuting benevolent labors by organized effort, and in their general familiarity with the principles and methods, which insure success in such undertakings, it had discovered a precious source for a regular, systematic, and bountiful supply of all that the soldier could need in the way of voluntary and supplemental aid. It was its constant effort during the war, so to direct their zeal in this work, and so to instruct them in regard to their labors, that the greatest possible practical benefit should result to the soldier. It was wholly unnecessary to stimulate this zeal, or urge to self-denying labor, in so sacred a cause. The intense feeling of nationality, characteristic of all classes, the ardor of which no reverses or discouragements could chill, burned with ten-fold intensity in the hearts of the women of the country. Denied a participation in the actual toils and dangers of the strife, they eagerly sought to manifest the depth of their sympathy, by work suited to their sex. If they could not lead those they loved in battle, they could, almost before its smoke had cleared away, bind up their wounds, minister to their sufferings, and set them an example of heroic courage, patience and self-sacrificing devotion, which would inspire them with fresh and undying enthusiasm for the cause.

Strong as was the love of country as a motive for persistent and intelligent effort for the relief of the soldier, there was another which, appealing more peculiarly to their household affections, served constantly to keep alive their zeal. The vast majority of those who had gone forth to fight the battles of their country, went from well-ordered and comfortable homes. While they carried with them into the Army, the healthy influence of such a training, that influence was constantly preserved, by the consciousness that they were the objects of the anxieties and prayers of wives and sisters, who sought to relieve their overburdened hearts by working for those loved ones, who were absent and in danger. The sentiment of profound love of country aided in almost every instance by an impulse of personal affection towards some one at least who might suffer in its cause, was soon crystalized into those organizations which did such wonderful and effective service during the war. It produced more than seven thousand Aid Societies, tributary to the Sanitary Commission, composed wholly of women, all of whom were engaged in the common work of Army relief. Its material result was the collection and distribution of supplemental supplies, valued at many millions. The estimated value of the

Nature and motive of this sympathy.

stores distributed by the Commission to the Army during the war was about fifteen millions of dollars. Of this sum at least four-fifths was made up by the value of the contributions in kind from the homes of the country. To how many a weary sufferer in the Hospitals or on the battle-field these supplies gave life and strength and comfort, none but the Recording Angel can tell; what an influence for good, this generous and constant stream of bounty flowing directly from the homes of the country to the Army, exerted in improving the *morale*, and stimulating the patriotic devotion of the soldier, it is not difficult to conjecture. In all this work there is positively nothing of which history has given us an example. The women of our country bore no resemblance to that type of ancient virtue, the Spartan Mother, who as she delivered the shield to her son, on the eve of battle, uttered the deepest wish of her heart, as she told him, " Either with this or upon this;" their work claims no praise for reasons for which we are asked to admire the Roman Matrons, who, while their husbands were absent in the Army, occupied themselves in their own homes, preparing clothing for their slaves and dependents; their influence was quite unlike that of woman in the days of chivalry, when a romantic sentiment of devotion impelled to deeds of heroic courage. But in all that invests the social position of woman in our day with real dignity, valuing her sympathy with Truth and Right as a mighty moral power, it was a work full of a significance as novel as it was consoling.

This appeal to the women of the country to aid the Government with supplemental Hospital supplies, was

Objections to Volunteer and supplemental aid considered. of course based upon the assumption, that either it could not do, or was not doing, all that the necessities of the case required. There was a natural objection to this plan of volunteer aid, which had occurred to many reflecting people, and which had been fully considered by the Commission before embarking in so important an undertaking. It was said, that it was the duty of the Government to meet all these wants in the fullest manner, and that any attempt, outside its agencies, to eke out its deficiencies, would result in a relaxation of zeal, on the part of the authorities, in the performance of their proper functions. It was also feared by many, that the distribution of these gifts of the people would embarrass the officials in the due exercise of their authority, especially in the Hospitals. These were objections made at the outset, and reiterated with great apparent plausibility as the war went on, and as the Government standard of providing for the sick and wounded improved. Still the Commission, watching constantly for an opportunity of throwing this labor on the Government, where in theory it properly belonged, was never able to do so without neglecting its duty. So entirely was this the case, that after hostilities had ceased, and more than three months after Lee had surrendered, the Commission was called upon to supply antiscorbutics for a corps of 25,000 men which had been sent to Texas, unprovided with any means of guarding against that form of disease, to which it must have been known by some one in authority, they were peculiarly liable in that part of the country. But at the outset of the war, or at least as soon as the vast armies called for by the Government, began to take the field, there was no pretence that there was any adequacy of provision on its part for the humane care of the suffering soldier. At that time, owing to the enormous and sudden demand, deficiency was the rule, a regular or abundant provision the exception, in all the Supply Departments of the Army. When arms and clothing could not be furnished for the newly raised regiments, when the Quartermaster-General was forced, in the month of October, 1861, publicly to solicit donations of blankets for men in active service, it is not to be wondered at, that articles of the first necessity were wanting in the Hospitals and on the battle-field. Hospital clothing there was none, the supply even of the commonest medicines was exceedingly scanty and irregular, and no provision had yet been made for a suitable Hospital diet. The only dependence aside from voluntary offerings for such delicacies as were needed by the sick, was the " Hospital fund," a precarious resource, arising from a commutation in money of the value of that portion of the ordinary ration not consumed by the patient,—a fund which in most cases under the management of inexperienced officers was not productive. There was a universal complaint of neglect in the Hospitals, and the question was, not whether they were well provided for by the Government, but how best to supply their acknowledged deficiencies without impairing the responsibility of the officers in charge of them. This was indeed the only question, for, as we have had occasion so often to remark, the impulse of the roused benevolent feeling of the people towards the Army, was wholly irresistible.

All that could be hoped for, was, so to direct and control it, that it might produce a result in some measure commensurate with the zeal, generosity and energy, which were its main characteristics.

If this irrepressible energy was not to be wasted, trustworthy information from some recognized autho- **Necessity of** rity was needed as to the real wants of the **studying the** soldier, and judicious advice as to the best **special needs of** **the soldier.** mode of supplying them. The natural impulse with those who had friends in the Army was of course directed first, to the aid of some particular soldier, while the zeal of a neighborhood was quickened by the desire to help the men who had gone from its immediate homes. But it was soon found, that it was impracticable to reach the soldier in this way. It was discovered that, in the movement of an army, all the resources of the government were taxed to the utmost to furnish transportation for the men themselves with their indispensable provision of shelter, food and arms. The order to advance was the signal for leaving behind every pound of superfluous baggage, which, if taken, might encumber the march. Of course it was impossible for the soldier to carry with him such articles for his comfort, as had been sent to him from his home, and experience proved that on a long march the men would often rather throw away their blankets and their overcoats, and even their rations, than endure the fatigue of carrying them. Thus it happened that a large portion of the gifts of the people, sent directly to their friends in the Army never reached their destination or contributed, in any way, amidst the privations of active campaigns, to their health and comfort.

But even if this difficulty could have been sur-
mounted, there was found in the natural ignorance
that prevailed concerning the real wants of the men
and their comparative importance, another obstacle to
the practical usefulness of all this well meant zeal.
As no one knew anything, by experience, of a soldier's
life, and as it was so difficult to find out exactly how
far the government proposed to care for them, the
imagination of the kind-hearted took the widest range
in seeking for methods to relieve his necessities.
Who has forgotten those strange appendages to
the head gear of the first three months' men called
" Havelocks," the work of so many busy hands and
warm hearts, remembered now, only as an illustration
of the wasted labor and energy of a true but misguided
zeal ?   Who does not recall the strange medley of
articles called delicacies, which, together with many
things of essential value to the suffering soldier, were
poured indiscriminately into the Hospitals, during the
early months of the war, or the indignation of excitable
philanthropists,—men and women,—when they were
told that the patients could not be the recipients of
their peculiar care, but must be left in the charge
of the Surgeons, who, alone, could be permitted to
provide for their treatment and regulate their diet?
The nature, then, of the supplies and the mode of
distributing them, were soon found to be practical
questions, not to be solved by a mere sentiment of pity,
or even by a spirit of devotion to the welfare of the
soldier, no matter how pure its motive, but solely by
considerations growing out of the exigencies of the
military service.   There was here a wide field for the

23

exercise of the truest humanity, but it was a field, utterly unlike that in which any one had heretofore labored, and its proper and successful cultivation required a special instruction.

The Commission, therefore, recognizing with all the world the need of supplemental supplies, sought to {Council of women held in Washington.} organize a system by which those most needed should be provided in abundance, and distributed in such a way as to accomplish the best practical result for the common benefit of the whole Army. As a means of securing a concert of action among the women of the country, the Commission invited certain societies, from which it had hitherto received its principal contribution of supplies, to appoint Delegates, who should meet in Washington, and after fully discussing the subject in all its bearings, advise the Commission as to the best mode of effecting its object. This conference, or " Women's Council," as it was called, was held in November, 1862, and was attended by ladies representing the chief auxiliaries of the Commission in different parts of the country. Its plans and methods were laid before them by Mr. Olmsted and Dr. Newberry ; the peculiar relations of women to the war, and the aid which might be rendered by them to the sick and suffering by means of a system of organized effort were earnestly discussed. With entire unanimity the Council agreed that it was the duty of the women of the country to provide assistance and consolation for the sick and suffering " abundantly, persistently, and methodically," and that such aid should be as far as possible an expression of pure patriotism and love of the Union. To perform this duty properly, they resolved, that associations should be formed in every village and town with this distinct purpose in view, and that whatever was thus provided, should be thrown into a common stock for the relief of all soldiers who might suffer. They decided also that the best system for the distribution of these gifts, was that adopted by the Sanitary Commission, by means of which relief was as freely afforded at points most remote from loyal communities, as at those nearest to them. This was the great source of the wonderful supply organization of the Commission, and out of it, owing to the zealous, enlightened, and unwearied labors of the societies which were represented in this Council flowed a stream constant and abundant, the vast proportions of which were only less remarkable than the perpetual refreshment it administered to the sick and weary of the Army. These Councils or conventions of representative women were held from time to time, as the changing circumstances of the war seemed to require them, and they always resulted in perfecting the details of the general organization, in stimulating those engaged in work for the soldier to renewed zeal, and in confirming the loyalty of the women of the country to the principles and methods of the Commission.

As another step towards carrying out their plans for a supply organization, the Commission invoked the powerful aid of a body of men throughout the country whom they had appointed Associate Members. At the beginning of the year 1862 more than four hundred such members, representative men in their respective communities,

Aid of the Associate Members of the Commission invoked.

had been selected. Their duties were defined in a circular issued in June, 1861, "to consist in efforts to promote the establishment of auxiliary associations and so to direct the labors of those already formed, for the aid and relief of the army, that they might strengthen and support those of the Commission." When the depôts were established by the General Secretary at the various points already referred to for the reception of supplies, the Associate Members residing at those places were requested to take charge of these depôts, to see that they were constantly replenished, and to hold the stores accumulated in them subject to the order of the central office of the Commission. In pursuance of the request contained in this circular, the "supply business," as it was called, was actively entered upon by the Associate Members.

In accordance with the policy of the Commission, as has been already stated, their efforts were principally Action of the Associate Members in different parts of the country. directed towards aiding their country-women to methodize and enlarge their plans of gathering supplies, and in organizing a system by which the depôts, at all the large centres, should be kept replenished. In Boston, the Associates of the Commission transferred their work, at an early Boston. day, to the New England Women's Auxiliary Association, an organization conspicuous, during the whole war for its vigor and energy. By its active efforts, Aid Societies, tributary to its depôt, were established throughout all the eastern portion of New England, and it thus became, to use the words of General Meade, "one of the principal sources whence flowed the inestimable blessings and benefits conferred by that noble association (the Sanitary Commission,) upon the sick and suffering soldiers." In New York, as has been already stated, the work of Army relief was begun by that great society, the Women's Central Association of Relief. Its managers soon New York. became convinced of the wisdom of the plans and methods adopted by the Commission, and made a formal application to be recognized as one of its Branches, stipulating only, that all the stores accumulated in its depôt should be subject to the orders of the proper officers of the Commission. Their request was granted, and the success of their efforts in gathering supplies was as great, as that spirit of perfect faith in the methods of the Commission, and that harmonious co-operation with it in all its work which marked the whole period of its history. It laid under contribution the state of New York, and a part of New Jersey, and it soon succeeded in establishing a network of auxiliary organizations of singular efficiency and influence throughout those states. In Philadelphia, the work of gathering supplies from benevo- Philadelphia. lent societies and individuals, made but slow progress, while under the direct charge of the Associates. Their zealous efforts to support the general policy of the Commission were rewarded, however, by the contribution of large sums of money, by which, supplies of a kind needed in the army, and not provided by the homes of the country, were procured. Following the example of Boston and New York, it was determined to transfer the whole business of collecting supplies in Pennsylvania, Delaware and Western New Jersey to a number of ladies who afterwards took the name of the

"Women's Pennsylvania Branch." This society prosecuted its labors with great zeal during the continuance of the war. It established, in the district under its special jurisdiction more than three hundred and fifty Aid Societies tributary to it. From these societies a vast amount of valuable contributions was received which aided materially in the support of the great supply work of the Commission. These three associations became the great centres of supply, by which such wants of the armies operating east of the mountains as could be provided for by contributions in kind, were met.

While the Associate Members in each of these three cities aided and encouraged by their influence the prosecution of this supply work after its active management had passed into the hands of the women, the co-operation in it of those resident in Philadelphia was more direct and constant than anywhere else. "The Women's Pennsylvania Branch" industriously engaged in that portion of it which embraced the collection of articles from its numerous tributaries, and the discovery of new sources of supply. The management and disposal of these supplies so as to meet the requisitions of the Central Office at Washington, and the wants of local military Hospitals, besides an important Special Relief work including the Hospital Directory, the Employment Bureau, and the War Claim Agency, remained under the direct control of the Associates. The details of this great business were managed by their Superintendent, MR. ROBERT M. LEWIS, a gentleman to whose rare judgment, wisely tempered zeal, and persistent earnestness of purpose was due in a great measure the impulse which resulted in gathering money and supplies of the value of more than a million and a half of dollars, as the share of Philadelphia and the district dependent upon it, in maintaining the work of the Commission. For more than three years he conducted the affairs of the Agency at that place with unceasing assiduity and consummate skill, abounding in labors, which had no fee or reward save the consciousness that he was among the foremost in that noble army of workers at home, which was the true reserve force and support of that in the field.

There were, besides these, a large number of societies, not affiliated with the branches, which preferred to send their local contributions direct to the Central Depôt at Washington.

In the West, also, the same great work was organized by the Associate Members of the Commission. In Cincinnati, in Columbus, and especially   In the West. in Cleveland, they exhibited a zeal and enterprise which resulted in the formation of Aid Societies directing nearly all the vast resources of the patriotic sympathy of the great State of Ohio towards the Army through the channels of the Commission. The unwearied zeal and personal toil of the Associates at Cincinnati after the battles of Fort Donelson and Shiloh have been already referred to,   Cincinnati. and they there set an example of a good work which stimulated the friends of the Commission throughout the West to similar efforts, as occasion called for them during the war. The extraordinary success of the officers of the Commission in Ohio in gathering contributions, and the wonderful energy which they dis-

played in placing them at the disposal of the soldier just when most needed, attracted the attention
of the Legislature of that state, and received its official
commendation and approval. The North-Western
Chicago. Branch of the Commission at Chicago was
one of the most efficient of all its auxiliaries in collecting
supplies, and its various tributaries scattered throughout the states of Illinois, Wisconsin and Iowa, did more
for the relief of the soldier, probably, in proportion to
their means, than those of any other section of the
country. Nowhere had the Commission warmer or
more enthusiastic friends than at Chicago. It was most
fortunate in enlisting at an early period the active sympathy of some of the most influential and trusted men
in that important place. The names of the gentlemen
who conducted the operation of its Agency there, Judge
Skinner, Mr. E. B. McCagg, and Mr. E. W. Blatchford, were alone a tower of strength to its cause throughout the North-West, and the Commission reaped the
benefit, in the vast contributions of that region, of
their wide-spread reputation and active exertions.

The history of these Aid Societies forms in itself a
wonderful chapter in the annals of philanthropic labor.
General results It has seemed to the Commission of such
of the supply or-
ganization. special interest and importance as to require,
for its full development and illustration, a distinct
volume in which a detailed account of the methods and
results of their operations should be presented. It is
impossible, in any other way, to do justice to the vast
labors of those who conducted them, or to present such
a lesson of this great mode of organizing popular benevolence as may be useful to posterity. These asso-

ciations, with their affiliated tributaries, formed, in an important sense, the main stem or trunk of the Commission, rather than its branches, for through them chiefly flowed that stream of life-giving nourishment which maintained the whole body in perpetual vigor. Without them, indeed, that body might have had but a dwarfish growth. It is not easy, therefore, to overrate the importance of their efforts as shaping the policy and results of one of the most important departments of the Commission's work. It might indeed be an interesting subject of speculation to discuss the probability of its success as an organization, had it confined itself wholly to its original design of securing the adoption of a thorough preventive service. Whether popular sentiment was at any time during the war so enlightened as to appreciate fully the paramount necessity of such a service, and to provide the means of carrying it on, to the exclusion of other forms of Army relief, may well admit of a doubt. But this appeal for articles to supply wants, which were obvious to the most unreflecting, made a deep impression on the great popular heart, and it resulted not only in obtaining means for supplying these special wants, but also, indirectly, in furnishing the Commission's Treasury with money, by which the other and more scientific portions of its work were supported. In this way, the labors of these Societies were of inestimable service in educating the public mind to a due conception of the character and value of the Commission's theory, and of the wide scope of its operations. It is impossible to do full justice to the patient and untiring energy, zeal and devotion of the members of these societies, or to the systematic,

24

intelligent, and successful methods of conducting their operations which distinguished them during the war. Where these qualities were so conspicuous among the multitudes engaged in this sacred work of self-denial, it is scarcely necessary to point to individuals as bright and shining examples of their influence, still justice and gratitude alike demand from the Commission the avowal of its conviction, that to the enlightened and zealous labors of such women as Miss May and Miss Stevenson, at Boston, Miss Collins and Miss Schuyler at New York, Mrs. Grier and Mrs. Moore at Philadelphia, Mrs. Rouse and Miss Brayton at Cleveland, Miss Campbell at Detroit, and Mrs. Hoge and Mrs. Livermore at Chicago, is due not merely a large proportion of the supplies distributed in the Army, but also much of that enthusiastic spirit of devotion to its general policy as an agent and exponent of popular sympathy, which pervaded all classes during the war.

When it was determined to induce these Soldiers' Aid Societies to become tributary to the Commission, and to adopt its channels as the best means of distributing their gifts, it was found that a larger number than was supposed had already sprung into existence, and were actively working. It needed but little effort to convince their members that the agency for which they had been seeking, as the best almoner of their bounty, was close at hand. The peculiar advantages which the Commission possessed for distributing wisely and with the best practical results, contributions for the relief of the soldier were set forth in numerous circulars and other documents. Very soon, most of these societies became auxiliary to the Commission, and their gifts soon swelled the amount of its stores to an extent far beyond what had been anticipated by the most sanguine. Various other means were taken to quicken and enlighten the zeal and labors of the members of these societies. A complete _{Canvassing} system of canvassing by means of special _{Agents.} Agents was adopted. These Agents made frequent visits to the societies, presented statements of the needs of the soldier, explained the modes adopted in giving relief, and frequently illustrated the value of the work in the Hospital, and on the battle-field by relating incidents occurring within their own personal observation. A constant correspondence was kept up concerning the work in which they were engaged between the officers of the great central receiving depôts and their tributary branches, and thus each remote society was kept fully informed of the special needs of the soldier at particular periods or in particular localities, as observed by the agents of the Commission engaged in the work of distribution. In order more fully to enlighten those upon whom the Commission depended for its stock of supplies, two periodical publications, one at the West, the _{Sanitary Reporter and Sanitary Bulletin.} Sanitary Reporter, the other at the East, the Sanitary Bulletin, were established. They were issued every two weeks, and containing in the letters and reports of the Agents of the Commission with the Army in the field, the latest accounts of its actual work, they carried to each society the evidence of the practical results of its labors. At the meetings of these societies, it was customary to read such portions of these publications as appeared most likely to interest and encourage those who were working for the soldier.

By these varied means, the zeal of the women of the country was kept alive, and their faith in the methods adopted by the Commission, was preserved and strengthened. The Village Aid Society or sewing circle soon became the nucleus of the patriotic feeling, and self-sacrificing efforts of the particular locality in which it was held. As the war went on, these societies, so far from diminishing in numbers or efficiency or in the amount of their contributions, actually increased in all these respects, with every increasing demand on their energy and resources. The extraordinary constancy which was maintained by most of them during the war, in their efforts to aid the soldier, was one of their most remarkable characteristics. The women had evidently enlisted for the war; there was nothing intermittent or spasmodic about their labors, their zeal kept pace with the triumphant march of their brethren in the field and there can be little doubt, that had the struggle continued for years longer, the women of the country would have been found just as persistent in their self-denying labors, as when their enthusiasm had been first roused. This unmistakeable feeling, thus exhibited, had, of course, a far deeper significance, and a far wider influence than that which resulted in merely sending gifts to the soldier. It can hardly be doubted that the existence and support of such a society, in any particular town or village during the war, exercised there a powerful effect upon public opinion in favor of sustaining the National cause. It was impossible to work

Influence of these Aid Societies in favor of the National cause.

constantly and in a self-sacrificing spirit, for the relief of the soldier, without imbibing a feeling of intense sympathy for the cause which he was defending. Such a spirit could not be confined to the women, and its legitimate result was, to encourage husbands and brothers in loyal devotion, by the example of their wives and sisters. Among the many influences which contributed to the general support of the Government during the war, especially in the rural districts, one of the foremost unquestionably was an intense desire, on the part of those who stayed at home to aid and encourage those of their friends, who were absent in the Army. In maintaining so healthy a sentiment, it will readily be seen, that these efforts of the women were not without a controlling power. Their labors indeed, viewed in this more general light, were very significant in another aspect. The Aid Societies of the Sanitary Commission worked for the National cause because they worked for the National soldier only. Nothing had been more difficult, at first, than to divert the warm impulses of the hearts of women from efforts to minister to the necessities of those, who, going from their own households, seemed to have peculiar and special claims upon their sympathy. But when they were convinced, not merely that distribution to particular individuals or regiments was impracticable, but also that a true and lofty conception of their duty required them to recognize all National soldiers as equally deserving their aid, they gave a practical illustration of their devotion to the National idea in its broadest sense. The heresy of state sovereignty with its natural fruit of local jealousies and a petty, narrow, unnational spirit, had its counterpart in much that was observed here while we were engaged in a terrible struggle to preserve our own life, by extirpating every trace of so poisonous an element. Some allusion has already been made to its hurtful influence as exhibited in the attempt of some of the State Governments to provide for the care of their own sick and wounded exclusively, and sectional jealousies and pretensions, as is well known, fomented too often by a pure spirit of demagogueism, appeared in a much more offensive form during the war. The imperious need of the time was the inculcation of a thoroughly National senti- ment which, above and beyond everything else, should recognize only one country and one destiny. This principle once thoroughly rooted in the popular mind, everything was safe, and the result of the struggle could not be doubtful. The Sanitary Commission, not only because it was a necessity in the practical admin- istration of its work, and because it was always re- garded by its officers as a species of bureau of the National Government, but because it anxiously desired to uphold National principles and a National policy, strove unceasingly, both in its appeals to its constitu- ents for supplies, and in its distribution of them in the Army, to recognize in every man who wore the uniform, a National soldier only. It can hardly be doubted that its constant adherence to this principle in all its methods and operations, contributed powerfully to foster that intense spirit of nationality, which, unweakened by the fierce strife of parties, brought us safely through the war.

The interest of the communities, in the midst of

which these societies were working, was further stimu-
lated by lectures, concerts and other exhibi- Powerful effect of this influence in certain locali- ties.
tions of various kinds, the claim of the
soldier on the gratitude of those who were
at home being always the inspiring theme on such occasion. By expedients of this sort, their treasuries
were kept filled, their contributions in clothing and
all kinds of supplies became abundant, and an unflagging spirit of devotion to the welfare of the
soldier, was perpetually kept alive. An intelligent appreciation of his particular wants, was also one
of the characteristics of these organizations. Did
scurvy invade the Army, and threaten to paralyze its
efficiency, circulars were issued from the Head Quarters of the Commission, asking for contributions of
fresh vegetables, in order that the dreaded evil might
be extirpated. In response to these appeals, contained
in what were called in the history of the Commission,
" Potato Circulars" and "Onion Circulars," thousands
of barrels of these esculents were gathered in a short
time by the members of these societies from the farmers
of the North-west, and sent without delay to the distant
fields of military operations, where the effect they produced may be inferred from the declaration of one of our
most distinguished Generals, that the Sanitary Commission had saved by these means the Army engaged
in the siege of Vicksburg. The ability to perform
such a work was due entirely to the perfect system
adopted by the Commission in organizing the benevolence of the country.

The ingenuity of the women in discovering new
methods of enlisting the sympathy and interest of the

Sanitary Fairs. people in working for the soldier, when the old ones had somewhat lost their freshness, was very remarkable. The ordinary, regular, steady work of these societies had resulted in very large contributions. As time went on, their production, as we have said, so far from diminishing increased, notwithstanding the gradual exhaustion of home supplies, and the constantly advancing price of materials. Still the wants which prevailed during the campaigns of 1863 had been so great and so urgent, and the prospect of an increasing demand in the future seemed so imminent, that it was determined to adopt a bold experiment for replenishing the funds of the Commission, and to test the strength of that public interest which had been awakened in the general subject of Army Relief. This was no less than an attempt to organize, on a grand scale, those novel exhibitions popularly termed "Sanitary Fairs," the unparalleled success of which was not only a most remarkable proof of popular confidence in the plans of the Commission, but also one of the most striking illustrations of the profound gratitude and affection felt by the popular heart towards the soldier which occurred during the war. It is not our purpose here to give a detailed account of these brilliant displays of patriotic sympathy. That task is in other and competent hands. The material aid which was furnished by these Fairs was hardly more opportune, than the evidence they afforded of the undiminished interest which was felt in the welfare of the soldier was gratifying. Beginning at Chicago in the autumn of 1863, these Fairs, held afterwards at Cincinnati, Cleveland, New York, Boston, Brooklyn, Philadelphia, Pittsburg, and Albany, added more than three millions of dollars to the funds of the Commission and its branches throughout the country.   It need hardly be said, that the whole conception of these great exhibitions was as peculiarly novel and American as their success was unexampled. Everything was crowded into them which the busy brains, or the warm hearts or the skillful hands of our country-women could create or gather as a fit offering of their gratitude to the soldier. The products of the farm, the manufactory, the machine shop, the delicate workmanship of the skilled artisan, works of art and beauty, of taste and utility, represented there the sympathy of all classes of the community for the suffering soldier. The months of previous preparation, necessary to perfect the arrangements for these gigantic exhibitions, the appeals to all classes through large districts of country for contributions, the stirring events of the campaigns in progress, all helped with wonderful effect, to turn the thoughts of every one into the same channel, and to keep alive an excitement and interest in the work, which soon became contagious, and from the influence of which few escaped. The quiet, unassuming but hard-working Village Aid Societies had suddenly become partners in a grand scheme which appealed not only to their long-tried sympathy for the soldier, but to their local pride, and to that love of novelty and excitement, which is so wonderful a stimulus of activity in all undertakings.   It was feared at one time, by the cooler and wiser heads of the Commission, that the extraordinary labors attendant upon preparing and conducting these great Fairs,

25

would inevitably be followed by a reaction, and that the old normal, steady system of gathering supplies, which had been in use since the beginning of the war, would seem tame and spiritless after the excitement had passed.   Such an apprehension, however, proved groundless.   It seemed, after all, that the efforts of the women, on behalf of the soldier were based on no transient emotions, but on sober convictions of duty. As long as the need lasted throughout the war, just so long were they ready, with warm hearts and full hands, to minister to him.   Thus, the surplus stock of the homes of country, in every description of clothing and bedding, and in articles of delicate food, intended for the comfort of the sick, was poured with a lavish bounty into the depôts of the Commission.   From many of these homes where the contributions in kind appeared smallest, the spirit which dictated the offer- ing was really the grandest and most self-sacrificing, for not seldom they represented the widow's mite, cheer- fully shared with those, who were supposed to be more needy than herself.

These were some of the means by which the Com- mission was able not only to rouse the patriotic sym- Other services pathy of the masses in different sections of Associate Members. of the country, but also, so to guide the strong impulse of home affection as to render it the great source of the power wielded by it in the work in which it was engaged.   The Aid Societies as has been already mentioned, were placed at first under the immediate charge of the Associate Members, residing in different localities.   Practically, however, after their work began, their relations were with the

Central offices of the Commission, from whom they received instructions as to special wants, and in obedience to whose requisition, they sent their accumulated stores to the distributing depôts. But the functions and duties of the Associate Members did not, by any means, end here. The valuable assistance, rendered by some of them, in the preparation of monographs on Medical and Surgical subjects, for distribution among the Army Surgeons, has already been noticed. As they were men of position and influence, in their respective communities, they were looked to, also, as Agents for devising means for replenishing the treasury of the Commission. A vast amount of money, was required, not merely to place the contributions in kind of the Aid Societies in the hands of the soldier, and to purchase those articles that could not be furnished by them, but also, for the support of the general work of the Commission. Each Branch had besides, its local treasury, and the funds belonging to it were used not only for the purchase of those articles, for which requisition was made by the central authorities, but also for the purpose of affording relief to local Military Hospitals, and in aiding soldiers in irregular circumstances. This last branch of their service, involved great labor in many parts of the country. In the large cities particularly, where numbers of troops were constantly passing and repassing, and Hospitals were established, which were crowded with patients during the war, the Branches found it necessary to establish Homes and Lodges, and Bureaus of information, supported by funds from their own treasuries. These various means of relief proved as useful to the particular objects of their care, as the similar establishments managed by the Commission at points nearer to the scene of hostilities.

CHAPTER VIII.

CONTRIBUTIONS FROM CALIFORNIA AND THE PACIFIC COAST.

WHEN the Sanitary Commission entered upon its undertaking, seventy-five thousand men had been called into the field, and it was hoped they would prove sufficient to put down the Rebellion. *Original design of the Sanitary Commission.* This army then seemed a very large one, and it was solicitude for only seventy-five thousand troops that called the Sanitary Commission into existence. Fifty thousand dollars, it was thought,—not without grounds,—would suffice to enable a scientific Commission to render all the services such an Army could require from a careful study of the whole subject of military hygiene, from thorough inspection, and such systematic appeals to the War Department and the Medical Bureau, as would keep the authorities accurately informed as to the dangers, wants, and deficiencies of each regiment, camp, and hospital, and secure the prompt and efficient supervision of the Military and Medical authorities over the health, life and comfort of the men.

It was with these hopes and views, and with this inadequate idea of the cost of its undertaking that the Sanitary Commission first got to work. For a few months its labors were *Limited amount of money required at the outset.*

197

very much confined to camp inspections, and to matters strictly scientific and preventive. To what belongs directly to camp police, it added a careful re-examination of the questions of diet and cooking, of quarters and tents, of uniforms and knapsacks and shoes, as affecting comfort and endurance, and examined an immense number of patented inventions having reference sometimes to camp equipage, sometimes to preparations of food. Its monthly expenses did not exceed for the first six months an average of five thousand dollars.

From the first, boxes and bales of comforts for the soldiers had been forwarded to the Sanitary Commission, but not in such quantities as to embarrass its small *depôt*, or to give any special trouble in distributing them. For the first six months neither the Eastern nor the Western Army went far enough from home to make any general agency indispensable. But in the second six months, the supplies poured into the hands of the Commission became cumbrous in quantity, and the Commission began gradually to feel how much it was depended upon to meet the wants of an ever-growing army, which the longer it was in the field, and the further it went from its base, became more deficient in the ordinary appliances of personal comfort and safety, more exposed to sickness, and more dependent on the nation's bounty to be extended to it through some vehicle more flexible than the Commissariat and Quartermaster's Departments.

There was a double embarrassment which the Sanitary Commission encountered at this stage of its existence. ·

Contributions of supplies.

Its own success in drawing to itself supplies, involved the necessity of a costly machinery of storehouses, officers, accountants, agents of inspection and distribution, of wagons and horses,—which it had no obvious means of creating and supporting. The people freely gave their supplies—made with their own hands, or raised on their own farms. But for one dollar in money they found it easy to raise and send forward ten dollars worth of supplies. Such was the disproportion of supplies to the cost of their distribution, that the Commission trembled at the responsibility it had assumed, and often thought the day near at hand when it must abandon its enterprise. Another embarrassment arose from the discovery that the more it did, and the better it did it—the more it must do. The field kept continually widening. As its labors became known and appreciated, it was more and more drawn upon by the army—and every successful effort it made to distribute its supplies, only made new and increased efforts necessary. The state of its treasury meanwhile compelled it to be most cautious. It could form no plans with boldness for the want of means. The people had not in the first year of the war, become accustomed to the immense expenses which war demands. The Governmental reports had not then familiarized their ears with hundreds of millions, nor had the expansion of the currency lessened their sense of the value of money. The Treasury of the Commission therefore, although always fed with a steady stream of small gifts, was still always threatened with exhaustion because its means ran out

More money required to meet its enlarged plans.

nearly as fast as they ran in, and the outlay seemed increasing out of all proportion to the income.

It was just at this crisis when the Commission's plans for a thoroughly national work were embarrassed with Contribution of the practical difficulties of a feeble and in-one hundred thousand dollars adequate supply of money—which there from California. appeared to be no adequate means of increasing; when a system of canvassing the country for money and supplies was hindered by the want of means to support canvassers in the home field; when the desire to prevent local associations and State Agencies from becoming their own distributors was thwarted by an inability to announce that the Commission had agents of its own in the military field, numerous enough and at so many different points, as to qualify it to assume the effective distribution of all the Nation's supplementary supplies; when the want of money in considerable advance of its current expenses forbade it from laying plans ahead, with that breadth, forethought and wisdom which it knew the case required—it was just at this point of time, and at this crisis in its history, when three months more of such trials as had embarrassed the Commission for the three months preceding, would have probably brought it to a premature death, that the news reached the public that the Mayor of San Francisco had telegraphed the President of the United States, that a hundred thousand dollars had been raised in that city for the benefit of sick and wounded soldiers, and had asked his advice through what channel this magnificent contribution should be applied. The President consulted the Surgeon-General, Dr. Hammond, who immediately

recommended that the Sanitary Commission should be
selected as the almoner of California's bounty.   The
President adopted the advice, and on October 14th,
1862, the President and Treasurer of the Commission
received a draft on Eugene Kelly & Co., of New
York, drawn by Donahoe, Ralston & Co., of San
Francisco, and dated September 19th, 1862, for one
hundred thousand dollars in current funds!

This hundred thousand dollars, with all it implied, was the making and saving of the United
States Sanitary Commission.   Up to that State of the
period the largest cash balance in the Commission's
treasury at that
treasury at the end of any month had time.
been twenty-four thousand three hundred and forty-
three dollars, (April 30, 1862).   The whole receipts
to October 1, 1862, had been within one hundred
and seventy thousand dollars; showing for fifteen
months and over, only an average sum of about
eleven thousand dollars of cash, to carry on the
work with.   The supplies were coming in very dispro-
portionately to the money, and without money to move
and manage them were useless.   On October 1st, 1862,
the balance in the treasury was only sixteen thousand
seven hundred and twenty-three dollars and ninety-
one cents, while the disbursements of the previous
month had been twenty-six thousand six hundred and
forty-six dollars and one cent, and the receipts only
twenty thousand nine hundred and sixteen dollars and
eighty cents.   With so small a margin of resources as
the Commission had during the first fifteen months of
its existence, it is easy to infer how contracted its enterprise, and constrained its policy necessarily were—and
26

how little vigor it had to contend with State Associations and local Relief enterprises.

When then on October 14, 1862, the Commission received the magnificent sum of one hundred thou- Effect of this sand dollars, as its first contribution from Contribution. California, more than half as much as it had received in all, up to that date, it can readily be understood how it was at once emboldened to break the fetters which doubt and anxiety had fastened upon its policy ; how strengthened it was in its ability to maintain its difficult and unpopular plan of resisting sectional schemes of Relief for special commands in the Army ; how much abler it was to contend with the jealousies and rivalries of at least one powerful Branch which was more than half-disposed to go into the field itself as an independent organization, and utterly destroy the unity of the Commission's operations ; how enlarged its capacity of extending and perfecting its machinery in all parts of the Army, so as to leave all Relief Associations without excuse for withholding their supplies on the ground of inadequate arrangements for their distribution, on the part of the Commission. .

The news of California's noble contribution to the United States Sanitary Commission arrested universal General atten- attention, and fastened the eyes and the contion attracted by fidence of the wavering upon it. It was the it. How it affect- ed its resources. first splendid thing in the way of beneficence which had been done for the soldiers. It excited emulation, and was at once imitated. It placed the Commission so far before all local Relief Societies in its resources, as to make it plain that rivalry with it was useless. And the moment that it appeared plain that the Commission was going to succeed, even the luke-warm were stimulated to place themselves among its supporters. The total receipts went up from October 1, to November 1, from twenty thousand nine hundred and sixteen dollars and eighty cents, to two hundred and thirteen thousand nine hundred and sixty-four dollars and twenty-three cents. And what was thus so grandly begun, continued. California pleased with her own humanity, and gratified with the enthusiastic reception her munificence had met, sent another one hundred thousand dollars fourteen days later. The receipts and disbursements of the Commission for the three previous months had been as follows:

	Receipts.	Disbursements.	Cash Balance.
August 1, 1862	$24,381 46	$16,613 50	$14,682 61
September 1, 1862	24,491 71	16,721 20	22,453 12
October 1, 1862	20,916 80	26,646 01	16,723 91

The receipts, disbursements and cash balances of the next three months will sufficiently exhibit the immense expansion which California gold had produced in the operations of the Commission, and which California gold from that date to the close of the war was the chief means of enabling the Commission to maintain.

	Receipts.	Disbursements.	Cash Balance.
November 1, 1862	$213,964 23	$43,876 93	$186,811 21
December 1, 1862	103,406 18	64,774 99	225,442 40
January 1, 1862	168,154 14	86,262 73	307,333 81

From this date, November 1, 1862, there was not for eight months, less than two hundred and forty-seven thousand dollars cash balance in the treasury at the close of each month, nor with the exception of two months (December and January, 1863–4) ever less than one hundred and twenty-two thousand dollars. With the money raised by products of the Great Fairs,—the other grand feeder of the cash resources of the Commission, and much later in its flow, not to say greatly stimulated by the example of the contribution from the Pacific coast,—the treasury from April 1, 1864 to the close of its active operations, January 1, 1866, while at one time it had a balance of one million two hundred and twenty-two thousand six hundred and sixty-nine dollars and thirty-three cents (July 1, 1864) and commonly over a half million, never had less than one hundred and ninety-nine thousand two hundred and twelve dollars and twenty-three cents, (August 1, 1865). The immediate effect of the California contribution upon the disbursements of the Commission (which fairly represent its activity and · usefulness) ·is most striking. From fifty-four thousand dollars the previous three months, the disbursements for the next three months, went up to one hundred and ninety-four thousand dollars, or nearly four times as much. And the possession of this money stimulated in far larger proportion the contribution of supplies in kind. For the means at hand to canvass, to advertise, to establish Sanitary Bulletins, to report the work of the Commission, swelled the number of Aid Societies and consequently the flood of supplies, and tasked to the utmost, the expensive machinery which the money-power of the Commission created, to apply the generous gifts in clothing and food to the ever increasing demands of our immense Army.

It is very doubtful whether if California and the other Pacific States, had not chosen the Sanitary Commission for their almoner, it would have been able so far to have secured the confi- dence of the country at large, as to have be- come the beneficiary of the great Fairs which supplied more than half its whole cash income. The immense national advantage in a struggle for unity, of a com- mon enterprise of humanity round which the homes of the country could rally, adding thus the united strength of the domestic feeling of the American people to its political and military power in the coun- cil and the field—would have been lost, if the United States Sanitary Commission had not succeeded. It was a desperate enterprise to attempt to unite by hu- mane feeling what was so disunited by distance and the disintegrating tendencies of local pride and interest, as the different states and communities of so broad a country. Neither the excellency of the plan, nor the ability of its administration, could have succeeded against the force of sectional pride and independence, and the truly American love of multiplying local asso- ciations. Desperate efforts to throw off the yoke of the United States Sanitary Commission would constantly have been made by its already half-independent Branches, and would have succeeded. Coaxing and compromising and humoring did wonders to bring about unity and co-operation. And we do not hesitate to say that the cash resources of the Commission which alone commanded and utilized its supplies, were mainly due to the largeness, the constancy, the per- sistency of the contributions from California and the Pacific Coast,—Nevada, Oregon, Idaho, and the Sand- wich Islands,—so that to California more than to any

State in the Union, is really due the growth, usefulness, success, and national reputation of the United
States Sanitary Commission.

Let us now turn to California, and see how it happened that the citizens of San Francisco adopted the
General sketch   United States Sanitary Commission as the
of California.   almoner of their bounty to the soldiers and
sailors in the war, and led the State and the Coast
throughout the national struggle, to pour such large
contributions into its treasury.

California, removed two thousand miles by land,
and five thousand by water, from the scene of the
war, was settled by American citizens only in 1848.
Its gold attracted a population of singular vigor,
and enterprise, from all parts of the country and
the world. In less than one generation, in seventeen years, it had attained through the most painful
process of emigration by which any country ever
gained a population, a half million of people, and had
built a city of a hundred thousand strong—a city
which, rising like an exhalation, had something of the
solidity and finish, the elegance and splendor of an old
capital. All modern improvements—gas-works, water-
works, street rail-cars, school-houses, churches, hotels,
elegant shops, great commercial houses and banking
establishments, splendid steamships at the wharves,
and beautiful steamboats in the rivers and Bay—at-
tested the cultivated tastes, the essentially American
ideas, habits, and energies, of the people of this new
State and young city. With a currency exclusively of
gold and silver, a business largely made up of mining,
in which great risks and great losses and gains were

constantly experienced, where the golden inducements to bodily labor with the pick and the shovel, the rocker and the "long-tom," overcame the reluctance of educated and refined men to physical toil, and made labor reputable,—where, too, men were often rich by luck to-day and poor by accident to-morrow,—and all were used from the very beginning to rough lives and great personal hardships, which they made light by good fellowship and brilliant hopes—it is impossible to name another country where money is so universally sought and so little valued; where everybody is in search of wealth, and nobody is miserly in the use of it.

California,—a country distinguished for the vastness of its features and the intensity of its contrasts,—in which are brought together snow-clad mountains and parched plains, terrible freshets and intolerable droughts, great heats and severe cold; where gigantic trees, monstrous fruits, and teeming harvests are confronted with nine months of sere and dusty yellowness—when greenness wholly disappears, while nothing corresponding to sod is ever found outside of artificial gardens:—California, rich in gold and silver, in quicksilver and lead—poor in iron and in coal; where the mines and the climate possess a similar uncertainty, and the seasons are spread, not over one, but over several years—as in the Egyptian times, when seven years of famine succeeded seven years of plenty, making one long summer and one long winter of the whole period;—California, where a sparse population has ransacked the immense territory, and the mark of the spade and the blast is left so legibly upon the face of the whole country, that the traveler would think millions of people at some time had occupied it; where towns, villages, and hamlets, forsaken by former occupants, present the same appearance which the desert might offer if the Bedouins had left standing forever the tents they occupied from night to night, as for generations they crossed its wastes each time by some new track;—California, with its wilderness at the city gates, and its civilization in the midst of the mountains; where luxury and want, refinement and coarseness, education and ignorance, have a twin-like co-existence, has impressed its natural features upon its population. They are broad-minded and aspiring, with large thoughts and free feelings; like their soil, underlaid with volcanic fires, and subject to earthquakes of sentiment. They have mighty freshets of enthusiasm, and burning heats of political excitement. Free-handed and open-hearted like Nature in their lavish valleys, they are ready to give all they have to any cause that moves their quick and contagious affections. Like their rains, that come in floods or stay away altogether, they move in mass if they move at all. As their fires devastate not a single house or block, but half a city at a time, so their charities sweep through whole communities and involve high and low, rich and poor, in their rush. Long unaccustomed to the society of women, the men of California developed many of the tendernesses of the other sex in their own mutually dependent hearts. Cooking for, and nursing each other in the mines, they grew gentle even while growing wild, and no cry of humanity was ever raised in vain among them in their rude camps and diggings.

The feverish nature of a mining life makes the

population of every such country greedy of excitement in all their concerns. Sensation Exciting nature of life in that is the lifeblood of such a people. When region. street fights and gambling in the open squares to the sound of bands of music have passed by, comes the splendid excitement of Vigilance Committees, with their solemn Lynch law and their Venetian secrecy and dispatch; then the era of fire companies, with their architectural engine houses and wide political and social dominion; of Masonic lodges and their rivalries in regalia and halls; next the rage and clash of political parties, headed by Bowery Boys turned scholars, gentlemen and statesmen, but wearing under their black vests the red shirt and the fiery heart of their antecedent sympathies; then the spicy personalities, pungent wit, and sublime extravagances of party and local newspapers—reeking with vigorous, improvised poetry, rollicking, unscrupulous fun, and stinging and often poisoned wit, but all alive with meaning and stir and courage; finally comes the era of amusements, when everybody in town knows the popular clown at the circus, the "Bones" at the Minstrels, the "double shuffler" at the Museum, and when the boldest daring in all things carries the day. Such a people are as capable of noble and self-forgetting enthusiasm, of contagious patriotism and uncalculating beneficence as of ignoble and frivolous excitements. They will stand anything but mediocrity. They will do neither good nor evil by halves. Their love and their hatred, their fun and their earnest, their pleasures and their charities, will be whole-souled.

To such a people, it can readily be imagined how

27

the news of the late war came. Added to the vastness of the excitement, which so great and world-moving a conflict brought to their sensational temperament, was the divided relations of the population of California to both sections of the country. San Francisco, the moral and commercial capital, had been early resorted to by many able Southern men, who had taken leading places at the bar, and established whatever social aristocracy existed there. The leading clergyman in the place for many years was a Southerner and a secessionist. A large foreign population naturally sympathized with English and French views of the war, and consorted with the Southern element in the city. The Army officers in command of the fortifications of the harbor and coast were Southerners. At the first news of the firing on Sumter, it was doubtful whether the stronger feeling in San Francisco, was sympathy with the South, or with the United States Government. It was by no means certain which side even the Army officers would take, and Alcatraz, the key of the port, was in immediate peril of being seized by its own officers, and held in the interest of the Rebellion.

How the people there were affected by the war.

It is true that the anti-slavery and pro-slavery struggle in California — thanks to Broderick — had years before this terminated in favor of liberty, and that the Republican party had been successfully formed, and had elected its own Governor. The State was supposed to be more Republican than the city. The press blew both ways. The fashion and wealth of San Francisco leaned strongly to the Southern side.

But California and San Francisco were no exception

to the common rule in finding their attachment to the
flag and national unity far stronger than Their patriotism.
they knew. Danger to the Republic roused the
sleeping patriotism in the cities and towns of every
free state. Sectional sympathies paled before the national sentiment which rose and flamed in the hearts
and eyes of those who had thought themselves indifferent or wavering. In those first days, to waver was
soon inevitably to incline to the National side. None
not deeply pledged before, went over to the enemy;
and many whose inclinations and sympathies were
supposed to be with the South, came boldly over to the
other side.

In no part of the country was the struggle one more
of feeling, and less of interest than on the Pacific
Coast. It was too far off to feel very bene- Its peculiar
ficially the protection or care of the United characteristics.
States Government. If any part of the nation
could have seceded without great inconvenience,
and with a very plausible claim to geographical
isolation, boundaries of its own and separate interests, it was that Pacific slope. But, distant and
independent as California was in its soil and topogra-
phical relations, it was nearer and more strictly bound
to the country, and the National cause, by the quick
and strong heart-strings of its American population,
—whose birth-places, and the graves of their parents,
and the altars of their childhood, were in the free North
—than the people were conscious of till the hour of
threatened separation came. The less of interest their
patriotism had, the more pure and exalting it was;
and distance, exile, yearning towards parents and

brothers who had flown to arms, and places they were never again to see, only quickened the pulse of love of country. Before this filial outburst no mere party or sectional feeling could live. Matched with the friends of the Union, as the opposition seemed at first, led too by social and professional leaders, by beautiful women, and by distinguished physicians and divines, no sooner had a few brave bugle-notes, rallying the National sentiment, been blown from the lips of whole-souled and inspired patriots, than California took her place in the National ranks, one of the most loyal, uncalculating, devoted and disinterested States in the Union, as lustrous as the brightest in the glorious sisterhood of stars that were never dimmed by treason.

The most gifted and inspiring of the patriots who rallied California and the Pacific coast to the Flag of the Union, was undoubtedly Thomas Starr King, Minister of the First Unitarian Church in San Francisco. Born in New York, but reared in Massachusetts, he had earned an almost national reputation for eloquence and wit, humanity and nobleness of soul, in the lecture-rooms and pulpits of the North and West, when at the age of thirty-five, he yielded to the religious claims of the Pacific coast, and transferred himself to California. There, in four years, he had built up as a public speaker from the pulpit and the platform, a prodigious popularity. His temperament sympathetic, mercurial and electric; his disposition hearty, genial and sweet; his mind, versatile, quick and sparkling; his tact exquisite and infallible; with a voice clear as a bell and loud and cheering as a trumpet, his nature and accomplishments were perfectly adapted to the people, the place and the time.   His religious profession disarmed many of his political enemies, his political orthodoxy quieted many of his religious opponents.   Generous, charitable, disinterested, his full heart and open hand captivated the California people, while his sparkling wit, melodious cadences and rhetorical abundance, perfectly satisfied their taste for intensity, and novelty, and a touch of extravagance.   It has been said by high authority that Mr. King saved California to the Union.   California was too loyal at heart, to make that boast reasonable.   But it is not too much to say that Mr. King did more than any man, by his prompt, outspoken, uncalculating loyalty, to make California know what her own feelings really were.   He did all that any man could have done to lead a public sentiment that was unconsciously ready to follow where earnest loyalty and patriotism should guide the way.

California was too remote from the seat of war to send troops into the field.   She asked the privilege, and actually proceeded to raise several California offers regiments.   But the Government wanted troops. all the troops that could be mustered on the Pacific coast to remain there against possible contingencies.   True there were a few troops, a company of cavalry and some infantry representing California actually in the field, but not enough to satisfy her ambition, and her ardor of patriotic feeling.   If then California wished to demonstrate and indulge her full feeling of devotion to the cause, it must be through succor generously supplied to the wants of the National soldiers and sailors, by uniting actively with those who were ministering in camps and hospitals to the comfort and protection of the sick and wounded.

The origin, growth, and triumph of this movement, is too important to the history of the Sanitary Com-
First efforts to raise contributions for army relief.
mission, and too honorable to California not to be recorded with all possible detail and fullness in this final record of the Commission's work. The contributions of the Pacific Coast have been of so exceptional a kind, and so vast in sum as to entitle them to an exceptional notice. We depart therefore from the condensed method which has guided us in this history, to lay before our readers the Report which the Secretary of the California Branch made to the Board of the labors and successes of the Citizen's Committee, in which will be found a more exact, interesting, and reliable account of the history of California's connection with the nation's beneficence towards the Army, and especially of her labors in behalf of the Sanitary Commission, than could possibly be got in any other way.

Gentlemen of the California Branch of the United States Sanitary Commission.

In accordance with a vote passed at the last meeting of the Soldiers' Relief Fund Committee, which organization you succeed, held on Thursday evening, August 11th, 1864, I have the pleasure of presenting to you the following report:

The first movement in this State, from which grew the more extended action of all the people, in behalf of the sick and wounded soldiers of the Union Army, took place in this city, in the latter part of August, 1862. The loyal portion of the community was then aroused by the constantly recurring dispatches that told us of the successive battles and defeats which our army suffered, under the command of Major-General John Pope, when attempting to stay the current of the rebel arms under command of General R. E. Lee. At that time, when the most earnest sympathies of the people were excited, it was felt that something ought to be done by us, by which we could, in some way, aid the cause of the Union. The State was too far distant from the seat of war to be called upon for volunteers to the army; and, even if we might send reinforcements, the Administration had not deemed it prudent to decimate the strength of the State, lest its isolation might demand all the forces it could muster in case of any complications with foreign powers. One evening a subscription paper was suggested by the impulsive loyalty of a few gentlemen, and, in a few hours, a considerable number of names were subscribed, pledging various sums, amounting, in the aggregate, to $6,600, for the relief of the suffering of our army. The movement was one that enlisted the sympathies of all; but it was conceived, upon reflection, that the movement should be systematized, made broader and more general, and in place of a few hundred, perhaps many thousand dollars might be obtained. Only a small portion of the money thus subscribed upon that occasion was therefore collected. The first public action towards a wider recognition of the people's duty to the Union and its noble defenders, was made at the next meeting of the Board of Supervisors, held Monday evening, September 8th. At that meeting, Supervisor John H. Redington offered a resolution, which passed unanimously, as follows:

Resolved, That this Board recommend that a public meeting of the citizens of San Francisco be called for Wednesday, the 10th inst., at 8 o'clock, P. M., at the chambers of the Board, to take measures for increasing, to the greatest extent possible, the Patriotic Fund, for the benefit of sick and wounded Union soldiers, and that the Clerk of this Board be instructed to advertise the same in the several daily papers of the city."

In accordance with this resolution, a meeting was held, of which Hon. F. H. Teschemacher, Mayor, was made Chairman, and F. MacCrellish and J. W. Bingham, Secretaries. On account of the meagre attendance of the meeting, it was moved that the meeting adjourn to the next evening to insure a fuller attendance. The motion was opposed by R. G. Sneath, Esq., who desired that an Executive Committee be appointed without delay; and that the whole State be communicated with. He believed that, by exertions, a large amount of money might be remitted East every month during the war, and the feeling prevailed that action should be taken at once. A slight discussion followed relative to the method of organization and the appointment of committees, participated in by Messrs. J. H. Redington, Eugene Casserly, D. C. McRuer, and Hon. M. C. Blake, which resulted in the appointment of a Committee of Five to report a plan of action and organization, and the names of a General Committee of Thirteen. The committee of five was composed as follows: Hon. M. C. Blake, Messrs. Eugene Casserly, R. G. Sneath, D. C. McRuer and E. H. Washburn. The meeting then adjourned until the next evening (Thursday, September 11th,) at 8 o'clock, at the chambers of the Board of Supervisors.

The citizens met again the next evening, according to adjournment, and Hon. M. C. Blake, Chairman of the Committee of Five, submitted the following report:

The undersigned, appointed, at a meeting of the citizens of San Francisco, held on the 10th instant, in accordance with a resolution of the Board of Supervisors, "to take measures to increase to the greatest extent possible the Patriotic Fund for the relief of the sick and wounded soldiers of the Union," a committee to report a plan of organization and action, and the names of a Central Executive Committee, would respectfully submit the following as their report:

Believing that the pending rebellion against the Constitution and Government of these United States, can and must be put down; that to that end the entire energies and resources of the nation should be devoted; that every individual should make the cause of the Constitution and the Government his cause, involving in its issue his honor, patriotism, and manhood, and should consecrate to it his entire self, fortune, and life—that present reverses only call for the exhibition of the might of a true and loyal people, which we and our enemies know full well, once aroused, will be irresistible—that right and truth and God are on our side—and that at the present juncture, a public declaration of their sentiments by the citizens of San Francisco, is eminently fitting and proper,—your committee recommend for your adoption the following resolutions:

1. *Resolved,* That this war must be prosecuted till the authority of the Constitution and Government of the United States is fully re-established over every foot of American soil.

2. *Resolved,* That we will sustain the Government in the most vigorous possible prosecution of the war, till we have conquered, for our common country, peace, union, and the supremacy of the Constitution.

3. *Resolved,* That present reverses do not dishearten us, but we see in them only a call for the arming of the nation.

4. *Resolved,* That we recommend a meeting of the citizens of San Francisco, at Platt's Hall, on the evening of —————— next, for a public declaration of their sentiments in regard to the war and its prosecution. [Amended so as to read: "On a day to be designated by the Committee of Thirteen."]

We make these recommendations, because they express our own views, and seem to accord with the views of the meeting by which we were appointed, and also because we believe their adoption will not only promote the cause for which this meeting was specifically called, but will confirm and establish patriotic sentiments in our community.

But our object is not talk, but action. What can we do? California is removed from the seat of war. We have peace and quiet and wonderful prosperity within our borders. We have not seen the march of armies, nor have we ever been called upon to pour out our treasure or to hazard our lives as have our brethren in the East. But we have a call now—we are beginning to hear it—it needs no eloquence of words—it is pressing its claims upon us by its own irresistible logic—a call manifest and distinct for material aid—a call from the sick and wounded in the hospitals and on the battle-fields of the Union. We ought to respond to this case and to every kindred case, for our country's sake, and not less for our own—ought to respond nobly, generously, patriotically, like men who have a country to save, and who are worthy of that high position; and we are sure California will do it.

We, therefore, recommend the adoption of the following resolutions as the organic laws of the San Francisco Committee of the Soldiers' Fund.

1. *Resolved,* That Messrs. F. H. Teschemacher, Wm. Norris, Henry Seligman, A. L. Tubbs, J. B. Roberts, Peter Donahue, John H. Redington, Horace P. James, James Otis, Herman Nichols, John N. Risdon, Eugene Sullivan and Wm. M. Lent be a committee to be known by the name of the San Francisco Committee of the Soldiers' Fund.

2. *Resolved,* That it shall be the primary object of the Committee to raise money for the benefit of sick and wounded soldiers and seamen of the army and navy of the United States, and to disburse it through the proper channels.

3. *Resolved,* That the Committee shall continue during the war—shall have power to fill vacancies in its body, to make all needful rules and regulations for conducting its business and accomplishing its objects; and, by a vote of two-thirds of its members, to change its organic law.

4. *Resolved,* That the Committee shall invite not only the aid and co-operation of the citizens of San Francisco, but of kindred organizations and of Union men throughout the States of California and Oregon, and the territories of Washington and Nevada.

5. *Resolved,* That in furtherance of its primary object, the Committee be requested to use its best endeavors to raise and forward, with the least possible delay, a sum of money large enough to make up, in some degree, for our past neglect, and to be an assurance of our present interest in the cause of the Union and its defenders; and hereafter, monthly, during the continuance of the war, such a sum that it may be truly said of California in this respect, she has done her whole duty.

All of which is respectfully submitted.
    M. C. BLAKE,
    R. G. SNEATH,
    E. H. WASHBURN,
    D. C. McRUER,
    E. CASSERLY,

        Committee.

The report was accepted and adopted unanimously.

28

The gentlemen named as the Committee of Thirteen accepted readily the positions assigned them, excepting Herman Nichols, Esq., who felt obliged to decline on account of his being a representative of a foreign power. In his place Mr. Jona. G. Kittle was immediately chosen. The Committee began at once to hold its meetings, and took immediate measures for carrying out the recommendations of the Committee of Five. At the first meetings of the committee, held on Friday forenoon and evening, September 12th, Hon. F. H. Teschemacher was chosen Chairman of the Committee, James Otis, Esq., Treasurer, and Alfred L. Tubbs, Secretary. Sub-committees were appointed to make arrangements and invite gentlemen to address a Mass Meeting which was appointed for Sunday evening, September 14th. At a meeting held on Saturday, September 13th, a communication was read from Louis McLane, Esq., of the firm of Wells, Fargo & Co., tendering the services of their agents throughout this State and Oregon, in aid of the objects of the committee, and offering to transmit all moneys collected in the Interior to this city, without charge. The committee was divided into sub-committees, to whom different classes, trades and professions were assigned for collections, for the purpose of facilitating the canvassing of the city, and all arrangements were made for commencing the work immediately, after laying the matter properly before the people.

On the evening of Sunday, September 14th, there was assembled in Platt's Music Hall, in response to the call of the committee, one of the largest gatherings ever held in this city. The meeting was appointed to be held at eight o'clock, but such was the interest already excited in the people, that an hour before that time, the Hall was filled with an audience that has, perhaps, never been excelled in this city, in point of intelligence and respectability. Every available space in the body of the Hall was occupied, and the gallery was filled with ladies. The meeting was called to order, punctually, by D. C. McRuer, Esq., and organized by the choice of Hon. F. H. Teschemacher as President, with seventy-seven Vice-Presidents and four Secretaries, selected from the most prominent citizens. After introductory remarks by Mayor Teschemacher, exceedingly earnest and eloquent addresses were made by Eugene Casserly, Esq., Frederick Billings, Esq., Hon. J. McM. Shafter, Edward Tompkins, Esq., and the late Rev. Thomas Starr King. After the addresses, upon motion of John Middleton, Esq., the following resolution was passed unanimously :

Resolved, That the action of a meeting of citizens, in selecting a Committee of Thirteen, composed of the following well-known gentlemen, F. H. Teschemacher, Wm. Norris, Alfred L. Tubbs, J. B. Roberts, Henry Seligman, Peter Donahue, Horace P. Janes, J. N. Risdon, John H. Redington, Eugene L. Sullivan, Wm. M. Lent, James Otis and Jona. G. Kittle, to collect and disburse funds for the relief of the sick and wounded soldiers and seamen of our army and navy, meets with the hearty approval and endorsement of this meeting, and that we will meet these gentlemen upon their coming, with open hands and liberal purses, and will cheerfully assist them to raise a fund that shall be creditable to San Francisco.

Mayor Teschemacher then stated, in behalf of the committee, that it being their intention to raise as large a sum as possible, subscription books would be submitted to all citizens in every portion of the city, that each person might have an opportunity to make a single cash contribution, or subscribe a certain sum, payable monthly, as long as the war should last.

The sub-committees, according to previous arrangement, immediately commenced the canvass of the city. All private business was ignored, for the time, by the gentlemen composing the committee, and the chief hours of the day given to this new and noble work. The whole city seemed to be thrilled as with an electric shock, and the talk of the groups on the streets, the merchants on 'Change, boys in the gutter, of men, women and children, was the movement for the relief of our sick and wounded soldiers; and every loyal man's heart beat in active sympathy with the work. The soldier's needs took such an energetic hold on the people that the committee, on their rounds, were not treated as unwelcome beggars, but greeted as men who were doing a work which it was each man's pride to see well accomplished. And they gave—all citizens gave—with such enthusiasm as one might expect from the recipients of good gifts, instead of givers of the wealth they had toiled for. And there was such singular unanimity as men see in no other great public undertaking. There was alive, to interrupt their action, no bias of political feeling, no conflict of religious opinion, no difference on grounds of nationality. Men gave their gold as the overflow of patriotic love. It was the blood of their giant protector —their country, native or adopted—that was flowing, and they came forth readily to stay its stream. Men of every political party gave—whether Democrats, Republicans, or even Secessionists; and there was no sect of religion that was not represented in this noble army of givers. The Christians gave with loyal self-denial; the Jews, as earnest sympathizers with the suffering; heretics, as citizens of a Republic to be saved; and men of no religion, with an ardor worthy the humblest religious devotee. The representatives of every nation living in our midst—English, German, French, Irish, Chinese, Italian, Hungarian, Russian, Spanish—gave with the fervor of native citizens. The canvassing committees met, after their first labors, on Wednesday evening, September 17th, and reported a list of subscriptions amounting to $66,000. They met again on Thursday evening, and reported an additional subscription exceeding $30,000. On Friday they reported more than $14,000, in addition.

The money began now to flow into the Treasury, but the question came with it, what was the best means of its disbursement to aid the sick and wounded soldiers? The United States Sanitary Commission was an institution little known in this city, and the committee were unwilling to trust the distribution of this bounty to any uncertain channel. The late Rev. T. Starr King, at this time, conferred with several members of the committee, and, at their suggestion, he was invited to meet the whole committee at the meeting of Thursday evening, September 18th. He readily complied, and displayed to the committee his familiarity with the workings of that noble organization. He gave an account of its origin, its objects, its progress, its administration, its endorsement by the United States Government, its relation to the same, and its wonderful prosperity and success. The familiarity which he showed, and the earnest confidence which he expressed in that institution as a most worthy almoner, decided the committee as to the channel of distribution.

The money, in answer to the subscriptions, poured so rapidly into the Treasury, that by steamer-day, (Saturday,) September 19th, the committee bought exchange for $100,000, and remitted the same at once, by telegraph, to Rev. Henry W. Bellows, D.D., President, and George T. Strong, Treasurer, United States Sanitary Commission, New York.

Notwithstanding the activity of the committee selected by the people, many were eager lest they should be behindhand in this loyal work, and handed their contributions—whatever they could give—

to the Treasurer, before the gentlemen of the committee could reach them. It seemed like a great festival of charity, at which all men united, even though they were "poor indeed." The employees of all the great corporations and manufacturing establishments, both private and those belonging to the Government, combined together and sent their offerings for the sick and wounded soldiers. The public and private schools of the city took on themselves the sacrifice of their own luxuries, and the names of almost all the children in the city appeared in the daily papers as givers of their mites for the relief of the soldiers.

The committee still continued their work, and reported at their next meeting, on Tuesday, September 23d, more than sixteen thousand dollars. The money subscribed was paid in so rapidly that by the next steamer, September 1st, the committee were enabled to make a second remittance of drafts for one hundred thousand dollars, and acquainted the head of the United States Sanitary Commission in New York by telegraph.

In view of the work of the Western Sanitary Commission, a distinct and independent organization, whose headquarters were at St. Louis, the committee directed that fifty thousand dollars ($50,000) of the last remittance be given to that body. Scarcely a fortnight had passed since the great mass meeting to arouse the people had been held, and already, through their efforts, the treasuries for the relief of the soldiers had been enriched by two hundred thousand dollars.

The question of inciting the whole State to the same noble work that the city was doing, claimed the early attention of the committee. A circular was immediately prepared, dated September 29th, 1862, addressed "To the loyal people of California," and sent to the postmasters and prominent citizens in every city and town of the State. It was liberally distributed also among the leading citizens of Nevada and Washington Territories, and the State of Oregon, and published in all the loyal newspapers of the coast. The interior had already been excited to admiration at the singular and spontaneous liberality of this city, and soon caught this wonderful fever of charitable giving. Money, in all sums, soon came pouring into the Treasury from every portion of the State. Pacheco, in Contra Costa county, sent one hundred dollars on the 20th of September; San Andreas, Calaveras county, four hundred and four dollars on the

22d ; Georgetown, Eldorado county, two hundred dollars, and North San Juan, Nevada county, two hundred and forty-two dollars, on the 23d, before the circular was issued. In the early part of the following month, the other counties began liberally to respond—Solano, and then Shasta, Los Angeles and Tuolumne, Placer, Santa Cruz and Tehama, and the other counties of the State, following in quick succession and making liberal contributions to increase the Soldiers' Relief Fund.

To make the Interior better acquainted with the work of the Sanitary Commission, and to offer specifically the services of this committee in forwarding the funds there collected, another circular was issued, dated October 20th, 1862, and widely distributed through the State.

Besides the subscriptions which were paid immediately, there were a number of persons in this city who subscribed and paid monthly during the ensuing year. Every month following the general movement, various sums were raised in the interior counties of the State, according to their several ability, and forwarded to the Treasurer in this city, as are particularly specified in the Treasurer's Report, preceding, in this pamphlet. The contributions from the city did not cease with the canvassing of the committee, but during the year numerous associations and individuals manifested their interest in the cause by various donations. After the first active labors, the current of remittances to the Treasury was constant.

At the time of the elections, in the early part of September, 1863, the sick and wounded soldiers were remembered, and at the polls throughout the State, boxes were placed to receive contributions. The happy result was, that the State at large gave the sum of eight thousand four hundred and ten dollars and eighty-six cents in coin, and eight hundred and eighty-one dollars in Legal Tender notes, and San Francisco five thousand two hundred and twenty-nine dollars and thirty cents in coin, and forty-three dollars in Legal Tender notes— making the handsome total of thirteen thousand six hundred and forty dollars and eleven cents in coin, and nine hundred and twenty-four dollars in Legal Tender notes, as a single day's contribution from the loyal masses of the State. During the period of thirteen months following the Mass Meeting, September 14th, 1862, the committee made fourteen remittances to the Treasury of the United

CONTRIBUTIONS FROM CALIFORNIA.

States Sanitary Commission, New York—thirteen being in drafts payable in currency, amounting to four hundred and fourteen thousand nine hundred and ninety-five dollars and fifty-eight cents ($414,-995 58 ;) and one draft payable in gold, amounting to fifteen thousand dollars ($15,000,) making a total of four hundred and twenty-nine thousand nine hundred and ninety-five dollars and fifty-eight cents ($429,995 58.)

At the end of that time the war was being still prosecuted with vigor, our army was suffering from wounds and disease, and the charities of our people were needed to continue the same noble work they had begun. The committee met again, after a long period of inactivity, to consult upon the best method of future conduct. The vacancies in the committee, occasioned by death and by absence from the State, were immediately filled. His Honor, Mayor H. P. Coon, was chosen Chairman in place of Hon. F. H. Teschemacher, former Chairman, then absent from the State. Communication was entered into with the President of the United States Sanitary Commission, asking him the condition and needs of the Treasury. The following reply was received by telegraph :

NEW YORK, Oct. 23, 1863.

The Sanitary funds are low. Our expenses are fifty thousand dollars a month. We can live three months, and that only, without large support from the Pacific. Twenty-five thousand dollars a month, paid regularly while the war lasts, from California, would make our continuance on our present magnificent scale of beneficence a certainty, We would make up the other twenty-five thousand a month here. We have already distributed Sanitary stores of the value of seven millions of dollars to all parts of the army, at a cost of three per cent. To abandon our work, or to allow it to dwindle, would be a horrible calamity to the army and the cause. We never stood so well with the nation ; but California has been our main support in money, and if she fails us we are lost. The Board imperatively urges me to go out to California and tell her all we owe her for past favors, and all we need and hope. But how can I turn open beggar to such a benefactor ? When California needs my presence for such an object she will ask for it. Meanwhile I know that you represent the soldiers' wants and our Commission better than I could do in person. So organize, if possible, a monthly subscription, and let us feel that California trusts and will sustain us in her past spirit to the end. Telegraph fully in reply. God bless California !

HENRY W. BELLOWS.

The committee, in answer to this appeal, determined to increase its numbers, and begin operations once more, and incite the people to repeat the earnest benevolence of the last year. A sub-committee issued a small circular, October 30th, 1863, to a hundred or more citizens, inviting them to attend "a meeting to be held in the Twelfth District Court room, Saturday evening, October 31st, at 8 o'clock, to hear a communication from Rev. Dr. Bellows, and to consult upon business connected with the Sanitary Commission."

In response to this call, a considerable number of citizens met together. His Honor, Mayor Coon, was made Chairman, and Wm. Sherman, Esq., Secretary of the meeting. The late Rev. Thos. Starr King gave a brief history of the United States Sanitary Commission, its operations, and what it had accomplished, and read a letter from Dr. Bellows, setting forth their acknowledgments to the committee and the people of California and the Pacific Coast, and stating the Commission's future needs. Various gentlemen discussed the matter of responding in the best manner to the wants of the Commission, and expressed their confidence in the patriotism and liberality of the people of California. The result of the meeting was the addition of twenty-two gentlemen to the old committee, and a recommendation that "the committee call a mass Meeting, issue a circular address to the people of California, and adopt such other means to accomplish the object of the committee as they may deem expedient." The committee thereafter, including a few gentlemen added to it at the earliest subsequent meetings of the committee, was composed as follows : H. P. Coon, James Otis, A. L. Tubbs, Jos. B. Thomas, R. G. Sneath, E. L. Sullivan, W. M. Lent, Albert Miller, John O. Earl, W. C. Ralston, A. Seligman, H. L. Dodge, W. M. Rockwell, J. P. Buckley, Jerome Rice, Alex. G. Abell, Wm. Sherman, F. A. Holman, Jonas G. Clark, Thos. Starr King, John H. Redington, Jas. B. Roberts, Jona. G. Kittle, Peter Donahue, Geo. W. Gibbs, John Sime, E. Cohn, F. A. Woodworth, J. N. Risdon, R. B. Swain, Seth H. Wetherbee, Wm. R. Wadsworth, R. B. Woodward, L. B. Benchley, Eugene Casserly, J. R. Hardenberg, Horace Davis, O. B. Jennings, W. H. Hook, N. P. Perine, W. H. Codington.

According to the suggestions of the meeting of citizens, the committee took measures for holding a Mass Meeting, and invited speakers for the occasion. As a preliminary measure, for the thorough canvassing of the city, immediately after the meeting, subscription books were prepared and sub-committees appointed, and special portions of the business community assigned to them.   The Mass Meeting was held at Platt's Music Hall, on Tuesday evening, November 10th. The people answered the call enthusiastically, and at the hour appointed for the commencement of the exercises, the Hall was densely crowded.   The Band of the Ninth infantry, U. S. A., was present, and gave interest to the occasion by its contributions of stirring patriotic airs.   At seven and a-half o'clock, the chairman of the committee, Hon. H. P. Coon, called the meeting to order, and, with a few eloquent remarks, introduced Hon. F. F. Low, Governor of the State, as President of the meeting.   The President was supported by an able and intelligent corps of Vice Presidents and Secretaries.   An introductory speech was made by Gov. Low ; and the Treasurer, Jas. Otis, Esq., followed with the report of the receipts, disbursements, and remittances to New York, since the formation of the Committee.   Interesting and patriotic addresses succeeded from Rev. D. B. Cheney, Wm. T. Coleman, Esq., Commander Selim E. Woodworth, Edward Tompkins, Esq., and the late Rev. T. Starr King. The same earnest sympathy was manifested by the hearers in the cause of the suffering soldier, and the same ardent enthusiasm seemed to prevail as when the object was first approached in the year previous.   It was evident that the loyalty and generosity of the people had not become exhausted, nor the ability to do noble deeds for our country.

The sub-committees immediately waited upon the people of the city, who received them with no less cordiality than the year before. Looking to a long-continued flow into the Treasury, and to a fulfillment of the request of the President of the Commission, contained in his dispatch, the committee now asked especially for monthly subscriptions.   These they received from many, while the impulsive generosity of others induced them to give at once the donation they would make for the following year.   At the first meeting after the canvassing began, the committee were able to report the sum of thirty thousand dollars subscribed, payable immediately, and four thousand five hundred dollars payable monthly ; at the next meeting, seventeen thousand nine hundred and seventy-five dollars, in cash subscriptions, and two hundred and fifty-five dollars payable monthly.   It was soon apparent that San Francisco would do her part towards fulfilling the request from the East.

29

The effectiveness of appeals to the people of the interior of the State, had been abundantly proved by the experience of the past year. The committee, this year, had adopted the same course, and issued, at the time the work was begun in this city, for interior distribution, a circular "Appeal for Relief of Wounded Soldiers," dated November 9th, 1863; and the country began to answer with their former alacrity and generosity.

The success of the committee in this city was such that the following dispatch was soon sent to the President of the United States Sanitary Commission:

SAN FRANCISCO, Dec. 12, 1863.

REV. HENRY W. BELLOWS,

President of the U. S. Sanitary Commission:

San Francisco will furnish the Sanitary Commission Two Hundred Thousand Dollars during the year 1864, to be paid in New York in monthly installments. We are not yet informed what amount may be expected from the balance of the State, but believe that One Hundred Thousand Dollars more will be assured the Commission as soon as organizations can be effected for that purpose. This will give Twenty-five Thousand Dollars per month; and by steamer to-day we send you Fifty Thousand Dollars for January and February.

With assurance of our continued fidelity to the cause, and sympathy for those who suffer in its defence,

In behalf of the Committee,

H. P. COON, Chairman.
JAMES OTIS, Treasurer.

To which, a few days after, the following telegraphic reply was received:

NEW YORK, December 17th, 1863.

HON. H. P. COON, AND JAMES OTIS, ESQ.:

BROTHERS:—I wonder that your life-giving telegram, charged with Two Hundred Thousand Dollars ($200,000), did not find me in my travels, and shock me into immediate consciousness of the splendid news. But just returned to New York, I see my table illumined with this resplendent message, and in my haste to acknowledge such a glorious and patriotic continuance in well-doing, I can only stutter—Noble, tender, faithful San Francisco, City of the heart, commercial and moral capital of the most humane and generous State in the world!

If God gives to you, so you give to others. Your boundaries will not hold the riches and the blessings in store for you; they must needs overflow into the hands of the needy and suffering, and make your name the balm and cordial of want and sorrow. "I was sick, and ye visited me." This is the nation's thought, as she sees herself wounded in every hero that languishes in her hospitals, and then gazes at the Pacific, at California, with San Francisco at their head—the good Samaritan for the first time appearing in the proportions of a great city, of a whole State, of a vast area.

HENRY W. BELLOWS.

The Treasurer's Report amply testifies to the success which the appeals of the Committee met with throughout the extent of our loyal State. The towns of the State came hastily into the line, and were strenuous each to outdo the other in their gifts. Most paid their contributions at once; a few made occasional contributions during the year. The town of Columbia, Tuolumne county, and the Gold Run Relief Society, of Placer county, are prominent, as making handsome contributions, for several successive months, into the Treasury.

No direct appeal having been made to the Interior for specific monthly contributions, it was deemed expedient that the matter be brought to the notice of the people, that it might be known what definite amount might be expected monthly from the whole State. A circular was accordingly prepared, but was delayed in being sent away. In the early spring of 1864, one of the committee—late Rev. T. Starr King—had determined, and had so announced to the committee, to go personally into the most prominent counties of the State, appeal directly to the people, and ask of them fixed contributions to the Sanitary Fund every month. That purpose he was unable to fulfill; for, at the time he had proposed to begin the work, he was taken sick, and after a few days' illness, died on the 4th of March, 1864. In his death not the Sanitary Commission alone, but every good and noble cause, lost an able advocate; not the City and State alone, but the Nation lost an ornament and support—a strong arm and noble heart. On the 8th of March the committee met to take notice of the loss. After a few remarks upon the character of Mr. King, Mr. F. A. Woodworth offered the following resolutions, which were passed unanimously.

As co-laborers with the late Rev. Thomas Starr King, in the cause of the suffering among the defenders, in the field and on the wave, of our Nation's honor and integrity, it is fitting that the Soldiers' Relief Fund Committee give public testimony of their appreciation of his services. It is therefore

RESOLVED, That in his death they deeply feel the loss of a toiler, most earnest and energetic, in the field of their labors—a soul ever ardent with love of a country in anguish, full of eloquent sympathy for the dying on the battle-fields, the sick and wounded in the hospitals of the nation; unwearied in his work of filling other men with a just estimate of their duty in the cause of mercy, of charity and of country;

That he has gone from among them when it would seem he could least be spared, just ready, as he believed himself to be, once more to seek the interior counties of the State, and plead the cause of the soldier;

That in his going, the City has lost a most worthy citizen; the State an able upholder of law and government; the Nation a Patriot, whose uncompromising loyalty won the honor and admiration of all good men, the fear of traitors and their abettors; Humanity and Charity and Mercy a supplicant, whose asking was not greater than his own bestowment; Learning and Culture and Literature, a scholarly disciple, whose constancy taught others much of the alphabet of Truth; Religion, a bright exemplar, whose fervor and piety found joyful testimony in a noble life, a heroic and triumphant death; all good men and true, and all causes of progress and truth, a laborer, who has early gone to receive his well-won reward;

That, as friends of the man, and lovers of his virtues, they trust in Him who called him away, believing that only a bright crown awaits him who could so humbly meet the decree of God, could go so manfully into "the valley of the shadow of death," proclaiming, as he stepped from the Life Present to the Life Eternal, that he was "happy, resigned, trustful."

The active labors of the committee in this city were finished, and there was need for meetings only occasionally, until the arrival of Rev. Henry W. Bellows, D.D., President of the United States Sanitary Commission, in the last of April, 1864. Although the committee was merely a local organization, and disconnected in every way with that of which he was the head, the work for which it was formed and its constant communications and remittances, had placed it in the position of nearest sympathy with him. He met the committee soon after his arrival, was in constant intercourse with them, and placed himself, so far as communication with the people of the city, under their immediate auspices. But the people needed no medium between them and the eloquent head of the great charitable organization with which they had long been familiar. They had become immediate friends through the eloquent and thrilling messages which he had often sent during the past two years, by telegrams and letters, in answer to the remittances which the committee had been constantly making. He wished early to meet the people, and accordingly, under the direction of the Committee, he addressed the citizens of San Francisco, on Friday evening, May 13th, at Platt's Music Hall.

At a meeting of the committee, on Saturday evening, June 4th, an offer was received, through Mr. Sneath, from Messrs. Steele Bros., to make a mammoth cheese, of 4,000 pounds weight, to be exhibited and finally sold for the benefit of the Sanitary Fund. They desired the expenses attending the preparation of the same for exhibition, to be met by this committee, and upon its completion it would be handed over to them. The proposition was immediately acquiesced in, and the expenses assumed by the committee. The matter of the cheese was referred to a committee, by whom arrangements were subsequently made, upon its reception, for its exhibition in the pavilion of the Mechanics' Institute, erected for the Industrial Fair, and open to visitors in the first of September.

Since the Treasurer made his Report of the previous year, at the Mass Meeting of November 10th, 1863, up to August 11th, 1864, remittances had been made to the Sanitary Commission, in answer to the appeal of Dr. Bellows in October, 1863, for $25,000 per month; seven drafts, amounting to one hundred and thirty-six thousand three hundred and seventy-one 47-100 dollars ($136,371 47,) payable in currency; and two drafts, amounting to twenty-one thousand two hundred and thirty-six and 71-100 dollars ($21, 236 71,) payable in gold. In the month of March, the Treasurer remitted to the Western Sanitary Commission, at St. Louis, a draft for seven thousand five hundred dollars ($7, 500,) payable in gold—making the total of remittances since the Treasurer's Report, one hundred and sixty-five thousand one hundred and eight 18-100 dollars' ($165,108 18.) The amount of remittances since the first movement, September 12th, 1862, was five hundred and ninety-five thousand one hundred and three 76-100 dollars ($595, 103 76.)

In addition to these remittances, in the month of June, 1863, in answer to representations concerning the condition of the United States soldiers upon this coast, the Treasurer paid to R. C. Drum, Assistant Adjutant-General, five hundred dollars ($500) for disbursements for their relief.

The total receipts from forty-two counties of this State, and a few donations from Nevada territory, Oregon, and Washington Territory, from September 14th, 1862, to August 13th, 1864, were four hundred and eighty-four thousand one hundred and eighty-nine 23-100 dollars ($484,189 23,) in coin, and seventy-two thousand and ninety-two 62-100 dollars ($72,092 62,) in currency—making a total of five hundred and fifty-six thousand two hundred and eighty-one 85-100 dollars ($556, 281 85.)

The apparent excess of remittances over receipts is explained by the fact, that a large portion of the coin collected was converted into currency, by the purchase of drafts, payable in New York in current funds.

The whole expenses of the committee, during the two years of their existence, including Mass Meetings, office rent, circulars, printing, and expenses of all kinds, amounted to $4,789 93, no one of the members of the committee having received any compensation for their services. The exchange paid for coin drafts, was $2,018 33. The balance in the Treasury, August 13th, at the time the name and functions of the organization were changed, was twelve thousand five hundred and fifty-nine 28-100 dollars ($12,559 28,) in .coin, and three hundred and fifty-five dollars ($355) in currency; total, twelve thousand nine hundred and fourteen 28-100 dollars ($12, 914 28.)

The probability of the still further continuance of the war, and with it the need of money for the relief of our suffering soldiers, instigated, during Dr. Bellows' sojourn, the re-organization of the committee. That the charities of the whole State might be more thoroughly collected, it was deemed best that a State organization be founded, through which local organizatious in every populous community of the State might be formed, and to which they should all be tributary. The committee, therefore, at the meeting held August 14th, 1864, accepted the suggestions of Dr. Bellows, ceased to be a local organization for the direct collection of funds in this city alone, and under his approval and authority, assumed the character and name of the California Branch of the United States Sanitary Commission, of which persons residing iu different parts of the State, should be invited to become members. They thereupon elected Hon. F. F. Low, Governor of the State, President, and chose an Executive Committee, upon whom the chief conduct of affairs should devolve, composed of Hon. D. C. McRuer, Chairman; R. G. Sneath, Abraham Seligman, George W. Gibbs, F. A. Woodworth, Albert Miller, and A. L. Tubbs. Here ended the work of the original organization as such. Its functions, and others of wider scope, were assumed and are now continued by the larger organization.

Respectfully submitted,

A. L. TUBBS,
   Secretary.

GEO. B. MERRILL,
   Ass't Secretary.

SAN FRANCISCO, Dec. 7th, 1864.

This admirable and spirited Report brings the history of the movement in behalf of Army relief in California down to December 7th, 1864. As its object, however, was mainly to give the history of the Citizens' Committee, it passes lightly over the labors of the California Branch, established by the President of the Commission, Dr. BELLOWS, after his arrival in San Francisco, April 30th, 1864. The labors of the energetic and admirable Committee of Citizens had somewhat slackened after Mr. King's decease. His death had prevented his cherished purpose of canvassing the State in person. This duty fell to Dr. Bellows. Moving about the State and addressing the citizens in many of the principal towns, he became convinced that the interest of the people was not abated, nor their liberality exhausted. He had studied the fruits of organized effort too well not to believe that, great as the pecuniary yield of California had been, it would have proved twice as great if a thorough system of canvassing had been adopted from the start, and all the towns of the State brought under the admirable method which was pursued in San Francisco, where committees went regularly from store to store, through whole blocks and streets, giving no one in all that generous city an apology for evading his fair share of the burden of humanity. The mere presence of a known and authorized officer of the Sanitary Commission in California stimulated patriotic beneficence to such a degree, that over two hundred thousand dollars were spontaneously poured into Dr. Bellows' hands for the soldiers, during his short stay of four and a half months on the Coast. Not knowing

California Branch of the Commission. Visit of Dr. Bellows.

how long the war might continue, and feeling that every day, with the depleted resources of the North and West, it was becoming more and more difficult to raise money for the use of the sick and wounded, on the 11th August, 1864, the President of the Commission organized the California Branch with the officers enumerated in the closing paragraph of the above Report.

The Rev. O. C. Wheeler, largely known in the State, was made Secretary, and proceeded under the direc-

Organization of
Aid Societies.

tion of the Board to send agents into most of the counties, to establish Aid Societies, whose members should pledge themselves to a monthly stipend of any amount from a half-dollar (the smallest form that charity ever takes in California) to five, ten, and even a hundred dollars. Over two hundred of these Aid Societies were formed, chiefly through the faithful and indefatigable exertions of Rev. Mr. Chapin and Mr. R. N. Bellows, to whom, it is conceded, the triumph of this plan was mainly due. The organization was a complete success. The Aid Societies were many of them small and feeble, and all required occasional visitation from the agents who had formed them, but as a whole, they contributed with surprising freedom, regularity, and persistency to the Treasury at San Francisco, which was thus enabled to continue its monthly remittances to the Central Treasury at New York with amazing punctuality and fullness to the very end of the war. The proposition to disband the California Branch and cease collections and remittances did not proceed from California, who never showed impatience to throw off the burden. At the earliest moment, when the Commission could dispense with her aid, her President notified the California Branch (July, 1865) and all the Pacific Branches, that their labors might cease.

The rich experience in California, Oregon, Nevada, the only States which were thoroughly canvassed and organized systematically for money contri- System of canbutions, teaches that if the Sanitary Com- vassing on the Pacific Coast. mission had adopted in all the loyal States Its results. the method it employed on the Pacific Coast, twice the large revenues they enjoyed might have been realized: a fact recorded for its instructiveness to future laborers in this field, and not because of any regrets that it was not adopted, since the means employed proved adequate to the wants of the Commission, which after the first fifteen months of its existence was never (for five years) without stores and money commensurate with its demands and wants.

It would be impossible to exaggerate the debt of gratitude due to the gentlemen composing the original Committee of Citizens in San Francisco, or the Board of the California Branch for their faithful and protracted labors. The President of the Commission was a grateful witness to the zeal and generosity of each and every member of the latter Board. The Mayors of the city, Mr. Teschemacher and Mr. Coon, who were Presidents of the Citizen's Committee, and Hon. D. C. McRuer, M. C., President of the California Branch, James Otis, Esq., Treasurer of the Citizens' Committee, and R. G. Sneath, Treasurer of the California Branch, deserve particular mention for their laborious services.

It would leave a great blank in the history of this
30

movement if we failed to name some of the peculiari-
Means resorted
to to stimulate
public interest. ties in the methods adopted on the Pacific
Coast for raising money for the Sanitary
Commission. Ingenuity, grotesqueness, extravagance
were never taxed more freely or to better effect, or in
so worthy a cause. Places of public amusement,
churches, schools, agricultural fairs, lyceums, private
parties, public elections, in short, any assembly of
human beings of any kind, and at any time were considered proper occasions and places for calling upon
the people present to raise money for the Sanitary
fund. No public gathering was sanctified unless something had been done for the soldiers. It mattered
little whether notice had been given or not; the more
sudden the call, often the more successful it seemed.
It was enough for somebody to rise and propose a collection for the Sanitary fund to put everybody into
good temper, and a giving disposition. If they were
excited by a political speech, they let off their enthusiasm in a Sanitary collection; if a favorite at the
circus or the theatre specially flattered their humor,
it was turned in some way in aid of the Soldiers' Fund.
If they went to the polls, it was with a ballot in one
hand and a half-eagle in the other, the one for the candidate who was to represent them in Congress, the other
for the wounded soldier who had represented them in
the field.

But it was at meetings called for the purpose, at
pic-nics and fairs usually on some "high day," and
Sales at auction. specially on the Fourth of July, that the peculiarities of California life and character showed themselves in their most gorgeous extravagance and generous

oddity. Then it was that they resorted to their favorite method of selling at auction such gifts in kind as might have been added to their contribution in money, —it might be a picture, a specimen of gold quartz, a live pullet, a revolver, a watch, a hose-carriage, an autograph,—any thing which the means or convenience or humor of the donor might have sent in which was knocked down to the highest bidder, with the implied understanding, that after paying for it, he was to give it back again to the auctioneer to be re-sold to the same company. Often have we seen one article—a white pullet, for instance,—not intrinsically worth a dollar, sold to five or ten successive " highest bidders" for sums varying from five to twenty dollars, until the sum realized amounted to over one hundred dollars. A box of strawberries of herculean size, presented to the President of the Commission at the Sacramento pic-nic in a solemn and beautiful wood of oaks, named in his honor " Bellows Grove," was sold for a gold dollar for each strawberry, (each the size of a pullet's egg,) while the biggest was sold for one hundred and twenty-three dollars! On the same occasion, the train of the Pacific Rail Road (where some twenty cars were linked together) which carried the company to the grounds, being delayed for an hour by an unexpected obstruction, some enterprising passenger who had brought his fowling-piece, stepped out into the chapparal and shot a hare, and then entering at the rear car, passed through the whole train, selling it to one after another, until he came out at the front with one hundred and fifty-seven dollars for the fund—the greatest amount, we make bold to say, for which a hare was ever yet sold and by a plan which only an enthusiasm "as mad as a March hare" could ever have ventured upon.

Perhaps, however, the wildest and most successful extravagance ever practised in the interests of the Sanitary fund was started at Austin, Nevada, in the wildest part of the desert, half-way between Virginia City and Utah. There the two candidates for the mayoralty of a city not two years old, but with five thousand inhabitants, had each agreed if defeated to carry a sack of flour on his back from Austin to a neighboring village, in broad day. Accordingly, when Mr. R. C. Gridley lost his election, he prepared to fulfill his engagement. Headed by a band of music in a wagon, leading his little boy clad in the National uniform by the hand, and with the sack of flour on his back, followed by a mongrel procession of miners and citizens, Mr. Gridley took up his foot journey to the appointed place. Arrived there, the thought struck him, that the gay spirits and the patriotic feelings of the crowd that grew as he traveled, might be turned to humane account. He instantly proposed to sell the now famous sack of flour to the highest bidder. The humor took. The sack was sold again and again, netting five thousand dollars. The amount realized fired Mr. Gridley's enthusiasm to make the most of his lucky idea. Accordingly he started for a journey of three hundred miles to Virginia City with the sack in company. Arriving on a Sunday, and finding a Sanitary meeting going on in the Opera House in the afternoon, he proceeded to the place, got admitted to the stage, and there telling the story, sold the sack to the audience for five hundred and eighty dollars. The next morning, having procured a band of music, he proceeded to make the tour of the neighboring towns, Gold Hill, Silver City, and Dayton, selling the sack wherever he could find bidders, and adding the price to the amount labelled on the face of this more than Fortunatus' purse. At Gold Hill, the sack sold for five thousand, eight hundred and twenty-two dollars and fifty cents; at Silver City for eight hundred and thirty dollars; at Dayton for eight hundred and seventy-three dollars. Finally, returning to Virginia City again, the sack putting forth all its attractions, won a prodigious subscription of twelve thousand and twenty-five dollars! Mr. Gridley, pursuing his successful way, not in pursuit of the golden fleece, but in actual possession of it, arrived at Sacramento, one hundred and fifty miles further west, just as the Sanitary pic-nic at Bellows' Grove was in progress. In the midst of the festivities he marched into the crowd, a band of music leading the way, a stalwart negro walking by his side carrying the sack, and an extempore procession following him, which grew larger every minute and presented himself for new conquests to the officers of the day, and the President of the Commission. The sack did not fare as well here as before. Several fresh wrinkles of humor had broken out in the face of that occasion. Among others, a good woman, finding a small island of a few rods square in the swamp, had erected a bridge of one plank, and established such a rate of toll, that to see nothing there cost the curiosity of some hundreds a half-dollar each. Then the President of the Commission was invited to shake hands with some hundreds of the company, who bought the privilege at from fifty cents to a double eagle a-piece, making his hat their *till*, until it was literally half full of silver and gold. Under these rival excitements, the sack was not favored with its wonted success. Carried thence to Sacramento, it was sold again at a public lecture by Dr. Bellows for several hundred dollars, and finally, transported to San Francisco, it added moderate gains to its enormous harvest even in that comparatively staid community. Six months afterwards, what was the surprise of the recorder of this strange history, to find the sack with its irrepressible owner in New York, and on its way to the great Fair at St. Louis! Plans already existed for carrying it across the ocean to England, and it would not astonish us to learn that it had appeared in Sydenham Palace, or even in the great Paris exhibition of 1867! The sum realized by it to the Sanitary fund cannot have been less than forty thousand dollars.

It would be unjust not to name expressly the peculiar zeal and persistency which some of the towns in Sacramento. California exhibited in this work of mercy. Perhaps not even San Francisco outstripped Sacramento in generosity, if we consider their relative importance and wealth. The Sacramento Valley Soldiers' Aid Society was a separate organization, which began early and continued late in the service, and was always dropping magnificent and unexpected gifts into the treasury of the United States Sanitary Commission. The ladies and gentlemen of that hospitable city, the fair capital of the State, were among the warmest and most constant friends of the Soldier, and the special cause of the

Commission. Under Messrs. Carroll, President, and Crocker, Treasurer, there was no room for lukewarmness and no possibility of failure. Their names, with a hundred others of that generous city should be kept in everlasting remembrance.

It must not be forgotten that while San Francisco was the head and centre of all this movement, the whole state was alive with interest and effort, and at least fifty counties, and a hundred towns, are worthy of having their history written were time and space allowed.

Nevada Territory (now the State of Nevada) early took up the cause of the National Soldier   Nevada. and the support of the Sanitary Commission. Under the admirable leadership of Almarin B. Paul, a well known and most energetic Miner and Banker in Gold Hill, that new constellation of gold and silver villages and towns, lying round Virginia City, all shed benignant beams—and very substantial ones—upon the Central Treasury.

A great success attended the labors of the Original Committee, and of the Nevada Branch afterwards organized. Mr. Paul indefatigable himself, was supported by energetic men in each of the Counties of the Territory and State and silver and gold in bullion and in coin rolled into the hands of the treasurer, Mr. Black. The President of the Commission passed ten days in the Territory with great pleasure to himself and advantage to the Commission, addressing crowded audiences for seven successive nights in seven different places, and forming a very high idea of the generosity and patriotism of the people. The amount of money sent forward by Nevada, was in currency one hundred and seven thousand six hundred and forty-two dollars and ninety-six cents, which considering its population of not over fifty thousand is an astonishing contribution of over two dollars for every man, woman and child in the State.

Oregon, too, a state not rich in mines or in money, but in lands and in forests, early showed that its Oregon. fidelity to the Union was perfect, and its zeal for the Army enthusiastic. Hon. Amory Holbrook was the first to communicate to the Commission the substantial proof of Oregon's devotion to the National Cause, and the zeal and success of his endeavors appear to have contributed very much of the original impulse to the work. Later, the Governor and other friends took up the laboring oar. It is difficult to do full justice to noble, enterprising, vigorous Portland, after San Francisco the most important place on the Pacific coast, and which steadily poured its largess into our Treasury; to Salem, Albany, Oregon City, Eugene City and other towns which vied with the commercial capital in their constancy and zeal, if not in their ability. Oregon sent seventy-nine thousand three hundred and seventy-one dollars and nineteen cents to the Treasury of the Sanitary Commission, more money than any Atlantic State, as such, except New York, Pennnsylvania and Massachusetts.

Washington Territory, too, with her very scattered population, sent the extraordinary sum of twenty Washington thousand nine hundred and eighteen dollars Territory. and ninety-two cents, thanks to the zeal of Vancouver and Olympia.

The Sandwich Islands, proved an unexpected fountain of supply. The few Americans there seemed unwearied in their joy at giving. Captain The Sandwich Makee's gift alone cannot have fallen short of Islands. five thousand dollars, while the sum total reached the extraordinary amount of fifteen thousand nine hundred and sixty-eight dollars and fifteen cents. We must here acknowledge the great indebtedness of the Commission, to its correspondent in Honolulu, Alex. J. Cartwright, through whose patient and long-continued faithfulness, all the moneys from the Hawaiian Islands have been forwarded.

Idaho, sent five thousand three hundred and one dollars and thirty-one cents. Colorado one thousand and twenty-five dollars. Vancouver's Island Idaho, Colorado, Vancouver, two thousand one hundred and ninety-five Peru, Costa Rica. dollars and sixty-one cents. Peru, two thousand and two dollars. Costa Rica, eighty-four dollars.

We have then this extraordinary show of liberality from Americans on the Pacific Coast and General result. adjacent islands.

California	$1,233,831 31
Nevada	107,642 96
Oregon	79,371 19
Washington Territory	20,918 92
Sandwich Islands	15,968 15
Idaho	5,301 31
Colorado	1,025 00
Vancouver's Island	2,195 61
Santiago de Chili	5,066 62
Peru	2,002 00
Costa Rica	84 00
	$1,473,407 07

Thus it appears that nearly a million and a half of

31

the whole five millions of cash received into the Treasury of the Sanitary Commission, came from the Pacific Coast.   Of the remaining three and a half millions, two million seven hundred and thirty-six thousand eight hundred and sixty-eight dollars and eighty-four cents were the results of Fairs, leaving only about seven hundred thousand dollars as the total amount contributed in cash by all other sources of a spontaneous kind.

It will not be forgotten, that the other sections of the country supplied stores to the amount of fifteen General conclu- millions of dollars in value, and gave its sions. most precious wealth, the lives of two hundred thousand men to the conflict, risking a million and a half of its sons in the perilous fight.   But the Pacific Coast would as gladly have given its men and its supplies, if they could have been received, and would not have withheld its money either.   The noble generosity of its contributions must be remembered forever.   No such splendid beneficence of a state to distant objects, for general purposes under unknown almoners, over whom the State had no control, and where no visible monument was to remain, was ever yet recorded.   The consent of the people in a common effort, which no jealous sectarian or political rivalries could alienate them from, their confidence in the United States Sanitary Commission and constancy to it to the last, are extraordinary proofs of their trusting, unsuspicious temper, thorough disinterestedness and sympathetic patriotism.   California may rightly put upon her State shield, the claim to have been the largest, promptest, most efficient helper and nurse of our sick and wounded soldiers in the great War for National Unity and Life. Considering her distance and her youth, what more honorable and lasting memorial of her splendid part in the war could she have, or ought she to desire?*

* See appendix No. 5 for a detailed account of the contributions from California and the Pacific Coast.

CHAPTER IX.

DISTRIBUTION OF SUPPLIES—GENERAL AND BATTLE-FIELD RELIEF.

HAVING thus traced the principal methods by which the vast contributions of Hospital supplies confided to Different forms of Army Relief. the Commission during the war were gathered, it remains to explain in what manner, and upon what principle they were distributed for the relief of the sick and suffering of the Army. The word " Relief," as used by the Sanitary Commission, was a technical term, and embraced a number of distinct modes of ministering to the necessities of the soldier, according to the different circumstances in which he might be found requiring assistance. Thus, the work of relief was divided into General and Special relief. The first concerned the wants of the inmates of General, Field and Regimental hospitals, and of men in camp or on the march; the other, the care of sick and needy soldiers in the vicinity of military depôts, discharged men, paroled prisoners, and that vast class of sufferers known as soldiers in " irregular circumstances" or, in other words, those that had no legal claim upon the ordinary provisions of the government for assistance. Another distinct form of relief was what was called, Battle-field relief, a term which sufficiently explains its object.

244

In undertaking to administer these different forms of Relief, it was necessary in accordance with the Commission's theory, to ascertain accurately the real wants of the Army, so that aid *Principle upon which relief was bestowed.* should not be afforded, even where it seemed needed, unless it was withheld for some reason which justified intervention outside the Agencies of the Government. It was important to distinguish carefully, between those wants for which the only radical remedy could be found in an improvement of the military administration, and those which, inevitably occurring, even under the best administered system, might be properly relieved by the contributions of public benevolence.

This subject had been carefully studied by the Commission in the light which had been shed upon it by the reports of its Inspectors, and as *Its design to supplement the Government service.* experience rendered the practical working of the Army system more familiar, a very clear view was gained of the true sphere of the Government on one side, and of the Commission's special field of labor on the other. Its fundamental principle was to *supplement*, not to supplant the government. The necessity of supplying the government deficiencies was apparent, but when, and how, and under what circumstances this was to be done, so as not to impair the responsibility of the officials, and so as to afford the truest relief to the soldier, was in practice, an exceedingly delicate and difficult problem. It was impossible to establish any uniform rule by which the same apparent wants should always be supplied in the same way. Theoretically, the Government undertook of course, to provide all that was necessary for the care and comfort of the soldier in the Army and in the Hospital. The Government standard in this matter was always fluctuating, generally advancing and improving; but at no time was it true, and perhaps in the nature of things could not be that it provided fully for the particular necesity of each particular man. Even had the system been one upon which a reasonable expectation could have been founded of abundant and regular supply, the good intentions of the Government were liable, at any particular point, to be frustrated by the inefficiency or incompetency of its own officers. Still it was considered essential, that in no case should stores entrusted to the Commission be distributed in the Camps or in the Hospitals, until it was clearly ascertained that Government had failed to make adequate provision for the supposed need. It was therefore an established rule of the Commission, that none of its supplies should be issued in ordinary cases, unless *first*, the need of them was apparent, *secondly*, unless some satisfactory explanation was given of the manner in which the need had arisen, and *thirdly*, unless a written voucher or statement was presented by the Surgeon applying for assistance, showing why the Commission had been called on. These rules were strict, but their observance was essential if the distribution of supplies by the Commission was not to be hurtful in many cases to the men themselves, and if that distribution was not to be made the occasion for the introduction of those loose notions of discipline into the Army, which would have resulted in tenfold greater injury to it than any good which could possibly have arisen from an irregular mode of relief.

How different this system was from many of the schemes of relief which had been suggested, both in its view of the true relations of a volunteer or- *How it differed* ganization working in concert with the Army *from other sys-* *tems of Army* officials, and in its practical results in main- *relief.* taining the proper responsibility of those officials, it is not difficult to perceive. The clamor, during the war, among many well-meaning but indiscreet persons, was for personal ministrations to the suffering, to be bestowed by those in no way connected with the military service, and of course wholly irresponsible. An opinion prevailed that the Surgeons and Hospital Stewards could not be trusted to dispense delicacies and luxuries provided by sympathizing friends at home for the use of the patients. Prompted by this suspicion, and perhaps disposed to gratify the natural desire to receive expressions of gratitude from the suffering, many persons forced themselves into the Hospitals, interfered with their discipline, and too often by their injudicious kindness provided the patients with articles of food which destroyed all chances of their recovery. The Commission pursued the opposite course. Thinking, of all evils, the worst that could befall an Army because it included all others, was a relaxation of salutary discipline, and of a just sense of official responsibility, it subordinated all its plans, even for the relief of suffering to the maintenance of that discipline in its strictest form. While its own methods were elastic, and intended to meet any possible emergency, it never forgot that the great purpose of an Army organization was to train men to fight and to conquer. To effect this object, perfect subordination and accountability were essential; and just as it was impossible that an Army which had gained a victory should be delayed in the pursuit of the retreating enemy in order to look after its wounded, so it determined that if the relief of the suffering required a violation of those rules of military discipline upon the observance of which the safety of all depended, the sacrifice should be made for the general good. There were many cases during the war in which the officers of the Commission seriously differed in opinion with the Government Agents as to the proper care of the suffering, but they never forgot this fundamental principle of non-intervention beyond their legitimate sphere; so far from it, they were unceasing, by their example and counsel, in their efforts to make all in the Army understand that they were there, not to embarrass the Government officials, but to aid them when their aid was invoked in the appointed way. They sought to teach the soldier that the Government was his best friend, desirous of doing everything for him, and failing, as all Governments had done sometimes, from occasional and accidental causes. They never joined in the foolish cry, so common during the war, against 'red tape' and Army regulations, for they were persuaded, that without the strict accountability which it was intended to secure by these means there would soon have been no Army to take care of.

These were some of the principles upon which what was technically called General Relief was administered by the Commission to the soldier, who was subject to the ordinary and usual care of the Personal minis-
trations to the Medical Authorities. Everything was done suffering. through the Surgeons or other responsible officers, nothing without their knowledge and implied sanction. In the other branch of the department, that known as Special Relief, where the soldier was, for the time out of his normal practical relations with the authorities, the rule was just the opposite; and here the personal services of the agents of the Commission and its supplies were freely given. To minister to the wants of a single class of these men,— those discharged from the service, and therefore from the care of the Government, and obliged to remain for a few hours or days, owing to their feeble condition or their desire to collect the amount of pay due them, at some point *in transitu* to their homes,—the Commission maintained during the war, at different points, forty Homes and Lodges, which received more than a million and a half of inmates, and provided them with more than four millions of meals. This branch of the Commission's service, however, was so novel in its character, and attained such vast proportions that it will require special consideration hereafter.

The principle of distribution being thus settled, it is necessary to describe the machinery by which the gifts of the people at last reached the soldier, and Machinery for
the distribution the means adopted for ascertaining his wants of supplies. at a particular time. The contributions of the various Aid Societies were sent in the first place to sub-depôts, ten in number, in various parts of the country, where they were assorted and repacked, articles of the same kind being placed in separate cases, and were held sub-

32

ject to the requisitions of the officers of the Commission in charge of the great central distributing depôts. These depôts, during the war were at Washington and Louisville, they being the great gateways, through which passed all supplies, of every kind, for the use of the principal armies, operating against the enemy. Both in these sub-depôts and in the distributing depôts a rigid system of accountability was maintained in the reception, care and issue of the goods. So completely was this system carried out, that it could not be ascertained after the most careful investigation, that of the many thousands of boxes sent to the depôts during the war, more than a very insignificant portion had failed to reach their destination. At the distributing depôts, these articles were accumulated, not merely to supply the current wants of the army, but also for the purpose of forming a reserve stock to be made immediately available in the event of great battles, in which case delay in forwarding them from points distant from the scene of conflict might involve the loss of many lives. This wise prevision was abundantly justified by the events of the war. Amidst the horrors and confusion of a battle-field all ordinary means of Relief, Government or supplemental, are soon exhausted, and the immense distribution of supplies with its life-saving results, which took place after Antietam, Gettysburg, and the bloody battles of the Wilderness Campaign would not have been possible had a different policy been pursued.

To each Army sent upon a distant expedition, and generally to each column of the main Armies operat-
Relief Agents. ·ing in Virginia, and in the Southwest, was

assigned an Inspector, as Superintendent of the Commission's work with a competent staff of assistants, known as Relief Agents. This corps was permanently attached to the Army as an integral part of its organization, and accompanied it in all its movements. Connected with it and under its charge, was the Commission's depôt of supplies, larger or smaller according to the actual or prospective wants of the Army. Wagons and teams, and where needed steamboats also, were provided by the Commission, not only to transport such supplies as might be required in the Hospitals attached to the Army while encamped, but also to accompany it with a suitable stock of articles when on the march. The business of the Inspector, who was always a Medical man, was to visit constantly the Hospitals within his jurisdiction, to ascertain their wants, to make suggestions to the Surgeons in charge in regard to evils which were observed requiring correction, and to assist them by an offer of such supplies for the use of the sick as might be needed, but which the Government had failed to provide. There never was a time during the war when the Surgeons were not too glad to avail themselves of this assistance, and they never hesitated to make requisitions on the Commission in the form required by its rules for any articles of which they happened to be destitute, and which could in any way promote the comfort or hasten the recovery of the patients under their charge.

It is most gratifying to remember that there was no occasion during the progress of the war, at least after the organization of the Supply Department, Vast scale upon which relief was afforded. and the arrival of the first instalment of the golden treasure from the Pacific Coast in the autumn of 1862, in which the resources of the Commission were not found sufficient for this call for supplemental aid. Whether the wants of the Army of the Potomac were confined to suitable Hospital clothing and Hospital diet, whether General Rosecrans' army before Chattanooga, or that of General Grant before Vicksburg was wasting away from the terrible effects of scurvy, whether General Gilmore's army on Morris Island was perishing of disease aggravated by the use of brackish water, or that of General Weitzel in Texas was suffering from a total deprivation of vegetable food, the stores of the Commission were always found abundant for supplying the particular necessity, and were conveyed to the sufferers with a promptness and with an abundance, which never failed speedily to restore their shattered strength. It seemed indeed just as easy with the means at the disposal of the Commission, and with the thorough organization of its system to forward cargoes of ice and anti-scorbutics to South Carolina or Texas, or to transport thousands of barrels of onions and potatoes from the distant Northwest to the Armies of General Rosecrans or General Grant, as to send a few cases of shirts and drawers, and of Hospital delicacies from Washington to the Army of the Potomac. Relief on this vast scale was the ordinary regular work of the Commission, and was designed to meet the constantly recurring wants of an Army in the field. It was totally distinct and independent of that form of relief afforded after great battles and known specially in the work of the Commission, as Battle-field relief, but its extent and the wonderful results which followed from its bestowal may be inferred from the vast territory which it embraced, and the great resources required fully to meet the unceasing demand. Although the Commission's work on battle-fields became more conspicuous because public attention was naturally more directed to it, the money and supplies required to maintain in thorough efficiency, a system which sought to promote the health of the men while in camps, in order that they might afterwards fight battles successfully, required tenfold greater labor and resources.

This constant, never-ceasing care for the health and comfort of the Army, the absence of all improper intermeddling with the officers, the vast extent of the work and its perpetual activity, soon produced, as was natural, a profound impression upon the military authorities. They discovered, not merely that it was conducted on principles which they could recognize and approve, but also that in unforeseen emergencies, which often threatened serious disaster, the Commission was always at hand, prompt and ready and able to afford the needed remedy. Commanding Generals, the success of whose operations depended so much upon the physical condition of their men, lost their natural jealousy of extra official co-operation, and not only testified publicly and most warmly in favor of the inestimable value of the Commission's services, but aided its efforts in every way by granting to its agents in charge of supplies, means of transportation, and by affording them various facilities for the prosecution of their work which were denied to other associations engaged in similar labors.*   Even the officers of the Medical Department itself, convinced by their own personal observation that it was possible

---

* "HEADQUARTERS DEPARTMENT OF THE TENNESSEE, ⎫
           Vicksburg, Miss., Sept. 28, 1863. ⎭

"Commanding Officer, Cairo, Ill.:

"Sir,—Direct the Post Quartermaster at Cairo to call upon the U. S. Sanitary agent at your place, and see exactly what buildings they require to be erected for their charitable and humane purposes.

"The Commission has been of such great service to the country, and at Cairo are doing so much for this army at this time, that I am disposed to extend their facilities for doing good in every way in my power. You will therefore cause to be put up, at Government expense, suitable buildings for the Sanitary Commission, connecting those they already have, and also put up for them necessary outbuildings.   *   *   *   *   *   *

         "(Signed)   U. S. GRANT,
                         "Major General."

"HEADQUARTERS 14TH ARMY CORPS, ⎫
   "DEPARTMENT OF THE CUMBERLAND, ⎬
        Nashville, Dec. 11th, 1862. ⎭

"The General Commanding, appreciating the vast amount of good which the soldiers of this Army are deriving from the Sanitary stores distributed among them by the United States Sanitary Commission, directs:

"That all officers in this department render any aid consistent with their duties, to the agents of this society—and afford them every facility for the execution of this charitable work.

       "By order of
           "MAJ. GEN. W. S. ROSECRANS."

"DEP'T OF THE SOUTH, HEADQ'RS IN THE FIELD, ⎫
     "MORRIS ISLAND, S. C., SEPT. 9.   ⎭

      "*General Orders, No.* 73.

"The Brigadier-General commanding desires to make this public acknowledgment of the benefits for which his command has been indebted to the United States Sanitary Commission, and to express his thanks to the gentlemen whose humane efforts in procuring and distributing much-needed articles of comfort have so materially alleviated the sufferings of the soldiers.

"Especial gratitude is due to Dr. M. M. Marsh, Medical Inspector of the Commission, through whose efficiency, energy, and zeal, the wants of the troops have been promptly ascertained, and the resources of the Commission made available for every portion of the Army.

       By order of
               Brig.-Gen. Q. A. GILLMORE.
"ED. W. SMITH, A. A. G."

so to conduct a volunteer organization in the Army as really to aid and not embarrass them, entered into those cordial relations with it which had been from the first its anxious desire to establish, and many of them became its warmest friends.

The machinery by which these plans of distribution were carried out was very simple but very effective. In regard to Hospitals at the base of military Field relief operations or in large cities, in which the Corps. wants of the patients were more readily provided for than in the remote Field and Regimental Hospitals, the duty of the Inspector was easy, and the demand on the stores of the Commission for supplemental aid, particularly after the reorganization of the Medical Department, comparatively light. The officers of the Commission, enlightened by their experience of the ever varying but unceasing wants of the Army, made constant efforts to perfect its system of distribution. At first, as we have seen, a single depôt had been established near the Headquarters of each Army, and from thence was issued, under the requisitions of the Sanitary Inspector all that was called for throughout its various divisions. It was found, however, that in order to accomplish its work more thoroughly a somewhat different arrangement of labor was necessary. The plan adopted was substantially one suggested by Dr. Lewis H. Steiner, one of the most valued and experienced Inspectors of the Commission, and he was placed at the head of the new corps, with instructions to organize its work. Under the general superintendence of Dr. Steiner, a body of Agents was formed, called the Field Relief Corps, one of whose number was assigned to each Army Corps. He had charge of the whole of the Commission's work in the particular corps to which he was attached. He had under his charge Agents and supplies intended exclusively for the service of that particular portion of the Army, and was provided with wagons and horses, in order to render that service more complete and effective. He remained constantly with the corps, accompanied it on its march, and in every way became thoroughly identified with it. In the Army of the Potomac there were six such Relief Agents, all working in harmonious co-operation with the Medical Authorities under the orders of the General Inspector or Superintendent. They replenished their stock of supplies, as it became exhausted, from a central depôt established at the military base, which depôt was in turn kept filled by requisitions on the storehouses at Washington.

The efficiency of this system depended much, of course, upon the character of the Agents employed, Character and and their exact observance of the rules laid instruction of down by the Commission for conducting its the agents. operations. These Agents had been selected with the greatest care with special reference to their peculiar qualifications for this particular duty. The policy of the Commission in this, as in all the departments of its work, was to secure the permanent services of capable and well-trained men. It was satisfied that its plans could never be thoroughly or efficiently carried out by the temporary, spasmodic, and irresponsible labor of mere volunteers. During the war there were a vast number of persons, who, influenced by motives of humanity, and sometimes by those less praiseworthy, were desirous of spending a few weeks in the Army with the hope of rendering aid to the suffering soldier. Many of these persons were such, as by previous training and habit, were wholly unfit for any relief service whatever, and all of them were so fettered by the claims of their ordinary duties at home, that they were unable to remain long enough in the Army to acquire that familiarity with its system and life which would have made them really useful. The practice of the Commission was wholly opposed to any such irregular and irresponsible method of labor. It was satisfied that the work it had to perform was of such peculiar novelty and difficulty, that it required for its faithful execution not only men of the highest character for intelligence and zeal, but that it involved the necessity also of a thorough course of training. No one was ever placed in the responsible position of a Field Relief Agent until he had received some instruction, and acquired some experience in a subordinate post. It was understood also, that those who entered the Commission's service should engage to remain in it for a lengthened definite period. The Agents were all instructed before they entered on their duties, in a knowledge of the general principles of Army organization, in the special functions of its different departments, in the usages of Army life, and in the peculiar relations which the Commission, bore to the Military Authorities. Until they showed some proficiency in such matters they were never placed in positions in which their ignorance could compromise the reputation of the Commission, or embarrass the discipline of the Army. As they gained experience, or

33

showed peculiar aptitude for their new duties, they were promoted from subordinate posts, and invested with larger responsibilities. Thus the Commission had always at its command a body of well trained and experienced men, thoroughly imbued with the spirit of its work, and competent faithfully to perform it.

As a means of attaching permanently to its service, such a body of capable Agents, a moderate compensa-
System of paid tion was paid to all of them. It would
Agents. hardly seem necessary to say one word upon the superior effectiveness, and greater real cheapness of paid labor in the kind of work in which the Commission was engaged during the war, had not its policy in this matter been not only questioned, but vehemently assailed by many well-meaning persons. Nothing could well be more lofty, than the scorn which was so often expressed during the war for those who would consent to receive money for their services in such a mission of mercy as this, but the Commission felt at the outset, and experience soon confirmed it in its opinion, that it had entered upon a work altogether too full of toil, drudgery, and repulsive reality, to be upheld by any mere sentimental pity or sympathy for the poor soldier. Its object was to help the suffering by the best practical methods it could discover, not to give an opportunity for sympathizing friends at home, to relieve their overburdened hearts, by spending a few weeks in the Army Hospitals in busy yet fruitless attempts to aid him. The work of relieving the soldier was found in practice to be a very hard, continuous and prosaic one. The best mode of doing it was not learned by inspiration, but was to be acquired only by

patient and long-continued watchfulness and labor. No man was fit for it who was not moved to undertake it by a principle of duty, but it was a novel idea that that duty was less conscientiously performed, and its lofty nature degraded by those who received compensation for their services. The great object which the Commission had in view of course, was to secure the best services of the best men. The whole practice of the military service as well as that of every association or individual having work to do, and needing the help of Agents to do it, was opposed to the assumption that any man's zeal and devotion in the performance of any duty is unfavorably affected by his receiving a salary. Why the rule heretofore universally recognized that paid services have always been more steady, regular and abundant in results than those of mere volunteers should be reversed in the matter of Army relief, it is difficult to say.

One of the great advantages which this system presented, was that it maintained discipline and proper ideas of subordination in the service. The Discipline of the Field Relief Corps. Commission knew exactly how much it should attempt, because it knew accurately its means of doing it. Its unfortunate experience in the transport service of the Peninsular Campaign with volunteer nurses and assistants, has been already spoken of. The failure of that experiment confirmed its Managers in their determination never again, in the ordinary administration of their work, to trust to the services of any man whom they could not at all times rightfully command. A single exception to this rule was made in the case of the great emergencies of battle-fields. At such times the demand upon the Commission for supplies was so great, that it was found impossible to meet it with the limited number of its permanent Agents attached to the Army, and in such cases, temporary volunteer aid was sought for, on the principle, that on the whole, it was better in relieving the wants of such an exceptional condition, to employ inexperienced hands than none at all.

Of all the conditions of human suffering experience has shown that that which occurs after great battles, is the most difficult adequately to provide for. This is inevitable, not merely because the number to be cared for is ordinarily great and their wants pressing, but because battles are often fought at a distance from the base of supplies, because the means of transporting such articles as are needed by the Surgeons are generally taken up with sending forward food and ammunition, and because it is impossible to maintain in the normal organization of an Army such a system as will fully meet the needs of a general engagement which even, in active campaigns is an occasional exigency only. During the war of the Rebellion there occurred more than six hundred conflicts between the hostile forces. Many of these were serious battles or bloody skirmishes, but comparatively few of them rise in dignity to what are known distinctively in history as " great battles." These struggles of giants with more than one hundred thousand men on each side are, fortunately for humanity, as rare in their occurrence as they are decisive in their results, not only of the campaign but of the whole contest. When these great battles do occur, however leaving their tens of thousands of wounded on the field, no Government system however provident, no official machinery however elastic, and no popular sympathy however burning with zeal or abundant in its resources, can do much more than mitigate the inevitable horrors attendant upon them. Owing to the general advance of Christian civilization, however, the battle-field has now become something more than a spot where humanity shudders at a consciousness of its own helplessness, as it witnesses the terrible suffering, it is powerless alike to prevent or relieve. It was one of the glories of the late war, that numerous as were its battle-fields, and immense as were the difficulties of fully relieving the wants of their victims, public opinion not only always insisted that the Government should maintain a high standard in its care of the wounded, but the people themselves were ever ready and anxious, by the offer of personal services and voluntary gifts, to assist in this humane service. This was the universal feeling and practice from the earliest period of the war, and although popular zeal may, at times have been indiscreet, experience gave it method, and immense practical efficiency and value. It should not be forgotten that the standard of comfort for those wounded in battle is necessarily very much lower than that maintained in long-established military Hospitals. Much of the misery which ensues on such occasions is, in the nature of things, inevitable, and the relief of this misery can be relative only. If, indeed, the relief afforded by the Government and by all popular voluntary contributions, and the value of personal services rendered at such times had been tenfold greater than it really was, the condition of the wounded would still have been one of terrible privation and agony. Into this unpromising field nevertheless, the warm current of popular sympathy was constantly turned during the war. What results followed in that portion of this field under the charge of the Sanitary Commission, it is for us to tell.

The first campaign in which its system of battle-field relief was methodized, and assumed the form The battle of which it retained during the war, was that in Antietam. Northern Virginia and Maryland which terminated in the great battle of ANTIETAM. There was probably no campaign throughout the war which was conducted under greater disadvantages in respect of supplies of all kinds. The Army with which the campaign opened under General Pope had been driven back defeated on Centreville, with immense loss of men and material. It was reinforced by the Army of the Potomac which had been sent to its assistance, in all haste, from the Peninsula. Thus united, several sanguinary battles were fought, which did not result in victory to the Union arms, and which had the effect, not only of disorganizing the Army, and demoralizing the men, but, to a very considerable extent of exhausting its supplies also. Washington the great base, it is true, was near, but owing to the confusion arising from a series of unsuccessful battles, and a change in the command of the Army, a very inadequate supply of stores reached it. A large portion of those sent forward, including forty wagon loads of medical supplies, was captured by the enemy, and for some days the utmost anxiety and alarm prevailed in Washington lest the means of providing that Army, upon whose success the fate of the nation depended with food and ammunition should fail. The enemy having withdrawn from the neighborhood of Washington with the design of invading the Northern states, the Union army passed through that city into Maryland. These events occurred within a period of a few days, and it was necessary that the Army should move with the utmost expedition, in order to oppose the advance of the rebels north of the Potomac. Its supply trains were, of course, replenished in passing through Washington, but the loss and destruction of wagons and horses during the brief campaign in Northern Virginia, had been so great, that its disposable means of transportation were very limited, and there was no time to replace the loss which had been sustained. The railroad bridge over the Monocacy River also had been destroyed, so that the Army was deprived, at least temporarily, of the great channel by which its supplies might have been rapidly forwarded. Thus, from a combination of causes, not often occurring together,—the immense losses and terrible exhaustion of a week of battles, the consequent confusion and disorganization, and the impossibility of providing adequate means of transportation for the most necessary supplies, the Army which fought at Antietam was placed in the worst possible condition so far as its ability to care properly for its wounded was concerned.

The result was precisely what might have been confidently anticipated. The battle was fought on the 17th of September, 1862, and resulted in leaving on our hands nearly ten thousand of

Suffering of the wounded for want of supplies.

our own wounded, besides a very large number of the enemy, abandoned by his defeated and retreating army. Hospital accommodation of the rudest form could not be provided for any considerable number of these sufferers, and after every house, and barn, and church, and building, for miles around had been appropriated for the use of the wounded, many remained shelterless in the woods and fields, for want of tents. The number of Surgeons was wholly insufficient for the demands upon them, and until they were reinforced by Medical men in civil life, who came from all parts of the country and volunteered their services, the condition of the wounded whose first wants had not, in many cases, been attended to for days after the battle, was most distressing. The supplies of the Medical Authorities were not one tenth of what was absolutely needed. A large stock had been accumulated in Baltimore, ready to be despatched to the battle-field. But it must be remembered that the Medical Authorities had no independent means of transportation, but were forced to rely on the Quartermaster's Department for the performance of that essential part of its service. That Department, charged with the responsibility, not merely of sending means of succor to the wounded, but also of supplying the Army with everything it needed in the way of food, clothing and ammunition, naturally considered it more important to provide for the wants, of those who were still able to fight, than for those who had been placed *hors-du-combat.* In this way, the supplies which had been accumulated by the Surgeon-General were delayed, and even the small portion which was sent forward did not reach the battle-field for many days, owing to the destruction of the bridge over the Monocacy. The serious injury resulting from these, perhaps unavoidable, delays can be estimated when it is remembered that on such occasions, the first two days are more important than the next ten, to the saving of life and relief of misery.*

The Commission was perfectly aware of all the circumstances in this campaign which would call for its utmost exertions, and it employed all its resources in preparing for the emergency. It was foreseen, that the grand difficulty on the part of the Government in promptly succoring the wounded, would be a deficiency in the means of transportation. The Commission determined, therefore, wisely, to place all its supplies in its own wagons, in charge of its own Agents, who should move with the Army during this campaign. Two large wagons, each accompanied by an Inspector, were kept constantly well up to the "front," and distribution of stores was made on the march, whenever needed. When these stores became exhausted they were replenished from other wagons following in the rear. In anticipation of the battle, a wagon-train laden with suitable supplies was despatched every day, from Washington to the Army, during this brief campaign, so that

Preparations of the Commission for this battle.

---

* It is a curious fact as illustrating the extremely limited amount of supplies, with which every department of the Army which fought at Antietam, was provided, that there was serious cause of alarm during the battle, lest the ammunition should become exhausted. Information of this state of affairs was at once sent to Washington, and in consequence, a train of cars laden with ordnance stores was forthwith dispatched from Baltimore to Hagerstown *via* Harrisburg and the Cumberland Valley Railroad, making the trip of about one hundred and twenty miles in less than three hours. If the same energy had been shown in sending forward relief for the wounded how many noble and precious lives would have been saved at Antietam !

34

after the battle occurred, relays of these trains arrived at intervals, during several succeeding days at Head-quarters. In this way the Commission was enabled to supply at once the first wants of the wounded, and by Friday, the 19th of September, it provided abundantly for the most pressing necessities of the thousands who were imploring succor. During all this time, and for nearly two days afterwards, that is to say, during four days after the battle, the Medical Director received no supplies. They were stored in abundance in the cars near the broken bridge over the Monocacy, and on the railroad between that point and Baltimore, but they could not be got forward by the ordinary means of Government transportation. What the condition of the wounded at Antietam would have been, without the timely succor furnished by the Sanitary Commission and other volunteer organizations, it is horrible to imagine. Chloroform, opiates, instruments, bed-pans, everything, in fact, required for the treatment of the wounded, was wanting. Had there been no voluntary supplemental supplies these sufferers would have been forced to depend wholly for food upon the coarse rations furnished by the Commissary, and for clothing and shelter upon such means as the inhabitants of the country, recently plundered by the Rebels, could provide. Within a week after the battle of Antietam there were dispatched to that field by the Sanitary Commission and distributed by its Agents, the following articles:

" Twenty-eight thousand seven hundred and sixty-three pieces of dry-goods, shirts, towels, bed-ticks, pillows, &c.; thirty barrels of old linen bandages and lint; three thousand one hundred and eighty-eight pounds farina; two thousand six hundred and twenty pounds condensed milk; five thousand pounds beef stock and canned meats; three thousand bottles wine and cordials, and several tons of lemons and other fruit, crackers, tea, sugar, rubber cloth, tin cups, and hospital conveniences."

In addition to these issues, strange as it may seem, the Commission succeeded in transporting from the Medical Purveyor's office in New York to the Government depôt at Frederick, four thousand sets of hospital clothing, and one hundred and twenty bales of blankets. It is certainly a circumstance well worthy of consideration, as showing how the theory of the ability of the Government, always fully to provide for the wants of the soldier, will sometimes break down, that the Commission succeeded on this occasion through the energy and determination of its special Agents, in overcoming the difficulties and delays which had beset the transportation even of Government Medical stores by the ordinary channels. Perhaps the greatness of the emergency may justify the Commission in this single instance of departure from its ordinary policy of non-interference with Government plans.

Transportation of Government supplies from New York.

The wonderful success of the Commission's methods of succoring the wounded at Antietam, was due, not merely to the wise and comprehensive system of relief which it adopted, but also to the extraordinary fidelity, energy and intelligence exhibited by the Agents employed in their

Success of the Commission's plans of relief after this battle.

execution. The Board was holding its regular session at Washington, during the progress of the campaign, and its presence and example inspired all its officers with a spirit of renewed activity and devotion. Dr. C. R. Agnew, one of the Commissioners, accompanied the Army on its march, superintended the movement of its wagon-train and the distribution of its stores. For more than a week he was constantly in the advance, in close communication with the Medical Director, having the best opportunity of knowing the relative wants and necessities of the wounded, and the blessed power, for several days, of fully ministering to them. The subordinate Agents rivalled each other in the unflagging zeal they displayed, and in the cheerfulness with which they bore unceasing toil and privation, in carrying out the details of this humane and merciful service.

One there was who died a martyr to his devotion for the relief of the suffering on that field, whose name and services deserve commemora-
William Platt, Jr.
tion, for he was one of the true heroes of the war. WILLIAM PLATT, Jr., at that time superintendent of the Philadelphia Agency of the Commission, had gone to Washington, in the early part of September with a view of arranging plans for the more rapid transmission of the supplies in the Philadelphia storehouse to the point where all felt that the great conflict was impending. On his arrival there, he found every one busy, packing and forwarding stores to the army. Inspired with an earnest wish to occupy that post where

he could render the greatest service, he volunteered to take charge of one of the wagon trains, which the Commission was about despatching to " the front." He hastened forward with the utmost expedition, and reaching Middletown at eleven o'clock at night on the 17th of September, the day of the battle, he pursued his journey during the whole night, quickening his speed as he came within the sound of the cannon, leading the way with a lantern in his hand, and compelling the reluctant drivers to follow. He reached the Headquarters of the Army at nine o'clock the next morning, when the stores he had brought, the first and for nearly two days the only ones, which reached the Army, were distributed, to the inexpressible relief of the suffering. But his labors did not end here. As the wounded were brought in in the ambulances, he carried many of them in his arms to the Hospital, and performed for them all the gentlest offices of a nurse. Thus employed he overtasked his strength, and contracted a disease which soon brought his short but well spent life to a close. The Sanitary Commission has its roll of martyrs,—as what noble cause has not?—men who have sealed with their blood their belief that there are many things in this world more valuable than mere life, yet, there is no one of those who "laid down their lives for their brethren," whose memory is held in more grateful and loving reverence than that of this modest yet earnest gentleman, this pure-minded and faithful Christian, this ardent and steadfast lover of his country. He died, as he himself would have chosen, at the post of duty in the highest service of humanity.

The battle of Perryville in Kentucky, which occurred shortly after that of Antietam, furnished, if
The battle of possible, a still stronger illustration of the
Perryville. fact, that the wants of the wounded were
neglected after great battles, not through any fault of
the Surgeons, but because the Medical Department had
no control whatever over the means of transporting the
supplies necessary to relieve them.   The want of independent means of transportation continued to embarrass the action of the Medical Officers in the field
throughout the war.   The aggravated suffering which
was due to an absence of this provision caused a
constant appeal to the Commission as the great
Agent of relief, and required a corresponding increase
of its resources.   Owing to the necessity of limiting
as much as possible the transportation of any stores
which could impede the rapid march of the Army
which fought at Perryville, an order was issued
by the General commanding, forbidding even Regimental Surgeons to carry medical supplies.   Such
an order may have been justified by military necessity,
but its consequences were none the less shocking to
humanity.   The battle at Perryville left nearly twenty-
five hundred of our men wounded upon our hands.
The Surgeons were destitute, of course, of almost every
thing which could minister to their relief, and the supplies which had been forwarded by the Medical Director at Louisville, only eighty miles distant, did not,
for some reason, reach Perryville until several weeks
after the battle.   But the Commission did not allow its
operations to be embarrassed by any such obstacles.
On the receipt of the news of the battle at Louisville,

Dr. Read, the Inspector in charge, borrowed from the Medical Director three large army wagons and twenty-one ambulances, and loading them with stores from the depôt in that city, proceeded forthwith to the battle-field. The condition of things when he reached there was deplorable in the extreme. It was the same sad story of agony and misery resulting from the casualties of war, not even mitigated by the commonest modes of relief, and intensified, if possible, by the utter want of Hospital accommodation. What could be done, of course, was done. The resources of the Commission were abundantly poured out, but great as they were, they could make but a small impression upon such a mass of suffering. It was a burning disgrace to the country, and to the administration of the military service, that the lives of men who had fallen in defending the National cause, and who were lying in their agony within eighty miles of the great military depôt of the West, should be confided for weeks to the care of a mere voluntary, benevolent organization.

The fearful suffering on battle-fields, preventible as it seemed to the Commission, by the adoption on the part of the Government of very simple means of succor was a subject which commanded the anxious attention of its members during the whole war. It made constant efforts to secure the great *desideratum*, the control by the Medical Authorities of independent means of transportation. These efforts proved unavailing, for reasons deemed satisfactory by those at the head of the military service. These reasons were based upon the theory that every-

<small>Independent transportation for medical supplies.</small>

thing in an Army must be subordinated to its capacity to fight battles, and as that capacity was reduced by whatever impeded its rapid march, and by any division of authority in the matter of forwarding supplies, the neglect of the wounded, which it was admitted resulted from existing arrangements, must be accepted as one of the inevitable evils of a state of war. No argument, founded on considerations of humanity could induce the military authorities to change the system, and consequently all that was left for the Commission to do was to attempt to mitigate the evils which it never ceased to deplore, but which it was wholly powerless to remove.

The systematic method which was characteristic of the Commission's work in its other forms of relief, Auxiliary Relief Corps. was, as we have seen, somewhat necessarily relaxed when it was called upon to afford succor to the wounded after great battles. Still the ignorance of Army regulations and usages on the part of that portion of their corps of Agents, who coming fresh from civil life, had volunteered their services for the emergency, the misdirected zeal of some, and the carelessness and inefficiency of others, all causing a waste of labor and of stores, led it to seek for some means by which its invaluable services could be bestowed in a more systematic and therefore more effective manner. After the question had been much discussed, and all the light which could be borrowed from nearly three years' experience in this peculiar work had been shed upon it, it was decided to introduce a more orderly system into the Commission's work even amidst the confusion of the battle-field. With the view of trying this experiment, a corps was organized, in anticipation of the campaign upon which the Army of the Potomac entered, in May, 1864, which should be charged specially with battle-field relief during that campaign. This corps was called the AUXILIARY RELIEF CORPS. The design was that the new organization should not interfere in any way with the functions of the Field Relief Corps of the Commission, whose duty, as we have stated, was to accompany the Army on its march and supply its ordinary and current necessities. That work was to be continued in all its vigor at the " front," while the new corps was to look after the wants of the wounded sent to the Hospitals after an engagement, and left behind by the Army on its onward march. The expediency of organizing such a corps for such a service had been suggested by Mr. FRANK B. FAY, of Chelsea, Massachusetts, who had had during the war much personal experience in Army relief as an independent worker. He was accordingly placed at its head, and proceeded at once to organize it. Fifty agents were first selected, most of them young men, principally theological students. It was agreed that they should enter the Commission's service for at least four months, and bind themselves to observe its rules and discipline.

The great object in view was to secure personal ministrations to the wounded by chosen men who should be responsible members of an organ- Peculiar duties ization directed by those who were familiar of this Corps. by experience with the regulations of the Army, and the needs of the suffering. They were to be relied upon, in strict obedience to the orders of the Superintendent, to meet the wounded as they were carried in

35

ambulances from the field, and see that they were provided with proper food and stimulants; they were to
assist, when called upon, in conveying them to the
Hospitals, to wash and cleanse them when necessary,
and to provide them with fresh clothing.   If it happened, as it often did, that the buildings which were
occupied as Hospitals required a thorough renovation
and cleansing, in order that the patients might be properly treated, and their chance of recovery promoted,
they were expected cheerfully and promptly to undertake this menial and scavenger work.   They were to
give themselves, day and night, unreservedly to the
care of the particular wounded men placed under their
charge.   When, by these means, the sufferings of their
bodies had been alleviated as far as practicable, they
were to give their attention to their other wants. They
were to write letters for them to loved ones at home;
they were to supply them with reading matter when
their condition permitted them to read; they were to
enliven their tedious hours with cheerful conversation
and expressions of sympathy; they were to minister
to the dying the sublime consolations of a Christian
faith, and they were to perform for the dead the decent
rites of a Christian burial.   In short, these young men
were expected to consecrate all their powers for a
definite period to this exhausting labor of humanity
and mercy.   A spirit of devotion was required of them,
not unlike that exhibited by those noble men and
women who, bound by religious vows, have braved the
worst terrors of the pestilence in their efforts to relieve
the sufferings of their fellow-creatures.   Instances, of
course, were not wanting of heroic self-devotion and

most arduous self-imposed labor, upon the earlier battle-fields of the war, but in most cases the service was too short to be absolutely exhausting, and in all, there was the stimulus of uncontrolled action, which, powerful as it was, was wholly unlike that needed to keep ever fresh and active a zeal for the regular, systematic, and continuous performance of a service repulsive to every instinct save that of humanity and Christian duty.

The Agents composing this Auxiliary Relief Corps were gathered together in Washington in the early days of May, 1864, and the nature of their duties was fully explained to them. They *It enters upon its duties.* were told that their zeal and ardor, however impatient, must at all times be controlled by the orders of the Superintendent, which were based upon a careful study of the wants they would be called upon to relieve, and were framed with the intention of avoiding all possible conflict between the Commission's labors, and those of the military authorities. They also received instructions in their duties as nurses, and in general Hospital work. They were then formed into squads or companies of six, each under the charge of a captain, who was responsible for the work of his particular company to the General Superintendent. Each of these squads was provided with what was called a " relief box," which contained a limited supply of food suitable for the wounded, and a great variety of articles which experience had proved were not only essential in suddenly improvised Hospitals, but which were most difficult to procure when most needed.

The corps left Washington on the receipt of the

news of the battles of the Wilderness, and its first
Work at Belle Plain and Fredericksburg. duty was the establishing at Belle Plain of Feeding Stations, whence food could be dispensed to the famishing, wounded men, who were slowly and painfully conveyed in ambulances stretching out in lines many miles long, all moving towards the water base of the army. But their services were soon required nearer to the " front." Walking to Fredericksburg, ten miles distant, they found more than twenty thousand wounded men crowded into that place. These were the worst cases which had been sent from the battle-field, so bad indeed, that it was deemed unsafe to transport them further. To the inexperienced eyes of the members of the Corps, those whom they had met on the shores of the Potomac seemed to have reached the utmost verge of human misery, but their condition was positively comfortable compared with that of those with whom they were now brought in contact. The whole place was actually encumbered with a mass of human beings, undergoing physical torture and agony under every conceivable variety of form. For days the public buildings, the private houses, and even the streets of the town, were filled with these wretched victims of war, imploring food and succor.

By the time the Corps reached Fredericksburg, its numbers had increased to nearly one hundred and fifty
Work at Fredericksburg continued. persons, embracing, besides its regular members, many volunteers who placed themselves under the orders of the Superintendent. Mrs. General Barlow, Miss Gilson, and several other ladies took charge of the special diet kitchens of the Hos-

pitals and supplied the requisitions of the Relief Agents. As soon as practicable, each squad or company was assigned to a distinct Hospital, and reported for orders to the Surgeon in charge. As usual, the arrangements of the Government for feeding and caring for the suffering men were wholly inadequate. For some reason, which has never been very clearly explained, the authorities at Washington had supposed that the wounded would have been removed from the battle-field to the Hospitals in that city by railroad, and trains of cars had been dispatched from Alexandria to the Rapidan River to transport them thither. Instead of this arrangement, however, the wounded were all poured into Fredericksburg, where, as their coming was unexpected, no preparations had been made to receive them. It is impossible to imagine anything more frightful than the confusion and destitution which followed. Many days elapsed before anything like system could be introduced into the management of affairs.

There were three things to be observed in the midst of it all, which went to prove how wise a measure the establishment of such a disciplined body by the Commission as its Auxiliary Relief Corps had been, and how providential was its interposition just at that particular juncture. In the first place, the stores of the Commission, owing to its possessing more than forty four-horse wagons were readily brought forward from Belle Plain. Had these stores, in the state of utter destitution which then prevailed, been placed without specific instructions in the hands of irregular, independent, and irresponsible workers,

Peculiar advantages of this form of relief.

men prompted only by an intense natural desire to relieve the agony of those immediately around them, their distribution might have been injudicious, and would certainly have been wasteful. In the second place, owing to the previous organization of the corps into companies, it was easy to assign each company to a distinct Hospital, where it could work effectively, and thoroughly, and with a definite purpose. In the third place, it seemed that during the whole war no instance had occurred in which the regular authorities so much needed the aid of a trained body like this to assist them in their special duties, the larger number of the Surgeons being, of course, obliged to accompany the Army in its onward march, and those who were left behind being completely overworked, and entirely un-provided with proper means of relieving those under their charge. The members of the Corps worked in perfect harmony with these Surgeons, and carried out faithfully their instructions in everything concerning the care of the patients. They not only performed all the duties of nurses, but strove, in a variety of ways and under the most discouraging circumstances, to provide for the comfort of the patients, acting as Stewards of the Hospitals and preparing their food in the special diet kitchens. It was not intended by the authorities to make Fredericksburg a point for the establishment of permanent Hospitals. The vast multitude of wounded which had accumulated there was transported as soon as practicable to the General Hospitals at the North. The Auxiliary Relief Corps followed the water base of the army first to Port Royal, then to White House, and last to City Point. To each of these places the wounded of Spottsylvania, Cold Harbor, and of the battle-fields in front of Richmond and Petersburg were brought, and were cared for temporarily until they were either sent to General Hospitals, or so far recovered from their wounds as to be able to rejoin their regiments. The peculiar work of the corps was unceasing, and most beneficent in its results at these points. The intensely personal character of its ministrations, and the actual contact of the gifts of the loyal people of the North with the misery they were designed to relieve, are well described in an extract from a letter of one of the most active participants in the work, Mr. Orange Judd.*

* "These hands of mine are hallowed by the hundreds of pairs of socks, the shirts, the drawers, the arm-slings, the crutches, the pillows, the ring cushions, the slippers, etc., etc., that they have been permitted to give to these heroes during five weeks past. And every hand that has helped to make these things, or helped by work, or dimes, or dollars, to buy them, is a nobler hand therefor. I wish I could give a thousandth part of the items. I have said nothing of the tens of thousands of cups of good coffee, prepared with pure milk brought condensed in cans, and sweetened with good sugar, of other thousands of cups of tea, of milk-punch when stimulants were most needed, of farina, of beef or chicken broth, which modern invention enables us to carry fresh to the field. Imagine at least a hundred persons constantly preparing and bearing these things to our sick and wounded brave men, far from home and home comforts and care, and again with me thank God that it was put into the hearts of the people, to work in Fairs and at home for our soldiers, and that you and I have been privileged to bear some part in this noblest enterprise of this or any other age. Shall I speak of a single day's work of my own in illustration? The men had for thirty-six days been away from their usual access to sutlers, or other sources of supply. I found a great eagerness for tobacco among those accustomed to use this narcotic; the longing seemed to be intensified by their condition. Yesterday I went around with a basket on each arm, and a haversack on my neck. A rough estimate of the day's work, from the morning and evening stock on hand, showed that I had given out writing paper and envelopes to about seven hundred men. Pencils to ninety. A large lot of newspapers sent direct to me by Mr. Felt, of Salem, Mass. Crutches to one hundred and thirty-six wounded below the knee, who were thus enabled to get up

When the armies operating before Richmond and Petersburg became stationary, and a siege of those

Work in the Hospitals at City Point.

places commenced, the same practice of transferring the sick and wounded from the Field Hospitals at the "front" to temporary Hospitals at the water base, which had existed during the whole campaign, was continued. The same personal ministrations became therefore necessary on the part of the Auxiliary Relief Corps in the Hospitals at City Point, for although, of course, these Hospitals were much better supplied than those which had been improvised in the rear of battle-fields, still there seemed, after all, practically no limit to the distance which existed between the standard of Government ideas of comfort, and that which popular sympathy for the soldier was anxious to maintain. The Commission determined on this, as on all occasions, to do all in its power to improve the Government standard, striving, always, how-

and move about. Arm-slings to one hundred and fifteen wounded in the arm. (Perhaps *you* made one of these, reader.) A piece of chewing tobacco each to about three hundred and seventy. Smoking tobacco and matches to about four hundred and fifty, and pipes to seventy-three who had lost theirs. (A wounded man seldom brings anything from the field except what is in his pockets.) This is the only day I have attempted to keep an account of the work done. With my outfit of baskets, etc., I looked like, and was not inappropriately dubbed a "Yankee Pedler." I doubt if any other Yankee Pedler ever did a better business in one day, or one that *paid* a thousandth part as well. The pleasant running conversation kept up all day was cheering, to myself, at least, and the "God bless yous" and cheerful "good mornings" or "good evenings," responded from every tent as I left it, was *good* pay. Everywhere I met others of our "relief agents," bearing other things, or bending over the fallen men, dressing their wounds, and Samaritan-like "pouring in oil and wine." The sleep of that night was sweetened by bearing out thirty-eight nice warm new blankets to as many blanketless men whom I found, as I came from a distant part of the camping-ground at a late hour in the evening. These men had been brought in after dark, and had got separated from the rest of their train.

ever, not to embarrass that official care upon which, it well knew, the main dependence of the soldier must after all rest. It persevered in this peculiar method of supplemental aid, until the last hour of that campaign which the surrender of General Lee brought to a close. It was, on the whole, satisfied with the experiment which it had made. Some of its Agents might have been more earnest and active, a more thorough discipline might, perhaps, have lessened the immense issue of supplies without affecting, unfavorably, the real benefit derived from their distribution, but still imperfect as the system was, it was clear that it had done a work of beneficence of untold value to the sixty thousand wounded of the Wilderness campaign, a work which it did not seem possible to have accomplished in any other way.

The fidelity and devotion of nearly all its members to their duty under circumstances of extraordinary privation and exposure, and the sacrifice of the lives of several of them, caused by exhausting service in a malarious region, have *Fidelity and devotion of the members of this corps.* made the history of this Corps more illustrious in many respects than that of any body of men connected with the service of the Commission. During the summer of 1864 no less than four persons, members of this Auxiliary Corps, sealed their devotion to its pure and holy ministry with their lives. One of them, WILLIAM WILSON, the youngest, perhaps, *William Wilson.* of all its members, a mere boy, had nevertheless done a hero's work in ministering to the wants of the wounded. He was treacherously shot while on board a steamer, in the service of the Sanitary Commission

36

and bearing its flag, by guerillas concealed on the shore of the James River. He fell a victim to that barbarous policy of the enemy, which always refused to recognize as entitled to immunity and protection those who were not only non-combatants, but those who had always proved the best friends of their own helpless wounded when the fortunes of war placed them in our hands. Another, CHARLES H. STANLEY,

Charles H. Stan-ley.   was preparing for the service of that Divine Master whose teachings have inspired us with the highest motive for all humane effort. Impelled by such motives, and in such a service, no fear of danger could daunt his ardor, and no privation, or toil, or exposure were accounted obstacles to the full performance of a high Christian duty. But, as it often happens, the spirit of a martyr and a hero was enshrined in a weak and feeble body. In his pure and unselfish zeal, he discovered too late the limit of his capacity for doing good. Never faltering while a feeble remnant of strength remained, Stanley was at last prostrated by a fever, induced by his unremitting devotion to the wounded, and went home to die a Christian's death, fit sequel to his pure and noble Christian life.

There were two others, the story of whose lives, freely risked and at last yielded up for the sake of the Prof. Hadley.   soldier, will always serve to dignify, ennoble and exalt the history of the labors of the Auxiliary Corps. One of these was a man, and the other a woman, and they were both the highest types and representatives of that extraordinary combination of intense love of country, with a spirit of pure, unselfish devotion to the needs of those who were suffering in its cause, which prevailed everywhere during the war as the strongest and most striking characteristic of popular feeling. Professor Hadley, Hebrew Professor in the Union Theological Seminary at New York, a Student, a man of quiet and retiring habits, utterly unpracticed from the nature of his life and tastes, in the toil and drudgery of personal ministrations to the suffering, nevertheless thought it his duty to devote his time and strength to this peculiar service. With this intention, he went to the James River in June, and enrolled himself as a member of the Auxiliary Relief Corps. He gave himself up to his new duties with all the earnestness and energy of his nature, and his feeble body not being able to meet the demands made upon it by his heroic spirit, he soon sank into an early grave. His life was characterized while in the service of the Commission, by quiet but incessant work. *He never went to the front* to gratify a curiosity so natural to those who for the first time visit an Army engaged in an active campaign. He toiled on unwearyingly in the sad Hospital, for he had come to help the helpless, and not to witness "the pomp and circumstance of war." He thus endeared himself to all who had been the objects of his merciful care. When he was borne, sick and dying to the steamer, the greatest interest was manifested in his condition by those whom he had nursed, and who were then convalescing. They eagerly inquired after the welfare of the "Sanitary man," as they called him, their grateful hearts pouring out blessings upon him who had been to them the noblest type of practical Christian love and sympathy. The death of such a man in such a cause, not only invests his memory with peculiar tenderness and reverence, but it hallows and ennobles the cause, the success of which rendered necessary so precious a sacrifice.

The last of this glorious band who laid down their lives for their brethren, was ARABELLA GRIFFITH BARLOW, whose life from the very commencement of the war, resembles more that of those holy women whom the Roman Catholic Church has canonized as Saints for their unshrinking devotion to the relief of human suffering in its saddest and most repulsive forms, than like that of one reared among the influences of the hard, material, and artificial state of society in which we live. Mrs. Barlow was the wife of Major-General Barlow, one of the most brilliant and heroic officers of the Army. They were married on the day of his departure for Washington, whither he went as a private in one of the New York regiments in which he had enlisted. She was a lady of rare personal attractions, of highly cultivated intellect, of the best social position, beloved and sought for by a large circle of friends, full of life, spirit, activity and charity. Her husband's extraordinary merit led to his rapid promotion. He went through the Peninsular Campaign as Lieutenant-Colonel of his regiment, and his wife was one of those women who worked hard and nobly, as close to the terrible battle-fields of that campaign as they were permitted to go. She again appeared as an angel of mercy at Gettysburg, where her husband in command of one of the Divisions of the Second (General Hancock's) Corps, added by his

Arabella Griffith Barlow.

skill and bravery fresh laurels to those he had so dearly earned. At the commencement of the Wilderness campaign, she identified herself, as we have seen, with the peculiar labors of the Auxiliary Relief Corps at Fredericksburg, superintending the important work of preparing proper food for the wounded, in the special diet kitchens established in the Hospitals. While thus occupied, she could hear distinctly the roar of the storm of battle in which her husband was exposed to extremest danger, but this served only to stimulate her to renewed activity in succoring those around her who had already fallen victims to its fury. Her mind, fruitful in resources, was always busy in devising some means of alleviating the miseries of the wounded, and many a fractured limb rested on cushions improvised from materials, which she alone was able to discover and make serviceable. She was the last to leave Fredericksburg, and passing to Port Royal and White House, she actively continued her beneficent and life-saving work in the Hospitals at those places. Arriving at City Point, she went at once to "the front" in the lines before Petersburg, and there gave herself up to incessant labor in the Hospitals. This perpetual toil and privation proved, at last, too much for her strength, and a fever was induced by it which soon after terminated her pure and noble life. Mrs. Barlow was a true heroine, the record of whose career is that of one who sought, by personal service, to mitigate those horrors of war which are appalling, even to the perfect spirit of devotion which is so characteristic of her sex. Her motives were the worthiest and the loftiest which can stir the human heart, and she appears at all times to have been wholly unconscious of the promptings of a spirit of self-indulgence, and love of ease. With this intense and absorbing desire to relieve the suffering soldier, she combined that ardent love of the cause for which he was fighting, which sustained and cheered her in the midst of the most toilsome and forbidding labors. She and her noble husband were true types of the grandest moral ideas which the war developed—a pure love of country combined with a perfect spirit of self-sacrifice. " There are many glories," writes one who knew them both well, " of a righteous war.   It is glorious to fight or to fall, to bleed or to conquer, for so great and good a cause as ours ; it is glorious to go to the field in order to help and to heal, to fan the fevered soldier and to comfort the bleeding brother, and thus helping, may be to die with him the death for our country.   Both these glories were vouchsafed to this bridal pair."

CHAPTER X.

SPECIAL RELIEF SERVICE.*

NOTHING can better illustrate the flexibility of the system adopted by the Sanitary Commission than the history of the rise, progress, methods, and wonderful results of that department of its work denominated the SPECIAL RELIEF SERVICE. Established on the scientific basis that preventive means were the best general means of curing the evils which threatened the Army with danger, the Commission did not ignore the fact, that either before such means were generally adopted, or because they would not be constantly enforced, a vast amount of suffering would ensue which would require methodical and large measures of relief. The plans, therefore, of the Commission embraced both prevention and relief. Its chief attention was given at the outset, as has been said, to the former, because it was thought that prevention was the best mode of diminishing the necessity of relief. Its experience, however, was uniform, that

Nature of the special relief work.

---

* It may be proper to repeat here what has been already stated in the Preface that the Commission deems the history of its Special Relief Service of such interest and value, that it proposes to present it to the public in a distinct volume now in the course of preparation by Mr. Frederick N. Knapp. The following chapter gives only such an outline of its work as will enable the reader to form a harmonious view of the general system adopted by the Commission.

notwithstanding its strenuous efforts to insure the adoption of preventive measures and the partial success of those efforts, there was always a wide field for labor open throughout the war in behalf of those who were not properly cared for by Government methods. Hence arose its whole system of Relief in Camps, in Hospitals, and on Battle-fields, requiring the elaborate machinery of Hospital Visitors, Field Relief Corps, and Auxiliary Relief Corps, with an immense outpouring of voluntary supplemental supplies. Yet, while each of these agencies was working faithfully and most usefully in its appropriate sphere, it was felt that there were many and peculiar needs of the soldier which were not supplied by any one of them. This obvious deficiency induced the Commission to establish a distinct department of its work called the Special Relief Service. It was first suggested by an observation of the vast suffering endured by men, who in their relations to the Army were, without any fault of their own in what may be called "irregular circumstances," those whose simplest but most urgent wants were, for the moment, either beyond the reach, or beneath the notice or, at any rate, out of the range of the ordinary means of care provided by the Government.

The necessity of the existence of some provision for wants of this kind was obvious from the very beginning of the war. Owing to the manner in which the troops had been raised, Regiments were often confided to the care of officers who were utterly unfitted to be entrusted with the control of a thousand men for any purpose, and least of all, qualified to provide for their wants in accordance with

What induced the Commission to undertake it.

the rules and usages of the regular Army. The incompetency of these officers, as we have elsewhere endeavored to show, was painfully conspicuous on the arrival of the Regiments at Washington. The Government officers, those of the regular Army, were, it must be confessed, at first, singularly backward in assisting the new Commissaries and Quartermasters in gaining a knowledge of their duties. One of the results of this state of things was that in the early days of the war, Regiment after Regiment arrived at Washington, and marched to camps several miles distant, while the sick men belonging to them were left without any attendants in the cars, to shift for themselves, and became thus dependent upon the humane bystanders, or the people in the neighborhood of the station for a supply of food.

The inhumanity of this state of things it is difficult to explain, and impossible to excuse. At one of the earliest meetings of the Commission, on the 21st of June, 1861, a resolution was passed calling the attention of the authorities to this subject, and suggesting that buildings properly fitted up should be erected near the Station for the reception and care of the exhausted men of regiments arriving at Washington. The application was long unheeded. When, at last, the Government erected a building it was not designed to be occupied by sick or exhausted men. There were no beds, no proper food, and besides, an order forbidding any one to remain longer than six hours in the building was rigidly enforced. It was evidently supposed by the Authorities that any show of comfort at this halting-place would

Action of the Commission on the subject in June, 1861.

37

prove too great a temptation to those of the newly-arrived men who desired to avoid their duty. This action may have been grounded upon proper ideas of military discipline, but it produced nevertheless as the inevitable consequence, a mass of real misery which was unrelieved except by volunteer aid. On the 9th of August, an Agent of the Commission, Mr. FREDER-ICK N. KNAPP, whose name is imperishably associated with the history of the organization and practical working of this peculiar form of relief, found in the cars at the Station, thirty-six sick men of an Indiana regiment apparently abandoned by their comrades, who had moved out to their camp. These men were so utterly unprovided for, that during twenty-four hours they had had nothing to eat but a few crackers. This large-hearted man, as quick in action as he was generous in impulse procured from a boarding-house close by, two pails full of tea, and soft bread and butter, with which he refreshed and made comfortable these exhausted men, until their Surgeon, who so far from abandoning them, had been absent many hours striving in vain to find some means of removing them to a Hospital, returned. Thus began the Sanitary Commission's work of Special Relief, and thus were given the first of the four million five hundred thousand meals provided by it during the war, for sick and hungry soldiers. The next day, more than thirty men of another Regiment who had dropped down from sheer exhaustion during a forced march, were found lying near the Station. There was no one to care for them, for their Regiment had passed on; they were of course, weak and hungry, when fortunately for them, they were found out and cared for by this same good Samaritan. Such instances occurred every day. Every variety of suffering which can be endured by a sick stranger in a strange place, without money and without friends, was undergone by many of the most heroic men who went forth to fight our battles in the early days of the war, whose strength was not equal to their courage.

It became necessary, of course, for the humane treatment of these men, most of whom were nearly exhausted from the fatigue of the journey, and were suffering from no disease which a rest of a few days and proper food would not cure, that they should be at least provided with beds and proper attendance. At first, the Commission was permitted to afford them this relief in a corner of a building near the Station known as the " Cane Factory," but in a few days its Agents were driven out of this place by the Provost Marshal, who, with equal stupidity and inhumanity, insisted that the arrangements there made were converting the building intended merely for the reception of troops into a Hospital. Thus baffled by a want of co-operation on the part of the authorities, a house in the neighborhood of the Station was secured by the Commission, and completely fitted up for its benevolent purpose. This house was appropriately called " The Soldiers' Home." It was the Head Quarters of the Special Relief Service at Washington, and as its plans became gradually enlarged to meet the new wants arising in the progress of the war, it extended a form of relief to the needy, which may be classified under ten distinct heads. Its objects were,

" First. To supply to the sick men of the regiments

arriving such medicines, food, and care as it was impossible for them to receive, in the midst of the confusion, and with the lack of facilities, from their own officers. The men to be thus aided are those who are not so sick as to have a claim upon a General Hospital, and yet need immediate care to guard them against serious sickness.

" Second. To furnish suitable food, lodging, care and assistance to men who are honorably discharged from service, sent from General Hospitals, or from their regiments, but who are often delayed a day or more in the city before they obtain their papers and pay.

" Third. To communicate with distant regiments in behalf of discharged men, whose certificates of disability or descriptive lists on which to draw their pay, prove to be defective—the invalid soldiers meantime being cared for, and not exposed to the fatigue and risk of going in person to their regiments to have their papers corrected.

" Fourth. To act as the unpaid Agents or Attorneys of discharged soldiers who are too feeble, or too utterly disabled to present their own claim at the paymaster's.

" Fifth. To look into the condition of discharged men who assume to be without means to pay the expense of going to their homes ; and to furnish the necessary means, where we find the man is true and the need real.

" Sixth. To secure to disabled soldiers railroad tickets, at reduced rates, and, through an agent at the railroad station, see that these men are not robbed, or imposed upon by sharpers.

" Seventh. To see that all men who are discharged

and paid off do at once leave the city for their homes; or, in cases where they have been induced by evil companions to remain behind, to endeavor to rescue them, and see them started with through tickets to their own towns.

"Eighth. To make reasonably clean and comfortable, before they leave the city, such discharged men as are deficient in cleanliness and clothes.

"Ninth. To be prepared to meet at once, with food or other aid, such immediate necessities as arise when sick men arrive in the city in large numbers from battle-fields or distant hospitals.

"Tenth. To keep a watchful eye upon all soldiers who are out of hospitals, yet not in service; and give information to the proper authorities of such soldiers as seem endeavoring to avoid duty or to desert from the ranks."

Upon carefully examining this classification, it will be observed that none of the persons embraced in it were the proper objects of that sort of care, which was bestowed by the ordinary agencies of the Army organization. Those who were sick, were not sick enough to be sent to a General Hospital, and those who needed aid in various ways required services which, in no sense came within the proper scope of the duties of the military officers. But still aid and comfort from some quarter were essential to these suffering men. It was demanded upon considerations not merely of humanity, but of patriotic sympathy and gratitude also, and the Commission came forward to supply the obvious need with its Special Relief Service, which in extent and practical value rivalled, in the end, that of any portion of its work.

Such is a meagre outline of the nature of the particular kind of succor afforded by the Special Relief Department at Washington during the war. Encouraged by the success, and guided by the experience of the Soldiers' Home and the various Lodges attached to it at that place, the work was gradually extended to other points where soldiers were to be found in similar needy circumstances. Soldiers' Lodges and Homes were established by the Commission in Boston, Hartford, New York, Philadelphia, Cleveland, Cincinnati, Cairo, Chicago, and other places in the loyal States where destitute soldiers in large numbers were congregated, and where relief of the same kind was administered, on the same general principles as governed that bestowed in Washington. But it was at the great gateways of the principal Armies where certain forms of this kind of succor were chiefly dispensed. We have spoken of Washington, the last station on the route to the Army of the Potomac, but substantially the same work was performed under the auspices of the Commission at Louisville, at Nashville, at Memphis, at New Orleans, and at various other points in the rear of the armies which were advancing into the enemy's territory. During the war, the Commission maintained forty Homes or Lodges. scattered throughout the field of its operations from Washington to Brownsville in Texas, and from Louisville to Port Royal in South Carolina. They were indeed beacons in a desert waste, shedding a cheering and steady light amidst the darkness and desolation

Soldiers' Homes established at various other Points.

of war. In these refuges, the soldier, when he had no one else to care for him was, as we have seen, furnished with more than four millions and a half of meals, and provided with more than a million nights' lodgings, while assistance was given him in collecting from the Government nearly two millions and a half of dollars, his hard-earned wages.

There were two features in the mode of administering relief at these Homes which well deserve attention. In the first place, the service rendered was Characteristics of the relief afforded by them. eminently a personal service, bringing the Agent of Relief into actual contact with the particular need of the individual soldier. One popular objection to the methods of the Sanitary Commission to which we have had occasion to allude, was that it distributed its gifts through the Surgeons for the general relief of sufferers in mass, and thus, that it could not know certainly that the soldier actually received them, while the moral influence of that sympathy which was supposed to be so grateful to him, and which would have been secured by personal ministration, was necessarily lost. Experience proved that the advantages of this personal service in Hospitals had been as much overrated, as the likelihood of the misappropriation of articles intended for the use of the soldier, had been exaggerated. But the Commission based its non-interference with the care of the patients in Hospitals upon the higher ground of military discipline. While that discipline was to be upheld when its necessity was apparent, the rule which forbade interference was not only relaxed, but wholly disregarded in those numberless conditions of suffering and want which unfortunately occurred where the soldier was for the moment as far beyond the reach of military control, as he was without the circle of official care. The result was, that although the Commission never interfered with the case of any man whose wants were being cared for by the proper officers of the Government, except to aid those officers at their own request and in their own way, its experience proved that beyond this well-defined limit there were occasions for employing personal ministration in aid of the special and individual wants of the soldier so numerous, as to demand of its Agents a far greater amount of work than that required in any of its other various forms of Army Relief.

Another feature of this Special Relief Service which was somewhat remarkable, is that it should have been *Military discipline maintained.* found possible to conduct it without weakening the bonds of military discipline. At first, as we have seen, it was feared by the authorities that these Soldiers' Homes might prove lurking-places for malingerers and deserters, who would seek their shelter to avoid doing their duty. It must be admitted that, had the hospitality offered by the Commission been abused, either purposely, or through the carelessness of its Agents, there would have been great reason to fear that these establishments so close to the lines of the Army would have proved prejudicial to discipline. When it is remembered that for a long period during the war the average number of men, all in some way or other connected with the Army, who were lodged nightly in these Homes, was nearly twenty-three hundred, it is apparent that there existed grounds for such an apprehension. Here, however, that same regard for military discipline which had its harsh side perhaps, in refusing to interfere in behalf of individuals in properly organized Hospitals, was of great value in solving the delicate problem how to relieve the soldier, without at the same time impairing his sense of the duty which he owed the Government, or lessening the responsibility of those who were officially charged with his care. The efforts on the part of Managers of these Homes to exclude from a participation in their benefits all who had no proper claim upon them soon inspired the military authorities with entire confidence in the wisdom of their administration. The absolute necessity for the maintenance of such establishments at certain great centres of military movement, became, in the progress of the war so apparent, that the highest authorities facilitated and encouraged this peculiar form of relief in every way in their power. Thus the Government permitted the "Home" at Washington to draw Army rations for its inmates; at Nashville, where more than two hundred thousand men were cared for in the single year of 1864, buildings were furnished for the use of the Home without charge, while at Cairo, by order of General Grant, the Quartermaster erected at Government expense a suitable Home with all the necessary offices, "the Commission," to use the language of that illustrious General, "having been of such great service to the country, and at Cairo are doing so much for this Army at this time, that I am disposed to extend their facilities for doing good by every means in my power."

Another most important branch of the Special

38

Relief Service, technically so called, was the care and
Feeding stations feeding of wounded men *en route* from the
for sick and dis-
abled men. battle-field to the distant General Hospitals.
This work was distinct from that performed on the
field itself, which consisted chiefly in providing the
Surgeons with supplemental supplies at the earliest
possible moment, and was under the charge of the
Field Relief Corps. But as the policy of removing
the wounded as rapidly as possible from battle-fields
to General Hospitals prevailed throughout the war in
all portions of the Army, and as owing to the vast
numbers of the wounded, as well as to difficulties of
transportation fearful suffering often ensued, it was
necessary to adopt some means of succor specially
adapted to relieve the wants of these men during their
journey. This gave rise to the establishment, as we
have seen, in the rear of all the great Armies engaged
in active campaigns, and upon their lines of communication, of posts occupied by the Relief Agents of the
Commission, and called Feeding Stations. It will appear when we come to speak of the work done in the
different campaigns, how essential such a service was
to those, who were forced to make a journey of several
days before they reached a place of rest and comparative comfort. Most of the great battles of the war, as
is well known, were fought far away from the supply
base of the armies engaged in them, and it is not easy to
overrate the agony endured by those heroic men, who
with mangled limbs, and utterly exhausted by fatigue
and hunger, were slowly borne to the rear. These sufferers were rendered as comfortable as possible previous to starting by contributions from the Commis-

sion's stores. At convenient points they were met by its Special Relief Agents, and were supplied by such food and stimulants—coffee, soup, and soft bread—as would serve to refresh them and keep up the strength necessary to enable them to reach their journey's end. The thousands who were thus relieved by these good Samaritans of the wayside at Fredericksburg, at Gettysburg, at Acquia, at Port Royal, at White House, and at various points on the line connecting Nashville with the theatre of war in southern Tennessee and northern Georgia, are the best witnesses that there are many occasions in the life of the soldier when he needs succor quite as much as when he lies wounded on the battle-field. Nothing is more remarkable in the history of the war than the persistent care with which the American people followed their soldiers wherever they might be in need. Ministrations on a battle-field may be due to a love of excitement, to the novelty of the situation, or to the effect of a deeply roused but transient sympathy, but this organized system of relief in the rear of armies kept up during months of active campaigns, and supplying the wants of the soldier as they occurred, during his long and painful journey from the 'front,' is a novel feature in Army relief peculiar to the American war.

The work done at some of these Feeding Stations was immense in kind, and inestimable in value, and it was not confined wholly to the relief of the Their great masses of wounded men accumulated after value in certain emergencies. a great battle. Owing to the suddenness and unexpected character of military movements, it often happened that Field Hospitals were abandoned by the Army, and it was necessary to remove their inmates in large numbers, with the utmost promptness to a place of safety. Thus when the army evacuated Leesburg in the summer of 1862, the patients in the Hospital there, five hundred in number, were with the greatest difficulty removed to the canal which leads to Washington. There were no means of transporting supplies to them, and it was supposed that the men would have sufficient strength to reach the Washington Hospitals, where they would be provided for. Some friend of humanity, who had misgivings about the perfection of Government arrangements, telegraphed to the office of the Commission, " Five hundred sick and hungry men are on the canal boats on their way to Washington. Can you do anything for them ?" Wagon-loads of food were at once dispatched to Georgetown, and on their arrival there, these men who were in a deplorable state of exhaustion, were all fed and cared for. Hours elapsed before ambulances could be collected to transport them to the Hospitals, and it is easy to imagine what would have been their condition during the delay had it not been for this timely relief. So when the Army of the Potomac moved northward from Fredericksburg, in June of the next year, the patients in the Hospitals to the number of ten thousand were hastily transferred to Washington by steamer. On their arrival at the wharf, they found the Agents of the Commission busily engaged in preparations to meet their wants, a kitchen having been established, huge cauldrons of hot beef soup and coffee being kept constantly ready, and served to all as soon as they arrived. More than eight thousand men were thus fed in two days, and most of them then received the only nourishment they had obtained from the time they left their camps on the Rappahannock.

Among the establishments connected with the Army organization which grew out of the necessities of the war, none presented a more important field Convalescent of labor for the peculiar work of the camp. Special Relief Corps than the Convalescent Camps. These establishments were neither Hospitals nor Camps, but partook of the nature of both, and formed a sort of halting-place for the soldier midway between them. They received men from the Hospitals who had so far recovered as no longer to need medical treatment, but who were yet not well enough for active service in the field. These men remained in the Convalescent camps until they regained their strength, or it became apparent that they were wholly incapable of further service, and then, as the case might be, were either sent to rejoin their regiments, or were discharged as disabled. In the course of time, however, these camps became general rendezvous for the distribution of troops, to which were sent not only convalescents from Hospitals, but recruits to fill up the old Regiments, substitutes, stragglers of all kinds, deserters, and that large class of men who were found by the Provost Marshal's guard wandering away from their proper commands without permission. It will thus be seen that a heterogeneous mass of men representing almost every condition of a soldier's life, was collected in these places. The vast number thus separated for a time at least, from their regular place in the army may be gathered from the statement that during the years 1863 and 1864, more than two hundred thousand such men passed through a single one of these convalescent camps, that in the rear of Alexandria. The proper management of such a place was an exceedingly difficult task. A permanent, effective, organization was almost impossible as the inmates were constantly changing, and as they belonged to nearly every Regiment in the service, and to all the staff departments of the Army. The consequence was that there could be no proper military duties regularly performed or steady discipline kept up, as the men were liable, from day to day, to be discharged. For a long time the natural fruits of idleness in the soldier were apparent, and although some improvement was effected as experience was gained, still, these Convalescent Camps were always one of the most unsightly offshoots of the military system. The wants of the men gathered in them were numerous and exceedingly various, far more so than those of the same number of men enrolled under ordinary conditions in the Army. It was peculiarly a case in which personal service, judiciously bestowed, might prove of inestimable value.

The Commission found, in a lady, MISS AMY BRADLEY, the qualities which rendered her peculiarly Special Relief suited for superintending the multiform and in these camps. perplexing Relief work of a Convalescent Camp, and the record of her labors in that near Alexandria during two years and a half, proves that she performed the delicate, difficult and responsible duty imposed upon her with wonderful skill and fidelity. Her labors may be classified under the following heads:

" 1. Distributing clothing among the needy.

" 2. Procuring dainties for the sick, and administering to their comfort by furnishing gruel, stimulants, etc.

" 3. Accompanying discharged soldiers to Washington, and assisting them in obtaining their pay, etc.

" 4. Distributing note paper and envelopes, and writing letters for the sick in hospital.

" 5. Receiving and forwarding money for soldiers to their friends at home. This done by draft without cost to the soldier.

" 6. Answering letters of Inquiry to Hospital Directory.

" 7. Obtaining certificates for arrears of pay for soldiers, and getting erroneous charges of desertion removed.

" 8. Distributing reading matter, such as newspapers and periodicals throughout the camp

" 9. Telegraphing to the friends of soldiers very ill in hospital.

" 10. Furnishing meals to feeble soldiers in barracks, who could not eat the food prepared for stronger ones."

In addition to the work of distributing supplies among the needy, and of affording relief in various other forms, this one woman assisted more than twenty-two hundred men in collecting the arrears of pay due them, amounting to more than two hundred and ten thousand dollars. Most of these men were utterly disabled, and not only without any means of providing for their wants, but so feeble or so ignorant as to be unable either to bear the delay, or comply with the rules of the Paymaster's office. Miss Bradley accompanied them in the ambulances in which they were conveyed to Washington, and never left them until, through her intervention, and by the assistance of the other Agents of the Commission, they received their pay, and were sent on their way home rejoicing.

Another opportunity for the active exercise of the peculiar kind of work performed by the Special Relief Service was afforded by the return of our soldiers, who had been Prisoners of War in the hands of the enemy. Great efforts were made during the confinement of these men to relieve the horrors of their captivity, by sending through the lines in accordance with arrangements made between our authorities and those of the enemy, articles of clothing and of sustenance. Although there can be little doubt that a portion of these gifts failed to reach their destination, it is certain from the evidence given by many of the men after their exchange, that there was not as much misappropriation of them as was at one time supposed. The sufferings of the Prisoners in the Libby, and of those confined at points in communication with Charleston, were unquestionably much alleviated by the supplies sent forward both by the Commission and by the Government. It was the desire and intention of the Commission to render this provision for our suffering men constant and abundant, but its plans were defeated by the policy of the Government, and unfortunately relief of this kind was limited in amount, and of short duration. When, at last, arrangements for a general exchange of Prisoners was settled, and there was a prospect that a large

Relief of men returning from Rebel prisons.

number of these men would reach our hands in a state of destitution and exhaustion, preparations were made to receive them, as soon as they were restored to freedom, as such a way as to manifest the practical sympathy of the American people towards those who had been victims of the barbarity of the enemy. In October, 1864, a fleet of steamers sailed from Fortress Monroe to the Savannah River for the purpose of receiving those of our paroled, invalid prisoners who were to be delivered to us by the rebels. Each of the vessels of this fleet was accompanied by an Agent of the Commission, supplied with suitable stores. When the exchange actually took place, and the men were received on board it was felt that no devotion could be too tender, and no provision too large, to give full expression to that sympathy which the spectacle of their sad condition excited. Many of them were unable to walk, most of them were barefooted, and without underclothing, and their thin, wasted forms were covered with dirt and vermin. They were made as comfortable as possible according to the Government standard, by our authorities, ordinary rations and blankets being issued to them, but it was felt that their past suffering and present destitution deserved a somewhat more kindly recognition. From the stores of the Commission they were supplied with milk, tomatoes and nourishing soup. Shirts, socks, slippers and other articles were dealt out liberally to them, and before they arrived at Annapolis, each one was provided with a complete suit of under clothing. When they landed at that place they were sent to Camp Parole, where they received the constant attention and care of another

39

corps of the Commission's Agents as long as their enfeebled condition required it. Annapolis was the great rendezvous, during the war for paroled prisoners, and their camp, while it presented the clearest evidence of the shocking cruelty of the rebels, was a great field in which the active practical benevolence of the country had the fullest scope for its exercise.

But not alone at Annapolis was the Commission called on to perform this great duty. On the Red River and at Wilmington, especially, the same harrowing sights were witnessed whenever our men returned from the rebel prisons. At the last named place, early in the spring of 1865, more than nine thousand of these wretched men arrived in a condition the result of cruel treatment and neglect, aggravated by positive starvation, such as it makes the heart sick to recall. These men also were made the peculiar objects of the Commission's care. A large amount of supplies had been shipped from New York in anticipation of the arrival of General Sherman's army on the coast of North Carolina. These articles in consequence of the capture of Wilmington, were not needed for that special purpose, and fortunately proved a most timely means of succor to these miserable men. With equal promptness and energy, Dr. Agnew, who had gone in charge of the supplies, designed for General Sherman's army, directed that they should be used for the relief of the prisoners. Four thousand suits of woolen clothing were at once issued, and the sufferers were supplied with proper food during a period of nearly three weeks. Army rations were abundant, but it was, of course, necessary to provide men who were just emerging from a state of starvation with a diet of quite a different kind, and nourishing broth and vegetable food, staple articles in the Commission's supply list, were fortunately, just such as their condition required.*

As the war went on, the sphere of operations at the different Homes and Lodges became enlarged as the wants of the soldier became better known, Hospital Direc- and the efforts for relieving them were bet- tory. ter organized. One feature of the work, which grew almost of necessity out of the nature of the military service, was the HOSPITAL DIRECTORY. In the constantly changing movements of large armies it is impossible that the track of the individual soldier can be always followed by his friends at home, and it often

---

* The intense and wholly unnecessary suffering endured by our men in the rebel prisons, and the barbarous and cruel treatment which they received during their confinement at the hands of the rebel authorities, was the subject, above all others, which roused most deeply, public indignation during the war. As it seemed important that the truth in regard to this matter should be ascertained, in order that the weight of the public opinion of the whole civilized world should be brought to bear against the continuance of such practices, the Commission requested some of the most eminent men of the country in the different professions, to examine into the matter and report the facts and their conclusions. These gentlemen, Dr. Valentine Mott, Dr. Delafield, G. M. Wilkins, Esq., of New York, and Dr. Ellerslie Wallace, Honorable Judge Hare and the Rev. Mr. Walden of Philadelphia, went to Annapolis, examined many of the returned prisoners there under oath, and made a report founded upon the information thus obtained which will remain a monument of disgrace to a people who claim to be governed by the ordinary maxims of humanity. The facts stated in this report in regard to the cruel treatment received by our men have never been successfully controverted. On the contrary, they are all confirmed by the evidence given, on the trial of the wretched Wirz, the keeper of the Andersonville Prison. See " *Narrative of privations and sufferings of United States soldiers while Prisoners of War in the hands of the rebel authorities.*" Published by authority of the United States Sanitary Commission.

happened during the war that these friends were unable for months at a time, to discover his position, and not unseldom, that they were without the means of knowing whether he was alive or dead.   The Commission, as the great medium of intercommunication between the people and the Army, was constantly applied to to cause inquiries to be made through its Agents with the different Armies.   At first it was the duty of the officers of the Special Relief Department to make these inquiries, but their number became so great, and the subject had so important a general interest, that it was decided to establish a bureau which should have special charge of what was called a Hospital Directory.   In this bureau was kept a complete record of the names of the inmates of the Army Hospitals, whether becoming such by disease, or by wounds received in action.   The Central Office at Washington was opened to the public on the 27th of November, 1862, and shortly afterwards branch offices were established at Philadelphia, Louisville, and New York. Returns were constantly received at these offices from every General Hospital in the Army, two hundred and thirty-three in number, and the Directory therefore contained not merely the names, but also information officially obtained, and within recent periods, concerning the condition of the vast multitude of invalids contained in them.   The labor involved in a constant correspondence with the officers of these Hospitals, in transferring the immense mass of information thus received to the pages of the Hospital Directory in an orderly and systematic form, and in answering inquiries in regard to soldiers who were missing, or whose condition was unknown, was, as may be supposed, no light one. Still, in some respects, it was the work perhaps of all others, the results of which were the most gratifying of any undertaken by the Commission, for, in relieving the anxiety of friends at home concerning the fate of those who were dear to them, it roused the deepest feelings of gratitude in a large and important class towards an organization which gave such a practical proof of its humane spirit and enlarged methods. The Hospital Directory contained in its four offices the names of more than six hundred thousand men, with the latest information procurable in regard to the position and actual condition of each one of them. After great battles, the anxiety on the part of those at home to ascertain the fate of their friends serving in the army was, of course, intense. The officers of the Commission did not wait until the wounded were transferred to General Hospitals before they discovered their names and condition. On the contrary, as soon as the roar of the battle had ceased, the Agents of the Directory Bureau accompanied those of the Supply Department in their ministrations to the wounded on the field, and while bodily suffering was relieved by one class of agents, every effort was made by the other to cheer and encourage the sufferer by an assurance that his friends at home should know, at once, his exact condition. Nothing is more remarkable as showing the energy and humanity of the American people or the enlarged method of operations adopted by the Commission as its representative, than this double service, differing so essentially in the objects proposed to be accomplished, but guided by the same humane spirit, and performed at the same time amidst the confusion and horrors of the battle-field.

The mode of obtaining the information afforded by the Directory was very simple. The applicant com-

The mode of consulting it and its value. municated to the Bureau the name, rank, and regiment of the person inquired for, and the point at which he had been last heard from. With these indications a search was immediately made, and the result communicated without delay. The average number of successful inquiries made is estimated at about seventy per cent. of the whole number. The interest awakened in this work of the Hospital Directory among all who had friends in the Army, was constantly expressed as their own personal experience testified to its value. " Mothers write of their ' undying gratitude' for the simple announcement that their boys are doing well in hospital; others 'invoke the blessing of God upon the labors of the Commission,' and sisters 'will cherish the warmest gratitude while memory lasts.' The eagerness with which inquiries were made was scarcely less touching : ' By the love you bear your own mother tell me where my boy is !' 'Only give me some tidings!' 'Is he dead, and how did he die ?' 'Is he alive, and how can I get to him ?' ' I pray you tell me of those two nephews I am seeking for. I have had fourteen nephews in the service, and these two are the only ones left.' "

The Commission's PENSION BUREAU AND WAR CLAIM AGENCY was another department of its work

War Claim Agency. which grew out of the constant necessities of the discharged soldiers who found refuge in its Homes and Lodges. It appeared that nearly every one of these men who passed through the Home at Washington, had a claim either for arrears of pay or for bounty, or arising in some other of the various ways in which the Government becomes indebted to the soldier. The rules of the Paymaster's Department were, necessarily, very strict, not merely in regard to the evidence required to substantiate claims but also in regard to the form in which they were to be presented. It was not, of course, to be expected, that men so utterly ignorant of official routine as private soldiers, and withal so enfeebled in their condition as to render their discharge from the service necessary, could prosecute their claims with any hope of a speedy settlement where there was the slightest complexity in their character. Men in this condition, found at the Homes and Lodges, a ready aid and assistance from officers of the Commission detailed for that purpose. Their papers were put in proper form, and their defects supplied by those who were familiar with the requirements of the Pay Office, and thus the soldier was enabled to receive his hard earned wages with as little delay, and the smallest amount of inconvenience possible. To such a refinement of care for his comfort was this system carried at Washington, that the Commission established one of its Lodges, directly opposite to the Paymaster's office where those who were too feeble to wait their turn in the crowd, but whose presence was necessary in order to obtain their pay might remain and rest, until the officials were ready to attend to them. At this Lodge a table which would seat fifty persons, was kept constantly supplied with suitable food, and some one was always in attendance to give such information and assistance, as might be needed by the discharged soldier in securing his money. This work was not confined to Washington, but was actively carried on at all the great military centres. The result was that more than two million five hundred thousand dollars due discharged soldiers were secured to them in cases where the papers had been examined and perfected by the Agents of the Commission at its Lodges.

As the war went on, claims of all kinds, against the Government, became so numerous, and the aid of the The same sub- Commission in prosecuting them was so ject continued. constantly invoked, that it became necessary to establish a distinct department having in charge one particular class of these claims, applications for pensions. The Free Pension Agency of the Commission, as it was called, commenced its operations on the 10th of February, 1863. Applications for invalid pensions made through the Commission were presented by it to the proper Government Bureau, the necessary papers filed, and the business prosecuted to a settlement. It' had the twofold object of saving the applicant from imposition, annoyance and a vast deal of trouble in ascertaining whether he was legally entitled to a pension, and afterwards of securing it without any expense on his part. The Agency was so well managed that it soon became the principal channel through which claims of this kind were presented, and its usefulness was afterwards extended by including under its charge claims of all kinds against the Government, held by the soldiers of the Army. Towards the close of the war, its name was changed to that of

the " Army and Navy Claim Agency," and its operations were extended by means of more than a hundred
sub-agencies in direct communication with the central
office, to every part of the North and West. By means
of this Agency and its affiliated branches, between fifty-
five and sixty thousand claims for pensions to soldiers,
their widows, mothers, or orphans have been presented
to the proper Government officers, and the evidence in
support of them arranged and preserved. These claims
form nearly one half of the whole number presented to
the Government Pension Office, and all the labor connected with their prosecution being rendered gratuitously as, it is needless to say, are all the other services of
the Sanitary Commission, the amount saved to these
most deserving of all the creditors of the Government is represented precisely by the fees which
would otherwise have been paid by them to Claim
Agents. The claims for pensions entrusted to the
Commission's Bureau are supposed to represent a
money value of about seven million five hundred
thousand dollars, and the saving thus effected to those
who present them exceeds half a million of dollars.
With the close of the war, the operations of this
Bureau did not cease, but on the contrary became more
widely extended, because until . the Army was disbanded a large number of soldiers entitled to pensions
had had no opportunity for presenting their claims.
It is still kept open at Washington although its
Agencies at different points have been discontinued
and their business transferred to the Central Office,
and it is intended that this humane and beneficent
work, one of the most grateful in all its aspects of any
40

in which the Commission has ever been engaged shall go on until all the claims confided to it have been finally disposed of.

There was a great variety of work undertaken by the Special Relief Department of the Commission less Other forms of conspicuous in its character, perhaps, than Special Relief. that which we have described, but still having a direct and important bearing on the welfare of the soldier. Thus, provision was made at the Homes Care of the wives at the great military centres for the accom- and mothers of disabled sol- modation of the wives and mothers of sol- diers. diers, whose anxiety concerning their relatives in Hospitals had led them to come to their relief. Those who appreciate the natural impulse of affection which prompts such journeys, and who understand the anomalous position of a woman in an Army, as well as the limited means of most of those who came upon such an errand, will not be slow to recognize the humanity of some provision for their decent accommodation. This was one of the needs developed by the progress of the war which certainly had not been foreseen, and for which it was clearly not the duty of the Government to provide. The whole policy of the Commission in regard to such needs was what may be called a shifting one, adapting its methods of relief to the endless catalogue of difficulties, embarrassments and sufferings which beset a soldier's life. Thus it Fresh Hospital appeared, that the barren market at Wash- supplies at Washington. ington was wholly unable to supply the vast Hospitals there with fresh provisions of a good quality, and at a reasonable price. The Commission, at the request of the Surgeon-General, in the spring of 1863 undertook to procure these provisions in the much more abundant market of Philadelphia, and to send them daily in proper condition to Washington. This service was regularly and faithfully performed during a period of nine months, and the result was that the Hospitals at Washington were far better supplied and at a very much less cost than they had previously been. No one suffered by this arrangement unless the Hospital Stewards, whose perquisites were affected by it, and the hucksters in Washington whose exorbitant gains were cut off, may be considered proper objects of commiseration. The actual outlay made by the Commission for this purpose, was, of course, reimbursed from the Hospital Fund, but the labor and responsibility of the service, involving the purchase and transportation of more than one thousand tons of food, were very serious, but nevertheless, had their full reward in the improved condition of the patients.

The plans of the Commission for the welfare of the soldier embraced a minute attention to all his possible wants which was very remarkable. Thus Employment of Detectives were employed by it, whose busi- Detectives. ness it was to watch the sharpers who, like evil birds of prey, were always ready to rob the soldier as soon as he left the Paymaster's office. Then, again, Couriers were employed who accompanied the trains Couriers. going North from Washington, looked after the wants of the sick and feeble soldiers in the cars, many of them just discharged from Hospitals, and took care that they were provided for at one of the various Homes of the Commission on the route, if their strength was insufficient to enable them to prosecute their journey.

This multiform work of Special Relief deserves attention and study quite as much on account of the novelty of its methods, as from the peculiar nature of General results the care it bestowed upon the soldiers. of Special Relief Service. Who ever read, in the history of any war waged since wars began upon the earth, that the worn out soldier as soon as he was turned adrift by the Government, far away from his home and utterly helpless found a friendly hand outstretched to supply his first wants,—those of food and shelter? Where do we find any record of a voluntary system thoroughly organized and conducted on an extensive scale, by which the soldier was aided without fee or reward, in obtaining from the Government the money due him? Where was ever before practically developed into action that beautiful thought, the outgrowth of a large humanity, which prompted the same organization to convey to anxious relatives information concerning the condition of those who were dear to them, when absent and in danger? Who ever thought before of caring for the wives and mothers of soldiers when their affection induced them to brave hardship and privation in order that they might be near their suffering husbands and sons? The possibility of accomplishing a tithe of all that was actually done in this direction during the war would have been regarded by those who were guided by the experience of former wars as the dream of an enthusiast. The truth is, this mighty work was the genuine product of American civilization, in all respects novel and peculiar, but at the same time, in perfect harmony with that spirit which is the true life of American institutions. The soldiers of the Republic were no hirelings in the opprobrious sense in which that term might be applied to those composing European Armies. They were "bone of our bone, and flesh of our flesh," and it was certain, therefore, that in some way they would become the objects of that humane spirit which has been so largely developed everywhere in modern times, but which guided and controlled by the popular ideas of this country exhibited such extraordinary activity and usefulness during the war. A constant effort was made by those at home to prove to those in active service how complete and practical was the sympathy which existed with them in all their trials and sufferings. This was done, not on the ground of humanity alone, but because such was the confidence in the intelligence and self-sacrificing spirit of the soldier, that it was felt that such manifestations formed the highest incentive to renewed zeal on his part. Such men were not to be bribed to do their duty by the distribution of a few gifts, but their moral purpose was immensely strengthened by the evidence these gifts afforded of the intense and anxious interest with which every step of their progress was watched by those they loved. The history of events proved most conclusively that the American people had not been mistaken in the character of their soldiers, and particularly in the mighty influence which the sacred idea of home exerted over them. Disbanded soldiers in other countries, and in former wars have been regarded almost as outcasts, spreading terror and dismay by their wild license in the quiet communities which they re-entered. In other countries they have been as little under moral restraint as escaped convicts, their passions long repressed by the brute force of an arbitrary military discipline, and once again allowed free play, leading to frightful excesses of all kinds. Hence, the disbanding of even a small Army has often been the signal of a vast and immediate increase of disorder and crime. Far different was the case here. The world has never witnessed a scene more striking and novel in its moral aspects than that which followed the disbanding of the American army at the close of the Rebellion. One million of soldiers, perfectly organized, under officers of the highest military capacity, flushed with recent and unparalleled victory, and capable, as the Duke of Wellington said, of the British Army in the Peninsula, " of going any where and doing anything," not only lay down their arms quietly, now that their work is done, without a thought of gaining any unpatriotic purpose by the enormous power they wield, but disperse gladly to their homes and fill up the places which had been kept open for them during the war, as if they were returning from some holiday pageant. The explanation of this extraordinary state of things lies deep in the peculiar spirit of American civilization, and certainly the event itself is one of the proudest monuments of its value. The truth is the soldier never ceased to be a citizen while he was in the Army. He became willingly subject to military discipline, because the work to be done could be performed, in no other way, and there cannot be a doubt that one of the most striking peculiarities of the struggle, in history will be, that it was one of those rare wars in which the private soldiers had as thorough an appreciation of its objects, and the sacrifices necessary to be made in order to bring it to a successful termination, as the Generals in command, or the most enlightened public opinion of the country in whose service they were fighting.

CHAPTER XI.

DURING the summer of 1862 the work of the Commission went on steadily increasing in value and effi-
General work in the West during the summer of 1862. ciency in the Armies of the West. After the battle of Pittsburg, Landing and the evacuation of Corinth by the enemy, there was a large accumulation of sick and wounded, who suffered greatly in the Hospitals located in the insalubrious region of South-western Tennessee. Perhaps at no time did the Army suffer more from diseases arising from the nature of the climate of the region which it occupied. This condition of things required in the opinion of the Medical authorities, the transfer of many of the patients to Hospitals north of the Ohio River. The numerical strength of the Army became so depleted by this process that the Generals became alarmed, and complained loudly. Yet it is certain that none of the Medical Officers, who alone were capable of forming a correct opinion on such a matter, deemed it possible to pursue any other course consistently with a proper regard for the lives of the men. The Agents of the Sanitary Commission, agreeing perfectly in opinion with the Medical Officers, and all suffering, in person, from the effects of the climate, assisted in this work of removing the patients acting

320

in strict accordance, of course, with the rules of Army discipline. The ill humor of the Generals at the loss of their men was, strange to say, vented upon these Agents. The course pursued by them, however humane in its results, was one for which they were responsible only as aiding the Medical authorities themselves. This is the true history of the ridiculous charge against the Sanitary Commission, attributed to a General of high rank, that it had "stolen" several thousand of his troops after the evacuation of Corinth.

Immediately after that event, the Army which had invested Corinth was divided, the original command of General Buell being detached with the view of making an attempt on Chattanooga, and the remainder under General Grant march-ing southwardly on the line of the Mobile and Ohio Railroad, having for its object, in coöperation with a force which was sent down the Mississippi under General Sherman, the investment and capture of Vicksburg. Both of these expeditions were unsuccessful, and in both the failure was due in a great measure to the difficulty of keeping open, while in the heart of the enemy's country, long lines of communication by which supplies in sufficient quantity could reach the Army. To maintain those lines unbroken has always been the first condition of success with the Armies operating in the South-west; how to do it completely, and thoroughly, was a secret not learned until nearly two years afterwards. The fatigues of these campaigns, owing to forced marches, were excessive, and the privations which the men endured in consequence of the insufficiency of supplies,

The Army of the Tennessee and the Cumberland divided.

41

so impaired the vital force of both armies that when that under Buell, then commanded by Rosecrans, rested at Murfreesboro, and that under General Grant, embarked at Memphis for Vicksburg, symptoms of a disease which, all experience has proved, affects more seriously the strength of an army than the casualties of the battle-field, began to prevail to an alarming extent.

This disease was the SCURVY, the natural and inevitable fruit of the conditions in which both of these Symptoms of Armies had been placed. The Medical and Scurvy appear. Hygienic history of Armies had led us to expect that, sooner or later, our Army would suffer from the effect of this malady, but it had also taught us that it was possible to guard almost wholly against the danger to be apprehended from it. This was just one of those conditions which the Commission had anticipated from the beginning, and its whole theory of action was based, as we have seen, upon the practicability of counteracting the wide-spread evils which would be developed by its unchecked prevalence. Faithful to its convictions, it had constantly endeavored to persuade the Government to adopt in time precautionary measures against diseases which, experience had proved, might be averted by such measures. Whatever else was omitted, this duty was never neglected. Every part of its relief system, vast as it was in its proportions and beneficent as it was in its results, was subordinate in its estimation to the necessity and value of these preventive measures. Thus during the first summer of the war, it had urged the adoption of true sanitary measures, including a provision of suitable food, as indispensable for preserving the new recruits from those forms of dysenteric disease which a novel and coarse kind of food eaten in a malarious region, would be certain to produce. Thus, previous to the campaign in the, Peninsula it was foreseen that long and exhausting marches in a country filled with swamps, where the water was impure, and where even an occasional supply of vegetables was not to be had, would produce that type of disease which afterwards, under the name of the Chickahominy fever, proved so unmanageable and so fatal to the troops. The recommendation by the Commission of such measures as it deemed essential to forestall the threatened evils of these campaigns was in a great measure unheeded, and it was left to deplore the sad results which it had been unable to prevent. In the West, however, in the beginning of the year 1863, there was opened before it a field for the employment of preventive measures on a grand scale, into which there was much encouragement to enter and labor.

The first appearance of the symptoms of scurvy in the Armies of the Tennessee and the Cumberland, roused the officers of the Commission to strenuous efforts to check it at the outset. Measures taken to check its progress. Their early call upon the farmers of the North-west for a supply of vegetables which alone could stop its progress and finally eradicate its poison, the wonderful alacrity with which these articles were contributed to the depôts of the Commission and sent to the " front," the extraordinary results which followed their use, the peculiar honor and gratitude which are due to this life-saving work in the absence of any suitable provision made by the Government to meet the emergency, all go to make up one of the most brilliant and instructive chapters, not only in the Commission's history, but in that of voluntary benevolent effort at any time.

The Army of the Cumberland under General Rosecrans after a vigorous campaign in Northern Mississippi and Southern Tennessee had marched to Murfreesboro, where on New Year's day, 1863, it fought the ever memorable battle of Stone River. This battle cost us eight thousand wounded men whose wants, and indeed those of the entire Army, were to be supplied by railroad transportation always difficult, and often precarious, from Louisville to the battle-field. Shortly after the battle the Army went into winter quarters, and then began to be observed the result of the terrible privations of the preceding campaign. Its discipline was excellent, and all accounts agree in saying that its condition, so far as it depended on the observance of such sanitary measures as were possible with its limited supplies, has never been surpassed by that of any Army during the war. But notwithstanding all this, the scorbutic taint was there, the seed of the poison had not germinated during the excitement of the march and the battle, but a short period of inactivity served to develope it in all its virulence, and the only means of checking its ravages, a supply of fresh vegetables, was not at hand, and it seemed impossible to procure them.

In order to show how well founded was the alarm of those who observed the appearance of the first symptoms of this disease in the Army, and what dangers were likely to arise from its

Condition of the Army of the Cumberland after the battle of Stone River.

The nature of scurvy.

continued spread and prevalence, it may be worth
while to state, in a few words, what scurvy is. " It is
then a chronic blood disease. Its essential characteristic is a decided and peculiar change in the constituents of the blood, in which the amount of water and
fibrin are greatly augmented, whilst there is a corresponding diminution in the number of blood-corpuscles,
in the amount of albumen, and in the quantity of lime,
iron and potash, in healthy blood. This blood-degenera-
tion is the consequence of defective nutrition ; and the in-
dication of cure is to furnish in available form for use
those elements in which the diseased blood is deficient.
Change of habit and surroundings, proper and increased attention to the conditions of health, effect
much—but a change in the diet is the great desideratum.
In fact, vegetables and their products, are the *medicines*
upon which the surgeon mainly relies in his treatment
of this disease."

The Government officers having ascertained beyond
question the existence and probable spread of this
fearful disease, at once gave public notice Efforts of the
that they were desirous of purchasing for officers to procure vegetables.
the use of the Army, fifty thousand bushels of potatoes
and a corresponding quantity of other vegetables.
Strange to say, their appeal met with no response, and
no proposals for a supply were made. Whether this
was due to a real scarcity of the articles asked for, or
to a fear of the result of a rigid government inspection, or to difficulties of transportation, we cannot say.
The fact is unquestionable that no one chose to become
responsible for the delivery to the Government, on any
terms, of the large amount of vegetables required.

The Medical Officers therefore of General Rosecrans' army, who had a most enlightened appreciation of the urgency of the want, found to their dismay, that no aid could reach them through Government channels.

It is a curious fact, as illustrating what false conclusions may be drawn from a reliance upon the operations of the ordinary routine machinery of an Army, that, during all this time, not only the Commander-in-chief of the army but the Corps commanders also, supposed that the soldiers were supplied with vegetables. The books of the Commissary General showed an issue of a hundred barrels daily, and the inference, of course, was that they were consumed by the soldiers. It appeared, on examination, however, that one-fourth in amount of· this issue went to the staff officers and their families at Head-Quarters, and that, of the remaining three-fourths, the Commissaries of the various Corps, Divisions and Brigades obtained the larger portion, so that the Regimental Commissaries who supplied the wants of the private soldiers were left almost wholly unprovided. An investigation by the Medical Inspector of the Army revealed the extraordinary fact that, although this very liberal daily distribution was shown by the books of the Commissary General, still the soldiers had not received, on an average, from the Government, more than three rations of vegetables, during the twelve months ending on the first of April, 1863. The injustice of this arrangement was so glaring, and the danger to the health of the troops from its continuance so imminent, that the Inspector suggested in his official

Vegetables issued to the officers but not to private soldiers.

report to the Commanding General, as the only remedy, that the private soldier should receive the first distribution, and that officers and their families should then be permitted to take what remained. This suggestion was never fully carried out, and the need of the soldier continued to increase.*

In this condition of things, the Medical Inspector on duty with that Army, Colonel Frank Hamilton, applied to Dr. Newberry, the Western Sec-retary of the Commission for assistance. He was informed by that officer that the subject had already been brought to his at-tention by Dr. Read, the faithful and intelligent chief of the Commission's service in the Army of the Cumberland, and that, in accordance with his request, shipments of vegetables had already been made from Louisville to the Army, and would be continued as long as occasion called for them. Dr. Newberry telegraphed, at once, to the depôts of the Commission at Cincinnati, Cleveland, Chicago, and Pittsburg, and, within one month, fifteen thousand bushels of vegetables were gathered from a portion of the country in which the Government had been unable to obtain any by purchase, and were sent forward to the Army. Thus an impending disaster was averted, and the claim of the Commission, to be the grand medium of communication between the homes of the country and the suffering of the Army, received a new and most striking vindication. Perhaps a more remarkable illustration, both of the need of supplemental voluntary aid in the

Application of the Medical Authorities to the Commission for aid—Shipment of vegetables.

* See Treatise on Military Surgery and Hygiene by Frank H. Hamilton, M. D. late Medical Inspector, U. S. A.

care of an Army and the practicability of doing by proper organization on a large scale, what the Government by its utmost efforts, through its ordinary agencies, had failed to do, was not afforded during the progress of the war. General Rosecrans, so far from hesitating to accept the invaluable aid tendered to him in this irregular and extra-official way, facilitated, in every manner, the transportation of these gifts of the people, to his Army. He ordered his Superintendent of railroads to transport without delay such vegetables as the Agents of the Sanitary Commission might desire to send. In a very few days after the first requisition had been made, a shipment of a hundred and twenty-five barrels of potatoes, which had been contributed by the Commission's branch at Pittsburg, reached the Army at Murfreesboro and were at once distributed to the Hospitals. Writing on the 16th of April, Mr. M. C. Read, the Commission's Inspector, says,

" You can say unhesitatingly to the donors at Pittsburg that, by this one shipment, setting aside all questions of humanity, they have done more to increase the efficient fighting strength of the Army than they would have done by securing a full regiment of new recruits. Let the supplies continue to come in as they have come for the last few days, and the scurvy, which has begun to show itself in very many of the regiments, will quickly disappear, and regiments of sturdy, stalwart men will be saved to the service at a very small part of the cost of recruiting untried men to fill their places."

To each Field Hospital, as the supplies came in more abundantly, eight barrels of potatoes, *per diem.*

were furnished, besides such a supply of Farmers of the West called upon for contributions—Results. other vegetables, pickles, sauer-kraut, etc., as the varying amount of stock on hand would permit. The other Hospitals and the Regiments in camp also received their due proportion of these invaluable anti-scorbutics. The result which was anticipated did not fail soon to manifest itself. Writing on the 8th of June, the same faithful Inspector says, "The external manifestations of scurvy have nearly all disappeared. The supply of vegetables distributed has greatly improved the health and efficiency of this Army. No greater amount of good was ever accomplished in so short a time, and at an expense comparatively so slight." The shipment of these articles was kept up during the whole summer, and their distribution was attended with increasing beneficial results. Every means was taken to keep alive public attention and sympathy throughout the West concerning this great want of the Army. Every farmer was called upon by circulars and appeals in the newspapers to send forward his surplus stock for the use of the soldier, and even children were asked to cultivate a portion of their gardens with special reference to a constant demand for this particular purpose.

"While laboring to supply vegetables for the immediate wants of the Army of the Cumberland in the early Spring, it was understood Hospital Gardens. that the supply from the North would in a few months fail, and that in the last months of summer the sick in that Department would be unsupplied, unless vegetables should be raised within it for their use. In the whole region occupied

42

by the Army, the country was almost a desert, and no dependence could be placed upon purchasing supplies of citizens. Vegetables could not be bought, they must be *raised*. Reliance, then, could only be placed upon *hospital gardens*, and to secure these, the cordial co-operation of the medical and military authorities with the Commission was essential. This was readily secured, and the work was commenced in the neighborhood of· the General Field Hospital, at Murfreesboro. This Hospital was situated under the guns of the fortifications, and in the neck of a peninsula formed by Stone River : the peninsula comprising some thirty-five acres of excellent land, well adapted to the growth of garden vegetables. This was immediately put under cultivation, protected from the intrusion of vagrant animals, and was soon wholly occupied by growing crops ; as was also some ten or fifteen acres subsequently enclosed on the opposite side of the river. The Sanitary Commission furnished seeds and garden tools, and about thirty thousand plants, purchased in Louisville and Cincinnati; and its agents exercised a general supervision over the work. The labor was performed by contrabands and convalescents, under the superintendence of a practical gardener. The ladies of the Soldiers' Aid Society, of Northern Ohio, sent forward a fine supply of flowering plants and seeds, to aid in ornamenting the hospital grounds ; and in all respects the garden was soon a complete success. The convalescents derived substantial benefits from the healthful exercise secured, and soon enjoyed an abundant supply of beets, onions, carrots, turnips, tomatoes, Irish and sweet potatoes, cabbages, peas, beans, sweet corn, melons, squashes, cucumbers, and all the other ordinary products of a vegetable garden."

A similar work was accomplished at Nashville, and these two gardens furnished a *full supply* of vegetables for the hospitals of the department during that part of the season in which they could not be supplied from the North. Mr. M. C. Read, writing from Murfreesboro on June 5th, says: " I visited the Field Hospital and garden yesterday. The garden is in good condition. The patients *all* have onions from it three times a week now, and yesterday all had green peas."

The wonderful success of this experiment of establishing gardens for the use of the Hospitals at Nashville and Murfreesboro led the Commission later in the war, to provide fresh vegetables for the troops, by the same means at Chattanooga, Knoxville and Newberne in North Carolina. These gardens became a peculiar and distinguishing feature of Army life in those remote and wasted districts, and thus by constant labor readily supplied by the Military Authorities, and with a favoring climate, abundant and wholesome food was provided, not only for the sick, but for those also who needed a properly varied diet to maintain them in vigorous health and activity.

Towards the close of the year 1862, the army of the Tennessee under General Grant, entered upon a campaign, the objective point of which was Movements of the capture of Vicksburg. At Memphis, General Grant's army. the troops were embarked on transports, and were sent down the river to a point in the neighborhood of

Vicksburg.   After an unsuccessful assault of the works
at that place they were forced to lead a life, for several
months, in a condition exceedingly unfavorable to the
preservation of their health and vigor.   During that
period, General Grant made no less than five unsuccessful attempts to place his Army in the rear of
Vicksburg.   That portion of the troops engaged in
these expeditions suffered terrible hardships.   They
were forced to make their way through rivers and
swamps and *bayous*, where the country was a wild and
tangled thicket, and where the navigation was impeded
by overhanging and interlacing trees, which often
locked and wedged in the boats.   The severest labor
was required to clear away the obstacles which hindered
the progress of these expeditions, and all the efforts
of the Army were, at last, rendered unavailing by the
characteristic tactics of the rebels, who, striking at its
rear, endeavored to block the way to its return.
Crowded on ill-arranged and worse-ventilated steamers, surrounded by an atmosphere filled with miasmatic poison, the depressing effect of the defeat before
Vicksburg, and the ill success of these expeditions
produced, as was natural, a gradual decay of that
spirit and energy which had hitherto characterized
the conquering army of the Tennessee.   The long delay necessary to perfect the plans which, carried out
afterwards, resulted in the glorious termination of the
campaign by the capture of Vicksburg, thus affected
seriously the moral as well as the physical condition
of the men.   But all felt that the interests at stake
were too vast to be abandoned until every possible
effort had been made to secure the prize and with per-

fect reliance on the indomitable will and fertile resources of its great Commander, the Army waited
patiently until he should lead it to victory.

During these dreary months, the Commission felt
that the troops were in peculiar need of a certain class
of supplies, which, if freely distributed, Work of the
Commission in
would materially assist in restoring their that Army. Co-
strength, impaired by a combination of operation of
General Grant.
unfavorable circumstances by which they were surrounded. Dr. Newberry, its Western Secretary, was
indefatigable in his efforts to send forward, from
Louisville, upon steamers chartered by him for that
purpose, the stores which had been accumulated there,
contributed by the people of the Western States for
the relief of their brethren struggling for the control of
their great river. In this way he succeeded in transporting, from January to July, 1863, to the army before Vicksburg, nearly fifteen thousand packages.
The extent of the amelioration of the condition of that
army, by these timely supplies, can only be estimated
by considering the influence on despondent, dispirited,
and ill-provided men, of gifts which not only relieved
their bodily wants, but had the powerful additional
effect of testifying to the constant interest and unwearied care of those at home. In this good work
the Commission was cordially encouraged and assisted
by General Grant, whose humane consideration for the
troops under his command has always been only less
conspicuous, than the masterly ability with which he
has led them in battle. By an order dated in March,
1863, he directed the Quartermaster to turn over to
the Commission a suitable steamboat to be called the

"United States Sanitary Storeboat," which should be used exclusively by it for the conveyance to the Army of such articles as would be calculated to prevent disease. He directed also, with a genuine appreciation of the true spirit of the Commission, that no goods should be transported on this steamer unless they were intended for the use of all the soldiers, without any distinction except such as was founded on their relative needs. By an unusual and exceptional order, he directed that the Sanitary Commission of all the Agencies employed in Army relief, should alone be provided with free transportation, thus clearly indicating not merely his approval of its methods, but also his conviction that it was fully able to meet the needs of the suffering. He thus showed a wise foresight in preparing his men for the severe and exhausting campaign in which he proposed to lead them; and there can be little doubt that the extraordinary vigor and success which characterized the operations of the Army during the five weeks in which it was cut loose from its base of supplies, and its transportation of stores was necessarily reduced to the *minimum* standard, was, in no small degree, attributable to the zeal he had exhibited in caring for its sanitary interests before it entered upon it.

During this campaign the Army marched through a country on the west bank of the Mississippi, rendered The Army in its almost impassable by swamp and jungle for march round Vicksburg. a distance of nearly seventy miles, then, crossing the river, they moved north by rapid marches, fought six important battles, in all of which they were victorious, and finally reached a point in the rear of

Vicksburg, whence they were able to communicate with their depôts. The number of grave cases in the Army Hospitals, as the result of these brilliant operations, scarcely exceeded one thousand. Well might the enthusiastic Inspector of the Commission at Vicksburg, in view of this wonderful result, declare "that its operations, in preparing that Army for that campaign, had modified history!" The gratitude of the men especially, when they had established once more communication with their base of operations by their circuit around Vicksburg was unbounded, and found expression in many letters of their officers to the Agents of the Commission. "When I told them," (the soldiers) says Chaplain Eddy, of the Thirty-third Illinois Regiment, "I had got from you ice, dried and canned fruits, lemons, spirits, shirts, drawers, slippers, sheets, bedticks, etc., etc., to make them comfortable, some of them have said, 'God bless the Commission!'— others would say 'good,' and others would use the very expressive phrase, 'bully!' I have been in the service nearly two years, and am glad to say, our sick were never so well cared for as now, and it is due to you to say, that we are indebted almost exclusively to the United States Sanitary Commission for the means of making them comfortable." Another of them, Surgeon Hill, in charge of a Division Hospital of the Twentieth Army Corps, writes,—"The battles- of Thompson's Hill, Raymond, Jackson, and Champion's Hill, more than exhausted the limited supplies of regimental surgeons, so that, had it not been for the Sanitary Commission, who met our victorious army as we arrived at Haines' Bluff, the sufferings of our wounded at the siege of Vicksburg would have been far greater than they have been. The wounded have been cheered and made contented, and many have been saved beyond all question."

The, peculiar condition, physical and moral, of the troops, after they had gone through the short but glorious campaign which terminated in the investment of Vicksburg on the land side, is well described by Dr. Warriner in a report to the Western Secretary, dated the 23d of June:

"I have been occupied for the last week with such inspections as circumstances would permit of the troops engaged in the trenches. They are all clustered in the ravines, and on the slopes of the hills descending *from* the city. A portion of the line now rests on the very slopes crested by the rebel works. The air in the ravines is most of the time still, hot and stifling. They live half buried in the ground for protection against the missiles of the enemy. The springs on the slopes and toward the summits of the hills begin to flag, and the principal dependence is now upon the water in the bottoms of the ravines. This naturally grows more and more impure from the drainage of extensive camping grounds, besides growing gradually less in quantity. In short, the surroundings of a large force thus situated, and occupied, are decidedly unsanitary. No one expects this state of things to continue many days longer, however, and, as the regiments are successively relieved from time to time, no considerable mischief has yet resulted from it. On the other hand, sickness is increasing slowly, especially

Report of Dr. Warriner.

intermittent fever and its allied ailments. This increase does not confine itself to troops in the trenches. It is doubtless in part but the consummation of effects that have been daily preparing from the commencement of the campaign. The excitement which has held the entire army up to such a key of resistance for these many weeks as to enable it to cope with both visible and invisible foes, is slightly on the decline. The men are sure of their prey. Nobody doubts for a moment the result. No one expresses discontent or discouragement. Add to this the fact that an abnormal tension of brain and nerve must of necessity exhaust itself at length, and one almost wonders that the keen edge held so long. Men obey orders now with a patient rather than exultant courage. An order to storm would change this suddenly enough, but meanwhile malaria and rather unwholesome lodgings and unwholesome water, (in many cases,) are beginning to show their legitimate effects. I could not but notice that the men in the rifle-pits and at work on the entrenchments wore a slightly jaded look, and were stimulated by their momentous and perilous labors barely enough to exercise the necessary caution for their own protection."

Immediately after the news was received of the achievements of Grant's Army, the profoundest admiration and sympathy were everywhere ex- Vast contributions of supplies for the Army after the fall of Vicksburg. pressed for these heroes, and a universal desire was manifested, throughout the West especially, to testify a grateful appreciation of their services by providing them - at once with such

43

articles of comfort as they were supposed to be most in need of.

"Pittsburg, whose Commission has from the hour of its establishment acted with great energy, forwarded five hundred barrels of potatoes, and many other choice stores, stimulants, etc.

"Cleveland, the presence of whose noble Aid Society has been felt through its generous contributions, as a benediction, on almost every field of suffering since the war began, sent four hundred packages,—and Buffalo showed her earnest and patriotic spirit in a very timely donation.

"The Cincinnati Branch fitted out a fine steamer, the Alice Dean, with seven hundred packages and a full corps of surgeons and nurses.

"The New Albany Branch sent a liberal supply by the steamer Atlantic.

"Davenport, Iowa, Quincy and Alton, Illinois, vied with each other in loading the Sanitary Steamer Dunleith, which at that time was on the upper Mississippi, having gone there to obtain a cargo of stores.

"At Louisville a public meeting was held under the auspices of the Kentucky Branch, and six thousand dollars were contributed by the citizens. The Governor of the State, through an admirable representative, J. B. Temple, Esquire, paid a beautiful tribute to the United States Sanitary Commission, and expressed his desire and purpose to make it the medium of conveying the State's contribution to the brave soldiers of the Union. The Jacob Strader, the largest and finest boat on the river, was chartered by Dr. Newberry, and most generously loaded with ice, vegetables, fruits, garments, and other things adapted to promote the welfare of the sick and wounded. Dr. Andrew was in charge of her, assisted by fifteen surgeons and attendants.

"The Chicago Branch acted with its usual promptness, and had a large contribution ready for the Strader on her arrival at Cairo."*

In reviewing the vast operations of the Commission in this Department of the Army, and in recalling the extraordinary success attending them, it is Character and services of the Commission's Agents at Vicksburg. impossible to over-estimate the value of the hearty coöperation of the Commanding General, and the facilities which were afforded by him for the full development of his plans. This was due

---

* The following table will show the nature and amount of articles issued from the Commission's depot, at or near Vicksburg, to the Army of the Tennessee during the four months ending September 1st, 1863. This, it will be remembered, does not include the supplies distributed from the commencement of the expedition until it entered upon its great campaign in May in the direction of Grand Gulf.

Groceries....................2,360 pounds.	Mattresses.....................199
Wines and Liquors........2,833 bottles.	Spices....................2,690 papers.
Butter.................. 5,839 pounds.	Comforts....................2,429
Apple Butter...................30 gallons.	Pillows....................4,357
Eggs.....................2,476 dozen.	Sheets 9,029
Pickles....................5,409 gallons.	Drawers...................13,230 pairs.
Molasses..............85 "	Farina....................2,125 pounds.
Sauer-Kraut.................1,532 "	Sago, etc....................2,022 "
Potatoes....................7,596 bush.	Bed Sacks...................1,121
Ale and Cider.............3,139 gallons.	Pillow Cases.................6,511
Ice......................... 47,367 pounds.	Shirts....................7,909
Crackers.................... 26,517 "	Dressing gowns................746
Codfish....................13,593 "	Socks....................4,218 pairs.
Corn Meal...................2,485 "	Slippers...................1,504 "
Tea......................1,589 "	Bandages......................50 bands.
Relishes....................662 bottles.	Fruit....................7,330 cans.
Lemons..................25,200	Dried Fruit..............45,205 pounds.
Hospital Furniture.......2,162 articles.	Dried Beef..................1,496 "
Fans....................4,700	Condensed Milk..........11,282 cans.
Crutches....................65 pairs.	

not only to the recognized ability of the Commission to perform the work which it had undertaken, and to the broad national principle it adopted in the distribution of the bounty of the people, but also, in a great measure, to the very remarkable zeal, capacity, and judgment of the Agents employed by it.   It is hardly possible to speak in too high terms of praise of the faithful and devoted service of these officers.   Dr. Warriner, the Chief Inspector, and his Assistants, exhibited in the highest degree qualities which are as rare as they are essential to the success of a work like this, and the truly humane spirit which animated them in their difficult and delicate task, made them, in the highest sense, exponents of the noble and generous policy which guided the Commission in all its work. In such an exhausting service, their health, of course, was imperiled and, in some cases, utterly broken. After the capture of Vicksburg, all the Agents were prostrated by disease, and it was necessary to remove them for a time from the field of their arduous labors.

The great interest in military operations in the West after the capture of Vicksburg centres in the campaigns of Chattanooga and Atlanta. The rebels had lost the Mississippi River, and despairing of any hope of regaining its control, combined all their efforts in the vain attempt to prevent the advance of the conquering National army into Georgia.   It was necessary, however, for us to retain a considerable force on points on the Mississippi and its affluents, in order to keep the navigation of those rivers free from interruption.   These points, unfortunately, were among the most unhealthy to be found along their whole course, and the recruits from the North stationed at them, sank rapidly from malarial fevers, and from diseases caused by defective nutrition. Scurvy, simple, or complicating all the diseases which attacked the men, prevailed to an alarming extent in these garrisons. The only suitable remedial means were vegetables, either fresh or pickled in vinegar, and these the Commission endeavored to supply. The steamer *Dunleith* was still in its service, and was kept plying constantly between Cairo and New Orleans. From the storehouse at Cairo she received immense cargoes of the needed articles contributed principally by the Branches in the North-west, and distributed them to the naval vessels on the Mississippi, and to the posts on that, and the White and Arkansas Rivers. In this way the hospitals at Memphis, Vicksburg, Natchez, Helena, Duval's Bluff, Little Rock, Pine Bluff, Brownsville, and Fort Smith were supplied, and whatever remained, was left in the hands of the Commission's Agents in New Orleans. This relief, small as it was relatively in point of amount, was of incalculable service to the wretched and suffering men at these remote posts, who found, that even in that desolate region, they were not forgotten by those at home, and were not beyond the reach of the Agencies they had provided for ministering to them.

CHAPTER XII.

CHATTANOOGA.

IN the latter part of the month of June, 1863, the Army of the Cumberland under General Rosecrans, The Army of the Cumberland moves southward. set out from Murfreesboro', the objective of the campaign being Chattanooga. In order to reach that point it was necessary, not only that it should defeat the large and well appointed Rebel army of General Bragg, entrenched in positions of his own choosing in the vast mountain range which guarded the approach from the North, but also that a safe line of communication with its base of supplies should be secured. If this supply question had been a difficult one, while the Army was stationary at Murfreesboro', those difficulties were increased in almost geometrical progression as it moved southward. There was but one badly constructed railroad between Murfreesboro' and Chattanooga, and from this the enemy must be dislodged, and it must then be repaired and securely held, for it was the only channel by which the supplies of the Army could reach it. The country between these two points was a continuous succession of mountain ranges, utterly barren of food for man or beast, and with no roads which would permit the passage of a large army with its supply trains. One who explored this region, after it had been made memorable by Rosecrans' great campaign, thus describes it:

342

" From near Tullahoma to Chattanooga, the whole interval is occupied with mountains of formidable height, terminating laterally in precipitous escarpements, separated by deep and narrow valleys, over which even a footman finds his way painful and perilous. In justice to those who planned and executed the military movements prior and preparatory to the late victories, I must say that our people of the Northern States have no proper appreciation of what our Army has done and suffered in reaching and holding Chattanooga, and I am sure if all could see what I have seen, of difficulties overcome, hardships endured, and privations so cheerfully suffered, there would be much less than there has been, of flippant criticism of the soldiers and Generals of the Army of the Cumberland."

As difficulties of transportation were the great difficulties of this movement—so great indeed as to threaten at one time its disastrous termination—it *materiel* of which a large army is made up. Materiel of the Army. Difficulties of transportation. In this way, perhaps, we may be able to form some adequate conception of what it requires to move it. The Army of General Rosecrans was composed of about eighty thousand effective, fighting men. Accompanying it were forty-two hundred wagons, and six hundred ambulances. There were twenty-two thousand artillery horses, three thousand private horses, and thirty-six thousand mules, in all sixty-one thousand animals, requiring, of course, for their subsistence immense supplies of food. If the Army had been stretched out in line, four abreast, with the usual distance of six feet between the ranks, that line would have been nearly twenty-four miles long; the wagons with their teams would have extended forty-seven miles, and the artillery and the ambulances with their horses would have reached nearly five miles further. This calculation makes no allowance for the cavalry, of which there was a large force with the Army. From this statement it will be seen that the daily consumption of food by the men, the horses, and the mules, must have been enormous. Nearly every pound of this food was brought from Louisville, a distance of nearly three hundred miles, and as the stock carried in the wagons of the Army could suffice for a few days' consumption only, it was necessary to keep up a continuous stream of supply from the depôts at the base to the Army in the field. Besides all this, the ordnance stores, necessary to maintain the Army in condition for constant and effective service, were necessarily very large, and their transportation required means of corresponding magnitude. So vast, indeed, was the amount of supplies of all kinds needed for the use of the Army, and so many were the difficulties surrounding an attempt to transport them in the enemy's country, that it became a serious question with those upon whom the responsibility of this service rested, whether it would be possible in the face of such obstacles to carry out the plans of the campaign. It is well known that the Rebel Authorities relied far more upon difficulties like these as a means of preventing a permanent occupation of their territory, than upon the chances of victory in battle. It is well to recall the embarrassments which beset every step of the progress of Rosecrans' Army towards Chattanooga, not merely to excite admiration for the energy, skill and perseverance by which they were overcome, but also to explain why, necessarily, during that campaign there must have been great suffering among those who needed for their sustenance anything beyond what are called " fighting rations."

The Medical Authorities took with them on the march a limited supply of articles for the sick but where the question was soon likely to Embarrassment of the Medical Officers. be how to avoid actual starvation, of course, no space could be given up for any reserve or surplus provision. All the dangers of the campaign likely to arise from the interruption of the line of communication with the Army had been fully considered and carefully guarded against, as far as possible by the Officers of the Quartermaster's Department, whose services in this, as in so many campaigns of the war, insured its success, yet after all the precautions had been taken, it was felt that the movement was on every account, one of singular peril. The failure of the campaign of General Buell in this mountain region the year before, owing mainly to the impossibility of getting forward supplies, and the straitened condition of this very Army of Rosecrans from the same cause after it reached Chattanooga, fully justified the fears of those who were deeply impressed with the danger of conducting military operations in regions far remote from supply depôts.

Such was the prospect of the Army of the Cumberland when it marched from Murfreesboro'. Bragg, who was strongly intrenched in the defiles behind Opening of the campaign. Duck Creek, awaited the assault, but Rose-

44

crans completely turned his position, and after a short fight at Shelbyville, in which the Union loss was very light, the Rebels retreated to Tullahoma. This place they soon abandoned and moved to Bridgeport, in Alabama, destroying, in their retreat, the railroad which connected these two places. Rosecrans, after being delayed nearly six weeks in repairing the road, indispensable as his line of supply, followed the enemy, who he found, had given up Bridgeport, and had concentrated at Chattanooga. Still following across the mountains, he found Chattanooga abandoned, and Bragg's Army in close proximity at Chickamauga. Here on the 19th of September Rosecrans assaulted him. In the battle which ensued a portion of the Union forces was broken and driven in confusion, and although General Thomas, with the remainder, well sustained his high reputation, and held his position at the close of the battle, yet it was deemed advisable to withdraw him the next day, and to concentrate the Army at Chattanooga. As soon as this was accomplished, the Rebels took possession of the heights of Lookout Mountain, opposite the town. This, of course, gave them control of the railroad to Bridgeport, and uncovered entirely Rosecrans' line of communication with his supplies at that place. Meanwhile, the enemy sent a cavalry force across the Tennessee River, above Chattanooga and destroyed an immense supply train, including seventeen wagons loaded with articles belonging to the Sanitary Commission, which was moving down the Sequatchie Valley to join the Army. The railroad between Stevenson and Nashville was also broken up temporarily by the enemy's raids, and thus an additional obstacle was placed in the way of the transportion of supplies.

It seems necessary to give the details of these operations in order to show how completely, by the course of events, the army of the Cumberland be- *Limited supplies* came blockaded at Chattanooga, and how *after the battle of Chickamauga.* limited, in such a condition of things, must necessarily have been its means of relieving the ten thousand wounded men who claimed its care after the battle of Chickamauga. For one month, and until the enemy were driven by the forces under General Hooker and General W. F. Smith from those positions on Lookout Mountain, which commanded the river and the railroad, the Army was forced to subsist on the rations which had been brought forward by that portion of the supply train which accompanied its march, and which were intended for a campaign of a few days only. Half and quarter rations only were issued to the troops. Ten thousand horses and mules died of starvation; the distress was extreme, and just before deliverance came, the danger of famine grew so imminent that it was thought necessary to make preparation for the retreat of the Army. In this untoward state of events it may be supposed that the Medical Department labored under the most embarrassing difficulties in the treatment of the sick and wounded. A portion of the Sanitary supply-train, composed of seven wagons loaded with condensed milk, beef stock, rags, bandages, and Hospital clothing reached Chattanooga with the first Army train which arrived there. Three wagons were afterwards got through with great difficulty. A store-house was at once procured, and arrangements made for the distribution of the stores in anticipation of the battle of Chickamauga. How opportune this distribution was, and how faithfully the Commission's agents labored in this hard service, is best told in the language of one of the best and most zealous of them:—"Not a great many wounded were sent back on Saturday, but on Sunday they came in in numbers, far beyond the ability of all the medical officers to provide even tolerably for their comfort. At the request of the Medical Director, Dr. Barnum took possesion of two large stores, cleared out the rooms, fitted them up temporarily for the wounded, supplying them with clothing, bandages, and edibles from our rooms, procured and put up stores, dressed the wounds of those most requiring immediate assistance, and superintended the providing and cooking of rations for the men. All of the rooms were soon filled, and by his untiring efforts from fifteen hundred to two thousand were rendered tolerably comfortable. On Sunday, I visited all the hospitals and temporary resting-places for the wounded, notifying the officers in charge of the location of our rooms and the nature of our supplies, asking them to send for everything we had, so far as it was needed. Returning late in the evening, I found a large church on Main street where services had been held during the day, and saw that the steps were crowded with wounded men. Entering the church, it was found filled with a congregation from the battle-field, crippled with every variety of wounds, with no medical or other officer in charge, without food of any kind, without water, and without even a candle to shed a glimmering light over their destitution, silent worshippers in the darkness, patient unmurmuring martyrs in a noble cause, apparently deserted by all except Him in whose sanctuary they had taken refuge. I immediately carried concentrated beef to the residence of Dr. Simms, near the church, a resident physician of rebel sympathies, but a generous, warm-hearted man, in whose office we had some days before found quarters, and where my brother superintended the preparation of soup, while I bought candles and a box of hard bread, had them carried to the church, and procuring water, distributed it to the thirsty. Never before had I so high an appreciation of ' nature's sweet restorer, balmy sleep.'"

These ten wagon loads of supplies constituted almost the entire dependence of the Hospitals until the Tuesday and Wednesday succeeding the battle, when Aid afforded by the train containing a portion of the Medi- the Commission. cal Purveyor's stores reached "the front." Immediate measures were taken to secure the transportation of a further supply from the Commission's depôt at Stevenson, and, after the most strenuous exertions, seventeen wagons were loaded and despatched from that place. These were the wagons which were afterwards captured and burned by the enemy in the Sequatchie Valley. The difficulties of forwarding supplies are thus described by the Chief of the Commission's service at Chattanooga: " By the destruction of the bridge at Bridgeport, and the occupation of Lookout Mountain by the rebels, we were deprived of railroad communication with Chattanooga on the one hand, and on the other were cut off from the best route for wagon transportation. Two wagon roads over the Mountain on the

North side of the Tennessee River, which would elsewhere and under other circumstances be considered almost impassable, furnish the only available routes for the transportation of the *materiel* of war, the subsistence of troops, etc. This has very much impeded the work of the Commission in connection with the movements of the Army beyond Bridgeport. Notwithstanding that every effort possible has been made at both ends of the route, the amount of transportation available for our purposes, has been far short of the demand upon our stores, and of our ability otherwise to meet these demands. On the 17th ult., as already mentioned, seven wagon-loads, on the 23d three wagon-loads, and on the 26th one wagon-load, and on the 29th fifteen ambulance-loads of stores were all that could be got forward to the 'front' during the month of September."

In order to provide for the necessities of the wounded on their weary journey over the mountains from Chattanooga to Stevenson, the Commission esta-

Feeding station established.

blished a Lodge and Feeding Station on the route of the ambulances midway between the two places. The privations and sufferings of those on the two trains which had already gone over that dreaded passage, had convinced every one of the necessity of the Lodge. It was expected that each ambulance train should so arrange its movements as to stop at that point, where there was an abundance of wood and water, and of wholesome, palatable food, and of kind attention, and where a good night's rest was provided when needed. This establishment proved literally a " Lodge in a vast wilderness" to multitudes of sufferers, who had been racked and exhausted while journeying in their wounded condition over the rough roads across the mountains.

But the struggle for the possession of Chattanooga was not yet over. In order to hold securely and permanently this great mountain citadel it was necessary to drive away from the neighbor- The battle of Chattanooga. hood the rebels, who, fully sensible of the value of the prize, determined to make us pay dearly for its coveted possession. The Army being largely reinforced, with General Grant at its head, and supplies arriving regularly, and with some degree of abundance, it was determined to make a grand effort to decide once and forever, who should hold the key of the great avenue of communication between the eastern and western portion of the enemy's territory. Accordingly, on the 22d of November, our forces advanced, General Hooker's to the assault of Lookout Mountain, and General Sherman's to that of Mission Ridge. Both the assaults were successful, and if the battle was one of the most glorious for the Union forces which occurred during the war, the defeat to the Rebels was, with the exception of the utter breaking up of Lee's Army, the most disastrous ever suffered by them. The battle was fought close by the intrenchments of Chattanooga, and within easy distance of well-arranged Hospitals. Every provision for the removal and care of the wounded had been made by the Medical Authorities. There was little, therefore, for the Commission to do, but that little was well done under the eye of the Western Secretary himself, who happened to be present.

After this great victory was achieved, the combined Army, under General Grant, remained in a condition Condition of the of comparative repose during the winter of Army during 1863–4. The Army of the Cumberland the winter of 1863-4. which had first occupied Chattanooga was reinforced, as we have seen, by the heroes of Vicksburg under General Sherman, and by a portion of those of Gettysburg, each of these immortal and decisive battle-fields, sending thus its representative in long tried and disciplined veterans to take part in that great campaign which was to terminate the struggle. The number of men thus concentrated at this remote point was, of course, much greater than it had been when it was found so difficult to supply the Army of General Rosecrans alone, and corresponding exertions were made by the Officers of the Quartermaster's Department to provide for the increased demand for food and clothing. There was, of course, less liability to interruption of the line of communication from the enemy's raids than there had been previous to the victory, but still the labor required to supply the Army regularly was immense, and may be estimated from the fact that no less than three thousand railroad cars were constantly employed in transporting from Louisville to Nashville what was absolutely necessary to its existence.

The physical condition of the Army was at that time in many respects peculiar, differing wholly from that Change in the of any large force which had entered upon a physical condition of the men. campaign during the war, and the supplies needed to maintain it in strength and vigor, and to prepare it for the coming conflict, were therefore of a somewhat different nature from those that had been found hitherto essential. There were few raw men in this Army. Most of them were hardy campaigners, inured to the toils and privations of a soldier's life, habituated to discipline, and accustomed to take care of themselves. The element of physical weakness which had existed in it, as in all newly raised Armies, had been rapidly developed by the extraordinary exposure and labor which it had been called upon to undergo, and disease and death, while they had thinned its ranks, had probably contributed to its real efficiency. The men composing it had all the vigor of veteran troops. From long habit they could be relied upon not merely for steadiness in battle, but they showed also toughness and powers of endurance on the march, passing unharmed through all the dangers attendant upon changes of climate, and insufficient food and shelter. The wants, therefore, of such a body of troops were likely to be very different from those of new recruits. Experience had also perfected many of the details of the Army organization which had been wretchedly mismanaged at the outset. This improved condition of things, as it affected the wants of the Army and the means at the disposal of the Government for supplying them, had been carefully observed by the Agents of the Commission, and was their guide in determining the amount and character of the articles issued by them. Nowhere can we find a more truthful and striking picture of the condition of the Army at that time than that drawn by one of these Agents, Mr. M. C. Read, whose opportunities for observation were only equalled by the zeal and fidelity which he exhibited in his efforts to improve them. Writing in June, 1864, he says: "Our brave soldiers in Chattanooga have exhibited the highest type of heroism. Inadequately clothed, many without blankets, with leaking tents or none at all, on half or quarter rations of the coarsest articles of army diet alone, their pitiful allowance of hard-tack, frequently wet and mouldy, gathering from the streets the scattered grains of corn to parch, and thus eke out their scanty allowance, encamped in a sea of mud, exposed to the constant fall rains, without fire, their encampment a daily target for the enemy's shells—their confidence in their cause and in their commander was unshaken, and the determination to endure this and more as long as it might be necessary, was universal. In riding through the camps complaints and murmuring were unheard, and I doubt not had the vote of the soldiers been taken in the most untoward circumstances, the decision would have been nearly or quite unanimous to die in Chattanooga rather than abandon it.

"After the battles of Chattanooga, the want of all means of transportation rendered another period of repose inevitable for that part of the Army which was confronting the rebel General Johnson. An effort was made to vary the hard fare of the soldiers by the addition of potatoes, pickles, onions, krout, etc. Never before in this department were so large amounts of these articles distributed by our Commission. They were made to reach the entire Army. Larger quantities than are ordinarily issued were forwarded to the Commission, and now when active operations are resumed, and our hospitals are again crowded with wounded, a marked change in the physical condition of the men is apparent. Patients are rapidly recovering from wounds here, who wounded in like manner in the battles of November would have certainly died."

The great enemy in the form of disease, against which the Commission struggled most persistently and most successfully in this Army, was Prevalent types that which exhibited itself in scurvy and of disease. chronic diarrhœa, diseases depending, as it is unnecessary to repeat, almost wholly upon the character of the food furnished to the troops. To combat this enemy successfully the greatest exertions were made, and there were distributed from the single depôt at Nashville during the month of January, 1864, three thousand four hundred and twenty-three bushels of potatoes, one hundred and fifty-seven bushels of onions, eight thousand seven hundred and forty-two gallons of sauerkraut, one thousand nine hundred and sixty-nine gallons of pickles, thirteen thousand six hundred and sixty-two pounds of dried fruit, etc., all antiscorbutics. During the succeeding months a large supply of vegetables, the produce of the Hospital gardens, which, with a wise prevision of coming events, the Commission had established at Chattanooga, aided very materially, improving the diet of the Army.*

* *Summary of Issues from the Hospital Garden of the United States Sanitary Commission, at Chattanooga, April 15th to November 14th,* 1864:

Lettuce, bushels, 1,289; beets, bushels, 1,563; onions, bushels, 1,407; mustard, bushels, 1,496; Irish potatoes, bushels, 904¾; radishes, bushels, 715; peas, bushels, 442; snap beans, bushels, 431; lima beans, bushels, 148; tomatoes, bushels, 1,269; sweet potatoes, bushels, 384; spinach, bushels, 133; turnips and winter radishes, bushels, 7½; cucumbers, doz., 2,693; summer squashes, 5,526; cabbage, heads, 10,761; table corn, ears, 107,562; okra, dozens, 177; peppers, dozens, 958; melons, 1,668; winter squash, 312; pumpkins, 1,152; flower seeds, papers, 5,779: estimated value at Chattanooga, $66,375 70.

During the campaign in Tennessee, the condition of the beleagured forces of General Burnside at Knox-
Relief to the ville had not escaped the anxious attention garrison at Knoxville. of the Western Secretary. Communication with his Army was, for a long time, simply impossible. Watching the very first opportunity, a train of wagons was despatched, *via* Cumberland Gap, laden with Sanitary stores, and after meeting incredible difficulties, caused by the condition of the roads, it reached Knoxville in safety, where the heroic garrison was found destitute of almost everything in the way of clothing and hospital supplies, The siege, however, was soon afterwards terminated by the events at Chattanooga. With General Sherman's army, which was sent to General Burnside's succor, the Commission despatched a considerable stock, its officers being ignorant, at the time, that the stores sent to Knoxville by the northern route had already reached there. A Hospital garden was soon after established at Knoxville by the Commission, and although it was not so large as those at some other places, its products were of incalculable benefit to the troops stationed at that point.

This systematic relief of the wants of the Armies engaged in active campaigns did not cause the Com-
Care of troops in mission to neglect those of the large force in garrisons in the rear of the their rear who were guarding their commu-
Army. nications, or the care of those of the sick and wounded, who were transported to Hospitals more convenient to the base of supplies. Each of the Commission's Agencies from Chattanooga to Louisville, Kelly's Ferry, Bridgeport, Stevenson, Murfreesboro', and Nashville became centres of activity, affording

relief to the sick and wounded soldier. So also in the camps and Hospitals out of the direct line of communication with the main Armies in Western Tennessee, and South-eastern Kentucky, its Agents were found investigating the needs of the troops, and distributing the people's gifts in order to relieve them. This relief was afforded at points near the Army, and on the route leading to it, by Feeding Stations, as they were called, and in the vast Hospitals at Chattanooga, Murfreesboro', Nashville, and Louisville, by means of Hospital visitors, who combined something of the functions of Inspectors, with personal ministrations to the special wants of individual soldiers. When it is remembered how vast the Army under General Grant became by successive reinforcements, it will be readily perceived, that the number who were disabled by the casualties of the campaign it had gone through, must have been proportionably great.

There were three successive stages of suffering through which each of these men was forced to pass before it was possible that he should reach that Three-fold nature of the relief condition where there was a fair chance of his afforded. recovery and return to the Army. In each of these the Commission was prepared to do its share in mitigating the inevitable misery caused by the war. In the first place, it was necessary that the sick or wounded man should be transported from the Field or Regimental Hospital to a more permanent establishment called a General Hospital, often hundreds of miles from the point where he had first become disabled. The arrangements made by the Commission for the merciful care of the maimed and suffering soldier, during his journey, by means of Hospital cars, have been already described. It would be difficult to Hospital Cars. over-estimate the comfort and relief which were afforded to these men by this improved system of transportation. No one can read the account of the aid that was given, and the suffering that was prevented by this means, without a feeling of justifiable pride that this great contribution to the general cause of humanity in military operations was purely an American contrivance, and that its invention, as well as its general adoption in the Army, were due to the persistent efforts of a member of the Sanitary Commission.

It was, of course, impossible to transport all, whom it was thought best to remove, by this means. The number of cars was limited, and their well appointed arrangements were reserved for the accommodation of the worst cases only. The great mass of helpless men was placed in common freight cars where they suffered, of course, not only positive discomfort, but often terrible agony. In order to meet their wants as far as possible, the Commission established stations Feeding sta- along the route, where its Agents met the tions. trains upon their arrival, and, were ready with coffee, soup, sandwiches, stimulants and such other articles as would be likely to revive the strength, and to keep up the courage of hungry and exhausted men. It is not too much to say that no one who had lost his health, or who had been wounded in his country's service, was transported to the rear of the Army of General Grant, without meeting these good Samaritans, always ready to pour oil and wine into his wounds, and to cheer him on his way. Thus, the disabled soldier passed through the second stage of his weary journey. When he reached, at last, the General Hospital where he was to remain until he recovered or died, the Commission did not lose sight of him. The larger number of the invalids from Grant's Army were received into the Hospitals at Nashville, nearly one hundred thousand men having passed through them, in one period of six months, during the war. The Commission employed at this point, as well as at others, men of kindly nature and self-denying zeal, who were engaged as Hospital visitors in ministering to the peculiar necessities of the patients. Hospital Visitors. Their duties were multiform as may be supposed, for they were obliged to listen to the complaints of many sick men, and to strive to remedy them when remedy was possible. They were brought thus into contact with the individual sufferer, ascertained his wants, supplied him with what would add in the opinion of the Surgeon to his comfort, communicated with his friends, encouraged him by kindly aid and sympathy to bear his sufferings patiently and, in short served as a link between him and his home. Men like the Rev. Mr. Ingraham and Judge Root, who, for a long time, were the Visitors of the Commission in the Hospitals at Nashville, proved themselves, by their discretion, by their Christian example and self-denying devotion, of the greatest possible service in the administration of those establishments. Their labors improved the tone, and kept up the spirits of the patients. They were gladly welcomed by the Surgeons as their best coadjutors, and the men who had been cheered by their counsel and active sympathy always regarded them as their truest friends.

The material relief afforded by these Hospital Visitors involved a large distribution of stores, Distribution of stores in Hospitals. not, of course, of the kind required, in such large quantities, at "the front," as a means of preventing disease, but including a variety of articles in the way of delicate food and home comforts, which would tend to improve the condition of the patient, and shorten his stay at the Hospital. This distribution was no indiscriminate pouring out of the gifts which had been confided to the Commission by the people. The whole business was administered carefully and judiciously, and with the same strict adherence to rule which was characteristic of all the relief methods of the Commission. The mode in which this distribution was made, and the persons to whom the articles were issued, are thus described :

" They were placed in store-rooms as convenient as possible to the Hospitals and camps, in charge of a competent store-keeper, and were given out by him, first and principally on the written request of the surgeon in charge, who in this request stated the number for whom he desired to procure stores, and their special wants.

"Secondly. The store-keeper issued stores on the application of the ladies in charge of what was called the " light-diet kitchen" in Hospitals. Those drawn by the surgeon were, as a general rule, placed in charge of those ladies, when the hospitals were so fortunate as to have such help. These ladies cooked, and distributed them to the sick.

" Thirdly. The Stores were given to " Hospital Visitors," agents who went to Hospitals and camps, seeking out from every possible source any special cases of want, and supplying them. Such visits were made as often as possible.

" Fourthly. The store-keepers filled all orders given by State Agents, for any soldier they might find to be needy, or who applied to them for relief. They also furnished to individual soldiers, who might apply to any of the agents for relief, as soon as it could be ascertained they were really needy. Under a general order from the Secretary of the Department, they extended to the agents of the Christian Commission the same privileges as were enjoyed by our own Relief Agents, distributing to them to supply any individual cases of neglect or suffering which they might discover.

" Fifthly. They furnished goods to the " Soldiers' Homes" and to the " Hospital Trains." When application was made by the surgeons or the soldiers, for such articles as the Government had for distribution, effort was made by the Agents of the Commission to have them supplied from Government stores."

The time had now arrived when a question, somewhat novel and of great practical importance, was presented to the consideration of the Commission. The number of the patients in the Hospitals at Nashville, and at other points in the rear of the Army, was, as we have said, very great, and during the winter large and constant demands were made upon the stores of the Commission for their supply. But at the same time, one hundred thousand men were concentrated at Chattanooga, pre-

Efforts to prepare Sherman's Army for its campaign in Georgia.

paring, under Sherman, for that great campaign which was to terminate in the capture of Atlanta. It was necessary, therefore, to decide to which of these large bodies of troops the stores of the Commission should be devoted, for it was obviously impossible with its resources fully to meet the necessities of both. General Sherman had desired that the larger portion of the Commission's stock should be accumulated at Chattanooga, in anticipation of the campaign. In accordance with his wish, and after the fullest consultation with the Medical Director at Nashville, who was satisfied that under the new system adopted by the Medical Department the wants of the patients there would be well cared for by the Government, large shipments of the reserve stock at Nashville were sent to "the front." Previous to the commencement of the campaign three thousand barrels of vegetables and a large supply of condensed milk, beef, stimulants, underclothing and bandages were sent to Chattanooga, and from the beginning of May until the end of July stores were forwarded to the same place at the rate of about one hundred tons per week.

During the campaign which followed, the Field Administration Hospital service was admirably organized, of the Hospital and was administered with the greatest service during the campaign. fidelity and exactness. " Each division of the army had a large number of wagons devoted exclusively to the conveyance of hospital tents and hospital stores, besides which there was a reserve train of over forty wagons for the Army of the Cumberland. These accompanied the troops, and moved up to the places selected for the Hospitals. This was usually so near the line of battle that the wounded might be carried but a little distance, and yet be out of reach of shot and shell, where they might not be disturbed, and the surgeons and nurses might work without danger. Suitable ground having been selected, men were detailed to make the necessary preparations. The Hospitals were established in dense woods, and one set began to cut up by the roots the thick underbrush; others to make brooms of the twigs, sweep and level the ground, and remove the stones; another set to pitch the tents or build arbors where there was not likely to be sufficient canvass to cover the wounded; others to make bunks of poles for the beds. Another set picked the green leaves of the oak, the chestnut, or the pine to fill the bed-ticks, or if the ticks were not to be had, the leaves were placed on poles or on the ground. In front of the tents large piles of leaves were laid, upon which the wounded were placed before they were examined and dressed. There were three piles for each division hospital, corresponding to the brigades, and before them were three strong tables, provided with a pillow and covered with a rubber cloth—"the operating tables." Over three hundred such Hospitals were established during the campaign, so long was the line of march, and so frequent the change of position. Every one of these Hospitals was visited by the Agents of the Commission, and during the ten days before the railroad at Ackworth was reached by the Army, no less than twenty-four large wagon loads of sanitary stores were distributed close to the line of battle. It is not easy to estimate the worth of such aid at such a time.

At the Feeding Stations established in the rear of the Army for the relief of the sick and wounded *in* Work at the *transitu*, at Kingston, Resaca, and Dalton Feeding Sta- tions. more than seventeen thousand meals were furnished up to the fourteenth of July. When it is remembered that the heroes for whom this beneficent provision was made belonged to an Army which had driven back a stubborn enemy more than a hundred miles, where every inch of the ground had been hotly contested, that it had taken seventeen lines of fortifi-cations, that it had built entrenchments more than a hundred and fifty miles in length, and had carried as strong natural positions as any in the world, we are at a loss which most to admire, the grandeur of the deeds themselves, or the practical manifestation upon so vast a scale of that profound affection and gratitude of those at home, which had been inspired by their brilliant courage and conduct.

The work of the Commission, and the character of its Agents had been so long familiar to all the officers in high command in that Army, and so exactly were its place and functions defined in the ordinary routine of Army life, that it had long been recognized as a permanent Army institution, almost as essential within its own sphere, as the Departments of the Surgeon and Commissary in theirs. So far from there being in that Army any complaint Appreciation of of interference with Officers in the dis-the Commis-sion's work by charge of their duties, there was throughout, the Command-ing Officers. not only a friendly feeling towards the Commission, but one of the utmost cordiality and co-operation with its work. This manifested itself on all occasions, not only in this Army, but in all the Armies of the West, and nowhere was it more conspicuous than in the perfect spirit of appreciation shown at all times for the labors of the Commission, by General Grant. The facilities afforded for the prosecution of those labors by his order on the Mississippi before Vicksburg, have been already spoken of, and when this illustrious man commanded a district, embracing nearly the whole of the Western country, he lost no opportunity of testifying his continued confidence in the system by which the operations of the Commission were conducted. "When, for instance," says the Inspector at Nashville, "General Granger, the Post Commander, doubting his authority, refused to issue rations or fuel for the "Home;" on application to General Grant, he replied, "Of course it must be done," and gave the necessary order, relieving us from that embarrassment. Soon after, our Agents at Chattanooga wrote us, that the authorities there were desirous to do all they could for us legally, but could find no authority to issue forage for our horses. We had then but two, but we must have them, and as it was almost impossible to supply ourselves, I again resorted to General Grant, who gave an order, that in all parts of his command, forage be issued on application of the authorized agents of the Commission, approved by the Post Commander. I have sent copies of this order to Chattanooga, Knoxville, and Louisville. For the past eight months, the Commission in Nashville has not been able to obtain comfortable quarters. The city is constantly crowded to overflowing.   A suitable building was hardly to be found.   After long delay I applied to General Grant, asking for a large house, and if practicable, plain furniture.   By the assistance of Mr. Scovel, our true friend, and a good Union man, such a house was found, and General Grant promptly put us in possession ; adding to the favor, that of paying the rent.   We receive such aid with gratitude, as substantial testimonials from the General, whom the nation delights to honor, of the value of our work."

In short, throughout the whole West, the affairs of the Commission had been managed with so much discretion and wisdom, and with such manifest advantage to the suffering, that the example set by their great Commander was followed by all his subordinates, and there, at least, was reached, at last, that ideal condition of friendly and confidential relations with all the Departments of the Army, which had inspired the original conception of the Sanitary Commission, and to secure which was its constant aim during the whole period of its history.

CHAPTER XIII.

FREDERICKSBURG—GETTYSBURG—THE WILDERNESS.

AFTER the battle of Antietam, the Army of the Potomac pursued its well trodden way in pursuit of the enemy along the base, and through the passes of the Blue Mountains. Arriving Improved condition of the Army after Antietam. on the Rapidan without succeeding in bringing him to an engagement, it was determined by General Burnside to make a sudden move to his left, and by gaining possession of Fredericksburg, interpose his Army between that of the rebels and Richmond. Accordingly, in the latter part of November, the Army of the Potomac was concentrated upon the heights opposite Fredericksburg, and preparations were made to cross the river, and storm the intrenchments which commanded the town. Great hopes were entertained of the success of this movement by those who were most familiar with the condition of the army. The long delay after Antietam had been employed in perfecting its organization, and in thoroughly refitting it, while the march from the Potomac to the Rappahannock not very severe in itself, had, with troops like these, improved not only their physical condition, but had developed in them some of the best soldierly qualities,— steadiness, obedience, and patient endurance. Experience in active campaigns had taught the leaders of the Army many valuable lessons. It had become a thoroughly trained and highly efficient body of men, and, notwithstanding there existed some dissatisfaction arising from the recent change in its Commander, it was full of confidence in its ability to win the victory. In no Department of the Army was the improvement more marked than in the medical service. Dr. LETTERMAN, the Medical Director, with uncommon capacity for organizing his work, had a very high appreciation, of the nature of the duties devolving upon him, and showed great energy in insisting that all the details of the service should be thoroughly and faithfully carried out by his subordinates. The Ambulance corps, which had been organized by him, under General McClellan's order before the Army left the Peninsula, had been thoroughly instructed in its duties, and at the battle of Fredericksburg was distinguished by a zeal, devotion, and success in the peculiar work assigned to it, of which there had been no example in previous campaigns.

In anticipation of the battle, eighteen Hospitals had been established for the special care of the wounded, First battle of one for each Division of the Army, and mi-Fredericksburg. nute instructions were issued by the Medical Director for their management. The vital matter of supplies, a point on which the Government theory of doing everything for the soldier had so often broken down in practice, had not been neglected. The Medical Purveyor's stores were kept constantly replenished, and in no considerable battle of the war was so complete a system of caring for its victims so thoroughly organized. The consequence was, that when the Army

failed to carry by storm the heights beyond Fredericksburg, there was as little confusion in the arrangements for the transportation and relief of the wounded,
as there was in the retreat of the Army itself. The
orderly manner in which both of these operations were
effected, and the whole Army with its ten thousand
wounded recrossed the river, was the best proof of the
existence of a true military spirit which needed only
better direction to have achieved the most important
results. When the condition of the Army which
fought at Fredericksburg is compared with that of
the same Army at Antietam, three months before,
the contrast is very striking. The difference, indeed,
was just that which must always exist between a disciplined and therefore truly effective body of soldiers, and
an imperfectly organized Army, exhausted by forced
marches, dispirited by frequent defeats, and unprovided with adequate supplies of any kind. Although
victory was the result of the first battle, and defeat of
the other, there can be but little doubt that for all
military purposes the Army of the Potomac was a
more serviceable and efficient army when it recrossed
the Rappahannock after the battle of Fredericksburg,
than it was when Lee recrossed the Potomac after the
battle of Antietam.

The Commission's Agents, as usual, accompanied
the Army during the campaign, but their duties, in
providing supplemental aid for the Hospitals Work of the
as may be inferred from what has been said, Commission after that battle.
were lighter than they had been called on to render on
previous occasions. When the Army reached Fredericksburg, the line of its communication was changed to

47

the Potomac River, and the central office at Washington, in anticipation of the impending battle sent forward a large amount of stores, and a number of Relief Agents, under the efficient superintendence of Dr. Douglas, to reinforce those already on the ground. They arrived at Falmouth, opposite Fredericksburg, just in time to witness the retreat of the Army, and the distribution of the wounded in the different Division Hospitals. A minute inspection of these Hospitals was at once made, and it was found that they had nearly all been amply supplied by the Medical Purveyor with those means of succor first needed by wounded men.

A contingency arose, just at this time, which had not been anticipated even by the provident and vigi-

Woolen clothing provided for the men in hospitals. lant care of the Medical Director, and which, fortunately, was fully met by the resources of the Commission. It so happened that the weather during the operations before Fredericksburg was unusually cold and stormy, and one of the first wants of those who had been disabled was not merely Hospital clothing, of which there was an abundance, but warm woolen clothing, of which the supply in the stores of the Purveyor was necessarily very limited. Here was another opportunity for filling up one of those gaps which, all experience proves, will occur in the administration of the best organized Army. As the Commission stood always ready prepared for this kind of service, this fact, if none other, should be a perfect justification of its claim to be considered an invaluable auxiliary to the Army methods of relieving the suffering. The Medical Director had provided all things in abundance which his experience taught him might be necessary. Ambulances, food, stimulants, surgical and hospital appliances of all kinds were ready at hand, but he could not have anticipated a snow storm at Fredericksburg in the early part of December, and therefore he was not prepared for the kind of suffering it occasioned. No sooner was this particular want made known, than the Commission placed at the disposal of the Medical Officers of the Hospitals, 1800 blankets, 900 quilts, 5,642 woolen shirts, 4,439 pairs of woolen drawers, and 4,270 pairs of woolen stockings. It is certainly unnecessary to enlarge upon the nature of the relief afforded to the patients at such a time by these articles.

It was the wise policy of the Medical Director to convey the wounded of this battle to the general military Hospitals at Washington and Point Lookout with the least possible delay, and such was the energy with which his plans were executed, that by Christmas Day, two weeks after the battle occurred, nearly all had been removed. The men were transported by railroad to Acquia on the Potomac, and from thence to the general Hospitals in steamers. To provide for the wants of those who might reach Acquia, hungry, exhausted, or needing care, Mr. Knapp, Superintendent of the Special Relief Service, was directed to establish a Feeding and Relief station close by the landing at that point. Although the work performed by him and his assistants was absolutely nothing, when compared with that called for by the wants of the suffering at the same place after the battles of the Wilderness in the next year, still on the first night after the station was established, more than six hundred wounded men, all more or less exhausted, who had been brought down by the cars, were fed and cared for.

After the battle of Fredericksburg the Army went into winter quarters, and, owing to its improved or-
Condition of the ganization, and its nearness to its base of
Army during supplies at Washington, it needed far less
the winter of
1862-3   supplemental aid than it had done at any previous time. It was thought by the officers of the Commission, that one good result of their presence and work in the Army which had been ardently hoped for, was very observable during this winter. There seemed to be a great eagerness on the part of the officials, not merely to profess their readiness to supply all the possible legitimate wants of the soldier, but an unusual effort to provide for them in abundance from the Government stores. The Commission, with pardonable vanity perhaps, attributed this renewed zeal, in part, at least, to the example which it had set. In this opinion, it was supported by one of the highest officers of the Government, and whether the improvement was due to this cause, or to the public clamor, which the alleged neglect of the suffering after great battles had roused, or to greater familiarity with the details of the Army service, or to unusual facility in forwarding supplies from the base, certain it is that the improvement was very marked and gratifying. It is now well ascertained, that at no time was the Army of the Potomac in better health, and better cared for in every respect than during the winter in which it lay before Fredericksburg.

While the demand upon the stores of the Commission, therefore, for use in the Hospitals, was limited, there was another branch of its service in Lodge at Acquia. which the duties of its officers were constant. During the winter, a large number of soldiers passed to and from the Army, either men returning from their furloughs, or sick and disabled men, who were sent to Washington to receive their final discharge. Acquia Landing, on the Potomac, was the great rendezvous and halting place for these men, all of whom were hungry, and many exhausted, and unfit to proceed further without that sort of care for which they had no claim upon the Government. Many thousands of these men were furnished with a comfortable meal at the Commission's Rest at that place, and many others, sick and destitute, who had served faithfully, but who had been turned adrift because they could march and fight no longer, found that the American people were not less disposed to recognize their claims upon its gratitude because they had become worn out in its service.

The movement of the Army which terminated in the battle of Chancellorsville was intended to be the commencement of a long campaign, but the Battle of Chancellorsville. unexpected result of that battle caused the Army to resume, within a few days, its former position on the north bank of the Rappahannock. Previous to the march, permission had been solicited by the officers of the Commission, to accompany the Army with a large amount of supplies. This permission had, at first, been accorded, but the exigencies of the service, requiring that the transportation should be reduced to the lowest point, it was afterwards withdrawn, and the Agents were obliged to carry what they could on pack mules. The difficulties of transportation, combined with the confusion of the battle, and the unexpected retreat of the Army, caused a serious, and deplorable, but perhaps unavoidable neglect of the wounded at the battle of Chancellorsville. Little could be done to relieve their agony either by the Medical Officers, or by those who proffered supplemental aid, although nowhere were the zeal and humanity of those whose special province it was to care for the wounded, more conspicuous. The horrors of the battle-field at Chancellorsville were perhaps more fearful than those of any other battle during the war, but they were of a kind least preventible, and least capable of being mitigated by official or extra-official methods of relief. The disastrous issue of the battle forced us to abandon many of our wounded into the enemy's hands, and some of them, it is feared, met with a worse fate, dying in the burning forest, from which it was impossible to rescue them.

Once more defeated, but not disheartened, the Army of the Potomac returned to its former cantonments to prepare for a new campaign. This time the first move was made by the enemy, who, abandoning his position beyond Fredericksburg marched towards the Shenandoah Valley, with the view first, of drawing General Hooker into some unfavorable position in the range of the Blue Ridge, and then, after defeating him invading the North. The plan of this campaign, it may be said in passing, was

The Army moves northward.

based by the enemy upon a very false conception of the real condition of the Army of the Potomac, which was supposed by him to be, both discouraged and demoralized. The forced marches which that Army made from Fredericksburg to Gettysburg, keeping within the inner portion of the circle while the enemy was moving round its circumference, the admirable state of discipline and efficiency which it exhibited during that march, the wonderful spirit, vigor and endurance which enabled it to gain the immortal victory of Gettysburg, and the ease with which it pursued the retreating enemy, all proved, that friend and foe alike had been mistaken in their judgment of that heroic, long-enduring and finally triumphant Army. A part of the Commission's Relief Corps accompanied it on its march, its wagons being constantly kept replenished from the depôt at Washington. Assistance was rendered day by day to the Surgeons in the care of those who were wounded during the frequent skirmishes, and of those who became ill in consequence of the fatigues and privations of forced marches in a desolate region during the heats of midsummer.

It soon became apparent that a grand conflict was at hand, a battle with nearly one hundred thousand men on each side, the result of which might decide the fate of the Rebellion. 'Accordingly, the most extensive preparations were made by the Commission to meet the terrible emergency. Experienced officers were sent to Frederick, Baltimore, Philadelphia, and Harrisburg, and a systematic daily communication was kept up between them, and the Agents

Preparations for the battle of Gettysburg.

accompanying the Army. Supplies were accumulated ready for movement at different points near the seat of war, and a large reserve stock was held at the different branch offices to be sent forward as soon as the news of the expected battle should reach them. A portion of the enemy's force, after crossing the Potomac occupied Frederick, on its march northward. During its stay, the Commission's stores in that town were carefully concealed, and after its departure the wagons moving with the supply train of the Union Army were replenished from them.

On the 28th of June, General Meade's Army was concentrated at Frederick, the Rebels being scattered

Battle of Gettysburg. Agents and supplies with the Army.

at various points in the Cumberland Valley, at Chambersburg, at Carlisle, and at York, near the Susquehanna. The Army marched northeastward to guard the approaches to Baltimore and Washington, and its advance guard, the First and Eleventh Corps, under General Reynolds, reached GETTYSBURG on the first of July. On that day it had an engagement with an overwhelming force of the enemy, and being driven in entrenched itself during the night on the Cemetery Hill, adjoining the town on the south. The Third and Twelfth Corps arrived during the night, and the remainder of the Army during the forenoon of the next day, Thursday, the 2d of July, and took up those formidable positions, from which during this and the succeeding day the Rebels made so many, and such vain efforts to dislodge them. All was quiet until four o'clock of the afternoon of Thursday, when a desperate assault was made by Longstreet's Corps upon our left wing, holding that portion of the field known as Round

Top Hill. The result was a disastrous repulse to the Rebels, and the wounding of many of our men. Two wagon-loads of battle-field supplies belonging to the Commission had arrived with the Headquarters' train, at Cemetery Hill, the night before. As soon as the assault commenced, these wagons were despatched to the left and were conducted, under fire, to the point at which the Surgeons had established temporary Hospitals, and to which the wounded were being brought from the field in large numbers. As these wagons, bearing the familiar inscription "*U. S. San. Com.*," (always so dear to the eyes of sufferers in the Army,) came in sight, a Surgeon who was standing at a point not five hundred yards in the rear of the line of battle, surrounded by sufferers for whose succor he had exhausted all the means at hand, exclaimed with joyful eagerness, "Thank God, here comes the Sanitary Commission; now we shall be able to do something." Brandy, beef-soup, sponges, chloroform, lint and bandages were at once distributed, and proved, no doubt, the means of saving many lives. The stock of supplies in these wagons was also sufficient to aid very materially in relieving the wants of the wounded in the Hospitals of the First, Second, Third, Fifth, Eleventh and Twelfth Corps, on this first day of a general engagement.

The wagons being thus emptied were sent at once to Frederick, so that their stock might be replenished and sent back to the field without delay. Agents of the Commission captured and held as prisoners of war by the enemy. They were reloaded at Frederick, and ready to leave that point early on the 4th of July. One of them was sent by way of West-

48

minster the other in charge of Dr. McDonald, who had the general superintendence of the Commission's work in the Army of the Potomac, was proceeding on the direct road to Gettysburg, when it was unfortunately captured by the cavalry of the retreating Rebels. Dr. McDonald, Rev. Mr. Scandlin, one of the Agents of the Commission, and two laboring men, who were in its service, and who were in charge of the wagon, were detained as prisoners of war, and marched to Richmond, where, for months, they endured all the loathsome horrors of the Libby Prison. This characteristic act of cruelty was committed by the Rebels, not only with full notice that the persons captured were, in the strictest sense, non-combatants, but also that they were conveying supplies to the battle-field, intended equally for the relief of friend and foe, and further that their own wounded men were, at that very time, receiving succor from the stores which these captured men were endeavoring to replenish.

The railroad approaches to Gettysburg on the east had been broken up, and the nearest point of commu- Supplies sent by way of West- minster. nication with the battle-field, in that direc- tion, was by way of Westminster, about twenty miles to the South-east. To that point, on the Fourth of July, the Agents succeeded in getting a car-load of supplies, from which wagons were laden, and sent to the Field Hospitals, which they reached early next morning. Immediately afterwards, five more wagon loads were despatched by the same route, and thus, before railroad communication between Gettysburg and the North was restored, the first, which are always the most pressing wants of the wounded, had been materially relieved. When the railroad to Gettysburg was opened, a vast amount of stores reached that place daily. Among other things, large quantities of fresh provisions, meat and vegetables, were sent every day from Philadelphia in "refrigerating cars," as they were called, or cars which had been converted into movable ice-houses. A glance at the table of issues from the Commission's storehouse during the ten days succeeding the battle, will give some idea of the magnitude of the relief extended to the wounded through its agency by the loyal people of the North.*

* The following is a statement of the quantities of the principal articles distributed by the Commission to the wounded upon the field at Gettysburg, subsequent to the battle. The perishable articles, (amounting to over 60 tons) were taken to the ground in refrigerating cars.

Articles of Sustenance, viz.:

Fresh Poultry and Mutton	11,000 pounds.
Fresh Butter	6,430 "
" Eggs, (chiefly collected for the occasion at farm houses in Pennsylvania and New Jersey.)	8,500 dozens.
Fresh Garden Vegetables	675 bushels.
" Berries	48 "
" Bread	12,900 loaves.
Ice	20,000 pounds.
Concentrated Beef Soup	3,800 "
" Milk	12,500 "
Prepared Farinaceous Food	7,000 "
Dried Fruit	3,500 "
Jellies and Conserves	2,000 jars.
Tamarinds	750 gallons.
Lemons	116 boxes.
Oranges	46 "
Coffee	850 pounds.

Articles of Clothing, etc., viz.:

Drawers, (woolen)	5,310 pairs.
" (cotton)	1,833 "
Shirts, (woolen)	7,158
" (cotton)	3,266
Pillows	2,114
Pillow Cases	264
Bed Sacks	1,630
Blankets	1,007
Sheets	274
Wrappers	508
Handkerchiefs	2,659
Stockings, (woolen)	3,560 pairs.
" (cotton)	2,258 "
Bed Utensils	728
Towels and Napkins	10,000
Sponges	2,300
Combs	1,500
Buckets	200
Soap, (Castile)	250 pounds.
Oil Silk	300 yards.
Tin Basins, Cups, etc	7,000
Old Linen, Bandages, etc	110 barrels.

The scene presented at the Commission's Depôt in
Scene at the the town for many days succeeding the
Commission's
storehouse in battle was a novel and extraordinary one:
the town. " Car-load after car-load of supplies were
brought to this place, till shelves, and counter, and
floor up to the ceiling were filled, till there was barely
a passage-way between the piles of boxes and barrels,
till the sidewalk was monopolized, and even the street
encroached upon. This abundant overflow of the
generous remembrance of those at home to those in
the Army was distributed in the same generous manner
as it was contributed. Each morning the supply
wagons of the Division and Corps Hospitals were before
the door, and each day they went away laden with
such articles as were desired to meet their wants. If

Articles of Sustenance, (continued.)			*Articles of Clothing, etc., (continued.)*		
Chocolate	831	pounds.	Water Tanks	7	
Tea	426	"	Water Coolers	46	
White Sugar,	6,800	"	Bay Rum and Cologne		
Syrups, (Lemon, etc.)	785	bottles.	Water	225	bottles.
Brandy	1,250	"	Fans	3,500	
Whisky	1,168	"	Chloride of Lime	11	barrels.
Wine	1,148	"	Shoes and Slippers	4,000	pairs.
Ale	600	gallons.	Crutches	1,200	
Biscuit, Crackers, and			Lanthorns	180	
Rusk	134	barrels.	Candles	350	pounds.
Preserved Meats	500	pounds.	Canvas	300	sq. y'ds.
Preserved Fish	3,600	"	Musquito Netting	648	pieces.
Pickles	400	gallons.	Paper	237	quires.
Tobacco	100	pounds.	Pants, Coats, Hats	189	pieces.
Indian Meal	1,621	"	Plaster	16	rolls
Starch	1,074	"			
Codfish	3,848	"			
Canned Fruit	582	cans.			
" Oysters	72	"			
Brandy Peaches	302	jars.			
Catsup	42	"			
Vinegar	24	bottles.			
Jamaica Ginger	43	jars.			

the articles needed one day were not in our possession at the time, they were immediately telegraphed for, and by the next train of cars they were ready to be delivered. Thus, tons of ice, mutton, poultry, fish, vegetables, soft bread, eggs, butter, and a variety of other articles of substantial and delicate food were provided for the wounded, with thousands of suits of clothing of all kinds, and hospital furniture in quantity to meet the emergency. It was a grand sight to see this exhibition of the tender care of the people for the people's braves. It was a bit of home feeling, of home bounty, brought to the tent, and put into the hand of the wounded soldier.''

But this work of distributing supplies to the Field Hospitals, grand as it was in its proportions, formed only a part of the general system of Battle- Special Relief Field Relief adopted by the Commission, and Work—Lodge and Feeding carried out so efficiently at Gettysburg. Ex- Stations. perience had taught its officers that the wounded suffered quite as much during their transportation to permanent Hospitals from hunger and exhaustion, and from the jolting of their mangled limbs over rough roads, as they did in the Field Hospitals themselves. This suffering was of a kind which the Medical officers could only measurably relieve. To mitigate it as far as possible, a Lodge and Feeding Station were established at the point to which the wounded were brought for embarkation on the railroad. At this place they were cared for and refreshed by the same means which had procured such inestimable relief to thousands in the Peninsula, at Acquia, and throughout the seat of war at the West.

On their arrival at the terminus of the railroad, that portion of the Commission's Corps which came through Nature and extent of the work done in them. by the first train, met a crowd of slightly wounded men gathered there, limping, dragging themselves along, silent, weary, hungry, and utterly exhausted. These wretched men were beyond the limit of ordinary Government care, and had wandered to the railroad, possessed, apparently, with but one idea, an anxious desire to escape from the horrors of the place which the battle had converted into a veritable Aceldama. The manner in which the ordinary routine of Army rule is thrown into confusion, after a great battle, when many of the suffering are left to shift for themselves, is well described by an eye-witness of the fearful suffering at Gettysburg.

" This is the way the thing was managed at first; The Surgeons left in care of the wounded three or four miles out from the town, went up and down among the men in the morning, and said, ' Any of you boys who can make your way to the cars, can go to Baltimore.' So off start all who think they feel well enough, anything being better than the ' hospitals,' so called, for the first few days after a battle. Once the men have the Surgeon's permission to go, they are off; and there may be an interval of a day, or two days, should any of them be too weak to reach the train in time, during which these poor fellows belong to no one, the hospital at one end, the railroad at the other, with far more than chance of falling through between the two. The Sanitary Commission knew this would be so of necessity, and coming in, made a connecting link between these two ends."*

The wise foresight of Mr. Knapp, who first organized the particular form of relief applicable to such cases as an integral portion of the Commission's general work, had provided in advance at Baltimore all the needed appliances for this service, and they were despatched by the Agents, who arrived by the first train. Tents were immediately pitched, cooking stoves put up, food prepared from the stores which had been sent forward, beds and bedding were found and arranged, so that that very night seventy-five suffering men were properly sheltered, and supplied with nutritious food. This, however, was only the beginning of the good work. It was continued for more than three weeks, gaining constantly in efficiency and practical value under the superintendence of two ladies who had acquired a large experience in this particular kind of service in the Peninsula. When it is remembered that these noble women did not permit one man of the sixteen thousand wounded, Union and rebel, who were transported during their stay to General Hospitals, to leave Gettysburg without a good meal, and without proper attention to their other and immediate necessities, it is not to be wondered at that the officers of the Commission should regard the record of its Special Relief work at Gettysburg as forming one of the brightest pages of its annals. To show the spirit with which it was carried on, we quote once more from that charming little *brochure*, "*Three Weeks at Gettysburg*," a sketch, which may safely be said to present the most

* See "Three Weeks at Gettysburg."

life-like and striking picture of the nature and value of volunteer relief work in the Army which the literature of the war has produced.

"Twice a day the trains left for Baltimore or Harrisburg, and twice a day we fed all the wounded who arrived for them. Things were systematized now, and the men came down in long ambulance trains to the cars; baggage cars they were, filled with straw for the wounded to lie on, and broken open at either end to let in the air. A Government Surgeon was always present to attend to the careful lifting of the soldiers from ambulance to car. Many of the men could get along very nicely, holding one foot up, and taking great jumps on their crutches.

"When the Surgeons had the wounded all placed, with as much comfort as seemed possible under the circumstances, on board the train, our detail of men would go from car to car, with soup made of beef-stock, or fresh meat, full of potatoes, turnips, cabbage, and rice, with fresh bread and coffee, and, when stimulants were needed, with ale, milk-punch, or brandy. Water-pails were in great demand for use in the cars on the journey, and also empty bottles to take the place of canteens. All our whisky and brandy bottles were washed and filled up at the spring, and the boys went off carefully hugging their extemporized canteens, from which they would wet their wounds, or refresh themselves till the journey ended. I do not think that a man of the 16,000, who were transported during our stay, went from Gettysburg without a good meal—rebels and Unionists together, they all had it, and were pleased and satisfied. "Have you friends in the

Army, madam?" a rebel soldier, lying on the floor of the car, said to me, as I gave him some milk. "Yes, my brother is on ———'s staff." "I thought so, ma'am. You can always tell; when people are good to soldiers, they are sure to have friends in the Army."

The ministrations of the Sanitary Commission on the battle-field of Gettysburg were not confined to the sufferers of our own Army. In accordance with its constant policy on such occasions, a policy dictated by the highest considerations of humanity and Christian duty, it recognized neither friend nor foe among the wounded. There were more than eighteen hundred of the enemy in our own Hospitals, cared for as our own men were cared for by our Surgeons. There were, besides, nearly fifty-five hundred of their wounded occupying Hospitals which had been established in the immediate neighborhood of the town previous to and during the battle, and filling besides, all the barns and houses for miles on the roads leading to Cashtown and Chambersburg. These men had been abandoned by their Army in its retreat, and were in a most deplorable condition of suffering and destitution. They were without Hospital supplies or even ordinary rations, and were saved from starvation only by the stores of the Government against which they were fighting. The state of these Hospitals claimed the attention and kind services of an organization, whose principles did not permit it to see an enemy in a suffering brother upon a battle-field, and although its means of relieving these men had been somewhat diminished by that barbarous act of inhumanity of which we have spoken, the capture of a

Relief to the wounded rebels at Gettysburg.

49

large amount of stores on their way to the battle-field
intended for the relief of all alike, still invaluable aid
was rendered to them for many days. Dr. Gordon
Winslow, one of the Inspectors of the Commission, was
charged with the duty of visiting these Hospitals,
ascertaining their wants, and offering such assistance as
might be required. He found the enemy's wounded
occupying twenty-four different camps within an area
of twelve miles. Most of the wounds were, of course,
severe, for those who had been able to move at all,
or who could be removed by the retreating Army
with its limited means of transportation, had been
carried off. Our own officers were too busily engaged
at that time in providing for the wants of their own
men, to bestow any other care upon those of the enemy
outside our own Hospitals than such as might keep them
from actual starvation. When, therefore, Dr. Winslow
called upon the Rebel Surgeons, explained to them
the nature of the work of the Commission, and offered
to supply their wants from its stores, the astonishment
and gratitude of those officers were expressed in no
measured terms. They eagerly availed themselves of
his offers, and one of the strangest of the many
strange and wonderful sights of which the Commission's depôt at Gettysburg was the scene after the
battle, was the mingling in that busy crowd of friend
and foe, National uniform and Confederate uniform,
Union army wagon and rebel army wagon, all engaged
in the common work of helping the suffering, and
seeking aid from a source which dispensed with impartial bounty its relief to the wretched victims of the
battle-field.

There is certainly nothing finer in its impulse, or more creditable to the civilization and humanity of the people of the North, than their willing- *Reflections on this service.* ness to share with their enemies the bounty which they had provided for their own suffering brethren. It is one of the many striking evidences which existed of the strong desire which that people always manifested that the war should be conducted upon every principle of humanity consistent with its successful prosecution. War is, necessarily, always a terrible agent of destruction. Its track is that of desolation and ruin, and its rule that of arbitrary force. Christian civilization may mitigate its horrors, but it can never change its essential cruelty. Every attempt to alleviate its misery consistent with its active prosecution should be recorded for the encouragement of those, whose best instincts teach them that they have not ceased to be men, and Christians, because war has caused them to become enemies.

The unexpected and timely aid furnished by the Commission to the enemy's wounded, made such an impression upon their Surgeons, and con- *Effect of this relief on the enemy.* vinced them so completely of the impartial spirit of humanity which guided its operations, that every one of those left at Gettysburg joined in a request to General Lee for the release of Dr. McDonald and the other Agents of the Commission who had been made Prisoners of war by his Army. The nature and character of the work of the Commission, the inestimable benefits which their own men had derived from it, and the relations of the captured Agents to it were fully set out in this petition. Strange to say, these representations of their own officers made no impression upon the Rebel Authorities, and these faithful Agents were permitted to languish in prison for months afterwards, and until influences of another kind effected their release.

The battle-field of Gettysburg was quite as remarkable for the striking opportunity it gave of proving Necessity of volunteer relief at Gettysburg. the indispensable necessity of volunteer aid in such an emergency, as for the amount of the supplies which were distributed, or the spirit of zeal and devotion which characterized all those engaged in this merciful work. The Commission's Officers, who had experience in this matter, always insisted that even where an Army after a battle did not move in pursuit of the enemy extra governmental relief was needed. But here was a battle-field from which the combatants on both sides disappeared within two days after the conflict ceased, leaving behind them more than twenty-two thousand men, whose condition required not only immediate, constant, and skillful care, but a large quantity of hospital supplies. The Army organization which, in theory, was to provide for all these wants, accompanied the onward march, leaving but a very imperfect representation of its various departments to look after those who had fallen. This was, of course, a matter of necessity, for it was evidently the duty of the Commander to press on with the Army prepared to meet just such another contingency as the battle of Gettysburg. General Meade himself has said, "I expected in a few days a battle at a distant point, and it was absolutely necessary I should carry away the greater portion of our surgeons and medical supplies, so that the wounded at Gettysburg were in a measure dependent upon such extra assistance as the Government could hastily collect, and upon the generous aid so cheerfully and promptly afforded by the Sanitary and Christian Commissions, and the various State, and Soldiers' Aid Societies. All the additional aid from every source was here most urgently needed, and it gives me great pleasure to say that, from the reports of my medical officers, I am satisfied the United States Sanitary Commission, as well as the others above mentioned, were fully up to the work before them."

On the whole, the record of the services of the Commission in the campaign which terminated in this great battle, is a highly satisfactory and encouraging one, and is especially honorable to the zeal and fidelity of the Agents by whose unremitting labor the work was done. Whether we look at the provident foresight which had accumulated at the centres of supply, a large reserve stock in anticipation of the battle, or at the determined energy with which these supplies were rapidly pushed forward to the field in spite of broken communications and limited means of transportation, whether we recall the faithful and untiring devotion of the Relief Agents, four of whom, as we have seen, were captured while in the discharge of their humane duties, and most of whom were exposed to the fire of the enemy while bringing succor to the wounded, or if, lastly, we consider the grand result of all this self-denying labor, the manifest relief afforded to more than twenty-two thousand victims of the battle, we are constrained to believe that

[marginal note: Commission's Agents on that battle-field.]

never has so vast a work of mercy been performed in a manner so satisfactory and efficient.

After the battle of Gettysburg the Field Relief Corps was somewhat reorganized, each Army Corps having permanently attached to it, for its special service a certain number of its members under a Superintendent, whose duties were confined to ascertaining and relieving the wants of the particular portion of the Army confided to him. This was not unlike the former system in principle. It was simply a more thorough division of labor, by which it was hoped greater efficiency would be secured. Under this organization, the Relief Corps crossed the Potomac with the Army, and accompanied it in its long and wearisome pursuit of the enemy to the Rapidan. The history of its services during the movement of the Army to Centreville, and back again to Culpepper, and during its long stay in winter-quarters, presents nothing very novel or striking. It was occupied in its regular, steady, current relief work by its ordinary means, and these have been so often described and the result was so similar to that which was observed on former occasions, that it is unnecessary to enlarge upon it further here. The Headquarters of the Commission were at Brandy Station, and here, were combined its methods of General Relief in the Hospitals, and the camps, with those of Special Relief, technically so called. This latter form of aid often proved a precious boon to those waifs and strays of the Army to whom, in their forlorn condition, a few meals and a night's lodging represented the highest form of practical benevolence.

The Army returns to the Rapidan.

The winter was passed by every branch of the Army service, and by all the benevolent organizations connected with it, in making large preparations Preparations for the Spring campaign of 1864. for the Spring campaign. The Chief Inspector of the Commission with the Army made a requisition on the Central Office for supplies based upon an estimate of what would be required for the wants of ten thousand wounded men. A large reserve stock, drawn from the sources of supply at the branch depôts, was accumulated at Washington, and arrangements were made to send forward stores either by land or by water, as either might be selected as the line of communication with the base. When the Army crossed the Rapidan, seven four-horse wagons containing food, stimulants, and clothing, in charge of the Field Relief Corps accompanied it. They were under the superintendence of Mr. WARNER JOHNSON, whose faithful, intelligent, and disinterested service during a period of more than two years and a half, forms one of the most striking examples of pure and unselfish zeal to be found in the history of the Commission. These stores were dispensed during the terrible battles of the Wilderness, and the wagons were sent to Belle Plain, *via* Fredericksburg, to be replenished. When the Potomac River was finally decided upon as the line of communication with the Army, the stores which had been accumulated at Washington were despatched to Belle Plain. In order to give some idea of the magnitude of the work undertaken by the Commission, and the means at its disposal for accomplishing it, we should state that at the opening of the campaign, two steamboats, and two barges were employed by it for the conveyance of stores from Washington to the base of the Army, that forty-four four-horse wagons constituted its independent means of transportation from Belle Plain to Fredericksburg, that by this means more than two hundred tons of stores were sent to points where they were most needed, while at the same time nearly two hundred Relief Agents, including the Field Relief Corps, the Auxiliary Relief Corps, and the Special Relief Corps, were engaged in giving their personal services to the wounded.

We have already described the condition of the wounded at Fredericksburg in the sketch presented of Work after the the peculiar work of the Auxiliary Relief battles of the Wilderness. Corps.* There was work enough in the dark days which succeeded the battles of the Wilderness, to occupy fully the most determined zeal of every man in the Commission's service, each in his particular vocation and ministry. There was not a moment from that in which the hero who was fighting for his country was disabled, until the comparative comforts of a General Hospital were reached, in which such relief as was afforded in this campaign by extra Governmental agencies was not of priceless value in soothing his agony.

The number of the wounded during this campaign was prodigious, far exceeding that which had been Vast accumula- anticipated by any one. Many of the tion of wounded —Their trans- wounds, of course, were slight, but they all portation. caused disability, at least for the time, and required attention. Nothing can better illustrate the

* See ante, page 276.

aggravated suffering which these wounded men under-
went, than some account of the embarrassments which
occasioned delay in sending them to a place where they
could be properly treated. The ambulances and
Army wagons, as they arrived at Belle Plain, filed
down in a long line on one side of a wharf of a
horse-shoe shape, when the wounded were removed to
the transports moored to it. The wagons having thus
discharged their living freight, passed to the other
side of the wharf, and were there laden in turn with
" fighting rations" for the troops in the field. It will
be readily seen that this process was inevitably a
tedious one, so much so indeed, that on one day, a continuous line of vehicles, laden with wounded men
stretched from the wharf at Belle Plain to Fredericksburg, a distance of nearly ten miles. The result, of
course, was an inextricable jam, which caused great
delay in the embarkation of the men, and added to
the suffering caused by severe wounds that produced by
hunger, exhaustion, and the rough jolting of the vehicles. To relieve completely such an immense mass
of misery was simply out of the question. To shorten
the agony of the wounded by embarking them as
rapidly as possible on the steamers was the task to
which the Medical Authorities, under the direction of
DR. CUYLER, Acting Medical Inspector-General of the
Army, devoted themselves. Hour after hour, for
days, this fearful procession of the victims of the
battle was kept up, and during all that time, Dr.
Cuyler's administrative skill, his quick and ready
humanity, his unselfish disregard of personal exposure
while striving to procure shelter for the wounded were

50

always conspicuous, and were beyond all praise. The Commission, anxious to do its share in relieving the wants of this particular class of sufferers, directed its attention chiefly to supplying them with such food and stimulants during their journey in the ambulances as their exhausted condition required. Between Belle Plain and Fredericksburg it established three Feeding Stations, where those of the wounded who were able to drag themselves to them were refreshed, and from which supplies of hot coffee, beef soup, and other kinds of nourishing food were borne to those who were unable to leave the ambulances. When we remember that this picture of the sufferings of the wounded on the route, frightful as it is, had its counterpart in the Hospitals in Fredericksburg, it will be readily perceived that the power of adequately relieving such misery far transcended all the means at the disposal of the Government, and all the volunteer aid, both in personal service, and in supplies which was proffered to it. Viewed in the light of the experience shed upon it, by the results of the battles of the Wilderness, the doubt, which has often been expressed whether there is a place for voluntary benevolent effort in an Army organization, seems like an insult to every humane instinct of the heart. Vast as was the work performed by the Government, and its volunteer, auxiliary helpers on this occasion, and laborious and self-denying as was the zeal of all who were engaged in the service of succoring the wounded, the mournful impression still remains when all was done, of the utter inadequacy of the best appointed means of mitigating, as the heart would fain desire, the horrors of scenes like these.*

In the onward march of the Army it became unsafe to send the wounded to the rear by way of Fredericksburg, as the roads were infested by guerilla bands, whose notions of humanity did not forbid their capturing the trains, and plundering the helpless. Port Royal, on the Rappahannock, was selected as the new base, and to that point were removed from Belle Plain the depôts of all the supply departments of the Army, including that of the Sanitary Commission. Timely notice of the intended change of base having been given to the officers of the Commission, its steamer laden with supplies, and conveying a large number of Relief Agents, was sent to Port Royal, and arrived there fortunately before any of the wounded reached that place. A Lodge and Feeding Station were at once established, and every preparation made for the reception and care of those who had fallen on the bloody battle-fields between Spottsylvania and the North Anna. Soon they came, these fresh victims of this terrible campaign, their wretched condition sickening the heart with the thought of the unending misery, and fearful sacrifice of all that is precious and noble which insatiate war demands, but rousing the deepest sympathy, and calling forth on the part of those in whose behalf they had suffered, the most persistent efforts for their relief. For a few days the usual busy scene was exhibited at the Commission's depôt at Port

The Army base transferred to Port Royal.

---

* From the 3d to the 12th of May inclusive, the Union Army sustained a loss officially reported at 3,300 killed and nearly 30,000 wounded. In this statement are reckoned the wounded of Spottsylvania.

Royal. The wounded, as they arrived, were fed, and refreshed, and made as comfortable as was possible in their condition, and were then transferred to the transport steamers in waiting for their conveyance to Washington.

The work at Port Royal did not long continue, as the advance of the Army towards Richmond required White House— the selection of another water-base in nearer Battles of Cold Harbor. communication with it. White House, on the Pamunkey, the well-remembered Headquarters of General McClellan's Army, during the summer of 1862, was the next point determined upon as a depôt of supplies, and thither the Agents of the Commission repaired with their stores, persisting with unwearied zeal in their determination of following the Army as long as there were wounded to be succored. During the first ten days of the month of June, the Army was engaged in a succession of sanguinary battles in the neighborhood of Richmond, known as the battles of Cold Harbor. It was the old story of the vain attempt, proved vain by the experience of both Armies throughout the war, to capture by assault a formidable entrenched position when defended by an adequate force. The loss, of course, on such occasions, falls most heavily on the assaulting party, and these battles added another ten thousand wounded to swell the ghastly catalogue of the victims of this campaign. These men were brought from the battle-field to White House, and there cared for by the Medical Authorities, assisted by the same unwearied devotion on the part of the Commission's Agents, and by the same abundant stores at their disposal, as had been so lavishly afforded on previous occasions.

In the meantime, a portion of the Commission's wagon-train which had proceeded overland from Fredericksburg and Port Royal reached White House, after having been exposed to imminent danger of capture on the route, a danger which was escaped only by the courage, energy and skill exhibited by Captain Harris, the officer in charge of it. It may be said in passing, as an illustration both of the practical difficulties attending any thorough system of Army Relief, as well as in just recognition of the services performed by the Agents of the Commission, that this wagon train was brought through the enemy's country from Fredericksburg to White House without losing a horse or a man. It was exposed as was the Army train with which it moved, to constant attacks of the enemy, and was frequently under fire, fortunately without receiving any great damage. During the occupancy of White House by the Union forces, a period of about two weeks, it was employed in transporting from that point to " the front," at Cold Harbor, stores designed to replenish the stock of the Field Relief corps.

About the middle of June, the Army of the Potomac crossed the James River to City Point, where in coöperation with General Butler's Army, an assault was made on the works which defended Petersburg. Although partial success attended this movement, the Army driving the enemy from his outer entrenchments, the defenses of Petersburg itself proved too strong to be taken by a *coup-de-*

main, and the Army soon after settled down to a condition of comparative rest. How much needed that rest was, may be inferred from the fact that it had fought desperate battles with an entrenched enemy during nearly every day since the beginning of the campaign, a period· of six weeks, that its march had been fatiguing and exhausting to the last degree, the troops often fighting all day and marching all night, and that its food had been an insufficient supply of hard crackers and salt pork. The wasting and destructive character of the campaign is further shown by the fearful loss the Army sustained in killed and wounded. From May 4th to June 20th no less than eight thousand four hundred and eighty-seven officers and men were killed and forty-four thousand two hundred and sixty-one were wounded. This is indeed a fearful record, one at which humanity shudders, and let us trust that the horror it should inspire will check forever the disposition to regard war in any other light than as one of the most terrible calamities which can befall the race.

The peculiar hardships of the campaign rendered it very apparent, that when the Army had fought its way Distribution of through, and reached a permanent base, its anti-scorbutics. vital force would be very much impaired, and a scorbutic taint would be found to prevail among the men. To guard against the dangers likely to arise from such a condition of things, the Commission had shipped to City Point, in anticipation of the arrival of the Army, a large quantity of preserved vegetables for distribution among the troops. During the month of June, there were forwarded no· less than 103 tons of canned tomatoes, 1200 barrels of pickled cucumbers, 18,000 gallons of pickled onions and tomatoes, 17,000 gallons of sauerkraut, and a large quantity of other anti-scorbutics. These articles, on true sanitary principles, were not intended chiefly for the sick and wounded in the Hospitals, but for those who were working in the trenches. The mode of distributing them adopted by the Commission was novel, and somewhat peculiar. Having obtained permission from the authorities, the wagons laden with these precious vegetables were driven along the line of the trenches, and the articles actually placed in the hands of the men who were to consume them. The eagerness with which they were received by the men is described by those who were eye-witnesses, as absolutely "frantic," and acknowledgements of the inestimable service conferred on the troops by their distribution poured into the office of the Commission at City Point from the Generals Commanding the different Corps, and from the Medical Officers attached to them.

We are thus brought to the close of active operations in that memorable campaign, known as the campaign of the Wilderness. We Amount of work done in this campaign—expenses. have endeavored to show that the Commission made ample preparations for the exigencies which arose, and that by means of its three branches of relief, Field, Auxiliary and Special, the best use was made of all its various appliances of succor. Never had the demand upon its resources been so great, or the services of its Agents, more ardent, prolonged, or continuous. Never also had a grander opportunity presented itself for testing the practical usefulness of its methods, and never had such an opportunity been so well employed. It only remains, in order to compléte the picture of the vastness of its work in this campaign, to state the amount actually expended in maintaining its operations in full efficiency. The money required during the months of May and June, to supply the wants of the Army in Virginia alone, exceeded the sum of five hundred and fifteen thousand dollars. It seems incredible at first sight, that so large a sum should be needed for the purchase of supplies within so limited a period, and equally difficult to understand where the money to carry on the work on this grand scale was procured. The sufferings of the soldier which were relieved by this distribution we have endeavored to describe. The distribution itself was made possible by the very large sum raised in the spring of 1864 by means of the Metropolitan Fair in New York, and by the steady current which poured the golden gifts of California into the Commission's treasury. This sum represents, of course, so far as the value of supplies is concerned, only those which it was necessary to purchase; a vast portion of the articles sent to the Army were contributions from the homes of the country, the money value of which we have no means of estimating. When it is remembered that in addition to this half million of dollars spent for the relief of the Armies operating against Richmond, it was necessary also to keep up the Commission's work in the Shenandoah Valley and throughout the Southwest, to say nothing of that in the General Hospitals, it will be seen that it is not difficult to answer the question which was so often asked during the war, " What does the Sanitary Commission do with all its money ?"

51

CHAPTER XIV.

MORRIS ISLAND—OLUSTEE—NEWBERNE.

THE combined naval and military expedition which was sent against Port Royal in South Carolina, towards Commission's Agents with the expedition against Port Royal. the close of the year 1861, was accompanied, as has been stated, by Agents of the Commission. Contrary to general expectation, the attack on Charleston, from the land side, was delayed, and the army remained in a state of comparative inactivity for many months. The first object of the authorities, after gaining a foothold, was to occupy all the important military positions on the coast from Morris Island to St. Augustine. The operations intended to accomplish this purpose were chiefly conducted by the navy, and although garrisons were established at eleven different points within the Department, little opposition was met with, and the troops were exposed to none of those privations and dangers, which marked the campaigns we have hitherto described. The Army was distributed in small detachments, having easy communication by water with its Headquarters at Beaufort, and with the North. It was composed mainly of New England regiments, and the men were intelligent, obedient to discipline, and trained to self-reliant habits. They were abundantly provided by the Commissary with the

402

ordinary rations and, owing to their small numbers, escaped danger from those multiform evils which lurk around crowded, ill-ventilated, and badly policed camps.

The fear which existed in regard to maintaining the efficiency of the troops was founded upon the enforced inactivity of the life they led, and the pro- Reputed unverbial unhealthiness of the climate of the healthiness of the Climate. region in which they were stationed. When it is remembered that the marshy inlets which form so much of the coast line which these troops occupied, has been long considered a district more exposed than any other on this continent to the deadly effect of malarious poison, it will be readily seen that this fear was well founded. Yet, strange to say, in a part of the country where, as we had always been told, no unacclimated white person could pass even a single night during the autumnal months, without imminent risk to his health and life, these northern troops remained for years, not only without showing any marked ill effect from the climate, but actually exhibiting a sickness rate less elevated than that of any division of the Army. Whether this result was due to the temperate character and habits of the men themselves, or to the unusually light duties, which, as soldiers, they were called upon to perform, or to the sanitary precautions which were adopted and enforced by the military authorities, or to all causes combined, it is not easy to say. One thing is certain, that the experience of the northern troops, not only on this coast, but in the Department of the Gulf where similar climatic conditions existed, seems to disprove the long cherished theory that it is impossible for white persons who are strangers, no matter what precautions they may take, to resist the deadly effect of the climate and, that, therefore, no such persons can live and perform manual labor in that region and yet retain their health and vigor.

In the early months of the year 1863 preparations for an attack upon Charleston, and the reinforcement

Movement against Charleston—Two Inspectors appointed.

of the Army by many unacclimated regiments, seemed to open a field for the systematic prosecution of the Commission's work of inspection and relief. Early in February, therefore, two Inspectors, one of whom, at least, proved himself afterwards to be a man of rare qualifications for the task assigned him, were sent to Port Royal. They found, as we have said, the sickness rate among the troops, especially among those who had been long in the Department, unusually and unexpectedly low. The narrow strip of territory then occupied by us had been so long in our possession, that the organization of the different branches of the service had assumed a measurable degree of completeness. The Hospital arrangements were excellent, under the charge of efficient and capable men, who were fully sensible of the absolute necessity of precautionary measures to insure the troops against diseases peculiar to the climate. Here, as elsewhere, the Agents of the Commission were cordially welcomed, and by their judicious counsel, and by the timely relief they were enabled to afford to those who were in need, they soon made themselves as indispensable in aiding to maintain a high standard of efficiency and comfort in this Army, as they had done in others. In pursuance of the or-

dinary method adopted by the Commission, the regiments at the different posts of the Department were
visited and thoroughly inspected, and Captains of companies were urged to apply to the store-house of the
Commission for whatever might be needed for the
comfort of their men.

In the absence of great battles requiring the peculiar kind of succor which had been so lavishly poured
out in Virginia and in the West, another Transportation
form of the many-sided system of relief of discharged
disabled sol-
adopted by the Commission did not fail to diers.
find its appropriate place. Here, as elsewhere, the soldier who, while in health had served his country faithfully, when discharged from the service of the Government because sickness or wounds rendered him incapable of performing that service any longer, passed
at the same time beyond its care. It is true, the
Government undertook to transport him to the North,
to the place where he had been enlisted, but he was
unprovided during his journey with that sort of convenient accommodation which his enfeebled condition
required, and which it would seem that the Government, out of consideration for his past services, if from
no other motive, was bound to give him. The care of
men in such circumstances had long been the work of
a distinct Department of the Commission, and the
same relief was afforded at Port Royal which had
proved of incalculable benefit to discharged men at
other points. At the suggestion of the Commission's
Inspector, General Hunter set apart a spacious steamer
with capacity for three hundred and twenty-five beds,
for the purpose of conveying these helpless men to

their destination at the North. To the equipment of this steamer the Commission contributed two hundred and fifty beds, and other necessary articles, and the success which attended this effort to transport the suffering with some humane consideration for their condition fully justified the experiment.

Meanwhile, preparations were going on for the first combined attack on Charleston, which took place in Landing on the month of April, 1863. Adequate arMorris Island. rangements were made for what promised to be a bloody conflict, but in consequence of the failure of the naval bombardment, the services of the land forces were not required, and of course there was no occasion for the battle-field relief of the Commission. Early in July, however, military operations in the vicinity of Charleston were renewed under another leader with great activity, and upon a large scale. General Gilmore removed his Army by transports to Folly Island, the object being to gain a foothold there, which would enable him to pass the strait which separated it from Morris Island, and thus assault Fort Wagner, one of the most formidable defences which guarded the approach to Charleston. This plan was, in the end, successfully carried out, but not without a display of persistent and heroic courage on the part of the troops of which there are few parallels in the history of the war, a courage which the Agents of the Commission, it will be seen, did much in their own way, to stimulate and to strengthen. So completely identified, indeed, are the labors of these Agents with the history of the siege of this great stronghold that no account of it can be complete without a reference to the very important part performed by them during its progress. The nature and methods of the relief afforded by them, and the difficulties and dangers through which they passed while engaged in their ministrations, constitute a chapter in the Commission's history of novel and peculiar interest.

On the 10th of July, the U. S. Brig Dolphin, with the Sanitary Commission's flag flying at its masthead, and laden with stores in anticipation of the coming battle, accompanied by Agents, ready to give their personal services to the care of the wounded, arrived at Folly Island. An assault was made on the same day on the lower works of Morris Island and was entirely successful, the enemy retreating to Fort Wagner at the other extremity of the island. On the next day, an assault was made on Fort Wagner, which resulted in a repulse, in which we lost one hundred and thirty-five men. The Agents of the Commission, Dr. Marsh and Messrs. Day and Hoadley, with their assistants, were untiring in their well-directed efforts to succor the wounded, administering to their wants in the temporary Hospitals, supplying them with clothing, accompanying the ambulances to the transport steamers, and furnishing such additional stores as might be needed on their voyage to Beaufort. From the 11th to the 18th of July, when the last memorable assault on Fort Wagner was made, the willing strength of the whole command was taxed to the utmost in making preparations for the conflict. The means of transportation on Morris Island were, of course, very limited, and were taken

up chiefly in conveying ammunition, and supplies of
food to "the front." Foreseeing the fearful destitution
of the wounded in the impending assault, and relying,
as experience had taught the Commission it must
always do in such exigencies, upon independent means
of transportation, Dr. Marsh had, during the interval,
used every effort to accumulate such stores as would
prove most serviceable immediately after the attack.
He succeeded in borrowing from the Quartermaster
some common row-boats, and taking a circuitous route
not less than seven miles long, through an inlet of
which the enemy held one bank, he brought his precious cargo to the proper point. On the evening of
the 15th, his tents were pitched, and his flag floating
at "the front." After consultation with the General in
command of the assaulting column, he determined to
supply every man in it with beef soup, tea and biscuit.
This he continued to do at intervals, and up to the very
hour of the assault. This provision was absolutely
indispensable owing to the temporary deficiency of the
ordinary rations, and many a poor fellow, no doubt,
fought on the terrible night of the 18th with renewed
courage from having been thus supported and strengthened.

The assault on Fort Wagner it will be remembered
was one of the most persistent and resolute recorded
Work of the in military history. Both officers and men
Commission dur-
ing these opera- seemed inspired with a strong determination
tions. to capture it, as the key to Charleston, cost
what it might. A portion of the column after crossing
under a terrific fire, but with the utmost steadiness, the
ditch which separated it from the Fort, and storming

the parapet, succeeded in gaining possession of one angle of the Fort, but not being properly supported, it was obliged to relinquish its hard earned prize. Meanwhile, the remainder of the force was exposed to all those terrible means of destruction, so readily employed by those who are sheltered in fortified positions, and so fatal to those who attempt to assail them. Grape and canister swept through their ranks as they began their onward movement; a sustained fire of musketry greeted them as they came nearer; as they pressed steadily on, they were raked by an enfilading fire from each side, while the bursting shells sent from distant Sumter, added to the horrors and dangers of that fearful night. In the midst of this terrible scene of carnage, the Commission's place was one which had been selected solely with a view of relieving the wounded, and with no more regard to the personal safety of its Agents than was shown by those whom a soldier's duty called upon to storm the work. All the arrangements had been made in advance. A portion of the corps acted as an auxiliary force in "the front" and in the Hospitals, another assisted the wounded in reaching the transport steamers which were to convey them to Beaufort, and a third was held in reserve for any unexpected event which might occur. During the assault many were wounded as they were mounting the parapet or face of the Fort. Just beneath them was a wide ditch, which, at high water, was filled to the depth of six feet. Into this ditch, therefore, many of those who had been stricken down on the parapet rolled, and were, of course, in their helpless condition in great danger of being drowned. But

52

here the Commission's helping hand was not withdrawn from them. During the assault, its Agents were stationed in boats, in this ditch, and as the wounded fell on the parapet directly above them, or rolled down into the water, they were instantly picked up by these brave and devoted men, and borne to the Hospitals. When it is remembered that these men had none of the excitement and stimulus of example, or the ambition of military glory to encourage them, deeds like these shine forth with a lustre as brilliant, in all the true elements of heroism, as that which is shed by the noblest achievements on the battle-field.

But the struggle for the possession of Fort Wagner was not yet over. The efforts to capture it by *coup-de-* {Siege operations against Fort Wagner.} *main* having met with a bloody repulse, it was determined to secure its possession by the tedious but sure operations of a siege with regular approaches. This process, always laborious and difficult, was rendered doubly so in this instance by the character of the soil of the island, consisting alternately of shifting sand-hills and pestilential swamps, through which it was necessary to construct the trenches. The scorching heat of the climate, and the debilitated condition of the men, worn out by difficult and exhausting labor, and disheartened by the failure of the first assaults, still further embarrassed its progress. Sickness began to prevail in an alarming degree among the troops. A decided tendency to scurvy became apparent, and very soon, in many of the regiments, only one-half of their number was fit for duty. It is, indeed, wonderful that siege operations could be carried on at all in the face of such obstacles, for all experience would seem to teach that no Northern Army in such a climate, in mid-summer, could engage in any active operations, least of all in the successful prosecution of a siege involving the extraordinary and long-continued labor which reduced Fort Wagner. In this alarming emergency every effort was made by the Medical Officers, and by those of the Commission, not merely to restore the health of those who had become disabled, but also to maintain the strength and vigor of those, upon whose ability to work regularly the success of the siege depended. Immense requisitions were at once made upon the Commission's store-house in New York for everything which would tend to promote this important result, and these requisitions were met with a liberal alacrity which aided essentially in imparting life and vigor to the whole command. Large supplies of vegetables, of curried cabbage, of pickles, onions, vinegar, and lime juice, soon arrived, and were distributed to the troops, not only in the Hospitals but in the trenches also, and it was not long before a decided and gratifying change in their condition was observable. Scurvy soon disappeared, the disease seemed not only checked but eradicated, and with it disappeared the more dangerous tendencies of other diseases.

The extraordinary services rendered by the Sanitary Commission in this campaign, the change produced in the general condition of the men by the distribution of its supplies was so noticeable, and the source whence this timely aid had come was so well recognized, that the Commanding General issued an order testifying his appreciation of its work, its flag was saluted by the grateful regiments as they passed it on their way to the intrenchments, and the Medical Director himself, echoing only the prayer which had gone up from the hearts of so many who had been cheered and sustained in their direst necessity, exclaimed with genuine fervor, " God bless the Sanitary Commission."

Another feature of the relief afforded by the Commission during this memorable siege deserves notice. Large supplies of ice furnished the troops by the Commission. A prolific source of disease on Morris Island was the bad quality of the water which was often brackish, and always impregnated with decayed vegetable matter, which rendered it not only very unpalatable, but very unwholesome. This was remedied, to a considerable extent, by the distribution of a liberal supply of ice, nearly four hundred tons having been shipped from New York for the use of the troops. Thus the frozen streams of Maine were made to cool, not only the burning lips of fever, but to assuage the thirst produced by exhausting toil in South Carolina. Meanwhile, the siege went steadily on, and at last the great prize which it had cost the lives of so many noble and heroic men to secure fell into our possession, abandoned at the moment when the resistless progress we had made would have forced its speedy capitulation.

This siege is, perhaps, the most remarkable in the whole history of the war, remarkable not merely for The siege memorable in a novel aspect. the engineering difficulties overcome, the scientific skill with which all its details were conducted, and the patient, persistent and heroic bravery of the troops, but remarkable also when its true history is known, for the essential aid which was rendered in bringing it to a successful termination by means of the voluntary, but well-organized sympathy of the American people.

After the capture of Fort Wagner, the operations near Charleston were confined for a long time to the bombardment of the city, which, fortunately for the sake of humanity, at least, caused a far greater consumption of ammunition than waste of life. In the interval between this period and the renewal of active operations in the field, the health of the troops, by rest and judicious treatment, was restored to the condition in which it had been previous to the campaign on Morris Island. When the Army was preparing, six months afterwards, for the expedition to Florida, it again presented the extraordinary spectacle of a body of northern troops operating in the unhealthiest region in the South, and yet exhibiting a sickness rate as low, at least, as that of any portion of the Army actively engaged in other parts of the country.

Low sickness rate among the troops after the fall of Fort Wagner.

From the want of adequate preparation of all kinds, it must be inferred that the expedition which was sent to Florida in February, 1864, under General Seymour, was not expected to encounter serious opposition. Jacksonville was occupied without resistance, and a column was pushed westward in the direction of Tallahassee. The expedition was accompanied, of course, by the Agents of the Commission, who, while sharing the general impression that the campaign would be a bloodless one, were nevertheless

Expedition to Florida.

determined to be prepared for all contingencies. How wise was this foresight we shall presently see.

The Army marched for several days without meeting the enemy, but, at last, on emerging from a long **The battle of** and narrow defile, it encountered him **Olustee.** strongly entrenched, and commanding with his guns the only avenue to its further approach. The marshy nature of the ground rendered the deployment of the troops impossible, and the head of the column having incautiously advanced without any suspicion of the presence of the enemy close to his position, was met by a terrific fire of musketry which soon drove it into a disorderly retreat. This produced, of course, confusion in the rear, where the Army was moving upon a narrow causeway, flanked as we have said by swamps, and the result was, that the repulse at Olustee was one of the most disastrous for the number of men engaged of any battle which occurred during the war. Seven hundred wounded and exhausted men thus suddenly required the care and services of the medical officers. As there had been no expectation of a battle, no preparations had been made for the casualties which attend one. It is a singular, but instructive, and noteworthy fact that the only medical supplies belonging to the Army in Florida at that time, were those of five of the regiments which made part of the expedition, and even these had been left behind at Jacksonville, more than fifty miles distant from the battle-field, for want of transportation.

This was an opportunity of doing good which the officers of the Commission did not fail to improve. They had proceeded with their stores to the terminus of the railroad, a point about fifteen miles Work of the Commission after that battle. from Olustee. There they remained to await events, and there they met the routed and demoralized Army returning, intent apparently only on escaping capture by the pursuing enemy. The wounded straggled in in a most pitiable condition, and in the absence of any other provision whatever, they were fed and clothed from the Commission's stores, and placed upon beds in the cars, improvised from bedsacks and hay. Six cars laden with these unfortunate men had been already despatched to Jacksonville, and a sufficient number remained to fill at least three more. At this juncture, General Seymour, expecting the immediate approach of the enemy, ordered all the government commissariat stores to be burned to prevent their falling into his hands, and strongly advised the Sanitary corps to abandon the wounded who remained, lest they themselves should be captured. These heroic and devoted men, however, fit representatives in the remote wilds of Florida, of the intense desire of the American people to minister to those who had suffered in their cause, nobly refused to quit their posts, and quietly proceeded in their work of transporting the wounded, who had been abandoned by the Army, to a place of safety. Fortunately they were enabled to embark them all on the cars, and, after incredible exertions, brought them in a comparatively comfortable condition to Jacksonville. Such invaluable aid, rendered under such circumstances, deserved a fitting recognition on the part of those who had derived benefit from it, and it was thus spoken of in an order of the General commanding the expedition :

GENERAL ORDERS—No. 10.

I. The Brigadier-General Commanding, gratefully recalls to the recollection of the troops of this command, the debt incurred by them, during the recent movements, to the Sanitary Commission and its Agent, Mr. A. B. Day. Much suffering has been alleviated, and many inconveniences removed, by the energy and promptness with which the supplies of the Commission have been placed at the control of our medical officers; and for those who have been so benefited, officers and men, the Brigadier-General offers his own and their most sincere thanks.

By order of Brigadier-General T. Seymour.

R. M. HALL,
1st Lieutenant 1st U. S. Artillery,
Acting Assistant Adjutant-General.

The work accomplished by the Commission after this battle is interesting and instructive on many accounts. It was not merely because a vast amount of misery and suffering was relieved by it, but also, because it furnished conclusive evidence of the necessity of the timely and opportune aid afforded by an organization, which seized upon every opportunity of filling the many gaps which experience proved were always left in the humane care of the suffering during active military operations. Here, for instance, was a battle fought near the close of the third year of the war, with troops who had been long in the service, and who must be presumed to have been tolerably well organized, and yet the Army suffers a defeat only fifty miles from its base of supplies, without possessing any means whatever of succoring its wounded. The excuse in this particular case may have been want of transportation, or the improbability of a battle, or inefficiency in certain

General Reflections.

branches of the service, but the true explanation is to be found in this patent fact, that the real business of every Army and every General who is in earnest, is to fight and to conquer, and not, except in the most general way, to concern themselves about the care of the wounded and non-effectives. This mode of regarding the matter has been characteristic of all Armies, since wars began on the earth. Victory, the defeat of the enemy is the grand purpose and aim of their existence. The triumphs of humanity gained in the merciful care of the suffering form no portion of the renown of the most famous Generals. Everything must be sacrificed to success. The well men, and even the horses must be fed, even should the wounded die of starvation and neglect. It is idle therefore to expect that the Commander of an army, in planning his operations, will ever be affected by questions about the disposition of his wounded. All this may be very inhuman, but it is simply War in its true spirit, and wise is the people who recognize it.

Any sketch of the relief afforded by the Commission to the troops stationed in the Department of the South which did not present some outline Agents of the Commission in this department. of the character and services of its superintendent, Dr. Marsh, would be very incomplete. No organization, certainly none of a benevolent kind, was ever served by men of more capacity, zeal and devotion than the Sanitary Commission, but in the long list of its faithful Agents it would be impossible to find one who was a fitter representative of its true spirit, than he who had charge of its affairs on the Carolina coast. From the first he thoroughly identified himself with his work. By his counsel and judicious conduct, he commended himself to the medical officers, and established relations of perfect harmony with them, while his wisely tempered zeal so won the confidence of those of other branches of the service, that there was no facility which he could ask for in the execution of his work of mercy, which they were not willing at once to accord him. The extraordinary service rendered by him and his assistants on Morris Island, and afterwards at Olustee, in promoting the health and comfort of the Army, gained him the universal affection of the soldiers, and received, as we have seen, a striking testimonial from their General. For more than two years he remained in that Army, broken in health, but pursuing his beneficent labors with unquenched zeal. In this long service, he had come to look upon the soldiers almost as his own children.   When a portion of the Army was transferred to Virginia, his interest in all that concerned their welfare remained undiminished. Hearing that the Tenth Army Corps, then at Bermuda Hundred, was suffering from a want of Sanitary stores, owing to some difficulty having arisen between the agents of the Commission and the Medical Authorities, he writes indignantly to the Associate Secretary, " It is too bad that the Tenth Corps should suffer. I have known them for a year and a half. There are no truer or braver men in the Army, and none more patient of suffering. They are noble men. Do not let them suffer. Send some resolute man to them, who will fear neither Dr. ———— nor the Devil. For my sake send a fearless man, and send him immediately. I cannot endure the thought that the heroes of Morris Island should need-lessly suffer."

The Army under General Burnside which captured Roanoke Island, and afterwards Newberne in North Carolina, was, accompanied by the Agents Work in North of the Commission, who remained with it Carolina. during the war, seeking by the usual methods to pro-mote its sanitary interests. The troops stationed in that Department were engaged in repelling the con-stant petty attacks of thé enemy, who seemed disposed to render their occupancy of the few miles of the coast which they had gained as uncomfortable as possible. They were not exposed, however, to the dangers, fa-tigues and privations of long marches, nor, after they had gained a firm foothold, except in comparatively few instances, to the casualties of the battle-field. But the unhealthiness of the climate proved, in the end, a foe far more formidable, and far more difficult to resist than the armed Rebels. The troops occupying this inhospitable coast were scattered, in small detach-ments, at isolated posts from Roanoke Island and Hatteras Inlet to Fort Macon, Beaufort, Morehead City, and Newberne, the last named town being the Headquarters of the Department. The climate of this region of sand-banks and sluggish rivers is prover-bially unhealthy, and during the autumnal months especially, miasmatic fevers prevail to an alarming extent. The dismal, tedious life led by the soldier at most of these isolated posts was one not calculated to maintain his *morale* at least, in that condition in which he might best resist the insidious poison of the atmos-phere. Some of the garrisons were so far out of easy communication with the North, that they were deprived of many of those articles by which the hard lot of the soldier, even in the most active service in other parts of the country was, to a certain extent, alleviated. The result was inevitable, and had been clearly foreseen. Scurvy and diseases owing their malignancy to a scorbutic taint became common.

It soon became apparent that what was most needed by the troops in that Department was not concentrated Hospital Garden food or stimulants, or even clothing, articles at Newberne. which figured so conspicuously on the Commission's Supply-list, but an abundant supply of vegetables. As it was obviously impossible to transport from the North these articles in sufficient quantities it was resolved to try the same experiment of establishing a Hospital garden at Newberne, which had proved so successful at Chattanooga, Murfreesboro', and Knoxville. The coöperation of the authorities was readily secured, and by order of General Peak commanding the Department, a plot of fifty acres of suitable land was assigned to the Commission for that purpose. Seeds were procured in New York, and sent forward, and the proper implements were provided. The success in cultivating this garden was very gratifying. In one week in the month of August, 1864, more than three hundred bushels of vegetables produced by it, were distributed among the troops, and the fertile soil, and skillful husbandry gave so constant a supply for a long time afterwards, that the unfavorable symptoms of disease which had appeared in the Army, were soon sensibly relieved. Two days in each week, the whole yield of the garden was devoted to the use of the Navy, at that time strongly represented in the waters of Albemarle Sound.

While the Commission was thus occupied in efforts to counteract the progress of scurvy, an insidious foe of another kind suddenly appeared, which *Yellow Fever at Newberne, in September,1864.* threatened, for a time, the complete extermination of the garrisons at Newberne and Beaufort. Yellow fever, that fearful scourge of the towns and cities on our southern coast, from the visitation of which our Army had been most happily and providentially spared for the most part during the war, broke out with great violence in the month of September, 1864, in the town and garrison of Newberne. The origin of the disease was clearly traceable to defective sanitary police arrangements, and its virulence during nearly six weeks was intense. The 15th Connecticut Regiment, which was doing Provost duty in the town, was first attacked and suffered most cruelly; the Quartermaster, the Commissary of the post, the Provost Marshal, the Post Master, many of the Surgeons and nearly all the clerks and employés in the various departments at Headquarters, were attacked by the disease, and many succumbed to it. Every one of the Sanitary Corps, except its zealous and efficient Superintendent Dr. Page, were prostrated by it, but fortunately all in the end recovered.

Dr. Hand, the Medical Director exhibited a heroic devotion to duty, and an unselfish disregard of all considerations of personal safety throughout these *Aid afforded by the Commission.* trying scenes, which did honor to the profession to which he belonged, and to the service of which

he was the head in that Department.   In his indefatigable exertions to relieve the suffering, he was zealously
assisted by the Commission's Inspector, Dr. Page.   Deprived as that officer was by the pestilence of the aid
of his subordinates, he seemed inspired with renewed
energy and devotion in this relief service.   Night and
day he attended to the wants of the sick, adding to his
personal services, such articles from the stores of the
Commission as would promote their comfort, and facilitate their recovery.   Under his direction, the Board of
Health was reorganized, three hundred negroes were
set to work to purify and thoroughly cleanse the town,
and although this measure had unfortunately been
adopted too late to prevent the outbreak of the disease, its result clearly proved that its origin was due
to the neglect of proper sanitary precautions.   The
inestimable services of this gentleman on this occasion,
form not only a title of peculiar honor to himself, but
the recollection of them was cherished with a feeling
of justifiable pride by the officers of the Commission,
for it proved to them that no danger, whether encountered in the form of the deadly pestilence, or amidst
the horrors of the battle-field, or in the less conspicuous, but often most perilous posts to which they were
assigned, ever deterred their Agents from the true and
faithful discharge of any duty.

CHAPTER XV.

DEPARTMENT OF THE GULF.

GENERAL BUTLER occupied New Orleans at the close of April, 1862. His Army, which was mainly composed of New England regiments of excellent material, had suffered much by overcrowding on the transports which brought it from the North, and afterwards from exposure and insufficient rations, while encamped on the barren sandy waste of Ship Island at the mouth of the Mississippi. The expedition had been poorly supplied with articles for maintaining the troops in an efficient condition, for those were the days of our early experience, and the Officers were charged with duties wholly unfamiliar to them, the nature and extent of which they were forced, according to the Government policy, to learn while the men suffered. Whatever inconvenience occurred during the voyage, however, or during the tedious delay which preceded the advance on New Orleans, was forgotten in the joyful enthusiasm with which the possession of that City inspired the Army. It was felt on all sides that its capture was by far the most important blow which the rebellion had yet received, and pleasing hopes were entertained by many that the end was now nigh. The loss of the City, however, seemed only to nerve the enemy to new desperation, and was the immediate cause of the strengthening of the fortifications of Port Hudson and Vicksburg, the reduction of which strongholds was to cost us so many precious lives, and to postpone for more than a year our control of the great Father of Waters.

General Butler's force was considered too small to attempt, immediately, expeditions into the heart of Sanitary pre- the enemy's country, and he occupied him-
cautions taken
by him—Results. self at New Orleans chiefly, in consolidating the fruits of the victory we had gained, and in efforts to render our possession of the City secure and permanent. Under his vigorous administration, the most effective sanitary measures were adopted, and enforced. The fear of the outbreak of yellow fever, during the summer months, and the danger to which a Northern Army would be exposed by its prevalence, acted as a constant stimulus to the most careful measures of precaution. Fortunately for the health of the Army, fears on this subject were so firmly rooted in the minds of the Authorities, founded as they were, on the familiar history of the effects of the epidemic in that region, that extraordinary efforts were made by them to remove all causes of preventible disease, and, as the result showed, with abundant success. The city was cleansed under General Butler's order as it had never been cleansed before, a rigid quarantine was enforced, the quarters of the troops in the Forts, and in the various camps were thoroughly policed, needless exposure to the fierce rays of the tropical sun, or to the deadly poison of the night atmosphere in the neighborhood of the swamps was avoided, a minute care was exercised with regard to the clothing and food of the

troops which was entirely unknown in other portions
of the Army, and as the result of all these precautions,
faithfully carried out, the summer of 1862 was passed
not only without the appearance of yellow fever, but
without any unusual sickness in that portion of the
Army which remained in the neighborhood of New
Orleans. Dr. McCormick, the Medical Director of the
Department, was an old Army Surgeon who had been
stationed at New Orleans for many years before the
war began, and knowing well, by experience, the
peculiar dangers to which the health of the troops was
exposed in that locality, and the proper course to be
taken to guard against them, employed with great
energy, all the means at his disposal for that purpose.
Under his administration the Sanitary Commission
found little to do in providing for the wants of the
troops in garrison, but it was thought advisable that a
thorough inspection of the various regiments should
be made so that the peculiar condition and history of
each might be known, as a guide in future measures of
relief should they become necessary. These inspections revealed a most extraordinary state of things in
regard to the health of the Army. Early in July, 1862,
the whole number of sick in that Department, in Regimental and General Hospitals, was only four hundred
and seventy-two out of a force of about twenty thousand men (nineteen regiments of infantry and seven
batteries) less than $2\frac{1}{2}$ per cent. This result was due
partly, of course, to light duties, and good rations, including vegetables, and an abundance of fresh meat,
but also, no doubt, to a great extent, to preventive
sanitary measures rigidly and constantly enforced in

54

the camps and garrisons. This favorable state of health among the troops in the Department of the Gulf was maintained during the whole war. In November, 1863, the experienced Inspector of the Commission, Dr. Crane, writes, " I have never seen so little disease among troops in the field. But little over four per cent. of the present force is on the sick list." This is another curious illustration of the fallacy of calculations made before the war as to the possibility of effectually subduing the rebellion, based on the alleged inability of Northern troops to resist the peculiar dangers of the climate. It is certainly very remarkable, that a far higher health-rate was maintained during the war among the troops on the coast of Carolina, and the Delta of the Mississippi, than in the mountainous regions of Tennessee and Virginia.

With the exception of the expedition which failed in the attempt to construct a canal opposite Vicksburg, General Banks and the severe battle which took place in assumes command of the the month of August at Baton Rouge, the Army. troops under General Butler were not engaged in offensive operations on a large scale during the remainder of the year. Towards its close, General Banks arrived with large reinforcements, and assumed the command of the Department. Active operations were soon afterwards begun in the country west of the Mississippi, the Army fighting its way through the Téche and Atchafalaya region, Alexandria on the Red River being the objective of the campaign. Its march was a series of victories, not gained, however, without some severe fighting on our part. In the early part of April took place the battle at Franklin, in which our

loss in wounded was considerable. Dr. The battle of
Crane, the Sanitary Inspector who had ac- Franklin.
companied the Army with his corps, was requested
by the Medical Director to look after the comfort of
these men during their transportation to Brashear City
and New Orleans. Having been placed in charge of
the steamer, he superintended the removal of patients
from the Hospitals, took care that they were well fed,
and properly attended to on board, and on their arrival
at Brashear placed them in railroad cars, and provided
them with such means of relief and sustenance as they
would need until they reached the General Hospitals
at New Orleans. The services rendered on this occasion did not differ from those which we have so fully
described as given to those who had suffered on the
battle- fields of Virginia. They are referred to here
merely to show the extent of the operations of the
Commission, and its thorough system of organization
by which it was enabled to afford the same priceless
relief at the same time, and by the same methods, at
points two thousand miles distant from each other,
in the wild and remote region of Western Louisiana,
and within sight of the National Capitol. It is, indeed, not a little remarkable that a scene such as is
described in the following letter could have been witnessed in the far Southwest, in a Department presumed
to be almost inaccessible to the reach of that kindly
succor which was constantly extended to the relief of
the Armies in Virginia and at the West.
    "   *   *   *   I have seen empty old build-
ings, as by magic, assume in a day the air of comfort
and order of arrangement of long-established city

hospitals. Not soon shall I cease to warm over the recollection of some of these transformations. For example, men to the number of several hundreds, after the fight at Bisland, were brought to Berwick City in flat-boats, skiffs, and little steamers, wounded in every conceivable manner. They had received all the attention that good medical skill could afford amid the din and smoke of actual conflict, but were, so dirty, black, and uncomfortable, as not to be recognized by their most intimate friends, until the renovating hands of tender nurses had washed away their blood and dust, and put on them and their beds clean clothes; all which, not excepting a piece of soap or a row of pins, were furnished by the *model department* of the Gulf, and the Sanitary Commission, sent thence eighty miles over a slow railroad, but in time to do all I have intimated. And I must say, that he who had looked, on the morning of April 18, at the interior of that deserted building in Berwick City, store below and tenements above, its large and small rooms, dusty, cobwebbed, gloomy, and also at the large hall of an adjoining building in the same condition, making in all a floor area of about 1,500 yards, had seen on the following morning every available yard of this space covered with wounded men, *our country's braves*, suffering anguish such as a wounded soldier only knows, without the shadow of comfort; on the same evening again seen all these sufferers arranged in trim rows, on iron bed-steads and good mattresses, clean wounds, clean bandages, clean lint, dressings, etc., clean shirts, clean drawers, clean sheets and pillow-cases, clean wards, with towels, and bowls, and brushes, and rows of pins in their places, tables supplied with vases of flowers, pitchers of ice water, tumblers, bowls, vials, packages, all in their places, and the poor sufferers sleeping quietly under their musquito nets, all order, all cleanliness, all beautiful. Anybody, I say, that saw, as I saw, all this, and was not moved with deep gratitude towards the institution that furnished the means for all this magic change, is a character for a cage in a menagerie."

After the occupation of Alexandria, General Banks returned with his Army to the Mississippi, and being joined at Baton Rouge by the forces under General Grover, commenced the siege of *Siege of Port Hudson.* Port Hudson. The two assaults which were made with the assistance of the fleet on that formidable stronghold were, it will be remembered, unsuccessful, while the impetuous courage of the troops engaged in them caused many casualties. The wounded were taken to Hospitals at Baton Rouge, not far distant, where the officers of the Commission aided the Surgeons in their care of them. There was nothing very striking or peculiar about their work there. Their place and functions on such occasions were now well understood; they had a duty to perform so well marked, that they went about their work as regularly and as systematically, as the Medical Officers themselves.

After the Mississippi was opened by the surrender of Vicksburg and Port Hudson, there followed a season of comparative rest for such of the *"Soldiers' Home" established at New Orleans.* troops as remained in the Department of the Gulf. The Commission took the opportunity of establishing at New Orleans its system of Special

Relief by means of a Home or Lodge, where soldiers discharged from the service on account of disability could receive temporary assistance, previous to their embarkation for their homes. Connected with the Home, was an office in which aid was given in preparing the discharge papers of soldiers, thus enabling them to receive the pay due them without inconvenience or delay.

A great practical grievance suffered by discharged soldiers at New Orleans at that time, was the neglect *Improvements in the transportation of disabled men.* of the authorities to provide them with suitable accommodations on the vessels which conveyed them to the North. As the route home, until long after the surrender of Vicksburg, was sea-going, on steamers which had decent arrangements only for a class of passengers who could afford to pay for them, the suffering condition of the discharged soldier in his sick and disabled state, forced to lie down among cotton bales, and without suitable food or any attendance, may be readily imagined. The passage on the boats on the Mississippi was perhaps less uncomfortable, but even there, the requirements of humanity were often unheeded. It was determined, if possible, to reform this condition of things. In February, 1864, the authorities placed in the hands of the officers of the Commission, at their request, a steamer to be properly fitted up as a transport. She was at once equipped on a plan which recognized private soldiers, even if discharged and non-effectives, as living human beings, whose transportation required a different arrangement from that adopted in the stowage of barrels of flour or bales of cotton. Each man had his own bed; proper ventilation and means of cleanliness were provided, suitable arrangements for preparing food were made, and last of all, but not least important, an Agent of the Commission whose special business it was to look after and care for those who were unable to help themselves, accompanied the boat on each trip to Cairo. This system once inaugurated, was continued during the remainder of the war. Many transports were thus employed, the Government authorities, after the Commission had once set the example, assuming their care and direction. The additional comfort afforded to these men, who deserved everything of their country, by this improved method of transportation, was very apparent. The part taken by the Officers of the Commission, in this great work, is best illustrated by the fact that one of the most faithful and efficient of all of them, Mr. EDGERLEY, fell a victim to disease brought on by his over exertion and zeal, while ministering to the wants of this class of sufferers.

The exchange of prisoners, in this Department, was also a business in which the Officers of the Commission took a very important and active part. *Exchange of prisoners. Relief afforded.* They accompanied the Commissioner of Exchange to the place of rendezvous, well supplied with articles, which were sure to be needed by those who had just been released from rebel prisons. At Galveston, for instance, a large number were received in a state of destitution and feebleness, which it was most painful to witness. They were almost literally naked on their arrival on board our vessels, and the officers of the Government had not thought it necessary to make any provision for their clothing, until they reached New Orleans. Here the Commission stepped forward at once to fill the gap, and the same hour which saw these men restored to freedom, found each one of them provided with a blanket, and other articles indispensable to his comfort. So on Red River, the Agents of the Commission were ready to welcome those suffering men who had passed so many weary months within the stockade at Tyler in Texas. They also were in a pitiable state of destitution, but in the midst of it all, it was most refreshing to observe the plucky endurance, and unquenchable love of country, which they had maintained during their captivity. The following incident, related by one of the Agents who was an eye-witness of it, will show that these noble men claimed the sympathy and aid of those who loved their country on other grounds besides those of mere humanity : " The color-bearer of the Forty-eighth Ohio, many of whose regiment were captured at Mansfield, had, when surrounded, stripped his flag from the staff, and secreted it around his body. When in the stockade in Texas, it being rumored among the rebels that such was the case, a diligent search was made for it, but our men had shrewdly buried it. After resting some time in rebel soil it was dug up, only slightly soiled, and stitched into the jacket of one of the captains, under the lining, and thus it passed *its* captivity. On the way down the river the men secretly made a flag-staff, so that the very instant they stepped on board our boat, after the exchange, they drew out from its long hiding-place their good old flag, spreading it to the breeze. The effect can be imagined better than described ; shouts, yells of defiance, and tears of joy followed, with no doubt many thanksgivings to God for his mercy in thus sparing them, to witness this triumph."

The ill-fated expedition to Red River gave the Commission another opportunity of accomplishing a very important relief work in the Army. The Red River Expedition. number of troops was so large, and the point which the Army proposed to reach (Shreveport) was so distant from the base of supplies, that it was deemed .advisable to send with it no less than six Agents who were provided with stores, equalling in capacity that of three hundred barrels. This ill-managed campaign came to an untimely end, and in two severe engagements beyond Alexandria, we lost more than twenty-five hundred wounded. No such result had been anticipated, and, of course, there was a great deficiency in the means of properly caring for these men. At this juncture, as on so many similar occasions, the stores of the Commission although far less in amount than could have been dispensed with the greatest benefit, still afforded a sensible relief to the sufferers. The first news of the disastrous result of the expedition reached New Orleans by a transport which brought a certain number of the wounded to that city. A good deal of excitement and some anxiety prevailed, but this soon gave way to earnest efforts on the part of the Authorities, who were well aware how inadequately the Army was prepared for such a contingency, to send forward with the least possible delay all the needed means of succor. The Mayor of the City, with a readiness which is the best evidence of the recognition of the nature and value of the Commis-

55

sion's work by those whose position best enabled them to form a judgment, at once applied to the resident Inspector for assistance. That officer was told that a boat would be dispatched to the Army within an hour, but in that short time, he was able to ship a considerable portion of the goods in the depôt, besides a certain amount of chloroform, sponges, lemons, etc., which had been purchased by him in the city. On the next day, another large invoice of supplies was forwarded, and by every boat which left New Orleans for " the front," during the next ten days, a ton of ice was sent to promote the comfort of the wounded. So prompt and invaluable had been the assistance rendered by the Commission on this occasion, that it called forth universal praise and gratitude, a sentiment which found expression in the form of a contribution of more than two thousand dollars to its treasury, the proceeds of an entertainment given at one of the theatres of New Orleans for that special purpose.

During the autumn of 1864 the Army was stationed in detachments at certain isolated points on Supplies of vegetables to the Gulf Coast. The great defect in the tables to the sanitary administration of these troops was garrisons on the the neglect to supply them with vegetables, Gulf Coast. either fresh or preserved. The regiments at Brazos Santiago, those in the forts in the front of Mobile, at Pensacola, at the Tortugas, and even at Key West, all suffered very severely in consequence of this neglect. The Commission made strenuous efforts to remedy this evil. Cargo after cargo of vegetable food was despatched by Dr. Newberry from Cairo to New Orleans, and placed in charge of Dr. Blake, the Commission's Inspector. By him, it was distributed in such quantities to the forces composing the garrisons, that it produced in a very short time the most favorable change in their general health, and once more the ravages of that inveterate enemy against which the Commission maintained so constant and so active a warfare ceased, at least, for the time.

From the slight sketch we have given of the work of the Commission in the Department of the Gulf it is clear that it was admirably administered. Character of the Its principal Agents at New Orleans were Agents. indeed men of no ordinary stamp. Dr. Crane who went out with the original expedition, and Dr. G. A. Blake who remained in New Orleans until the close of the war, so conducted its operations at this remote point, as to afford a practical illustration of the value of its plans and policy in no respect inferior to that exhibited on any other portion of the great field of war. Their labors were most arduous, and the embarrassments they met with sometimes very discouraging, but all difficulties were overcome by a wise and prudent conduct on their part, by a zeal always active but never indiscreet, and by that constant practical manifestation of sympathy with the wants of the suffering which brought great credit to themselves, and firmly established the reputation of the Commission with the Army serving in this distant region.

CHAPTER XVI.

SPECIAL INSPECTION OF HOSPITALS.

ALMOST before the smoke had cleared away from the great battle-field of Antietam, on the 21st of Septem-

Work enlarged in consequence of contributions from California. ber, 1862, a telegram from San Francisco announced that one hundred thousand dollars, the first instalment of California's golden treasure in aid of the work of the Sanitary Commission, was on its way to New York. How welcome this news was to those, who, in their efforts to relieve the mass of misery crowded into the preceding month, had almost exhausted the funds in their treasury, and were looking forward with the deepest anxiety to the prospect of abandoning the great work before them, may be readily imagined. When it was found that this large gift was only the precursor of still larger gifts, and that by its opportune arrival not only were present wants supplied, but a prospect of extended usefulness in new fields of labor was unfolded before them, the Officers of the Commission felt that now for the first time, it would be possible to expand and develope their plans in a way in some measure commensurate with their theory of the true functions of such an organization. All the old and well-tried agencies were reorganized upon a larger and more generous footing, and plans for new work were carefully discussed and studied.

436

At that time the most salient feature in the sanitary condition of the Army was the vast and rapidly increasing population of the Hospitals. The Condition of the Hospitals in Sept., 1862. campaigns during the summer on the Peninsula and in Northern Virginia, and the battle of Antietam had filled all the Hospitals in the Eastern Department, to overflowing. In the West, although no general engagement had taken place during the summer, the insalubrity of the country in which the Army was operating, and the excessive fatigues and privations to which the troops had been exposed from long marches, caused the number of sick in the Hospitals to be unusually large. To provide accommodations for so many patients, and to furnish them with suitable medical attendance and care, taxed severely all the resources of the Government, and required the utmost vigor and energy on the part of the Head of the Bureau. At that time there were, in the District of Columbia alone, forty-one General Hospitals, and a hundred and forty-three more in other parts of the country, while the number of sick and wounded under treatment in these Hospitals was not less than sixty-five thousand.

The popular notion as to what constitutes a Military Hospital is a very vague, and, in many respects, a very incorrect one. A certain number of Defects in the Hospital system at that time. beds, a certain number of surgeons, and a sufficient supply of food and medicines to provide all who may become sick or wounded with shelter, attendance and food, do not constitute by any means all that is requisite in such establishments. In all countries some such arrangements have been provided for the care of the sick, yet Hospitals supplied with all these things have often been pest-houses, where the sufferings of the patients have been aggravated rather than relieved. So true was this in former times, and so utterly unsuited have such places been proved by experience for the objects for which they were designed, owing to defects apparently inherent in the system itself, that an eminent writer on Military Hygiene, who had had the largest experience in the practical management of such establishments, asserted not fifty years ago, that " Hospitals were among the chief causes of mortality in armies ;" while another with equal opportunities of judging declared that they were " a curse to civilization." Unsuitable buildings, in unhealthy locations, the overcrowding of patients, want of proper ventilation, deficiency in drainage and water supply, want of a proper diet, the neglect or absence in short of all those essential conditions which are embraced under the general term of hygiene, these were some of the many causes which counteracted all the efforts of the Surgeons to treat sick men successfully who were sheltered from the weather, each of whom was provided with a bed, and abundantly supplied with such food as would have been nutritious to those in health. Ever since the beginning of the war in spite of our boasted advance in civilization, and in the true principles of humane care for the suffering, and with our increased knowledge of the requirements of such establishments, the management of some of the Army Hospitals was a crying evil. After inspecting one of them, Dr. Hammond, at that time acting as Medical Inspector of a military department, did not hesitate to

express his deliberate conviction " that such a condition of affairs did not exist in any other Hospital in
the civilized world," and that the Hospital in question
was " altogether worse than any which were such *op-
probria* to the Allies in the Crimean War." This
severe judgment was passed, it must be remembered,
not upon a Hospital improvised upon a battle-field, or
situated in the enemy's country, far remote from the
means which might have insured its proper administration, but upon one in a town within our own borders, and within easy reach of the great centres of
supply.

This unfortunate condition of things was due to a
cause similar to that which had produced such frightful confusion in almost every department of Efforts of the
Surgeon-Gene-
the Army in the early days of the war,—in ral to remedy
one word, to inexperience. No part of the this state of
things.
military administration requires for its successful practical management, a more thorough special instruction,
and greater experience than the complex machinery of
a vast hospital system. In this country, as we have
said, we were wholly without any experience in such
matters, the methods which had prevailed in the old
Army being worse than useless, because they misled us
in the vain attempt to apply them to wholly new circumstances. There were few men in the country who had
any well-defined conception of what a Model Military
Hospital should be, but one of these, fortunately for the
reputation of the country, and for the cause of humanity, was the Surgeon-General. From the beginning, the great object of his ambition had been to
inaugurate a Model Hospital system which should be

creditable to the age, and the country. He persisted, in the face of most serious obstacles, until his plans were accomplished. The result, which he had confidently predicted from their adoption, was fully attained, and among other great things worthy of the American name, which were done during the war, there is none of which we have greater reason to be proud, than that our sick and wounded were better cared for in every respect, in Military Hospitals, than ever before, and that the rate of mortality in them was far lower than had been observed in the experience of any Army since the world began.

As the views and intentions of the Surgeon-General were well known, as indeed they had been one of the principal grounds of confidence on the part of right judging men in his peculiar fitness for the position he occupied, the Sanitary Commission felt that he would not only willingly receive any suggestions which would assist him in his great work, but also, that he would gladly coöperate in any scheme having for its object a thorough and systematic inquiry into the peculiarities of the existing system. In this belief, it was not mistaken. Indeed, it may be said that the desirableness of a supplemental inspection of the Hospitals by competent medical men in civil life, came from the Surgeon-General, and every means which his official position and authority gave him were freely used to insure the faithful execution of this important object. Never was a better opportunity afforded than at this juncture for ascertaining how far the wants of the suffering were met by arrangements actually existing, and in what respects those arrangements were defective.

A special inspection of Hospitals proposed.

"While the strength of the Army had been nearly doubled, and the population of the General·Hospitals more than quadrupled, the Staff of the Medical Inspection had not been at all augmented. Under these circumstances it was obvious that intelligent assistance from civil life would be acceptable. This aid the Commission resolved to seek amongst the best and ablest members of the medical profession, soliciting, for short periods, the services of meñ unable to leave their responsible duties for any length of time, and yet ready to help the national cause, and that of humanity. This duty was assigned to the Medical Committee, who commenced immediately the organization of a scheme for the special inspection of Military Hospitals.* Invitations were issued to more than a hundred medical gentlemen of assured position, throughout the loyal States, and the services of Dr. Henry G. Clark, of Boston, were secured as Inspector-in-Chief."

Of this number, sixty entered upon this service at the request of the Commission, in the month of October, 1862, and during the next succeeding six months were busily engaged in the special inspection of the Military Hospitals in every part of the country. These gentlemen were assured at the outset, that their visits were made at the invitation of the proper authorities, and by the express desire of the Surgeon-General. They were further told that the general design of this movement was to secure a high standard of professional ability in the management of the Mili-

Corps of Special Inspectors organized.

---

* The Medical Committee of the Sanitary Commission was composed of Dr. William H. Van Buren, Dr. C. R. Agnew, and Dr. Wolcott Gibbs. The scheme for this Special Inspection of Hospitals originated in this Committee, and its details were carefully studied and organized by its different members. Dr. Clark acted under instructions from this Committee, and reported to it.

tary Hospitals, and to detect and remove such defects in their administration or care, as were susceptible of remedy or improvement. As it was not possible that men engrossed with the cares of a large private practice could absent themselves for a long time from their homes, it was proposed that each Surgeon accepting the invitation of the Commission, should devote but one month to the work of actual inspection. They were assigned by the Inspector-in-Chief to groups of Hospitals located in a particular region, care being taken, as far as possible, for obvious reasons, to confide this duty to those whose usual residence was remote from the points to be visited.*

Their instructions contemplated the investigation of a very wide field. The location, construction and Their instruc- general police of the Hospitals, the number tions. and character of the attendants, Surgeons and nurses, the number of the patients, the nature and gravity of the diseases from which they were suffering, the rate of mortality, the all-important question of diet with the means at the disposal of the Hospital to provide food of a suitable character ; drainage, water supply, and ventilation ; these were some of the general subjects which were to engage their minute attention and inquiry. They were expected to make a thorough and painstaking investigation into all these matters, and in order to stimulate them to efforts to render their reports full and accurate, they were informed that the results of their inquiries would be communicated confidentially to the Surgeon-General, who would base his official action upon them.

* See Appendix No. 7 for the names and residences of the Inspectors.

The inspections were commenced in the Hospitals at Washington and its vicinity, and were gradually extended to those in other parts of the coun- They enter upon try, until all the General Hospitals in the the work. Army, from farthest New England to the Department of the Gulf had been visited and reported upon. By the month of May, 1863, reports had been made by these Special Inspectors, which covered more than twenty-five hundred folio pages, and subsequently many additional reports were received. They contained a full, accurate and intelligent description of all the General Hospitals in the Army, and were filled with the evidence of that acute observation, sound opinion, and practical suggestion, which was to have been expected from the eminent reputation, in their profession, of those who composed the corps. These reports are taken up chiefly with detailed accounts of the Hospital administration, regarded from a purely professional and scientific stand-point, and although the views they present are of the highest interest and value, their discussion will find a more appropriate place in the medical history of the war, now in preparation by the Commission, than in the present volume. Still, the plan in itself was so wise and comprehensive, and its execution formed so important a feature in the general work of the Commission, that some outline of it seems necessary in order that some idea of the comprehensiveness of that work may be formed. It cannot be doubted that the information contained in these reports, coming as it did from trustworthy and independent observers, did much to build up our grand system of hospital construction and administration.

The Hospitals were found, in general, by these Inspectors in a far more satisfactory condition than had
General results. been anticipated. The prominent and ob-
Hospital build-
ings. vious defect existing everywhere, but especially observable in the West, was the want of suitable
buildings. At that time large and properly arranged
buildings on the Pavilion system, as it was called,
furnished with all the appliances for the proper treatment of the patients, in accordance with the latest and
best teachings of experience, were not yet completed,
although several were in the process of construction.
The testimony of all the Inspectors was uniform in
regard to the necessity of establishing Hospitals only in
buildings specially erected for such a purpose. In
their investigations throughout the country, they had
found every species of building from common dwell-
ing-houses, to hotels and churches occupied as Hospitals, and they never failed in their Reports to point
out the inherent unfitness of all of them for the purposes for which they were used. They found, at the
West particularly, that the Medical Officers complained
bitterly, that while money was profusely spent in other
parts of the country in supplying this acknowledged
want, no steps had yet been taken to provide proper
accommodation for the sick and wounded of the Armies of the Cumberland and the Tennessee.

The great object of this special Inspection was, as we
have said, to obtain such information with regard to
Character of the the practical management of the Hospitals
Medical Officers
in charge. as might suggest to the Surgeon-General
improvements in the system. The first result, however, was to increase the comfort of the patients who

were then under treatment. This was effected, partly by the intercourse of the surgeons in charge with eminent members of their own profession, whose counsel was naturally regarded by those who were in earnest in their attempt to perform their novel and responsible duties, as of very great value. The Inspectors had been cordially welcomed in almost every Hospital they visited, by the officers in charge. Every facility was afforded them for making a thorough investigation of their condition, and they did not hesitate to point out on the spot deficiencies in the service which met their observation. They found the Surgeons, as a class, faithful, earnest and skillful men, striving, frequently in the face of most serious obstacles, to do their utmost to relieve the wants of the suffering men under their charge. Many of these Surgeons had left their practice in civil life, at a great personal sacrifice, and had entered the Army, from purely patriotic motives. Few of them, it is true, had had any experience in the peculiar labors of Hospital practice, but it was surprising on the whole, how wonderfully nearly all of them had adapted themselves to the exigencies of their new position. There was found among them material for a most efficient corps of Hospital Surgeons, and all that was needed, as they themselves were the first to recognize, for establishing a satisfactory Hospital system, was some slight modification in the organization of the Medical Staff, and above all, suitable Hospital buildings and appliances for the relief of the patients. The suggestions contained in the reports of these Inspectors, says Dr. Clark, the Inspector-in-chief, " with regard to defects and evils found to be existing in any of the Hospitals, have, when transmitted by me, as they are frequently, by extracts, synopses, or verbally, to the Surgeon-General, invariably received his immediate and effective attention.

"An inspection of the reports of the different Inspectors, at different and consecutive dates, will also show, in many instances, a very marked and progressive improvement in the condition of the Hospitals inspected."

It must not be supposed that the work of the Commission in this particular department constituted the This Inspection only systematic inspection which the Hospi-Supplemental only. tals received. On the contrary, the eight Medical Inspectors attached to the Bureau were constantly employed in making official visits. But when it is remembered that in addition to the two hundred General Hospitals of the Army, these officers were charged with the supervision and the Medical and Sanitary care of more than eight hundred thousand men in active service, it will be readily perceived that the force was altogether too small to explore properly so wide a field. There were other reasons to which we have already alluded, for invoking the assistance in this work of the profession outside the Army, and an additional one may be found in the fact that, it was important in forming a judgment on disputed points to compare the opinions of those trained in the habits of civil life, with those who were naturally more affected in their views by purely military considerations.

Among the improvements suggested by these reports and afterwards adopted were some of such great practical importance that some mention must be Various Improvements suggested — Depôts of supplies. made of them here. In the first place, large depôts of Hospital supplies were established by the Authorities at great military centres where they were readily accessible at all times when needed. The former practice had been one utterly unfitting the character of the service, and had caused, in many ways, great inconvenience. When supplies were needed at any point, it had been usual for the proper officer to make a requisition upon the distant Purveyor who, after approving it, sent it to be filled by the still more distant Apothecary. The patients, meantime, were obliged to suffer from the delays caused by the state of the market, or the difficulties of transportation. The practical advantages of this change of system were felt immediately, and they were further increased soon afterwards, by the establish- Government Laboratories. ment of two large Government laboratories, one at New York, the other at Philadelphia, in which during the remainder of the war the principal medicines required in the Hospitals were prepared. The Medical Bureau was thus rendered wholly independent of mercantile houses, both as to the quality of the articles it dispensed, and the regularity of their supply. These laboratories were placed in charge of competent officers detailed from the Medical Staff of the Army, and were managed with great skill and fidelity. They saved also to the Government, the outlay of large sums of money, which would have been required for the purchase of the articles manufactured in them at a far lower cost than the ordinary market price.

A new and vastly enlarged supply-table or list of

articles which the Government would undertake to
New supply- provide for the inmates of the Hospitals was
table. also issued by order of the Surgeon-General, embracing many things essential to their comfort,
for the supply of which the Hospital Fund had been,
hitherto the only, and most precarious resource.   Hospital clothing, also, was furnished to the patients
under the new *régime*, a provision which, when their
Hospital cloth- condition in respect to personal cleanliness
ing. upon their entrance to the Hospital is considered, seems an indispensable pre-requisite to their
proper treatment.   But the measures of reform, introduced by the Surgeon-General, did not cease with his
efforts to provide for the material comfort of the
patients.   The condition of the Medical Staff excited
his most serious attention, and his struggles to maintain a high standard of professional excellence in it,
were never relaxed for a moment.   To effect this important object, he devised most generous and liberal
plans, some of which were adopted, and others failed
from a want of coöperation by the War Department.
They were all characterized by that comprehensiveness of view, which proved his thorough appreciation of the duties of his great office.   As a means of
securing the most competent men for the Medical
service of the Army, he reorganized the Boards of
Boards of Ex- Examination, and insisted upon a higher
amination. standard of attainment on the part of the
candidate.   He established also a new and complete
system of Hospital reports, which was designed to
Hospital Re- embody not merely a formal and barren
ports. statement of the number of patients in the

Hospitals, and of those who were discharged or died, but also such facts concerning their condition as would constitute valuable material for a Medical and Surgical history of the war. The interest and importance of such a history, not merely as a record of what had been done here, but as a valuable contribution to our knowledge of the general laws which govern the health and efficiency of Armies, are too obvious to need comment. In order further to accomplish this object, he instituted at Washington an Army Medical Museum, in which was collected and arranged a vast number of specimens from the different Hospitals, illustrating the nature of the peculiar diseases to which soldiers are liable, and the character of the wounds which are inflicted by the new missiles of war. The peculiarity of these wounds has essentially modified one of the most important departments of Military Surgery, and the specimens thus brought together in the Army Medical Museum, far exceeding in number and variety those of any other collection in the world, have served, not only to advance the cause of science and humanity, but have rendered the Museum a just object of national pride. But the great central want of the system, which left unsupplied, all the other improvements suggested by the Surgeon-General would have proved of little value, was the want of proper Hospital buildings. Fortunately for the completion of the circle of his plans, the necessary coöperation of those officers of the Government outside of the Medical Department who were charged with the erection of Hospitals was, at last, obtained, and a large number were constructed

Army Medical Museum.

Hospital Buildings.

57

on a vast scale in different parts of the country according to the Pavilion system. The peculiar advantages of this system, and the wonderful results which followed its adoption in the improvement of the sick and wounded of the Army is a subject belonging properly to the Medical history of the war. The best evidence we can give of the success of the experiment, is to repeat the statement of the simple fact, that the rate of mortality among the inmates of these Hospitals was far lower than has been recorded of the military Hospitals of any age or country.

The Sanitary Commission, without desiring to share the credit of any of the vast improvements made by the Surgeon-General, does claim not only to have fully sympathized with him in his enlarged and liberal views, but also to have aided him in carrying them out as far as any extra official coöperation could do. It seems, now, surprising that any obstacles should have been placed in the way of reforms obviously so much needed. But the truth is, that, from various causes, it required the persistent vigor and energy of a most determined man to advance a single step in the right direction, and the Surgeon-General always needed for his encouragement all the support he could get, in the Government, or out of it. The Commission felt that the best practical method of maintaining the health and efficiency of the Army was to secure the proper administration of the Military Hospitals, and it was only fulfilling the highest object of its mission by zealously coöperating in any plans which sought to accomplish this great object.

The Commission aids and encourages these improvements.

CHAPTER XVII.

THE COMMISSION'S BUREAU OF VITAL STATISTICS.

IT will have become evident to the reader that the fundamental principle which governed all the operations of the Commission was to make Value of General laws. its influence felt, as far as possible, through the agency of general principles and a general policy. Its action was controlled by a constant regard to those hygienic and physiological laws which are already known, and by an anxious desire to discover and apply such other laws as might affect the welfare and success of our soldiers in this or in other wars. The vast proportions of our national Armies, which doubtless reached during the rebellion the enormous aggregate of two and a-half millions of men, afforded facilities not likely to occur again, at least during the present generation; and it would have been most unfortunate had the opportunities thus afforded for the study of large number of men in their hygienic and physiological relations, been suffered to pass unimproved.

The employment of statistical methods of research is, in general, of comparatively recent date. Their peculiar advantages and restrictions have Early efforts of the Commission to acquire statistical information. been only lately appreciated; and it will be easily perceived that they must be used with great discretion, and with special limitations. But the exceeding importance of their results when properly interpreted, is continually impressing itself more and more upon students of both the moral and the physical sciences; and the opportunities which were presented during the war for the determination of important facts relative to the moral and physical characteristics and capacities of our soldiers, and of men in general, seemed to call upon the Commission to obtain such facts as seemed important to the welfare, not merely of our own country, but of the world. The earliest statistical inquiries of the Commission were directed toward forming the best attainable estimate of the condition, prospects and needs of the forces to be maintained in the field during the summer of 1861. It hoped thus to advise more effectively with the State authorities, and the general Government, as to modifications of the regulations, and such other measures as might tend to guard the troops against pestilence, and to mitigate the anticipated suffering from illness and wounds. For this purpose two series of inquiries were prepared by Mr. Olmsted; the one, relative to the organization and equipment of regiments, being sent to the Governors of States; and the other, pertaining to the sanitary condition of the regiments and their camps, being addressed to the Commanding officers of regiments.

Many of the laws of the physical as of the moral world are deducible only from experience, and the common judgment of mankind recognizes that experience as the most valuable which results from observation of the largest number of facts,

The nature and value of statistics.

the only restriction being in the exercise of a proper discrimination. Now when a very large number of facts bearing on any subject, are collected and systematically classified according to their proper relations, the classified results are called "Statistics," and inferences legitimately deduced from them occupy the same relation to those afforded by personal experience and judgment, that the number of cases collected and the systematic correctness of their classification bear to the number remembered by the individual, and the discrimination with which he forms his opinion. In short, the experience of thousands or hundreds of thousands of men may be substituted for that of one man, and the accuracy of numerical computation may thus supply the place of the rude estimate of personal opinion. Even here large opportunities for error exist in the unskillful combination of incongruous material; but as the fundamental facts are on record, such errors are always capable of subsequent detection and remedy.

From the classification and comparison of the answers to the inquiries propounded by Mr. Olmsted he anticipated useful information. Indeed they had begun to yield results of very considerable importance, when the encounter at Bull's Run solved the problems, exhibited the facts and enforced the conclusions, with a thoroughness to which a less disastrous experience, or years of sanitary inspection would have been inadequate.

Statistics concerning the Battle of Bull's Run.

Just at this memorable crisis the Commission was preparing enlarged and detailed series of questions concerning the condition and needs of the regiments in camp, near Washington, for the purpose of placing them in the hands of medical men especially appointed as Sanitary Inspectors ; and, at the same time, Mr. E. B. Elliott, known as one of the most zealous and well-informed statisticians of the country, came to Washington to obtain accurate statistical information regarding ·the character, number and health of our troops—subjects regarding which the whole nation felt so deep an interest, yet possessed so little knowledge. Mr. Elliott's services promised to be peculiarly valuable at that juncture, and when our Army arrived panic-stricken and disorganized at Washington, a most important field for his labors presented itself. No time was lost in instituting such researches as should best make manifest the causes which led to the calamitous result. The nature of these inquiries, and the value of the information derived from the answers to them, have been already referred to.*

The able report made to the Secretary of War by the General Secretary of the Commission, in Decem-

Statistical Bu- ber, 1861, and published as Document,
reau organized. No. 40, contains in the appendix some of the results of these inquiries. The system of sanitary inspection of regimental camps was at once extended, and was actively prosecuted. The Statistical Bureau was organized as a special Department of the Commission, and the returns of Camp Inspection were at once transmitted thither for tabulation and classification. Digests of more than four hundred of these reports were given in the report to the Secretary of War, just cited, showing the time of recruiting the

* See Ante, page 89.

regiments, the nativities and ages of the men, the thoroughness of their inspection at enlistment, the situation and hygienic characteristics of the camps, the drainage, tents, clothing, cleanliness, food, hospitals, discipline, remittances of pay, competency of medical officers, systematic recreations, etc. Of these Camp inspections one thousand four hundred and eighty-two were received, representing in all about eight hundred and seventy regiments or other organizations.

Immediately upon their reception they were subjected to a preliminary tabulation for office reference, and were so arranged as to enable the Commission to give such information as might be deemed proper, regarding the position and military condition of each regiment. They were then again classified in a condensed form by groups of regiments, in such manner as to exhibit at a glance the information needed for the purpose of the Commission in ameliorating the sanitary condition of the regiments or camps, and in correcting abuses. Thirdly, they were classified by States, and months, and summaries and aggregates of the results were prepared by months, seasons, States, and groups of States. The value of the materials thus collected and assorted is very great, and although their nature is such as to render it difficult to present condensed summaries of results in tabular form, this has still been done as far as possible, and the aggregated results afford sources from which copious information may be derived on many special points of hygienic importance. It is intended by the Commission that these materials, like the others of similar nature, shall be deposited for permanent preservation with some public institution, where those engaged in the investigation of any of the questions involved may find easy access to the information they require, in its most condensed and available form.

Some statement of the influence of these Inspections, and the action which was taken upon the reports Indirect influ- without delay by the Commission, may not ence of its work be without interest. Their indirect influ- in the early part of the war. ence· was of the greatest value. The very asking of the questions, and the sight of the printed blanks are known in a multitude of cases to have suggested to Surgeons and Commanding officers, for the first time, those precautions and sanitary measures, which the lack of previous experience had prevented them from taking. It will readily be perceived how strong a stimulus to the enforcement of official regulations—many of which were at first regarded as a dead letter, or as matters of simple form,—was given by the knowledge that a corps of medical civilians were actively at work, examining into the strictness with which these regulations were enforced, and the general sanitary condition of the regiments and the camps. But in addition to this weighty incentive thus brought to bear upon the officers concerned, the Commission took immediate steps to bring about a remedy through official channels in cases of manifest need; and here again the salutary influence of the reform of a single camp, especially when thus brought about, was felt more or less manifestly upon the other camps in the vicinity.

During the summer of 1862, the materials on file in the offices of the Surgeon-General and Adjutant-

General, were also drawn upon for informa- tion not otherwise accessible, and which the officers of these departments had no opportunity to elaborate.   The consolidated morning reports of the Hospitals in the different Departments, giving for each day, and each Hospital, the number of cases treated, the proportion of cures, and of deaths, were transcribed from the official documents ; and were combined and aggregated according to regions, and according to seasons.   A large amount of the material for this work was provided by the Hospital Directory Department, until at the close of 1864 the present Surgeon-General forbade the communication of farther material to the Commission.   The tabulated results had however already yielded highly valuable information ; and the assumption by the War Department of the responsibility of classifying and tabulating these important facts was the source of much satisfaction to the Commission, which welcomed the probable attainment of the desired end.   It was satisfied with the consciousness that its efforts had in all probability led to the performance of the work, although in this indirect manner.   In this connection, it may be added that not only was the system of Daily Hospital Returns adopted by the War Department first suggested by the Sanitary Commission, but that it prepared even the blank forms of these reports, which (with the slight change of horizontal for vertical lines) are still employed.   The files of the Statistical Bureau contained abstracts and summaries of the returns for both the General Hospitals, and the Hospitals for Contagious Fevers, arranged by months

58

and by departments, for nearly all the U. S. Military Hospitals during the greater part of the years 1863 and 1864. Upon the assumption of the work by the War Department, and the refusal of farther information to the Commission, the work of the Statistical Bureau upon these aggregates and averages was suspended.

The monthly regimental reports on file in the Adjutant-General's office, afford a means for deducing the sickness and mortality of the whole Army, or of any portion of it, at any time. These reports are usually made out by the Regimental Adjutant, and are directed to be forwarded monthly to the office of the Adjutant-General in Washington. They exhibit the number of sick in the regiment, and both for officers and for men the number gained and lost during the month, specifying the manner in which the accessions and diminutions have occurred. These reports were in the early part of the War quite irregular and incomplete, but as the Department gradually adapted itself to its enlarged duties, and exacted from its officers a stricter compliance with the regulations of the service, the returns became more complete and thorough, until, during the later years of the war, the rolls became as regular and complete as in all probability would have been the case with any old standing Army. The results of the statistical elaboration of these data for the nine months commencing with June 1861 were prepared by Mr. Elliott, and printed as Document No. 46, of the Commission's publications. The mortality rates for our volunteer armies by seasons, by rank, by States, by region of service: the constant

Tabulation of loss and gain returns.

sickness-rates for the Eastern and Western forces, careful comparisons between the proportions of sickness and mortality of the troops, East and West, as well as comparisons with the experience of our own army at other periods, and with that of the British Army during the Peninsular and Crimean Campaigns, were elaborately discussed, and the marked preponderance of sickness and deaths among the troops serving at the West was for the first time made manifest. To demonstrate such facts is to make a large advance in the direction of a remedy, and these careful computations bore rich fruit. They also furnished, so far as the experience of these nine months could yield it, the rate of recruiting requisite for supplying a given rate of diminution from mortality, discharges, sickness, desertions, &c., as well as the number of men requisite for securing a given constant force of available and effective soldiers.

While transcribing these valuable statistics, the records of the Adjutant-General's office permitted the ready collection of other material less strik- Ages of the ing in its applications to the immediate troops and physical character- needs of the Army, yet of high importance istics. indirectly. Such are the ages of the troops enlisted, and their physical characteristics, as deduced from the descriptive muster-rolls. These are capable of yielding results of great scientific value, which by combination with each other, and with facts previously known, will be important in determining the relative efficiency for military service of men at different ages, and of different physical peculiarities. The elaboration and discussion of these materials will probably

lead to the establishment of physical laws, before unknown, which in their hygienic application alone,
although this is not their chief apparent value, would
have been cheaply attained at one hundred-fold the
outlay of time and of money. Early in 1863 a new
class of examinations was undertaken, to ascertain
the relative physical condition of soldiers coming from
different parts of the country and of Europe. The results arrived at by these examinations will probably
afford the most important contribution of observations
ever made in furtherance of " anthropology," or the
science of man, considered in reference to his physical
nature. One Inspector was employed upon the examination and measurement of Union soldiers, while
another was similarly engaged with rebel prisoners.
Their birth-places, ages, strength, capacity of lungs,
statures, dimensions of chest, bodily proportions, pulse,
respiration, etc., were carefully noted, and the tabulation of these materials carried on in the office, those in
good health being distinguished from those not in their
usual vigor.

These tabulated records offer the means of intelligent and discriminating comparison between troops of
different nativities, ages, complexions, occupations, etc.,
and between American soldiers, and those of different
foreign countries, as regards their physical and social
condition, and will probably furnish results of which
it would be difficult to say whether their value in a
medical, military, or physiological point of view should
be regarded as the greatest.

In August, 1863, Mr. Elliott embarked for Europe
to attend a meeting of the International Statistical

Congress at Berlin, and for the ensuing year Investigations continued — Dr. Gould takes charge of the Bureau. the collection and tabulation of materials was continued by Mr. T. J. O'Connell, an accomplished and most excellent man, who had served in the Army until his health gave way, and rendered his discharge imperative. During Mr. O'Connell's management of the affairs of the Bureau, a large amount of additional material was accumulated, and arranged according to the rules previously laid down by Mr. Elliott, who in the mean time prepared and presented to the Statistical Congress an account of the methods adopted by the Bureau, together with some of their results, which excited great interest.

In July, 1864, Dr. B. A. Gould took charge of the Bureau, and has conducted its work since that time. The Collection of "Loss and Gain returns," which had been suspended for awhile, was now resumed, and much more extended investigations were instituted concerning the physical characteristics of our soldiers, black as well as white. Materials were drawn from the offices of the Adjutant-Generals of the several States, as well as from those of the Federal Government at Washington, in all of which, with scarcely an exception, the most ready courtesy and cordial aid were afforded, in the examination of their voluminous records. The results promise to solve many long-discussed problems of important practical bearing, such as the laws of human growth while approaching the maximum stature; of pulmonary capacity as dependent upon physical proportions and upon age; of strength as related to age and rate; of complexion, stature and previous occupation as affecting strength and endurance; together with numerous minor questions of high scientific value, as leading to the knowledge of laws controlling the development of man, and the relation of different human races.

A curious illustration of the practical recompense which is always found ultimately to reward the investigation of any physical or moral truth, has recently been furnished by the computations and researches relative to that one subject which seemed to be the least germane to the regular functions of the Bureau.   Mr. Elliott had commenced, and Mr. O'Connell had continued the collection, from the muster-rolls at the Adjutant-General's Office, of the ages of soldiers from the different States.   The ages of more than 750,000 men had thus been collected, almost all of them being those of the original members of volunteer regiments, enlisted previous to the introduction of descriptive muster rolls, and before any recourse was had by the Government to drafting.   The collection of these ages was continued until it included that of all the volunteer regiments enlisted up to the date when it was completed, making in the aggregate about a million of men.   The number of men enlisted at different ages was found to follow a definite mathematical law with marvellous precision,—so closely, indeed, that the number as given by this law as enlisted at any particular age is in all probability even more accurate than the recorded number.   In regard to enlistments at certain special years of age, where motives for misrepresentation existed, the amount of such misrepresentation is thus made evident and measur-

Marginal note: Interesting results in regard to the ages of the men.

able, and the little inaccuracies arising from the tendency of men to express their ages in the nearest round number, rather than with absolute exactness, is also actually recognizable, and made capable of numerical measurement. This, although very striking, is not surprising to the scientist, who knows from the experience of a lifetime that all great moral and social, as well as material movements and impulses, are subject to the control, or at least follow the action of determinate mathematical law. But it is surprising to find that this definite law which governed the enlistment of our volunteer soldiers, and served as a gauge of the existing impulse to take up arms for their country, was measurably the same for the far West, for the populous Middle States, and for the Atlantic sea-board.

This disproved the imputations of certain foreigners that our armies were largely recruited from elements not American, for were the tendency to enlist dependent in any considerable degree upon a foreign element, this tendency would vary in different portions of the country according to the different numbers of immigrants in the respective portions. Yet so far was this from being the case, that while the number of our volunteers at different years of age followed nearly the simple law of geometrical progression, —about four-fifths of the whole number being in conformity with this law,—the rate of this progression, or, in other words, the proportion of enlistments at each successive year of age to those at an age one year younger, scarcely shows any token of variation, whether the enlistments were made in Maine, in Pennsylvania, in Michigan, or in Iowa.

The American element shown largely to preponderate in enlistments.

The ages of the officers were found to follow an entirely diverse law, bearing no resemblance whatever Ages of officers. to that regulating the ages of the enlisted men. And on comparing these two laws with that of the population, this latter was found to be utterly dissimilar to that of either of the others. And a farther examination of the subject led incidentally to the discovery of what appears to be the law of population unknown before; and this in its turn to the algebraic formula which gives the "expectation of life" for any individual, in any country. Thus the Life Insurance Companies, which so generously contributed to the financial support of the Commission at the very outset of its activity, having at one period furnished nearly one half of the funds it received, may not improbably derive from this unexpected quarter a means of largely increasing their usefulness by a reconstruction of their life-tables. And the Commission has the satisfaction of thus contributing to human knowledge and to the progress of civilization, as a collateral and unforeseen result of the very humblest of all its statistical investigations. It may be added here that more than one-eighth part of our volunteers were in their nineteenth year, the youngest military age at the time of enlistment; about three-tenths were under twenty-one; one-half of all were under twenty-three and a half, and three-quarters of them were under twenty-nine and a half years of age.

Soon after the battle of Gettysburg another investigation Investigation concerning the effect of forced marches. gation was set on foot, for the purpose of ascertaining the effect of long marches, and especially of forced marches upon the health of the men who took part in that memorable engagement. Blank forms were prepared containing a series of questions, and three inspectors sent to collect replies. Returns were received from one hundred and forty-four of the regiments which were engaged in the battle, and the study of these, after proper tabulation, seems to show conclusively, that the efficiency of troops during and after the severest marches depends in great degree upon their diet, the exhausting effect of long and hurried marches being of small significance in comparison with the effect for good or ill of the diet provided for them on the way.

The regimental returns of Loss and Gain are now tabulated and aggregated from the commencement of the war to the close of the year 1864. The *The present condition of the material in possession of the Bureau.* collection of material at the Adjutant-General's office in Washington had reached this point, when, by directions from superior authority, in October, 1865, further access to the rolls was refused, at first without reason assigned, but subsequently on the ground that it would enable the Commission to anticipate investigations proposed by the Surgeon-General's Department. The returns had, at this date, been transcribed up to January, 1866, excepting a portion of those for three of the smaller States; and the ready courtesy of the Adjutant-Generals of those States has permitted the completion of the data without difficulties. It is naturally a source of regret that the materials are wanting for the last four months of the war, as also for the colored troops, whose losses in battle and by disease form an important part of the history of the later campaigns. And it is by no means unlikely that

59

the investigation by the Commission of the circumstances attending the fearful mortality of these troops by disease might have led to the detection of some of the fatal influences, and the suggestion of remedies. Still, notwithstanding these deficiencies, the historical value of this investigation promises to be great. During the continuance of the war great care was taken to make public no absolute numbers of the soldiers of any Army, or organization, or those of the killed, wounded or sick, and in all the publications of the Bureau only relative or proportional numbers were given. The returns of Camp Inspections are now classified and aggregated, and the tabulated results bound in volumes for permanent preservation. More than twenty thousand measurements and examinations of soldiers and sailors are on record, and are now undergoing investigation and comparison. The statistics of the age and stature and nativity of more than eight hundred thousand men are on record in the office, the numbers being properly tabulated and assorted. And it is confidently anticipated by the officers of the Commission, that it may soon be possible to assign, with close approximation to the truth, the nativities for our whole army—the ages at which full stature is attained, and the rate of growth in approaching this maximum, the distinctive physical characteristics of men of different nationalities, and also probably the relative efficiency and endurance which belongs to different ages.

The scientific value of these results cannot be estimated. Indeed they may be regarded as priceless, inasmuch as the opportunity for gathering such infor-

mation is passed, and not likely soon to return either in this country or abroad.   The
facts obtained, together with those collected and elabo-
rated by the Medical Committee, comprise that portion of the Commission's work which will remain capable of constant application, to minister to the welfare
of humanity in the future as in the past, increasing
our knowledge of the physical characteristics of men,
and thus tending to the mitigation of the suffering
caused by war, and to the welfare of our race in times
of peace.   And in future years it will unquestionably
be accounted not among the least of the services of the
Sanitary Commission, that it was thus made to contribute to our permanent knowledge of physical laws, as
well as to the maintenance of free institutions, to the
perpetuation of American nationality, and to the succor
of the brave men who offered their lives in defence of
their country.*

* The Commission has published from time to time papers of great general
and scientific interest, based upon the material collected in its Statistical Bureau, and prepared by its Chief. "Document, No. 46," already referred to, showing the Loss and Gain of our Armies, when read before the Statisticians
assembled at the International Congress, at Berlin, called forth general commendation.   Both there, and afterwards in England, when presented at a general meeting of the "Society for the promotion of Social Science" the results shown
by this paper, particularly in regard to the low state of mortality, were considered very remarkable, and produced a most favorable impression of the
strength of our National resources.   Another paper "On the Ages of the U. S.
Volunteer Soldiery," prepared by Dr. Gould, and recently printed by the Commission, containing the results of a most intelligent, accurate, and laborious investigation, based upon a calculation of the ages of more than a million of men,
forms one of the most curious, interesting, and instructive chapters of the history of the war.—ED.

CHAPTER XVIII.

FINANCIAL HISTORY OF THE COMMISSION.

THE first financial measure adopted by the Commission was to announce what it sought to do, and to lay **Appointment of** before the people the question whether they **a Central Finan-** **cial Committee.** would or would not be likely to save money by enabling it to carry out its plans. As a preliminary step, it was resolved that inasmuch as " the professional and scientific character of the members of the Commission make it dependent on business men for the collection of funds," certain gentlemen of the highest position in New York* be requested to act as a Central Financial Committee to raise funds for the Treasury of the Commission. The gentlemen were at the same time brought into relations with the Commission as "Associate Members."† They met from time to time during the Summer and Fall of 1861. Their high position and repute enabled them to raise what then seemed a large sum, (twelve thousand eight hundred and seven dollars and ninety-five cents), in aid of the Commission's work. Without their support it could hardly have survived the first six months of its existence. They issued an earnest and eloquent

---

* Their names will be found at p. 84.

† Sanitary Commission Document, No. 6.

appeal for funds in July, 1861, which was scattered broadcast over the country.

The earliest calls for aid published in the name of the Commission itself bear date June 21st, 1861, and are embodied in two brief papers,* one ad- First appeals dressed to the people at large, the other to for money. Life Insurance Companies. Both dwell mainly on the economic value of its work. Neither appeals to the humanity or charity of the country. Both urge the vast importance to the nation of preserving the National Army in health and efficiency. Both insist on the fact, then new to the public, that in active campaigns many soldiers die of preventible disease, for one destroyed by the casualties of war. Indeed every call for support ever issued under authority of the Commission, except during the summer of 1862, (and these calls were very few compared with the munificent support its work received,) rely mainly on the cold-blooded proposition that every National soldier is a costly piece of National property, worth a certain large number of dollars to the Nation, and that his death is a pecuniary loss to the Nation and to every one of its citizens. The Commission's claim to support by the people was thus put on the lowest possible ground. But the Commission knew the people. It was sure of their humanity and Christian charity. These required no stimulus. It put its appeals and arguments on this lower ground, because the people needed light only as to the money value of the work the Commission had undertaken.

Up to July 10, 1861—that is to say, within ten days

* Sanitary Commission Documents, Nos. 4 and 5.

after public notice that the Commission was in exist-
Result of these appeals. ence and needed funds—fifteen hundred and seventy-eight dollars had been contributed to its support.* This sum came from citizens and corporations of the City of New York, then the Head-quarters and vital centre of the Commission. Its members felt that contributions so large (as they then seemed) and made within so brief a space, formed a ground of hopeful encouragement. For they had as yet done nothing that entitled the Commission to pub-lic confidence, nor had they laid before the people any matured plan of operations. They had as yet devised no such plan, nor had experience yet enabled them to answer the grave criticism they were forced hourly to encounter, namely, that they were volunteering to do what Government was bound to do, and what its offi-cials were paid for doing.

The appeal to Life Insurance Companies was fruit-ful. Before November 1, 1861, the Commission had received considerable sums from many of these Insti-tutions.† It received from all sources, up to August 1, 1861, $7,423 00, and to September 1st, $13,630 03.

Its second call for funds bears date August 13, 1861.‡ This paper sets forth as the main object of the Com-

---

* The receipts of the Commission on the first day of its financial existence, June 26, 1861, may be worth recording. They appear on the first page of its Treasurer's cash-book, as follows: "George Townsend, $50 00; George C. An-thon, $20 00; John A. Stevens, $100 00; Robert B. Minturn, $100 00; Anony-mous, $5 00; J. Carson Brevoort, $10 00; A. N. Lawrence, $100 00; John C. Greene, $100 00; R. H. McCurdy, $100 00; J. S. Merriam, $10 00; Phelps, Dodge & Co., $100 00; Dr. Jacob Harsen, $100 00." This little springhead of less than a thousand dollars, as we shall see, swelled into a great flood of millions.

† See page 84.

‡ Sanitary Commission Document, No. 22, of which No. 24 is an abridgement.

mission, the employment of Sanitary Inspec- Its second appeal.
tors. Six were in the field, and the Commis-
sion ventured even then to declare that it could employ
three times as many with advantage to the Army.

In November, 1861, the Commission seemed near
the end of its resources. The balance in its treasury
on the first of that month was but $1,212 04. The
battle of Bull Run had made heavy drafts on its
Treasury, for the Commission found itself even then
somehow compelled to go beyond its original pro-
gramme of scientific investigation and advice—to hire
skilled Hospital nurses and to purchase extra Hospital appliances and supplies. But that day (then held
so disastrous) brought no increased flow of contributions to its Treasury, such as followed the great battles of subsequent campaigns. For the Commission
was as yet hardly known to the people, nor had it yet
been enabled to organize any system of battle-field
Relief on a large scale.

It opened its seventh session at Washington, Dec.
3d, 1861, and this session was thought likely to be its
last. But it was an active session. It urged upon
Government with ultimate success the advantages
of " Pavilion" Hospitals—mere temporary shanties—
over the hotels and warehouses that had theretofore
been perverted into Military Hospitals. It decided to
undertake the preparation of a series of medical and
surgical monographs for distribution among Surgeons
of the Army and Navy. These were meant to be
substitutes, however imperfect, for professional libraries, to which Surgeons in active service could seldom
resort.

A few days before the session opened, a circular letter (pp. 24) was printed in New York under au-
Circular letter of Dec. 1861.
thority of the Commission, to be signed by its members individually, and by them addressed to such persons as they might think likely to be influenced by its statements. It dwelt mainly on the mere money value to the country of the life and health of every soldier in the service of the country. It affirmed, moreover, that the " Medical Bureau" organized long ago for a little army of fifteen thousand regulars was naturally and necessarily disqualified by its habits for the gigantic work suddenly thrown upon it, of providing for the multitudinous hosts then enlisted or enlisting under officers fresh from the desk or the plough, and as inexperienced in camp life as the rank and file they were suddenly called on to protect from disease in camp and quarters. On these grounds it appealed to the people to sustain the Commission in its work as a temporary organization auxiliary to the Medical Bureau, and designed to aid that Bureau till it could be strengthened by legislation and made equal to the emergency.

This Circular somewhat strengthened the Treasury
Condition of the Treasury in the early part of 1862—Appre-hensions.
of the Commission. It received $19,682.95 during that month; $910.75 during January, 1862. Its balance in bank March 1st, 1862, was $7,249.39. During February, 1862, it had paid out 7,200.62. Its members inclined daily more and more to the opinion that their work must soon be abandoned. They saw it growing larger and more costly every day. But there was as yet no corresponding increase in the means to

support it. Such increase seemed at that time obtainable only by personal solicitation or by "sensational" appeals to the public. Neither method was to their taste. They could not foresee the unprecedented munificence of the Pacific States, and the equally unprecedented results of the "Sanitary Fairs." They felt, moreover, that Government was not giving them the support to which they were entitled under the order of June, 1861; that it was doing little or nothing to strengthen the Medical Bureau, or for the sanitary interests of the Army. They doubted, and not without reason, whether they could fairly ask the country to sustain any longer a costly volunteer organization, originally designed to aid Government in a sudden emergency. For the manifest defects which that organization was meant in some degree to supply, remained after nearly a year without correction, and almost without notice.

On the morning of March 10th, 1862, certain members of the Commission attended the Military Committee of the House, and were heard at length in support of a bill to reform the Medical Bureau. When they left the Capitol they found Pennsylvania Avenue blocked up by a great column of men, guns, caissons, and Army wagons moving towards the Long Bridge. The Army of the Potomac had assumed the offensive at last. Telegrams and letters were instantly sent to members of the Central Finance Committee in New York from the Headquarters of the Commission at 244 F street: " A forward movement had commenced—a great battle was probably at. hand. The Commission would need

New appeal for funds in March, 1862—Its failure.

60

large additional means. Ten thousand dollars should be raised in New York at once." The members of the Committee thus addressed responded coldly, and with abundant reason. "Capitalists had done enough to help Government through the emergency of last Spring. Government ought by this time to be able to take care of its soldiers without amateur help. No more money could be raised in New York." The Committee was not called together and virtually ceased to exist.

This response from the earliest and most generous supporters of the Commission was disheartening. Effect of this There were but about seven thousand dollars failure on the in its Treasury, and there was no prospect members of the Commission. that this small balance would be much increased. Active operations in the field such as now seemed commencing at last would quadruple the cost of its work. Its members would be held in some degree morally responsible for the sufferings and privations of men on the march and after every battle, and legally responsible, moreover, for such engagements and contracts as their exhausted Treasury should fail to meet. On the other hand, the Commission had already received voluntary contributions amounting to $53,720.45, and seemed gaining ground in public esteem. A motion to disband was anxiously discussed at Washington on the receipt of this chilling response from New York, and unanimously negatived. The question was reconsidered at a meeting of members of the Commission in New York, (March 28th,) and again decided in the negative. Every member of the Commission felt that his personal reputation, and whatever worldly goods he might possess were pledged to the prosecution of the work the Commission had undertaken.

War had now begun in earnest, East and West. Reports, often exaggerated, of the sufferings of wounded men and of defects in the equipment of Military Hospitals inflamed public sympathy with the privations of the Army. Hospital transport service. General attention was thus directed to the work of the Commission. But its HOSPITAL TRANSPORT SERVICE, organized in April, 1862, and maintained to the end of the lamentable Peninsular Campaign, first made the work of the Commission known to the whole people. That work became then visible to the North. Boston, New York and Philadelphia saw thousands of sick and wounded men brought home in spacious, well-ventilated transports liberally equipped with every sanitary appliance—fully supplied with comforts and even luxuries. Each of these transports had its staff of Physicians and Surgeons, of Hospital dressers chosen from among the elite of our medical schools, and of loyal women of the highest social grade serving as matrons and nurses. Contributions to the Treasury of the Commission rose from $7,382.43 in June to $24,381.46 in July. It had received in September, 1861, $430.81, and in October, $890.00.*

It must not be supposed, however, that the Commission bore the whole expense of this costly Transport service. It could not have maintained the Flotilla for

* Its comparatively large balances in November and December, 1861, were due partly to a liberal contribution from the people of New England ($10,000), sent in through Mr. J. Huntington Wolcott, of Boston, afterwards a most efficient member of the Commission, partly to drafts on the fund raised by the "Central Financial Committee" during the first months of the war.

How far the
Commission sus-
tained it from
its Treasury. a single week. Most of its ships and steamers were chartered by the Quartermaster-General. " Ordinary rations" for crew, officers and patients, were issued by the Commissary-General. But the Commission made the transports confided to its charge safe and wholesome. It set up ventilating apparatus, provided abundant stores of everything needed by sick and wounded men, engaged surgeons and nurses, organized special diet-kitchens and other offices, and thus gave many thousand disabled soldiers on their way home what Government could not or did not then provide them—wholesome quarters, suitable diet, careful nursing and skilled professional treatment. This work, while it lasted, cost the Treasury of the Commission about twenty thousand dollars a month. But its value became more and more visible and palpable to the North as one Hospital Transport after another cast anchor in a northern port. Contributions to the Central Treasury rapidly increased. During July and August, 1862, it received nearly fifty thousand dollars.

It may be mentioned here that the labor thrown on the New York members of the Commission by the Hospital Transport service, first compelled them to employ paid agents. They found it absolutely necessary to hire an office (498 Broadway) and engage a Cashier and Clerk. This office was soon thereafter removed to No. 823 Broadway, where the Treasurer's books and vouchers were kept, and the Standing Committee met daily till the end of the war.*

* It is no more than justice to name Mr. Benjamin Collins and Mr. Charles G. Lathrop and Mr. Samuel H. Stebbins as among the most faithful and devoted Agents of the Commission in New York.

But this Hospital Transport service was far the most costly work the Commission had ever undertaken. It was, therefore, obliged, during the dark summer of 1862, to call on the country for help once more. It did so with It asks for new contributions in the summer of 1862. more fervor of expression than ever before or ever afterwards. What it had already accomplished with slender means and imperfect organization, had shown its members that its work might be so enlarged and systematized as to render substantial service to the country. They saw that it was daily saving the country scores if not hundreds of lives, not indirectly and presumptively through advice to Army Surgeons and suggestions of Sanitary Reform, but directly and palpably by food and stimulants given to men sinking from exhaustion, and by the transportation to the healthy climate of the North, from pestilential swamps and from field hospitals, little better than swamps (and in some respects worse,) of thousands who were dying of malarious disease or of trifling wounds aggravated by a poisonous atmosphere.

Hence their "Appeal to all loyal people of the United States," (San. Com. Doc., No. 44, July 4, 1862,) for money and supplies, "at once and in abundance," dwelt on the sufferings and privations of the Peninsular Army in a tone unlike that of any other appeal they ever issued.

The Commission had not learned till then how much suffering the people could remedy, and what service the people could render the National cause through its agency. A few months later set in that great flood tide of Gold Treasury again exhausted by the demands of the campaigns of August and September, 1862.

from the Pacific Coast, which made earnest and impassioned appeals to the public unnecessary.   Gen. Pope's campaign in northern Virginia obliged the Commission to issue another call for funds (September 11, 1862.)   A third was issued (September 24, 1862) after the battle of Antietam.   They were generously answered.   But during September the Commission's receipts were only $20,916 80, and its expenses $26,646 01.   Its balance, October 1st, was less than seventeen thousand dollars.

The financial infancy of the Commission ended in September, 1862.   For fifteen months it had lived from hand to mouth.   It had been more than once on the point of death by inanition. It had never been entitled to count with confidence on sixty days of solvency.   But its work had prospered beyond the hopes of its founders.   The Treasurer reported at its Ninth Session, (Washington, September, 1862,) that its receipts to the tenth of that month had been $158,501 10.   Its list of contributions proved that it had the confidence of the most intelligent business men of the country, and many contributions of small amount from " the workmen of sundry factories," showed that the " masses" were beginning to trust it as their Almoner.   Its money receipts had been thus far chiefly from the Cities of New York, Philadelphia and Boston, but contributions now began to flow in from the whole country, East and West, some of them small in amount, but important as a sign of popular sympathy.   State, City, Town and Village organizations were springing up throughout the land to aid it with supplies of clothing, bedding and hospital stores.   These were equivalent to large con-

The sources and amount of contributions to this time.

tributions of money to its Treasury. The city of Troy, N. Y., and certain towns in Maine, deserve special notice as among its earliest and most generous supporters. Up to the fall of 1862 they had done more for the Commission than New York, Philadelphia and Boston together, if the relative wealth of these several communities be taken into account.

In October, 1862, came the first considerable instalment of aid from California. The Commission's receipts from October 1st to November 1st California's contribution. were $213,964 23, and its disbursements $43,876 93, more than double any previous outlay. Of these receipts $206,837 65 came from communities beyond the Rocky Mountains. Among the items that made up the balance contributed at the East appears, " Collection in Trinity Church, N. Y., October 8, 1862, on the National service of Humiliation and Prayer appointed by the House of Bishops of the Protestant Episcopal Church (during the Session of its Triennial Convention) $290 95." This endorsement of the Commission by the head of every Northern Diocese proves that it had then become known throughout the country as a National organization, working for National objects and working not wholly in vain.

The munificence of California and her sisterhood of Pacific States is the subject of another chapter, and need not be dwelt on here. It was unprecedented and unlooked for. The Its value direct and indirect. eldest of the States and Territories that thus lavished their bounty on the Commission as the National Army Relief Agent, had existed as a civilized community hardly seventeen years. The Army they so generously aided and relieved was fighting thousands of miles from their frontier. Between them and its battle-fields were mountain ranges and desert tracts, barriers practically more formidable than the Ocean that divides the old world from the new. But the people of the Pacific Coast were impelled in God's good Providence to help the National Army through the Sanitary Commission, and their work will hold high place in history. They so upheld and strengthened this novel and untried popular agency that it became generally recognized as the chosen almoner of the whole people. The great "Sanitary Fairs" of 1864, which brought millions into its Treasury and into the Treasuries of its branches, and which sustained it to the end of the war, would never have been organized had not the bounty of the Pacific States enabled the Commission to prove itself a National organization working on a National scale.

The battles of Fredericksburg, (Dec. 11th, 1862,) of Chancellorsville (May 3d, 1863), and of Gettysburg (July 3d, 1863), brought considerable reinforcement to the Central Treasury. Its receipts during that period were:

Contributions from December, 1862 to July, 1863.

		From the Pacific Coast.	Other Sources.	Total.
Dec.	1862,	$104,630 52	$62,523 62	$168,154 14
Jan.	1863,	47,790 44	2,191 22	49,981 66
Feb.	"	15,069 15	6,022 35	21,091 50
March	"	61,194 56	4,482 12	65,676 63
April	"	1,451 98	1,178 40	2,630 38
May	"	11,109 95	4,381 65	15,491 60
June	"	11,800 00	17,372 31	29,172 31
July	"		28,628 54	28,628 54

Every great battle was usually followed by a freshet

in the stream of public bounty. But after each came a still greater drain on the Treasury. For the purchase of supplies vast sums were expended by the Central Treasury and by the Branches East and West. But the stores thus bought were of small account beside the great mass of supplies furnished by the people in kind. Both were kept flowing southward in a steady current to every Military Station to the Rappahannock, to Charleston, to New Orleans, Nashville and Kansas.

All this involved very heavy outlay. During the last six months of 1863 the disbursements of the Commission were two-fold its receipts. It entered on the year 1864 with a balance of $41,725.28. During the preceding month of December it had spent $64,634.28. To support its work at this rate of expenditure seemed impossible. The ordinary contributions of the Atlantic Seaboard and the West were far too small. Another great flow of treasure from the Pacific States could hardly be hoped for. Certain great Fairs, in aid of the Commission, to be held at Brooklyn, New York, and Philadelphia, were talked of, but their result was wholly uncertain.

In view of its fast failing resources the Commission published (December 7th, 1863) the last formal appeal for funds that it was obliged to issue. (San. Com. Doc. No. 69, pp. 64.) This paper sets forth the results of its work, and insists, as usual, on the economic value of that work to the country. But it expressly declines to solicit contributions or to stimulate public sympathy by any recital of the many pathetic and touching incidents which the Commission

Vast increase in its expenditures for Army relief.

Last appeal issued in December, 1863.

could have put on record. It simply submitted to the good sense of the people a dry statement of the work the Commission was doing. "If means be freely supplied as heretofore," it says, "the work of the Commission will be kept up. If not, it will be abandoned; and to keep it up not less than two hundred and fifty thousand dollars must be raised before February 1st, 1864."

This avowal was meant by members of the Commission as public notice that the Commission would soon cease to exist. Stimulated by the unlooked for munificence of the Pacific States, that work had outgrown the support on which it could certainly and steadily depend. Yet the proofs of confidence given it by the people were never stronger than at this very time.

During the first ten days of December, 1863, many hundreds of "collections" ("Thanksgiving Day collections" mostly) were received by the Central and Branch Treasuries from as many churches and congregations scattered over all the loyal States. Many of these collections came from obscure hamlets and from thinly settled rural districts. They were mostly small in amount, made up of pennies contributed by small farmers and mechanics. But they proved that the work of the Commission had become known to the whole people and not merely to the capitalists and business men of our chief cities.

Before February, 1864, the Fairs projected in aid of the Central Treasury had assumed such dimensions as to promise it the speedy receipt of much more than "two hundred and fifty thousand

dollars." The Commission and its Branches had received many contributions from the proceeds of concerts, Fairs, Tableaux, and the like. But in the autumn of 1863, and thenceforward till the war was
over, these efforts in its aid assumed a magnitude beyond example. Some of them were designed to aid
the Central Treasury, that is, the Commission itself;
some to aid its Branches, and some for the benefit of
both. They began with the "Great North-western
Fair" of Chicago, October and November, 1863. It
produced nearly seventy-nine thousand dollars. No
part of its proceeds reached the Central Treasury.
They were spent by the Chicago Branch in the purchase and the "making up" of material to be dispensed on the field by agents of the Commission.
That so great a sum should have been so raised in a
city that was a wilderness thirty years ago seemed
marvellous in 1863. But the example of Chicago was
soon followed in all the cities of the land and surpassed in some of them.

The history of these "Sanitary Fairs" as they were
commonly called, need not be repeated here. The
aggregate amount thus contributed to the Proceeds of
many of them
Central Treasury (two · millions seven went into the
hundred and thirty-six thousand eight Treasuries of
the Branches.
hundred and sixty-eight dollars and eighty-four cents,)
may well surprise all who did not see for themselves
with what energy and talent these undertakings were
conducted. But the whole amount thereby contributed
toward the work of the Commission was very much
larger. The managers of some of the Fairs enumerated in the appendix applied the proceeds of their

work mainly to their own local supply system and sent only some small balance to the Central Treasury. The proceeds of many other Fairs were (like that of Chicago) wholly devoted to local work, and as these contributed nothing to the Central Treasury they do not appear in the appendix at all. But the many hundred thousand dollars thus raised enured nevertheless to the benefit of the Commission, for they kept its Depôts and Relief Stations steadily replenished with supplies, of immense value in money, and of value hardly to be estimated in money to the sick and suffering men they relieved, and to the National cause.

The first direct aid in money thus given the Commission was a most timely contribution of fifty thousand dollars from the "Sanitary Fair" of Boston in January 1864. Other and still larger contributions followed it. Before the summer of that year was ended the Commission had received more than thirteen hundred thousand dollars from the Fairs of Brooklyn and New York alone. It entered on June 1864 with a cash balance of more than a million.

In fact its work had now grown too large to be carried on without a great reserve fund. During May Some items of June and July 1864 the average monthly its expenditure at this period. expenditure of the Central Treasury exceeded two hundred and eighty thousand dollars. On the rosters and pay-rolls of the Commission, East and West, were the names of more than five hundred persons of every grade from Physicians and Surgeons of eminence to "contraband" teamsters and cooks. Its "Homes and Lodges" were everywhere. It was buying supplies for battle-field relief on a great scale while prices were rising fast and at a fearful rate.   It was building " Hospital Railroad Cars" for the transportation of disabled men from camp to Hospital and providing them skilled attendance on the way.   It had its own flotilla of Steamers, sailing vessels and barges on the Atlantic Coast and on Western rivers, chartered or owned by the Commission itself (and not by any department of Government, as in 1862) and its own wagon trains through which ship-loads of life-saving antiscorbutic stores were daily reaching men already tainted with scurvy as they lay in the trenches and rifle-pits before Petersburg or lingered in unhealthy camps along the southern sea-board.   Many thousand claims on Government for pensions, back pay and bounty had been entrusted to it for gratuitous collection—many hundred thousand men were registered on the books of its Hospital Directory and the convalescence, the discharge or the death of every one of these thousands was duly noted day by day.   It was in short carrying out the purpose not merely of its creation, (for that purpose was mainly scientific and advisory) but the farther purpose insensibly forced on it by the people, of doing or trying to do for the health, comfort and efficiency of the soldier whatever the inflexibility of Regulations forbade his officers to do for him and that could be done without prejudice to discipline and good order.

Other chapters of the Commission's final Report will show how far it was enabled to do its appointed work while the war lasted.   The history of its Funds henceforth sufficient. financial hopes and fears and of what little effort it made to obtain money for its work ends here.

The great fund put at its disposal by the "Sanitary Fairs" of 1864, wasted fast away under the cost of its multifarious agencies. But its Central Treasury was refreshed till the war was over by a steady stream of unsolicited popular bounty. Though this fell far short of its constant daily expenditure it was large enough to show that the Commission enjoyed the confidence of the people, and that if the war should be prolonged till the proceeds of the " Great Fairs" were exhausted, the Commission could appeal to the people once more in the sure and certain hope that its appeal would be generously answered.

In the spring of 1865 Richmond fell, and the slave-holders' Rebellion collapsed. July, 1865, found the State of its Trea- Commission with a quarter of a million in sury at the close of the war. its Treasury, but with much costly work still on its hands. Its Special Relief service in aid of discharged and disabled men could not be abruptly given up without producing cruel disappointment and wide-spread suffering, nor was it possible to close its Pension, Bounty and Back Pay offices, scattered over the whole North. Through these offices the Commission had undertaken gratuitously to solicit the claims on Government of some fifty thousand men who had been disabled in the National service and of women and children representing men who had died in the National service. Many of these claims could not be worked through the machinery of Government in less than two years. The Commission had on its hands also the " Lincoln Home,"* an establishment in which many disabled and deserving soldiers had long been

* Grove Street, New York.

supported, and another "Home" for the same object in Yates County, N. Y. It was, moreover, bound to publish some account of the great fund the people had confided to it. Whether the small balance now* in its Treasury will enable it to do all this is a question about which its members feel some anxiety.

If the record of the Commission possess any but a local and temporary value, it is because it shows how much a Free People can do for its Armies in Lesson taught the Field, and even during the actual shock by this financial history. of battle without impairing the rightful and necessary supremacy of discipline. No Army had ever before received such aid on a large scale and during a series of great campaigns. The military representatives of the Powers of Europe in " International Congress" assembled, at Geneva, in 1863, discussed the feasibility of popular unofficial relief to Armies in active service, and generally condemned the project as not only Utopian but mischievous and disorganizing.†

The aggregate amount of money expended through the agencies of the Commission, and the money value of the supplies contributed to the Depôts of The whole the Commission, cannot be stated with pre- amount of receipts. cision. The value of these supplies is estimated at

---

* May, 1866.

† Among the questions discussed was the following: It appears to have been suggested by M. Twining, de Londres, philanthrope eminent. "Lorsque l'étât d' un blessé sur le champ de bataille ne laisse pas le moindre espoir de guérison, convient il aprés lui avoir administré les secours de la Religion, et procuré, autant que les circonstances le permettent, un moment de recueillement, de mettre fin à son agonie de la manière la moins penible, et d'empêcher ainsi qu' il ne meure un peu plus tard, la fièvre dans le cerveau, et peut-être le blasphême à la bouche." This nice point of professional casuistry seems to have been left undecided by the Conference of Continental Soldiers and Surgeons.

about fifteen millions.   The cash receipts of the Central Treasury to May 1, 1866, were $4,962,014 26.

The receipts of the Branch Treasuries were never reported.   These Branches must have received and ex-

Receipts of the Branch Treasuries. pended two millions more at the very least.* With each of them were affiliated hundreds or thousands of " Sewing Circles" and " Soldiers' Aid Societies," established in every loyal Town, Village and country neighborhood through all the North.   Each of these raised a certain amount of money—larger or smaller for its own local work of gathering supplies—

* In order to give some idea of the vastness of the work of the Commission, we annex a statement published by one of its Branches—that at Philadelphia:

Summary of the Receipts and Expenditures of the Philadelphia Agency of the U. S. Sanitary Commission to January 1, 1866.

The total amount in cash contributed to the Treasury of the Philadelphia Agency, including the proceeds of the Great Central Fair, is..	$1,186,545 14
The total amount in cash contributed to the Relief Committee of the Women's Pennsylvania Branch, excluding $2,551 50, received from the Treasurer of the Philadelphia Agency, and $1,681 31 received by them from contractors for work done, is	29,744 00
Total amount of cash received by the Philadelphia Agency.....	$1,216,289 14
Cash value of hospital supplies, clothing, etc., received by the Philadelphia Agency...	306,088 01
Cash value of four hundred tons of coal, received by the Relief Committee of the Women's Pennsylvania Branch...............	3,000 00
Estimated value of volunteer labor and railroad and other facilities rendered free of charge...	40,000 00
Total contributions of all kinds to the Philadelphia Agency...	$1,565,377 15

This amount has been distributed as follows :

For the support of the work of the Sanitary Commission in Philadelphia and its vicinity, including cash remaining in the hands of the Treasurer of the Philadelphia Agency......	$303,554 63
For the general work of the Sanitary Commission.................	1,261,822 52
	$1,565,377 15

making them up and forwarding them to the " Branch" with which it corresponded. The aggregate of these comparatively small sums must be enormous, but it cannot be ascertained. The Commission has twice scattered over the country thousands of Circulars addressed to these little vital centres of humanity and patriotism, entreating each to report how much it had spent on its own local work, and reminding each how desirable it was that a complete record be preserved of the People's munificence during the war. But not one in five hundred ever responded to these appeals. They had done what they could and cared not whether their work were remembered or forgotten. The very few answers these Circulars called forth proved that full returns would have shown an aggregate of contributions, severally small, but exceeding all the cash receipts of the Branch and the Central Treasury together. Little hamlets in the Eastern States and pioneer settlements in the West, the very names of which were new and strange had laid out each its five hundred dollars or its one or two thousand dollars in the work of Army Relief over and above like sums sent to the Central Treasury of the Commission or to that of some one of its Branches.

Another most important contribution came from the Railroad, Telegraph, and Express Companies of the whole country, or more properly of that part of the country which was not involved in Rebellion. Many of these gave the Commission their services gratuitously, all or nearly all at greatly reduced rates. They thus contributed to its Treasury at least three-fourths the cost of transporting its bulky

Facilities afforded by Steamboat, Express, and Telegraph Companies.

stores to the front, and of forwarding its daily (and often hourly) despatches to every part of the country. The free transportation given the Commission by two Western Railroads was estimated in December, 1863, to have saved its Treasury two hundred thousand dollars. Efforts have been made to obtain from these several companies some statement of their contributions to the National cause through the Commission. But these efforts have been fruitless. The loyal newspapers of Northern cities either gave the Commission free use of their columns, or sent in their bills for advertising with a credit of " one-half donation." The Merchants from whom the Commission bought its manifold supplies, its medicines, stimulants, blankets, flannels, fresh vegetables, concentrated food, dealt with it liberally and seldom sought to make profit of the Army's necessity. These indirect contributions were equivalent to millions of money given the Central Treasury. Every " Branch Treasury" and every " Village Aid Society" bought, no doubt, on terms as favorable. Public charity, therefore, (using that word in its broadest sense) organized and administered by the Commission, its Branches and its affiliated societies, far exceeded in money value the mere receipts of its Central Treasury. The aggregate of those receipts— of contributions in money to its Branches and to their affiliated Societies—of contributions of money's worth in free transportation, etc., and in goods, cannot be less than twenty-five millions of dollars.

The disbursements of the Central Treasury were carefully watched and guarded against misapplication. Of course, no member of the Commission ever asked or received compensation, though there were among them medical men in full and lucrative practice who often abandoned that practice for weeks together to devote themselves to the Commission's work in Virginia or North Carolina. All that members of the Commission ever received from its Treasury was a part* of their expenses when attending its Sessions, or traveling in its service.

So scrupulously did they confine the disbursements of their Treasury to work directly aiding the Army, that when it seemed desirable (January, 1862) to lay before the people through the newspaper press of New York an elaborate report submitted to the War Department by their General Secretary, (San. Com. Doc. No. 40,) they held the cost of its publication not a legitimate charge on the Treasury of the Commission. It was published, however, and filled six or eight columns of the prominent daily papers of New York as an advertisement at a reduced rate. One of these papers, however, (the N. Y. Times,) afterwards contributed to the Treasury what members of the Commission had paid it.

The Commission always maintained a close watch over the disbursements of its Central Treasury. At every session its first business was its Treasurer's Re-

---

* The vouchers of the Treasurer's office show that these expenses were never wholly refunded. " Extras" were always deducted from Hotel Bills, and under the name of Traveling Expenses only Railroad and Steamboat fares were allowed. The many other little items that swell the cost of travel were always excluded. This seems hardly worth mentioning. It is mentioned only because a newspaper attack on the Commission, in 1861, charged its members with living sumptuously at the Hotels of Washington on money contributed for Army relief. The slander has never been repeated to their knowledge, and is now probably forgotten, but may as well be thus formally contradicted.

Methods taken to insure exactness and fidelity. port and the appointment of a committee to examine and audit it. This committee always reported in writing before the session was closed. The Commission sought from the first to secure the supervision of its financial affairs by intelligent and influential business men. When it invited the aid of an outside "Central Financial Committee" in the summer of 1861, it requested that Committee to keep itself informed of the receipts and disbursements of the Commission and to pass on its accounts. A sub-committee (Messrs. David Hoadley and C. R. Robert) reported in writing to the "Central Financial Committee," Nov. 27th, 1861, that they had examined and audited the accounts of the Commission up to the 20th of that month, and had found them accurate and properly vouched. This Committee did not meet (as already stated) after the spring of 1862. In 1864 the Commission invited the supervision of another Committee—an "Auxiliary Finance Committee"—Messrs. A. A. Low, Jonathan Sturges, and J. J. Astor, Jr.) These gentlemen consented to serve. They advised the Commission from time to time as to the best and safest investment of its temporary surplus, went carefully through all its books and vouchers with the aid of professional accountants and certified to their accuracy. Their last report appears in the Appendix.

This financial history of the Commission is most imperfect. It ought to include a list of all the contributions received by its Treasury, with notes and commentaries showing how much patriotic and charitable self-denial was embodied in many even of the least of them. For many of them came unasked from very poor men, poor women and poor children.   There were many, in sums of a dollar or two, from soldiers in the field and from seamen lying in front of rebel batteries, though all Agents of the Commission were charged to discourage contributions from men in the National service.   Such contributions were now and then received under the name of " payment" for clothing or supplies.   These were always made the subject of special inquiry and returned to the contributor whenever he could be found out.   There should also be a detailed statement of the multifarious methods through which the Commission's funds were used, not only to provide battle-field supplies, anti-scorbutics and extra hospital appliances, but also to dig wells for posts that had no sufficient supply of water, to build wholesome guard-houses for regiments that had to turn soldiers under arrest into a filthy, pestilential " bull pen," to furnish men on monotonous duty at frontier posts with little collections of books called " libraries," to buy seeds and tools for the establishment of anti-scorbutic gardens in the South-west, and in short, to do every thing for the Army which could be done by the people through a flexible voluntary organization, but could not be done through the rigorous and inflexible system by which military officials are necessarily governed.*

* See Appendix No. 6 for two statements: one showing the " Receipts and Disbursements of the Commission from June 29, 1861 to January, 1866 ;" the other, " Monthly Receipts and Balances showing Contributions from the Pacific States, Sanitary Fairs, and all other Sources, from October 1, 1862 to May 1, 1865."

CHAPTER XIX.

INTERNAL ORGANIZATION.—RELATIONS WITH THE GOVERNMENT.

No history of the Sanitary Commission would be complete without some general view of the machinery
The Commission combined various methods to accomplish its object. of its internal organization. In reviewing its work, the great variety of the forms of relief. it bestowed, and the unity of plan by which they were so combined as to accomplish the common object of promoting the health and efficiency of the Army, are quite as remarkable as the vast extent of the field occupied by its labors. Two great principles, it is true, underlaid its whole work, the value of the preventive system, and the absolute necessity of harmonizing its relief operations with the requirements of Army discipline, yet the methods by which these principles were applied in practice differed in almost every department of its labors. Thus, as we have seen, its Inspectors had a distinct province assigned to them, differing wholly from that in charge of the Relief Agents. So also the various forms of relief which it administered—General, Special or Battlefield—had each its peculiarities, which were so arranged, that the efficiency of the whole service depended upon a division of labor thoroughly organized, and constantly maintained. To harmonize the operations of

all the different modes of Army Relief which we have described, in such a way that they should mutually support each other in effecting the great common object, was no easy task. The problem was not, how to bestow relief indiscriminately, but how to give full scope to the carefully prepared plans of a voluntary organization without, at the same time, unduly interfering with the ordinary routine, and necessary discipline of an army. This problem, always difficult of solution, became still more so as the war went on, and the new wants of the Army seemed to call for closer relations between its life, and the popular zeal for its welfare. The great principle which the Commission adopted in all its operations was, as we have seen, to supplement, and not to supplant the Government, and we come now to consider the machinery by which relief was afforded in strict accordance with this principle.

By reference to the Plan of organization, it will be observed that it was designed that the Commissioners appointed by the President, and such others *The Board. Its* as they might associate with themselves, *composition and functions.* should compose the Board or Legislative council of the new organization. This Board was never, strictly speaking, a representative body, although great care was taken as soon as the full scope of its powers was developed in practice, to give it a thoroughly national character by introducing into it as members, gentlemen of position and influence residing in different parts of the country. At first, when its operations seemed likely to be confined to a special field of inquiry, and to be of limited duration, the number of its members was small, and was made up chiefly of those who had urged its appointment on the Government. These gentlemen, as we have seen, were mostly residents of the city of New York, but shortly afterwards, new members were added, so that during the war Massachusetts was represented in the Board by three members, Rhode Island by one, New York by six, Pennsylvania by three, Ohio and Illinois by two each, Kentucky by one, Washington by one, and the military service of the country by three. These gentlemen were all men of weight and influence in their respective communities, and in their well-known devotion to the National cause, and in their perfect freedom from partisan influences, the public found a guarantee that the great powers entrusted to them would not at least be abused for selfish ends. When it is remembered that they all differed widely from each other in their personal characteristics, in their previous training and habits, in their professions in life, and in their opinions on many important subjects, political and religious, and that they were forced in carrying out their plans, at least at the outset, to grope their way very much in the dark, the harmony of their deliberations, and the unity of plan which they were able to preserve during the whole war become very remarkable. It is certainly most creditable to their earnestness, candor and thorough appreciation of the great objects of their appointment, that so many independent thinkers thus brought together were so fully inspired with a common impulse in effecting the grand object all had in view.

During the early months of the war, and until the

details of the service were well settled, the Board met in Washington every six weeks, but after Meetings of the Board. Nature of the business transacted. the first year, its sessions were held quarterly. It had been designed originally, as will be observed by a reference to the Plan of Organization, that the Commissioners themselves should take an active part in the Executive service, and for that purpose, an elaborate machinery of committees was prepared, intended to facilitate the investigation of various subjects, relating to the condition of the Army. These subjects were embraced in two divisions, the one concerning Inquiry, the other, Advice. It soon became manifest however, that this arrangement was unsuited to a body whose sessions were not permanent, and whose action to be in the highest degree efficient, should be characterized at all times by great flexibility and promptness. It was found, therefore, that in practice the functions of the Board itself would be confined to a general supervision of the work, and to the settlement of a policy to be pursued, while it would become necessary to confide all the details of the Executive service to subordinate Agents. During the war the Board held twenty-three sessions, most of them in Washington, but occasionally elsewhere. Many of its members came regularly from their homes, hundreds of miles distant, to attend these meetings, and spent usually four or five days in an earnest discussion of the reports of the Agents of the Commission concerning its operations in the different Armies, and in the various departments of its work. These meetings were always full of interest to those who had at heart the welfare of the Army. A carefully prepared report of the operations of the Com-

63

mission since its last session was made by the General Secretary to the Board, presenting a sketch of the actual condition of the work, founded upon the reports made to him by his subordinate Agents, and containing suggestions as to the future policy of the Commission. Reports from the Heads of the various Bureaus, Inspection, Statistics, Special Relief, the War Claim Agency, the Hospital Directory, were also read. The Treasurer always presented at these meetings, a full account of the receipts and expenditures of the Commission, which during the session was duly vouched and audited. In this way, the Commission gained a full knowledge from the most authentic sources of the practical working of its plans, and was able to modify them when they seemed defective, or to abandon them altogether, if they appeared to conflict in any way with its general policy. A meeting rarely took place in which some practical question of grave importance concerning the operations of the Commission was not submitted to the consideration of the Board, and decided by it after the most pains-taking and exhaustive discussion. It was soon found, however, that these questions constantly arose during the recess of the Board, and that they required a prompt solution. Their decision involved too grave a responsibility particularly, in regard to the expenditure of money, to be assumed by any one of its officers, and it became therefore necessary that a body should be constituted, which should possess in the intervals of its sessions all the authority of the Board, and be, in short its permanent representative.

This body was the Standing Committee of the Board,

composed first of five and afterwards of six of its mem- bers,* upon whom was conferred by its vote absolute power over the affairs of the Com- mission when the Board was not in session, accountable, of course, to it for the due exercise of that power.   When the Standing Committee was ap- pointed the larger number of the members of the Com- mission, including its President and Treasurer, were residents of New York.   Its meetings were held in that city simply because that was the most convenient place.   These meetings took place daily during a pe- riod of nearly four years, and its members were con- stantly engaged in arranging plans for improving the Commission's service, in settling the many embarrass- ing questions which arose in its current operations, and applying promptly its resources to meet the exigencies which occurred in the progress of the war.   The vast labor and responsibility of managing the financial affairs of the Commission, of devising methods of raising money for the continued prosecution of its work, and of expending it wisely and economically in the purchase of supplies needed in the Army, and in supporting the general work of the Commission, also devolved upon this Committee.   It was kept constantly informed by the reports of its Agents of the nature and extent of the needs of the Army in the different portions of the field, and by its order, supplies vast in amount, and of a kind suited to the peculiar wants of the soldiers at the time, were shipped to Morris Island,

Appointment of the Standing Committee. Its duties.

* The original members of this Committee were: Rev. Dr. Bellows, Dr. William H. Van Buren, Professor Wolcott Gibbs, Mr. George T. Strong, and Dr. C. R. Agnew.   In October, 1864, Mr. Charles J. Stillé, of Philadelphia, was added to it.

to Texas, to City Point, or to Washington, as the case might require. The position which this Standing Committee occupied was, as will be readily supposed, a most important and commanding one. It was the living representative of the Commission with the public at large. Its members watched with the keenest interest not only over all the details of the Commission's service, but also over the varying changes of public opinion in regard to its different operations. It was necessary, of course, in order that the work should be maintained in its fullest activity, that the interest of the people in it should be constantly stimulated. This result was produced by the unceasing labors of the Standing Committee. When the funds in the Treasury ran low, an appeal prepared under its direction, showing the nature and practical value of its labors, never failed to meet a proper response from the patriotic sympathy of the country. When doubts seemed to prevail in certain quarters as to the wisdom of its policy, or some misrepresentation of its acts which was likely to affect its reputation, became current, an explanation of its real position was at once made to the public, and if we are to judge from the constant increase of its resources, never failed to inspire renewed confidence. The labor involved in such a duty was, of course, immense. It was shared by every member of the Committee, each one of whom gave up unhesitatingly during the war, time and strength of great value to him in his particular calling, to employ it in this disinterested work of helping the cause of his country. Each one of its members was burdened with professional cares of no ordinary kind, but if it was deemed necessary, as it often was, that some one of them should leave his ordinary avocations to address public meetings held in behalf of the Commission in distant parts of the country, or that others should visit battle-fields to give greater efficiency to the Commission's service, or that others should superintend the distribution of vast stores among famishing returned prisoners, no one hesitated to go, however great the sacrifice. While the only reward for this unceasing labor was the gratifying assurance of the success of the plans adopted by the Commission for the relief of the soldier, that labor was rendered possible by the unbounded confidence which each member of the Committee felt in the purity of motive, and earnestness of purpose of all his colleagues. The tie which originally bound its members was a common sympathy for a grand object, but it is a characteristic feature in the history of the Commission, that unlike that of many associations formed to carry out a benevolent design, this sympathy proved a solvent sufficiently strong to remove all obstacles to success due to the peculiar temper or idiosyncrasies of the individuals composing the organization. The members of the Standing Committee were men, all of whom were accustomed to take strong, decided, and independent views of subjects presented for their consideration and action, but it was found that their peculiarities, so far from conflicting in such a way as to affect unfavorably the general design, mutually balanced and corrected each other, and the result was in the end a harmony of purpose to which much of the success of the Commission's operations must be attributed. In practice it was soon found that each member possessed some striking qualification for the furtherance of the general design. While one seemed more peculiarly fitted to keep alive interest in the work by public addresses, and by means of a vast correspondence, and another was distinguished by that zeal and executive ability which led him to superintend the Commission's work on the battle-field, a third (to whose established reputation in the community in which he lived, for fidelity, exactness and skill in the management of trusts in which the care of large sums of money was involved, the Commission was under an obligation which it is not easy to exaggerate,) watched over its financial concerns, while all were conspicuous for the skill, prudence, and devotion which they constantly manifested in their efforts to uphold the Commission's general policy.

The chief Executive officer of the Commission charged with the details of its service, was the General Position and duties of the General Secretary. Secretary. His duties have been already defined. Practically, his work was not confined merely to seeing that the orders of the Board, the Standing Committee, and his own were duly carried out by his Agents, but he was looked to also, for suggestions of such modification and enlargement of its plans as might be derived from an experience founded on a constant observation of the needs of the Army. His position was a most responsible one, not only on this account, but also because he was brought into daily contact with high officials in Washington, and was constantly called upon to defend the policy of the Commission, and to explain its motives. The novelty, delicacy, and difficulty of this task have been already adverted to, and it was the peculiar honor of Mr. Olmsted that he was able to accomplish it so successfully during the first two years of the Commission's existence, in which he held the office of General Secretary. Mr. Olmsted remained in the service of the Commission until its general policy had been shaped by the events of the war, and its system of internal organization finally adopted. He resigned in September, 1863, and was succeeded by Dr. J. Foster Jenkins, a gentleman who, with great purity of personal character, and indefatigable zeal in the Commission's service, combined the important advantage of a thorough training for the special duties of his position, having held for nearly two years the very responsible office of Associate Secretary for the East. Ill health, resulting from too close an application to the duties of his office forced him to abandon it in the spring of 1865, when Mr. John S. Blatchford, who had previously distinguished himself in the superintendence of the Relief work undertaken by the Associates in Boston, was elected his successor. Although the return of peace shortly afterwards was, of course, the signal for bringing to a termination the active work of the Commission in most of its Departments, it will be readily seen that the speedy and final settlement of the complicated affairs of so vast an organization was a task which required for its successful execution great devotion, skill, and knowledge of business concerns. That task fell to the competent hands of Mr. Blatchford, and under his direction the gradual winding up of the affairs of the Commission has been characterized by the same orderly and systematic methods which marked its history, during the period of its most active operations. No service which had been undertaken in behalf of the soldier, which peace found not fully performed, was given up because the war had ceased. On the contrary, as has been seen, some of the most responsible duties which the Commission ever assumed, especially in the collection of claims upon the Government, were increased rather than diminished by the return of peace. These duties were faithfully and honestly performed under a system carefully organized, and conducted under the intelligent and watchful supervision of the General Secretary.

The General Secretary was charged with arranging plans for insuring the greatest efficiency of the Commission in all its departments, with making due preparation for campaigns and battle-fields, with the task of accumulating proper supplies at points near the Army to meet its current wants, and a reserve stock, in addition, to provide against emergencies, with devising the best means of getting these supplies forward when needed, and with determining the proper methods of relieving the wounded, and of transporting them to General Hospitals. Besides this, he was invested with the power of selecting all the subordinate officers of the Commission, a task which, when the anomalous nature of their position in the Army is considered, involved a very serious responsibility. The multifarious character of his duties will be better understood when it is stated, that he was not only expected to enlighten the Board as to the measures which should engage its attention, but was held responsible also for the due performance of its work in all its various departments, and for the character of the Agents he employed. In the organization of the Commission's service, there were two Associate Secretaries, one for the East and the other for the West, each charged with the details of the work in his own department, and each reporting directly and constantly to the General Secretary. So also there was, during the first three years of the war, an officer called the Chief of Inspection, whose special province it was to superintend the work of inspecting camps and hospitals. He also received his instructions from the General Secretary, and reported to him. The Statistical Bureau also was under his direct supervision. The Headquarters of the Eastern and Western Departments respectively, in charge of the Associate Secretaries, were established at Washington and Louisville. The offices at these places were important centres of activity, for not only was the immense business of meeting the requisitions for supplies made by the Inspectors and Relief Agents employed in the different Armies in the field, and in the Hospitals, transacted there, but connected with them were various Bureaus, each charged with a specific department of the Commission's work. Thus both at Washington and at Louisville, there were under the jurisdiction of the Associate Secretaries, a Supply Bureau charged with the movement of supplies, and a Special Relief Department with its Hospital Directory, Pension Agency, and Homes and Lodges.

The number of Agents on the Commission's roster varied at different periods from one hundred and fifty to seven hundred. The average number con-

64

Number and
character of the
subordinate
Agents.

stantly employed was about three hundred. It was thought important, for reasons which have been already stated, that these Agents should receive a moderate compensation. How moderate that compensation was may be inferred, when it is stated that they received on an average two dollars per day for labor, which was, at least half of it, highly skilled, sometimes of professional eminence, and worth from five to ten times that amount. Few of these men could be had for the money, but they worked for love and patriotism, and were content with a bare support. The Board, (all included, twenty-one in number)—President, Vice-president, · Treasurer, medical committee, standing committee—gave their services and their time gratuitously. They received nothing. Their traveling expenses alone were partly refunded them, and these were trifling, excepting in the case of one or two who went frequently on tours of observation.

Adaptation of
means to the end
in the History
of the Commis-
sion.

It will thus be seen that the machinery of the internal organization of the Commission was arranged with the utmost care to meet the exigencies of the service. Order, regularity, subordination, and discipline were maintained by a system of graded responsibility, in which each Agent had his position and duties exactly defined. The history of the war proved that this organization was perfectly adapted to accomplish the practical ends proposed by it. This result was, of course, much aided by the character of the Agents in whose selection and training much care had been exercised. They formed, at all times, a most faithful and intelligent body of men, and the success of their work is to be attributed, in no small degree, to the zeal and devotion with which they were inspired by the nature of the service in which they were engaged.

It will be seen, we trust, on a review of the work of the Commission, as we have presented it in this volume, that the Sanitary Commission accomplished substantially the object it proposed by the means which it had first suggested, as proper to be employed for such a purpose. The great end of its appointment was, as we have seen to aid the Government. If we consider some of the evil consequences which might have resulted to the country *The Commission's policy free from partisan influences.* and the Army had the great power intrusted to it been abused or unwisely administered, the impression of the purity and sincerity of the motives of those who conducted it will be strongly confirmed. The great objection in this country to an extra-governmental organization like this, aside from the danger of its interference with the ordinary routine of Army discipline, was the fear, lest with its immense resources, and with the powerful support of a large body of influential men throughout the country, it might become in time, perhaps almost unconsciously, an instrument to subserve partisan ends. The power which it wielded during the war was vast, and did not fail to attract the attention of politicians. Its officers might easily and plausibly have indicated their preference for this or that General, or their approval or disapproval of a particular line of policy, and thus have become a cause of serious embarrassment to the Government. But the Commission steadily refrained from any such interference, and we shall look in vain, not only to its official acts, but to the most confidential reports of its Agents for any expression of unkind criticism, (except where the sanitary interests of the Army seemed to require it,) upon any act of the Government or its officers. Its Agents were strictly instructed to avoid all discussions of military or political questions in their intercourse with the officers of the Army, and they were forbidden by one of its rules from corresponding with newspapers. The great effort of the Commission at all times was to identify its work thoroughly with the success of the National cause in the widest sense. Hence it appealed for support to men of all classes and opinions, religious and political, and the wisdom of this liberal policy is best shown by the fact that some of the largest contributions to its funds came from those who did not belong to the party in power. When we recall the fierce opposition to the Government during the war, the undisguised hostility of some, and the coldness and disaffection of many more, it is not too much to say that the enthusiastic support which the Commission received from all classes, in all parts of the country, was not only a striking illustration of the manner in which a desire to aid those who were defending our threatened nationality dissolved mere party ties, but a wonderful expression also of confidence in the purity and disinterestedness of the motives of those who proposed to relieve them.

While the success of its methods had thus inspired the public with a confidence which grew as the war Relations with the Government. went on, the attitude of the Government towards it was not so satisfactory. The officers of the Commission always felt that it was no mere volun-

tary and irresponsible association engaged in the work
of Army Relief, and at liberty to adopt any system
which it might prefer to accomplish that purpose. It
was regarded by them as a body specially commis-
sioned by the President, and invested with all needful
authority to do a particular thing in a particular way,
and pledged to do it in no other way. In these
respects, of course, it differed essentially from all organizations engaged in the work of Army Relief.
Some of these Associations concerned themselves with
subjects of great importance with which the Sanitary
Commission never interfered, simply because these
subjects were wholly beyond the scope of the authority
bestowed upon it by the President of the United
States. Deriving, then, its existence and all its power
from the special appointment of the Government, and
working wholly in aid of its service, it was natural to
expect at all times from its officers, support, encouragement, and sympathy. As has been fully shown in the
narrative of its work, military officers of high rank
who had had the best opportunities of observing its
practical usefulness never withheld that support and
sympathy. It is a noteworthy fact that every General
in command of an Army during the war, has placed
on record an expression of his appreciation of the
value of the Commission's services to his troops, while
very many of them actively aided and encouraged its
operations by all the means at their disposal. While
such were its relations with those with whom its
Agents were brought into daily contact, and whose
natural prejudices against any extra governmental interference in the Army had been overcome by the

evidence of its value, it must be confessed that there was a want of cordial coöperation with its plans on the part of those in the higher regions of official authority, which was on every account much to be regretted. The attitude of the War Department especially, towards it was never that of open hostility, but rather of neglect and indifference. It was never regarded by that Department as it should have been, as one of the great glories of the war, and as the most comprehensive and successful method of mitigating its horrors known in history. While the evidence abounded in the reports of its own officers of the vast improvement which had been made in the condition of the troops through its instrumentality direct and indirect, no word of official approval of a work which was exciting the wonder, admiration, and gratitude of all humane and intelligent observers at home and abroad, was ever vouchsafed by the Government whose Agent it was. Although this want of appreciation of their labors existed in the quarter where they had the right to look most confidently for aid and encouragement, the members of the Commission were not disheartened. Carefully abstaining from asking favors at Headquarters, it was found that practically their work suffered little, so long as it enjoyed, as it did during the whole war, the confidence of the commanding Generals, and the coöperation of the various staff departments of the Army.

It would be very unprofitable to discuss all the Causes of a want causes which might be assigned for this of sympathy on the part of the want of cordiality towards the Commission Government. on the part of the Government, and particularly of the War Department. One thing is certain, that during its whole existence no complaint was ever made to that Department, that the Commission had exceeded its authority, or neglected its duties. When it is remembered how intimate and delicate its relations with the Army officials were, how large, at all times, was its corps of Agents, and how embarrassing and difficult their position must often have been, this fact in itself is no small evidence of the wisdom of its policy, and the character of those employed to give it a practical shape. The simple, natural, explanation of the difficulty lies far deeper, however, than any mere suspicion that the Commission was not doing its duty, or even than that personal antipathy which was said to have existed between certain high officials of the Government, and its own, and which has sometimes been assigned as its chief cause. The truth is, the continued existence of the Sanitary Commission was a standing criticism upon certain of the methods employed by the Government, and a protest against the insufficiency of others. This was the great grievance. It was not pleasant for officers of Government to be constantly reminded, as they were by appeals made to the public asking for means of relief to the soldier, that the Army was suffering from the insufficiency of the ordinary methods, or their defective administration. The Government theory on the subject was that its system was a perfect one, that occasionally and from accidental causes, its methods might fail, but that it had both the power and the will to supply all deficiencies, and that all possible needs of the soldier were provided for by it as soon as recognized. That this was the ideal standard towards which the officers of the Government should constantly aspire no one doubted, and all good men, and especially the members of the Sanitary Commission, were unceasing in their efforts to uphold it.   But the error consisted in supposing that in practice, any such standard could be reached by our Government, or had been reached by any Government since the world began.   We have pointed out how utterly absurd was the pretence during the war, that the Army needed no popular intervention for its relief.   The officers in the field were the first to be convinced of this necessity, and abandoned their preconceived notions on the subject.   But it was natural, that those at the head of affairs, who were occupied with devising plans for the general improvement of the service, should often be irritated when they found that the more they did, the louder seemed the cry for help.   It is not wonderful, then, that some of these officers began to think, particularly after the reorganization of the Medical Department, that the Sanitary Commission, if it had ever had a mission to accomplish, had done its work, and that there was no need of its further existence.   The reasons why the Commission did not withdraw from the field have been already fully given, and it is unnecessary to repeat them here.   It was always desirous to retire when the object proposed by it at the outset should have been accomplished.   That time never came in its opinion, while the war lasted, and it remained, therefore, not only a representative of popular sympathy towards the Army, but a constant stimulant urging the Government to improve its own standard of the comfort and efficiency of the troops.

While therefore, it cannot be denied that the continued existence of the Sanitary Commission was a natural cause of irritation to certain high officials, it is quite clear that that irritation on the whole was a healthy one. It did good in two ways, for it constantly educated public opinion through the testimony of independent observers in regard to the real needs of the soldiers, and that opinion not satisfied, with merely voluntary efforts to provide for those needs, was all powerful in forcing the Government so to modify and enlarge its system that, the evils complained of might be remedied. All improvements in a form of Government such as ours, it should never be forgotten, are due to the exercise of a free spirit of popular criticism, and however mistaken that spirit may be in some of its suggestions, and however distasteful may be the changes which it demands to those whose habits and interests are identified with the existing systems, it is none the less the very life of all free Governments. This principle which has always been recognized in our history is of universal application. The Sanitary Commission was its representative during the war in all that related to an enlightened appreciation of the wants of the Army, and as there can be no doubt, that the impulse which carried us successfully through the struggle arose from the influence of popular enthusiasm on the Government, so there can be as little doubt that any credit due the country for an improved care of its soldiers should be ascribed to the irresistible force of popular

The Commission a healthy stimulant to Government.

organizations outside of the Government agencies. If we examine the facts, nothing can be clearer than that the great reforms in the Medical service of the Army, the value of which can only be measured by the wants of suffering men in future wars, would never have originated in official quarters. If there had been no enlightened public opinion in regard to the real wants of the sick and wounded, and no Sanitary Commission to direct it aright, we should probably never have heard of the re-organization of the Medical Department, of improved Hospital buildings and administration, of a system of thorough inspection, of humane methods of transporting the suffering, or of the numerous other methods of mitigating the horrors of war, of which we have set the example in history.

It seemed necessary to say thus much in explanation of the want of a cordial coöperation and active sympa-
Aid afforded by all officers on active service.— Quartermaster's Department. thy with the work of the Commission on the part of some of the highest officials of the Government. Practically, however, this indifference, for it rarely amounted to anything more, interfered very little with its plans. In the Armies engaged in active operations, it had, as has been stated, the constant aid and encouragement of the Generals in command, while every facility was afforded it for the prosecution of its work by their subordinate officers. It had especially a warm and enlightened friend in the Quartermaster-General, GENERAL MEIGS. That officer had, from the beginning the fullest appreciation of its scope and usefulness, and there was scarcely a suggestion for the improvement of the service made to him during the war the adop-

tion of which required his official sanction, which he hesitated to approve. His readiness to adopt the plans submitted by the Commission for the construction of Hospitals, and his willingness to aid in establishing the new system of railway ambulances, have been already referred to. But his kindly intervention did not stop here. Means for the transportation of its Agents and its supplies were of course essential to the usefulness of the Commission's work in the Army, and this was a matter which, within the lines of the army itself, and upon all the routes leading to it, was exclusively under the control of the Quartermaster's Department. This transportation was liberally provided by that Department in aid of the Commission's work in every part of the country. Steamers in the employ of the Government were placed for months at a time in its charge, so that its stores might be more speedily placed where they were most needed. Wagons and horses, for the same purpose, were loaned wherever they could be spared from the Government service, while its Agents were permitted to travel as freely on all the military routes as if they had been officers of the Army itself.* The Commission it is true, thought

---

* The Commission at its Session in July 1865 adopted following resolution :

"*Resolved*, That the Sanitary Commission about to close the labors which it has pursued during the last four years for the relief of the National forces, desires to record the sincere expression of its deep gratitude to MAJOR-GENERAL MEIGS, Quartermaster-General U. S. A., not only for his aid and kindness to the Commission, but for the invaluable services rendered to it by his effective coöperation during the whole period of its labors. The same spirit of intelligent and patriotic coöperation with the Commission, inspired by him, has pervaded constantly his whole Department, and we desire to tender to all its officers our grateful thanks for the services which they have rendered to us, and through us to the Armies of our re-established Republic."

it advisable in most of the campaigns to provide its own independent means of transportation, but this was done, not because any indisposition on the part of the Quartermaster's Department to aid it was observed. In all great emergencies during the war the need of transportation was urgently felt in all the Supply Departments of the Army, and in such cases as we have seen, according to the military theory, the relief of the suffering was necessarily postponed until those still able to fight were provided with food and ammunition. The independent means of transportation possessed by the Sanitary Commission was a most costly appendage to its system, but it proved during the progress of active campaigns, and especially on battle-fields, the right arm of its power.

We have now concluded our sketch of the origin, purposes and work of this great organization, and General conclu- have endeavored to show that the unexam-
sion. pled success which it achieved in mitigating the horrors of war was mainly due to the influence of popular ideas, and the peculiar forms of American civilization. In looking back upon the events of any great war those who are as near to the scene as we are to that of the rebellion, find little upon which the mind can dwell with unmixed satisfaction. The blunders of the Government, the mistakes of the Generals, the confusion and incapacity which are so often conspicuous in many branches of the service, impress us with all the vividness of a fresh reality, and we wonder that success was achieved at all in the face of so many formidable obstacles. But however opinions may differ in regard to the policy of the Government, or the stra-

tegy of the Generals during the late war, the organized sympathy and care of the American people for those who suffered in their cause stands out alone in its ever fresh beauty from the dark back-ground of civil strife, and must always, and everywhere call forth the homage and admiration of mankind. It is the true glory of our age and our country, one of the most shining monuments of its civilization. May it ever prove a beacon to warn, to guide and to encourage those who, in future ages, and other countries may be afflicted with the dire calamity of War!

LIST OF THE MEMBERS

OF THE

U. S. SANITARY COMMISSION.

		DATE OF APPOINTMENT.
Rev. H. W. BELLOWS, D. D	New York	June 9, 1861.
ALEXANDER DALLAS BACHE, LL.D	Washington, D. C	"
WILLIAM H. VAN BUREN, M. D	New York	"
WOLCOTT GIBBS, M. D	Cambridge, Mass	"
*ROBERT C. WOOD, M. D., U. S. A		"
†GEORGE W. CULLUM, U. S. A		"
‡ALEXANDER E. SHIRAS, U. S. A		"
SAMUEL G. HOWE, M. D	Boston, Mass	"
ELISHA HARRIS, M. D	New York	June 12, 1861.
CORNELIUS R. AGNEW, M. D	New York	"
GEORGE T. STRONG, Esq	New York	June 13, 1861.
JOHN S. NEWBERRY, M. D	Cleveland, Ohio	June 14, 1861.
FREDERICK LAW OLMSTED, Esq	New York	June 20, 1861.
Rt. Rev. THOMAS M. CLARK	Providence, R. I	July 30, 1861.
HORACE BINNEY, Jr., Esq	Philadelphia, Pa	July 30, 1861.
§Hon. R. W. BURNETT	Cincinnati, Ohio	Dec'r. 5, 1861.
Hon. MARK SKINNER	Chicago, Ill	Dec'r. 7, 1861.
§Hon. JOSEPH HOLT	Washington, D. C	Jan. 23, 1863.
Rev. J. H. HEYWOOD	Louisville, Ky	Jan. 23, 1863.
‖ FAIRMAN ROGERS, Esq	Philadelphia, Pa	Feb'y 6, 1863.
J. HUNTINGTON WOLCOTT, Esq	Boston, Mass	June 13, 1863.
CHARLES J. STILLÉ, Esq	Philadelphia, Pa	Jan. 15, 1864.
EZRA B. McCAGG, Esq	Chicago, Ill	Mar. 9, 1864.

* Resigned, December, 1864.
† Resigned, February, 1864.
‡ Resigned, December 17, 1864.
§ These gentlemen never took their seats.
‖ Resigned, 1864.

APPENDIX.

No. 1.

TO THE WOMEN OF NEW YORK, AND ESPECIALLY TO THOSE ALREADY ENGAGED IN PREPARING AGAINST THE TIME OF WOUNDS AND SICKNESS IN THE ARMY.

THE importance of systematizing and concentrating the spontaneous and earnest efforts now making by the women of New York, for the supply of extra medical aid to our Army through its present campaign, must be obvious to all reflecting persons. Numerous societies, working without concert, organization, or head, without any direct understanding with the official authorities, without any positive instructions as to the immediate or future wants of the Army, are liable to waste their enthusiasm in disproportionate efforts, to overlook some claims and overdo others, while they give unnecessary trouble in official quarters, by the variety and irregularity of their proffers for help or their inquiries for guidance.

As no existing organization has a right to claim precedence over any other, or could properly assume to lead in this noble cause, where all desire to be first, it is proposed by the undersigned, members of various circles now actively engaged in this work, that the women of New York should meet in the Cooper Institute, on Monday next, at eleven o'clock, A. M., to confer together, and to appoint a General Committee, with power to organize the benevolent purposes of all into a common movement.

To make the meeting practical and effective, it seems proper here to set 'forth briefly the objects that should be kept in view. The form which woman's benevolence has already taken, and is likely to take, in the present crisis, is, first, the contribution of labor, skill, and money in the preparation of lint, bandages, and other stores, in aid of the wants of the Medical Staff; second, the offer of personal service as nurses.

In regard to the first, it is important to obtain and disseminate exact official information as to the nature and variety of the wants of the Army; to give proper direction and proportion to the labor expended, so as to avoid superfluity in some things and deficiency in others; and to this end, to come to a careful and thorough understanding with the official head of the Medical Staff, through a committee having this department in hand.   To this committee should be assigned the duty of conferring with other associations in other parts of the country, and especially, through the press, to keep the women of the loyal States everywhere informed how their efforts may be most wisely and economically employed, and their contributions of all kinds most directly concentrated at New York, and put at the service of the Medical Staff.   A central depôt would, of course, be the first thing to be desired.

In regard to the second form of benevolence—the offer of personal service as nurses—it is felt that the public mind needs much enlightenment, and the overflowing zeal and sympathy of the women of the nation, a careful channel, not only to prevent waste of time and effort, but to save embarrassment to the official staff, and to secure real efficiency in the service.   Should our unhappy war be continued, the Army is certain to want the services of extra nurses, not merely on account of the casualties of the field, but of the camp diseases originating in the exposure of the soldiery to a strange climate and to unaccustomed hardships.   The result of all the experience of the Crimean war has been to prove the total uselessness of any but picked and skilled women in this department of duty,   The ardor and zeal of all other women should therefore be concentrated upon finding, preparing, and sending bands of women, of suitable age, constitution, training, and temperament, to the Army at such points and at such times as they are asked for by the Medical Staff.

A central organization is wanted, therefore, to which all those desiring to go as nurses may be referred, where a committee of examiners, partly medical and partly otherwise, may at once decide upon the fitness of the candidate.   Those accepted should then at once be put under competent instruction and discipline—(for which it is understood a thorough school will be opened at once by the Medical Faculty of the city)—and as occasion offers, the best prepared, in successive order, be sent, under proper escort, to the scene of war, as they are wanted.

It is felt that all who want to go, *and are fitted to go*, should have in their turn a fair chance to do so, and are not unlikely to be wanted sooner or later.   Of these, many may be rich and many poor.   Some may wish to go at their own charges, and others will require to be aided as to their expenses, and still others, for the loss of their time. But the best nurses should be sent, irrespective of these distinctions— as only the best are economical on any terms.

It will at once appear that without a central organization, with proper authority, there can be no efficiency, system, or discipline in this important matter of nurses—and there can be no organization, to which a cheerful submission will be paid, except it originate in the common will, and become the genuine representative of all the women of New York, and of all the existing associations having this kind of aid in view.

It is obvious that such an organization will require generous contributions, and that all the women of New York and of the country, not otherwise lending aid, will have a direct opportunity of giving support to the object so near their hearts, through the treasury of this common organization.

To consider this matter deliberately, and to take such common action as may then appear wise, we earnestly invite the women of New York, and the pastors of the churches, with such medical advisers as may be specially invited, to assemble for counsel and action, at the Cooper Institute, on Monday morning next, at eleven o'clock.

Mrs. Gen. Dix,
 "   Hamilton Fish,
 "   Lewis C. Jones,
 "   E. Robinson,
 "   Wm. Kirkland,
 "   Wm. H. Aspinwall,
 "   R. B. Minturn,
 "   Jas. B. Johnson,
 "   Judge Roosevelt,
 "   A. M. Bininger,
 "   W. C. Bryant,
 "   R. L. Stuart,
 "   D. D. Field,
 "   W. B. Astor, Jr.,
 "   M. Grinnell,
 "   G. L. Schuyler,

Mrs. H. K. Bogart,
 "   Charles Butler,
 "   C. E. Lane,
 "   M. D. Swett,
 "   R. M. Blatchford,
 "   S. F. Bridham,
 '   A. W. Bradford,
 "   W. H. Lee,
 "   Parke Godwin,
 "   H. J. Raymond,
 "   S. L. M. Barlow,
 "   J. Auchincloss,
 "   Walker,
 "   Elisha Fish,
 "   C. A. Seward,
 "   S. Osgood,

Mrs. Peter Cooper,
" Thomas Tileston,
" F. S. Wiley,
" R. Gracie,
" M. Catlin,
" Chandler,
" R. B. Winthrop,
" G. Stuyvesant,
" George Curtis,
" A. R. Eno,
" W. F. Carey,
" A. S. Hewitt,
" Dr. Peaslee,
" H. B. Smith,
" R. Hitchcock,
" F. F. Marbury,
" F. F. B. Morse,
" Judge Daly,
" Charles R. Swords,
Miss Marquand,
Mrs. G. Holbrooke,
" D. Adams,
" H. Webster,
" Moffat,
" H. W. Bellows,
" Stuart Brown,
" Ellis,
" J. D. Wolfe,
" Alonzo Potter,
" R. Campbell,

Mrs. Griffin,
" L. M. Rutherford,
" S. J. Baker,
" H. Baylis,
" John Sherwood,
" S. H. Tyng,
" Capt. Shumway,
" Edward Bayard,
" James I. Jones,
" Judge Betts,
" William G. Ward,
" H. E. Eaton,
" W. C. Evarts,
" Judge Bonney,
Miss Minturn,
Mrs. M. Trimble,
" S. B. Collins,
" R. H. Bowne,
" B. R. McIlvaine,
" N. Lawrence,
" John Reid,
" C. Newbold,
" J. B. Collins,
" J. C. Smith,
" Paul Spofford,
" C. W. Field,
" P. Townsend,
" L. Baker,
" Charles King.

NEW YORK, *April* 29, 1861.

No. 2.

AN ADDRESS TO THE SECRETARY OF WAR.

TO THE SECRETARY OF WAR:

SIR:—The undersigned, representing three associations of the highest respectability in the city of New York, namely, the Women's

Central Association of Relief for the Sick and Wounded of the Army, the Advisory Committee of the Boards of Physicians and Surgeons of the Hospitals of New York, the New York Medical Association for furnishing Hospital Supplies in aid of the Army, beg leave to address the Department of War in behalf of the objects committed to them as a mixed delegation with due credentials.

These three associations, being engaged at home in a common object, are acting together with great efficiency and harmony to contribute towards the comfort and security of our troops, by methodizing the spontaneous benevolence of the city and State of New York; obtaining information from the public authorities of the best methods of aiding your Department with such supplies as the regulations of the Army do not provide, or the sudden and pressing necessities of the time do not permit the Department to furnish; and, in general, striving to play into the hands of the regular authorities in ways as efficient and as little embarrassing as extra-official co-operation can be.

These associations would not trouble the War Department with any call on its notice, if they were not persuaded that some positive recognition of their existence and efforts was essential to the peace and comfort of the several Bureaus of the War Department itself. The present is essentially a people's war. The hearts and minds, the bodies and souls, of the whole people and of both sexes throughout the loyal States are in it. The rush of volunteers to arms is equalled by the enthusiasm and zeal of the women of the nation, and the clerical and medical professions vie with each other in their ardor to contribute in some manner to the success of our noble and sacred cause. The War Department will hereafter, therefore, inevitably experience, in all its bureaus, the incessant and irresistible motions of this zeal, in the offer of medical aid, the applications of nurses, and the contribution of supplies. Ought not this noble and generous enthusiasm to be encouraged and utilized? Would not the Department win a still higher place in the confidence and affections of the good people of the loyal States, and find itself generally strengthened in its efforts, by accepting in some positive manner the services of the associations we represent, which are laboring to bring into system and practical shape the general zeal and benevolent activity of the women of the land in behalf of the Army? And would not a great economy of time, money, and effort be secured by fixing and regulating the relations of the Volunteer Associations to the War Department, and especially to the Medical Bureau?

Convinced by inquiries made here of the practical difficulty of reconciling the aims of their own and numerous similar associations in other cities with the regular workings of the Commissariat and the Medical Bureau, and yet fully persuaded of the importance to the country and the success of the war, of bringing such an arrangement about, the undersigned respectfully ask that a mixed Commission of civilians distinguished for their philanthropic experience and acquaintance with sanitary matters, of medical men, and of military officers, be appointed by the Government, who shall be charged with the duty of investigating the best means of methodizing and reducing to practical service the already active but undirected benevolence of the people toward the Army; who shall consider the general subject of the prevention of sickness and suffering among the troops, and suggest the wisest methods, which the people at large can use to manifest their good-will towards the comfort, security, and health of the Army.

It must be well known to the Department of War that several such commissions *followed* the Crimean and Indian wars. The civilization and humanity of the age and of the American people demand that such a commission should *precede* our second war of independence—more sacred than the first. We wish to prevent the evils that England and France could only investigate and deplore. This war ought to be waged in a spirit of the highest intelligence, humanity, and tenderness for the health, comfort, and safety of our brave troops. And every measure of the Government that shows its sense of this, will be eminently popular, strengthen its hands and redound to its glory at home and abroad.

The undersigned are charged with several specific petitions, additional to that of asking for a Commission for the purposes above described, although they all would fall under the duties of that Commission.

1. They ask that the Secretary of War will order some new rigor in the inspection of volunteer troops, as they are persuaded that under the present State regulations throughout the country a great number of under-aged and unsuitable persons are mustered, who are

likely to swell the bills of mortality in the Army to a fearful per centage, to encumber the hospitals, and embarrass the columns. They ask either for an order of reinspection of the troops already mustered, or a summary discharge of those obviously destined to succumb to the diseases of the approaching summer. It is unnecessary to argue the importance of a measure so plainly required by common humanity and economy of life and money.

2. The committee are convinced by the testimony of the Medical Bureau itself, and the evidence of the most distinguished Army officers, including the Commander-in-Chief, Adjutant-General Thomas, and the acting Surgeon-General, that the cooking of the volunteer and new regiments in general is destined to be of the most crude and perilous description, and that no preventive measure could be so effectual in preserving health and keeping off disease, as an order of the Department requiring a skilled cook to be enlisted in each company of the regiments. The Woman's Central Association, in connection with the Medical Boards, are prepared to assume the duty of collecting, registering, and instructing a body of cooks, if the Department will pass such an order, accompanying it with the allotment of such wages as are equitable.

3. The committee represent that the Woman's Central Association of Relief have selected, and are selecting, out of several hundred candidates, one hundred women, suited in all respects to become nurses in the General Hospitals in the Army. These women the distinguished physicians and surgeons of the various hospitals in New York have undertaken to *educate and drill in a most thorough and laborious manner;* and the Committee ask that the War Department consent to receive, on wages, these nurses, in such numbers as the exigencies of the campaign may require. It is not proposed that the nurses should advance to the seat of war, *until directly called for by the Medical Bureau here*, or that the Government should be at any expense until they are actually in service.

4. The Committee ask that the Secretary of War issue an order that in case of need the Medical Bureau may call to the aid of the regular medical force a set of volunteer dressers, composed of young medical men, drilled for this purpose by the hospital physicians and surgeons of New York, giving them such subsistence and such recog-

nition as the rules of the service may allow under a generous construction.

It is believed that a Commission would bring these and other matters of great interest and importance to the health of the troops into the shape of easy and practical adoption. But if no Commission is appointed, the committee pray that the Secretary will order the several suggestions made to be carried into immediate effect, if consistent with the laws of the Department, or possible without the action of Congress.

Feeling themselves directly to represent large and important constituencies, and, indirectly, a wide-spread and commanding public sentiment, the committee would most respectfully urge the immediate attention of the Secretary to the objects of their prayer.

Very respectfully,
HENRY W. BELLOWS, D.D.
W. H. VAN BUREN.
ELISHA HARRIS, M. D.
J. HARSEN, M. D.

WASHINGTON, *May* 18, 1861.

LETTER FROM THE ACTING SURGEON-GENERAL TO THE SECRETARY OF WAR.

SURGEON-GENERAL'S OFFICE, }
May 22, 1861.   }

Hon. SIMON CAMERON, *Secretary of War:*

SIR: The sudden and large increase of the Army, more especially of the Volunteer force, has called the attention of this office to the necessity of some modifications and changes in the system of organization, as connected with the hygiene and comforts of the soldiers; more particularly in relation to the class of men who, actuated by patriotism, have repaired with unexampled promptness to the defence of the institutions and laws of the country.

The pressure upon the Medical Bureau has been very great and urgent; and though all the means at its disposal have been industriously used, much remains to be accomplished by directing the intelgent mind of the country to practical results connected with the comforts of the soldier by preventive and sanitary means.

The Medical Bureau would, in my judgment, derive important and useful aid from the counsels and well-directed efforts of an intelligent and scientific commission, to be styled "A Commission of Inquiry and Advice in respect of the Sanitary Interests of the United States Forces," and acting in co-operation with the Bureau in elaborating and applying such facts as might be elicited from the experience and more extended observation of those connected with armies; with reference to the diet and hygiene of troops and the organization of military hospitals, etc.

This Commission is not intended to interfere with, but to strengthen the present organization, introducing and elaborating such improvements as the advanced stage of Medical Science might suggest; more particularly as regards the class of men who, in this war of sections, may be called to abandon the comforts of home, and be subject to the privations and casualties of war.

The views of this office were expressed in a communication of May 18, 1861, in a crude and hasty manner, as to the examination of recruits, the proposed organization of cooks, nurses, &c., to which I beg leave to refer.

The selection of this Board is of the greatest importance.

In connection with those gentlemen who originated this investigation, with many others, I would suggest the following members, not to exceed five, to convene in Washington, who should have power to fill vacancies and appoint a competent Secretary.

REVEREND HENRY W. BELLOWS, D.D.

PROFESSOR ALEXANDER DALLAS BACHE, LL.D.

PROFESSOR WOLCOT GIBBS, M.D.

JEFFRIES WYMAN, M.D.

W. H. VAN BUREN, M.D.

It would be proper, also, to associate with this Board an officer of the Medical Staff of the Army, to be selected by the Secretary of War, familiar with the organization of Military Hospitals and the details of field service.

Respectfully submitted:

R. C. WOOD,
Acting Surgeon-General.

No. 3.

ORDER OF THE SECRETARY OF WAR, APPROVED BY THE PRESIDENT, APPOINTING THE SANITARY COMMISSION.

WAR DEPARTMENT, }
Washington, June 9, 1861. }

THE Secretary of War has learned, with great satisfaction, that at the instance and in pursuance of the suggestion of the Medical Bureau, in a communication to this office, dated May 22, 1861, Henry W. Bellows, D. D., Prof. A. D. Bache, LL.D., Prof. Jeffries Wyman, M.D., Prof. Wolcott Gibbs, M.D., W. H. Van Buren, M.D. Samnel G. Howe, M.D., R. C. Wood, Surgeon U. S. A., G. W. Cullum, U. S. A., Alexander E. Shiras, U. S. A., have mostly consented, in connection with such others as they may choose to associate with them, to act as " A Commission of Inquiry and Advice in respect of the Sanitary Interests of the United States Forces," and without remuneration from the Government. The Secretary has submitted their patriotic proposal to the consideration of the President, who directs the acceptance of the services thus generously offored.

The Commission, in connection with a Surgeon of the U. S. A., to be designated by the Secretary, will direct its inquiries to the principles and practices connected with the inspection of recruits and enlisted men ; the sanitary condition of the volunteers; to the means of preserving and restoring the health, and of securing the general comfort and efficiency of troops; to the proper provision of cooks, nurses, and hospitals; and to other subjects of like nature.

The Commission will frame such rules and regulations, in respect of the objects and modes of its inquiry, as may seem best adapted to the purpose of its constitution, which, when approved by the Secretary, will be established as general guides of its investigations and action.

A room with necessary conveniences will be provided in the City of Washington for the use of the Commission, and the members will meet when and at such places as may be convenient to them for consultation, and for the determination of such questions as may come properly before the Commission.

In the progress of its inquiries, the Commission will correspond freely with the Department and with the Medical Bureau, and will communicate to each, from time to time, such observations and results as it may deem expedient and important.

The Commission will exist until the Secretary of War shall otherwise direct, unless sooner dissolved by its own action.

SIMON CAMERON;
Secretary of War.

I approve the above.

A. LINCOLN.

June 13, 1861.

.

No. 4.

PLAN OF ORGANIZATION FOR "THE COMMISSION OF INQUIRY AND ADVICE IN RESPECT OF THE SANITARY INTERESTS OF THE UNITED STATES FORCES."

THE Commission naturally divides itself into two branches, one of *Inquiry,* the other of *Advice,* to be represented by two principal Committees, into which the Commission should divide.

I. INQUIRY.—This branch of the Commission would again naturally subdivide itself into three stems, inquiring successively in respect of the condition and wants of the troops :—

1st. What *must be* the condition and want of troops gathered together in such masses, so suddenly, and with such inexperience?

2d. What *is* their condition?—a question to be settled only by direct and positive observation and testimony.

3d. What *ought to be* their condition, and how would Sanitary Science bring them up to the standard of the highest attainable security and efficiency?

SUB-COMMITTEES OF BRANCH OF INQUIRY.

A. Under the first Committee's care would come the suggestion of such immediate aid, and such obvious recommendations as an intelligent foresight and an ordinary acquaintance with received principles of sanitary science would enable the Board at once to urge upon the public authorities.

B. The second Sub-Committee would have in charge, directly or through agents, the actual exploration of recruiting posts, transports, camps, quarters, tents, forts, hospitals; and consultation with officers —Colonels, Captains, Surgeons, and Chaplains—at their posts, to collect from them needful testimony as to the condition and wants of the troops.

C. The Third Sub-Committee would investigate, theoretically and practically, all questions of dirt, cooking, and cooks; of clothing, foot, head, and body gear; of quarters, tents, booths, huts; of hospitals, field service, nurses and surgical dresses; of climate and its effects, malaria, and camp and hospital diseases and contagions; of ventilation, natural and artificial; of vaccination; antiscorbutics; disinfectants; of sinks, drains, camp sites, and cleanliness in general; of best methods of economizing and preparing rations, or changing or exchanging them. All these questions to be treated from the highest scientific ground, with the newest light of physiology, chemistry, and medicine, and the latest teachings of experience in the great continental wars.

Probably these Committees of Inquiry could convert to their use, without fee or reward, all our medical and scientific men now in the army, or elsewhere, especially by sending an efficient agent about among the regiments to establish active correspondence with surgeons, chaplains, and others, as well as by a public advertisement and call for such help and information.

II. ADVICE.—This branch of the Commission would subdivide itself into three stems, represented by three Sub-Committees. The general object of this branch would be to get the opinions and conclusions of the Commission approved by the Medical Bureau, ordered by the War Department, carried out by the officers and men, and encouraged, aided, and supported by the benevolence of the public at large, and by the State governments. It would subdivide itself naturally into three parts.

1. A Sub-Committee, in direct relation with the Government, the Medical Bureau, and the War Department; having for its object the

communication of the counsels of the Commission, and the procuring of their approval and ordering by the U. S. Government.

2. A Sub-Committee in direct relation with the army officers, medical men, the camps and hospitals, whose duty it should be to look after the actual carrying out of the orders of the War Department and the Medical Bureau, and make sure, by inspection, urgency, and explanation, by influence, and all proper methods, of their actual accomplishment.

3. A Sub-Committee in direct relation with the State governments, and with the public associations of benevolence. First, to secure uniformity of plans, and then proportion and harmony of action; and finally, abundance of supplies in moneys and goods, for such extra purposes as the laws do not and cannot provide for.

SUB-COMMITTEE OF BRANCH OF ADVICE.

D. The Sub-Committee in direct relation with the Government, would immediately urge the most obvious measures, favored by the Commission on the War Department, and secure their emphatic reiteration of orders now neglected. It would establish confidential relations with the Medical Bureau. A Secretary, hereafter to be named, would be the head and hand of this Sub-Committee—always near the Government, and always urging the wishes and aims of the Commission upon its attention.

E. This Sub-Committee, in direct relation with the army officers, medical men, the camps, forts, and hospitals, would have it for its duty to explain and enforce upon inexperienced, careless, or ignorant officials, the regulations of a sanitary kind ordered by the Department of War and the Medical Bureau; of complaining to the Department of disobedience, sloth, or defect, and of seeing to the general carrying out of the objects of the Commission in their practical details.

F. This Sub-Committee, in direct relation with State authorities and benevolent associations, would have for its duties to look after three chief objects.

First: How far the difficulties in the sanitary condition and prospects of the troops are due to original defects in the laws of the States or the inspection usages, or in the manner in which officers, military or medical, have been appointed in the several States, with a view to the adoption of a general system, by which the State laws may all be assimilated to the United States regulations.

This could probably only be brought about by calling a convention of delegates from the several loyal States, to agree upon some uniform system; or, that failing, by agreeing upon a model State arrangement, and sending a suitable agent to the Governors and Legislatures, with a prayer for harmonious action and co-operation.

Second: To call in New York a convention of delegates from all the benevolent associations throughout the country, to agree upon a plan of common action in respect of supplies, depôts, and methods of feeding the extra demands of the Medical Bureau or Commissariat, without embarrassment to the usual machinery. This, too, might, if a convention were deemed impossible, be effected by sending about an agent of special adaptation. Thus the organizing, methodizing, and reducing to serviceableness the vague, disproportioned, and hap-hazard benevolence of the public, might be successfully accomplished.

Third: To look after the pecuniary ways and means necessary for accomplishing the various objects of the Commission, through solicitation of donations, either from State treasuries or private beneficence. The treasurer might be at the head of this Special Committee.

OFFICERS.

If these general suggestions be adopted, the officers of the Commission might properly be a President, Vice-president, Secretary, and Treasurer.

President.—His duties would be to call and preside over all meetings of the Commission, and give unity, method, and practical success to its counsels.

The *Vice-President* would perform the President's duties in his absence.

The *Secretary* should be a gentleman of special competency, charged with the chief executive duties of the Commission, in constant correspondence with its President; be resident at Washington, and admitted to confidential intimacy with the Medical Bureau and the War Department. Under him such agents as could safely be trusted with the duties of inspection and advice in camps, hospitals, fortresses, etc., should work, receiving instructions from, and reporting to him. He would be immediately in connection with the Committees A and B of the Branch of Inquiry, and of Committees D and E of the Branch of Advice.

The *Treasurer* would hold and disburse, as ordered by the Commission, the funds of the body. These funds would be derived from such sources as the Commission, when its objects were known, might find open or make available. Donations, voluntary and solicited; contributions from patriotic and benevolent associations, or State treasuries, would be the natural supply of the cost of sustaining a commission whose members would give their time, experience, and labor to a cause of the most obvious and pressing utility, and the most radical charity and wide humanity; who, while unwilling to depend on the General Government for even their incidental expenses, could not perform their duties without some moderate sum in hand to facilitate their movements.

The publication of the final report of the Commission could be arranged by subscription or private enterprise.

As the scheme of this Commission may appear impracticable from apprehended jealousies, either on the part of the Medical Bureau or the War Department, it may be proper to state, that the Medical Bureau itself asked for the appointment of the Commission, and that no ill-feeling exists or will exist between the Commission and the War Department, or the Government. The Commission grows out of no charges of negligence or incompetency in the War Department or the Medical Bureau. The sudden increase of volunteer forces has thrown unusual duties upon them. The Commission is chiefly concerned with the volunteers, and one of its highest ambitions is to bring the volunteers up to the regulars in respect of sanitary regulations and customs. To aid the Medical Bureau, without displacing it, or in any manner infringing upon its rights and duties, is the object of the Commission. The embarrassments anticipated from etiquette or official jealousy, have all been overcome in advance, by a frank and cordial understanding, met with large and generous feelings by the Medical Bureau and the Department of War.

> HENRY W. BELLOWS, *President.*
> PROF. A. D. BACHE, *Vice-President.*
> ELISHA HARRIS, M. D., *Corresp. Sect'y.*
> GEORGE W. CULLUM, *U. S. Army.*
> ALEXANDER E. SHIRAS, *U. S. Army.*
> ROBERT C. WOOD, M. D., *U. S. Army.*
> WILLIAM H. VAN BUREN, M. D.
> WOLCOTT GIBBS, M. D.
> SAMUEL G. HOWE, M. D.
> CORNELIUS R. AGNEW, M. D.
> J. S. NEWBERRY, M. D.
> GEORGE T. STRONG, *Treasurer.*

WASHINGTON, *June* 13, 1861.

WAR DEPARTMENT, WASHINGTON, *June* 13, 1861.

I hereby approve of the plan of organization proposed by the Sanitary Commission, as above given ; and all persons in the employ of the United States Government are directed and enjoined to respect and further the inquiries and objects of this Commission, to the utmost of their ability.

SIMON CAMERON, *Secretary of War.*

No. 5.

CONTRIBUTIONS RECEIVED FROM CALIFORNIA.

FROM FEBRUARY 24, 1862, to MARCH 1, 1866.

NOTE.—The contributions in gold have all been reduced in this Table to their value in currency at the time of their receipt.

1862.			Dolls.	Cts.
Feb'y.	24	Oakland Patriotic Fund, Oakland...	102	40
April	22	Olympic Club, San Francisco...	200	00
		Ladies' Patriotic Fund, San Francisco..	500	00
		Patriotic Fund, San Francisco, by Ira B. Rankin...............................	1,000	00
July	24	Proceeds of Treasury Note from "Lock Box 457," San Francisco P. O............	104	12
	25	H. F. Teschemacher, Mayor of San Francisco.....................................	2,125	66
Sept.	27	Contributions on Election Day, San Francisco....................................	3,785	00
Oct.	14	Citizens of San Francisco..	100,000	00
	28	Do. Do.	100,000	00
Nov.	3	Nevada City, California, by Hon. A. A. Sargent...................................	8,235	91
		Citizens of Marysville..	12,700	00
		Ladies of Santa Clara, by Mrs. T. Starr King.....................................	536	80
	11	Relief Society of County of San Joaquin, by H. B. Underhill, Sect'y, Stockton	7,222	36
	14	Citizens of San Francisco..	15,000	00
	15	" " California..	15,000	00
		" " Stockton...	650	00
		" " Monterey..	1,448	69
Dec.	6	" " California..	35,956	11
		" " California..	30,000	00
	8	Citizens of Marysville, by D. C. Benham, San Francisco.........................	6,400	00
		Yuba County..	8,960	00
	13	Citizens of Sacramento, by Messrs. Leland, Standford, S. Cross and H. Miller.	20,000	00
	15	Citizens of California..	30,000	00
	8	W. B. Brown, San Francisco...	500	00
	26	Citizens of Auburn, Placer County..	1,270	12
1863.	27	Charles Duncombe, Hicksville..	377	00
Jan.	6	Citizens of Sacramento, by Messrs. Leland Stanford, H. Miller and S. Cross....	1,260	75
		Citizens of California..	12,947	93
	10	Hiram Perham, Miner, Klamath County..	40	00
		San Joaquin Relief Society, by H. B. Underhill...................................	2,173	60
	17	Hon. Milton S. Latham...	250	00
	22	San Joaquin Relief Society, by H. B. Underhill...................................	730	00
	29	Citizens of Santa Clara Township, by James H. Morgan........................	2,022	02
	30	Citizens of San Francisco and interior towns, by James Otis, Treasurer........	20,000	00
Feb.	2	Thomas McConnell, Hicksville P. O., Sacramento County......................	190	00
	6	Citizens of Yuba County, by D. C. Benham, Treasurer.........................	1,855	00
	28	Citizens of Spanish Ranch, Plumas County, by Thos. McCormic. Marysville..	178	38
March	7	Woodland Soldiers' Aid Society, Woodland, Yolo County. Mrs. C. W. Lewis, President, Mrs. F. S. Freeman, Treasurer, and Mrs. G. D. Fiske, Sect'y... }	1,222	00
	13	George G. Briggs, Santa Barbara County...	100	00
	18	Citizens of California, by James Otis, Treasurer.................................	23,006	28
	27	Nicolaus, Sutter & Co., Sacramento..	1,122	00
April	6	Members of the Public School, Placerville, by J. A. Bartlett, President, and G. L. Fitch, Secretary.. }	50	00
	7	Ladies' Union Association, Santa Clara, by Mrs. B. F. Watkins.................	144	50
	20	C. K. Ercanbrack and C. H. Kelton, Watsonville, Santa Cruz County...........	30	00
May	6	Citizens of San Francisco, by James Otis, Treasurer............................	10,000	00
June	22	Lady Washington Society, Aurora, Moro County, by Mrs. S. E. Morse, Treasurer, Mrs. A. Mack, President, Mrs. L. Green, Vice-President, and Mrs. L. Hutchinson, Secretary... }	500	00
	26	Citizens of California, by James Otis, Treasurer.................................	10,000	00
Sept.	10	Do. Do. Do. Do.	5,000	00
	15	Lady Washington Society, Aurora. Moro County, by Mrs. A. Mack, President, and Mrs. S. E. Morse, Treasurer............................... }	118	00
	16	Woodland Soldiers' Aid Society, Woodland, Yolo County, by Miss C. A. Templeton, Sacramento... }	20	00
	28	E. B. Crocker, Sacramento..	25	00
	29	Napa Soldiers' Relief Association, Napa City, by Mrs. Thomas Earl, President, and R. E. Wood, Secretary... }	309	7
Oct.	12	Citizens of California, Contributions on Election Day, by Jas. Otis, Treasurer.	13,539	4
	17	Contributions on Election Day in Great Mogul District, Amador County, September 2d, by M. Scott.. }	235	2
	28	Citizens of California, by James Otis..	10,000	0
		Amount carried forward.........	$519,094	6

Contributions received from California—Continued.

1863.			Dolls.	Cts.
		Amount brought forward........	519,094	66
Dec.	4	Citizens of California, by James Otis..	1,000	00
	8	T. L. Baker, San Francisco, by F. A. Foster, New York............................	50	00
1864.	18	Yreka, (Curtis H. Pyle, P. M.)...	10	00
Jan.	4	Citizens of California, Font fund of Rev. T. Starr King, San Francisco, remitted by draft through W. M. Prichard, Esq., New York.................... }	360	00
	6	Citizens of California, by James Otis, Treasurer......................................	50,000	00
	23	Yreka, (Curtis H. Pyle, P. M.)...	5	00
	27	Ladies of Napa City, by Mrs. A. Y. Easterly, President; proceeds of Christmas Eve Festival.. }	700	50
	29	Ladies' Soldiers' Relief Sewing Society of Napa City, a New Year's Offering, by Mrs. E. G. Easterly, Secretary... }	140	00
	30	James McGlatchy, Sacramento, through H. Greeley, New York.................	10	00
Feb.	6	Yreka, (Curtis H. Pyle, P. M.)...	5	00
	16	Citizens of California, by James Otis, Treasurer......................................	50,000	00
March	5	Union Meeting of Presbyterians and Methodists, Cumberland Churches, Stockton, by Rev. R. Happersett.. }	91	50
May	3	Citizens of California, by James Otis, Treasurer......................................	50,961	53
	7	G. G. Briggs, San Francisco, through Fowler and Wells, New York..............	50	00
	10	Concert and Supper by Philharmonic Society, aided by Ladies of Sacramento City, by S. B. Leavett, Secretary and Treasurer......................... }	4,811	58
June	14	Citizens of California, through Macondray & Co.......................................	25,000	00
	30	C. P. Lolor, San Francisco, being amount paid by him for the "Gridley" Sanitary Sack of Flour sold at Auction, May 28, 1864......................... }	150	00
July	5	Sacramento Valley Sanitary Association, by C. Crocker, Treasurer..............	41,352	50
	6	Citizens of California, by H. P. Coon, Chairman......................................	25,000	00
	15	Do. Do. by James Otis, Treasurer........................	52,633	75
	19	Cabin passengers on board Steamer "Moses Taylor" on trip from San Francisco to New York, July 4, 1864, by R. S. Whigham, Treasurer........... }	781	95
		Cabin Passengers on board Steamer "Uncle Sam," July 4, 1864, through E. M. Jenkins, Purser.. }	714	00
	30	Citizens of Santa Clara; proceeds of Lecture by Dr. Bellows.....................	2,033	10
		Esmeralda Sanitary Association, by J. B. Saxton, President, (2 Silver Bars,).	11,473	18
		Citizens of Vallejo, through Dr. W. W. Chapman...................................	1,250	00
		Do. Howland Flat, Pine Grove and Potosi, through T. A. McFarland, Treasurer.. }	3,816	45
		Citizens of Eureka, North Sierra County, by J. Andrews...........................	1,506	00
Aug.	6	Citizens of California, through Dr. Bellows..............	349	00
	29	Children of Oroville, through George C. Perkins......................................	645	00
		Citizens of Santa Clara, balance of proceeds of Lecture............................	195	00
		First Baptist Church, Petaluma..	69	66
		Mr. Rolofson, San Francisco, one day's Photographing, July 4, 1864.............	606	30
		Horace Taber, Gibsonville..	154	80
		Santa Clara College, by Rev. Father Accolti..	302	50
		Hobbs, Gilmore & Co., San Francisco..	258	00
		Weaverville, Trinity County; proceeds of Festival, June 8, 1864, by Mrs. H. J. Howe, Chairman.. }	12,577	05
		John Gale (deceased) San Francisco, bequest in his Will, through Henry Edwards.. }	645	00
		Proceeds of Ball and Festival by Ladies' Committee, Placerville, through J. Wilcox... }	4,327	43
		Ladies' Sanitary Committee, Petaluma, by Mrs. K. Wilson, President..........	5,160	00
		W. S. Day, Auditor, Downesville, Sierra County; proceeds of sale of Jury Fee.. }	859	14
		Citizens of Taylorsville, Plumas County, by A. T. Blood, President, 4th July Committee.. }	8,824	60
		Citizens of Dutch Flat, by W. G. Brown...	34	83
		Citizens of Eureka, Humboldt County, by L. C. Schmiddt, President of Sanitary Fund Committee.. }	1,094	18
		Proceeds of 4th July, Barbecue of Military Companies in Napa City, through Mrs. E. G. Easterly.. }	1,032	00
		Ladies' Sanitary Commission of Amador County, by Mrs. T. A. Springer, Treasurer, Jackson.. }	2,665	14
		Proceeds of San Joaquin County Sanitary Fair, through C. O. Burton, T. R. Antony and others, for Committee, Stockton.. }	10,858	12
		Citizens of Fairfield, Solano County, through Miss S. R. Pearson...............	40	00
		Citizens of Vallejo, Solano County, through James Hillman......................	655	00
Sept.	26	Citizens of California, by Dr. Bellows..	11,256	46
	27	California Branch by R. G. Sneath. Treasurer..........................	35,631	00
Oct.	7	Citizens of California, by Dr. Bellows..	30	55
	8	Do. Do. Do.	16,080	00
		Joseph Britton, San Francisco...	2	00
Nov.	14	Citizens of Taylorville, Plumas County..	489	93
		Citizens of Jackson, Amador County...	84	42
		Amount carried forward........	$957,927	81

Contributions received from California—Continued.

1864.			Dolls.	Cts.
		Amount brought forward.........	957,927	81
Nov.	14	Citizens of Susanville, Plumas County..	147	21
		Citizens of Mokelunne Hill..	504	51
.		Citizens of Empire City, Coose County.................................	376	83
		Sacramento Union..	40	29
		Citizens of Sebastopol, Sonoma..	30	15
		Citizens of Vesaha..	275	88
		Miss Sarah Shafter and other Children, San Francisco....................	20	10
		Mrs. M. H. Holland, Skating Pond, San Francisco.......................	1,500	00
	5	California Branch, by R. G. Sneath, Treasurer........................	28,300	00
	7	Citizens of California, by Dr. Bellows................................	531	75
	15	Proceeds of Fair, Napa City, by Mrs. Emily G. Easterly, Secretary..............	3,552	77
		Citizens of California, by R. G. Sneath, Treasurer.....................	36,800	00
	19	Citizens of California, by Dr. Bellows................................	396	02
Dec.	22	Citizens of California, through Washington Office.....................	33	58
	9	Citizens of California, by R. G. Sneath, Treasurer...................	26,496	25
	12	Citizens of Sacramento, by C. Crocker, Treasurer...................	3,263	02
	24	Proceeds of sale of Silver Watch Chain from Santa Clara............	13	25
1865.	27	Citizens of California, R. G. Sneath, Treasurer....................	2,700	00
Jan.	5	Do. Do. Do. Do.	27,300	00
	16	Proceeds of Children's Fair, San Francisco, (Dec. 17th,) by Misses Sallie ⎱ Thibault, Florence Cornwall and Flora Haight, Committee.................... ⎰	360	12
	30	Loyal Voters of Placer County, by J. L. Browne......................	1,423	12
Feb.	14	Citizens of California, by R. G. Sneath, Treasurer..................	6,465	00
	9	Citizens of California, by Dr. Bellows...............................	105	50
	24	Citizens of California, by R. G. Sneath, Treasurer..................	35,820	00
March	8	Do. Do. Do. Do.	6,300	00
	9	Citizens of California, through Dibblee & Hyde, New York...........	4,508	00
	18	Citizens of California, by R. G. Sneath, Treasurer.................	18,045	54
April	7	Do. Do. Do. Do.	14,772	70
	10	Do. Do. Do. Do.	14,522	95
	13	Do. Do. Do. Do.	3,643	75
	14	Do. Do. Do. Do.	3,500	00
May	15	Arthur S. Barker, Almeda...	2	00
	19	Citizens of California, by R. G. Sneath, Treasurer.................	18,235	00
		Do. Do. Do. Do.	1,200	00
July	15	Do. Do. Do. Do.	293	80
Sept.	4	Do. Do. Do. Do.	14,425	00
Nov.	6	J. H. Chapin, San Francisco, am't of advance (in coin) refunded in currency.	146	50
1866.				
Feb.	3	Sacramento Valley Branch, by John McNeill, Secretary.............................	279	50
		Total amount......... $1,234,257		31

CONTRIBUTIONS RECEIVED FROM NEVADA.

From February 2, 1863, to January 1, 1866.

1863.			Dolls.	Cts
Feb.	2	Citizens of Ormsby County, by W. Stewart, Treasurer.........................	4,000	00
March	7	Citizens of Nevada, 8 Gold and Silver Bars.................................	29,921	04
May	4	Ladies' Social Benevolent Society, Gold Hill...............................	1,328	94
		Silver City Benevolent Society, by Melville Kelsey, Mrs. L. M. Barrett, Com- ⎱ mittee, and Mrs. H. J. Currie, President,............................... ⎰	449	25
Aug.	19	Washoe City, by P. E. Shannon,................................	623	75
Sept.	29	Loyal Citizens of Story County, by A. B. Paul, President, Virginia, (10 Gold ⎱ and Silver Bars).. ⎰	17,360	97
Oct.	20	Citizens of Douglass County, by Messrs. J. A. Harvey, Alexander Brinck- ⎱ man, C. M. Tuttle and P. Chamberlain, M. D., Committee...................... ⎰	460	80
1864.				
Feb.	16	408 Voters, Silver City, at Election for Adoption of State Constitution, by ⎱ N. P. Sheldon, President and C. B. Zabriskie, Treasurer........................ ⎰	2,236	50
		Proceeds of Ball, Silver City, Christmas Eve................................	404	17
May	9	Citizens of Dayton, by C. B. Zabriskie, Treasurer............................	176	70
	23	Proceeds of Ball, by Ladies of Carson Valley, through Henry Epstein..........	425	00
July	22	Proceeds of Ball, Douglass County, June 10th, by Henry Epstein.................	1,380	35
		Contributions at the Polls..	485	76
	30	Ladies' Sanitary Aid Society, Carson City...................................	5,020	00
		Amount carried forward......... $64,273		23

Contributions from Nevada—Continued.

1864.			Dolls.	Cts.
		Amount brought forward.........	64,273	23
July	30	Citizens of Austin, by E. S. Davis, President...	9,544	02
Nov.	9	Employes of Gould and Currie Mine, Virginia City, (1 Silver Bar.)................	10,888	76
	14	Citizens of Story County, by Dr. Bellows..	11,055	00
1865.				
Jan.	25	Citizens of Nevada, Contributions on Election Day.....................................	3,751	45
May	10	Citizens of Lynn County, by N. P. Sheldon, President.................................	5,089	50
	27	Citizens of Washoe County, by A. B. Paul..	1,700	00
July	28	Proceeds of Social Parties, Dayton, Lyon County, through E. H. Dean...........	165	00
Oct.	4	Nevada Branch, by A. B. Paul, Treasurer...	1,176	00
		Total amount.........	107,642	96

CONTRIBUTIONS RECEIVED FROM OREGON.

FROM OCTOBER 11, 1862, TO JANUARY 1, 1866.

1862.					Dolls.	Cts.
Oct.	11	Citizens of Portland, by Amory Holbrook......			1,662	65
	13	Do. Do. Do.			2,300	00
	20	Citizens of Oregon, by Amory Holbrook...			1,875	00
		Grand Lodge of Free and Accepted Masons of Oregon for the Relief } of Sick and Wounded Masons in the Army.............................. }			1,000	00
Nov.	7	Citizens of Oregon, by Amory Holbrook...			3,575	00
	26	Do. Do. Do.			2,120	10
Dec.	4	W. L. Adams, Astoria...			30	00
	6	Citizens of Oregon, by Amory Holbrook...			2,560	00
1863.	16	Do. Jacksonville, by Do.			2,913	40
Jan.	22	Do. Oregon, by Do.			1,384	19
Feb.	10	Do. Do. Do.			1,965	00
March	10	Do. Do. Do.			377	84
June	29	Ladies of Portland, by Amory Holbrook...			1,300	00
Aug.	19	Ladies' Oregon Sanitary Aid Society, by Amory Holbrook................	705	00		
		Citizens of Oregon, by Amory Holbrook...............................	175	00	880	00
Sept.	17	Canemah Oregon Ladies' Aid Society, by Amory Holbrook...............	126	00		
		Corvallis Presbyterian Church, by Amory Holbrook.........................	33	00		
		Portland Ladies' Sanitary Aid Society, collected in part at Methodist, } Presbyterian, Baptist, Congregational and Episcopal Churches... }	455	00		
		Dallas Congregational Church..	54	00		
		Ames Chapel Neighborhood...	102	00	770	00
Nov. 1864.	14	Proceeds of Entertainment by Young Men of Color at the Dalles, } through Lewis Tappan, New York................................... }			117	60
Jan.	7	Thanksgiving-Day Collections in four Churches...............................				
		Portland, by Amory Holbrook..	800	00		
		Citizens of Ames Chapel Neighborhood, by Amory Holbrook...........	70	00		
		Congregation of St. Paul's Chapel, Oregon City, by Amory Holbrook.	38	00	908	00
	30	Jacob Kann, Portland, through Wakeman, Gookin and Dickinson, } New York.. }			100	00
Feb.	6	Citizens of Salem, by John H. Moores...			342	63
	1	Sanitary Aid Society, Salem, by John H. Moores...............................			800	00
	4	Ladies' Sanitary Commission, Astoria..			122	00
	11	Ladies of Portland and Citizens of Oregon City, Vancouvers and } Milwaukie, by A. Holbrook.. }			622	87
March	19	Sanitary Aid Society, Oakgrove, by William H. Goodwin, Treasurer....			55	00
	29	Mrs. Flora G. Davenport, Silverton, Marion County.............................			36	00
	31	Ladies' Aid Society, Portland, by A. Holbrook...................................	300	00		
		Citizens of Oregon, by A. Holbrook...	500	28	800	28
April	19	Do. Do. Do.			500	00
May	23	Do. Do. Do.			500	00
	28	Ladies' Society of Portland, through Ladd & Tilton, New York.........			1,100	00
June	9	Ladies' Sanitary Aid Society, Astoria, by Mrs. Col. J. Taylor, Mrs. } J. Ross, and Mrs. W. H. Gray, Committee, Mrs. Mary Ross, Treas. }			136	00
July	15	Citizens of Lafayette, by E. Cartwright...			200	00
	20	Citizens of Portland...			435	00
	30	Linn County Sanitary Aid Society, Albany, by John Barrows, Se- } cretary, and J. J. Thornton, President................................... }			815	75
		Amount carried forward.........			$32,304	31

Contributions received from Oregon—Continued.

			Dolls.	C.
1864.		Amount brought forward.........	32,304	31
July	30	Ladies' Sanitary Aid Society, Portland....................................	1,578	79
		Citizens of Oregon, by Amory Holbrook..............................	2,000	00
		Do. Salem, by J. H. Moores.	537	09
		Do. Jackson County, by C. C. Beekman..............	1,079	25
		Do. Scottsburg Do.	210	00
		Do. Josephine County. Do.	546	00
		Do. Oregon, by A. Holbrook..............................	126	47
		Linn County Sanitary Aid Society, by J. Barrows,..........	105	33
Aug.	29	Do. Do. Do. Albany, by J. Barrows..............	1,290	00
		Ladies' Sanitary Aid Society, Portland, by Mrs. H. Low.....	1,206	92
		Citizens of Ames Chapel, through James Davis..............	96	01
		Citizens of Eugene City, by D. M. Risdon, President..........	776	72
		Unknown Town, through Mrs. A. C. Gibbs, Portland...........	61	92
		Citizens of Portland, by A. Holbrook..............................	3,634	01
		Citizens of Canemah...	50	00
		Peter Paquet, Oregon City...	16	00
		Citizens of Lafayette, Yam Hill County.........................	170	00
		Do. Albany, Linn County, by J. Barrows.................	104	45
		Do. Umatilla, through Mrs. A. C. Gibbs.................	1,023	00
Oct.	7	W. H. Corbett, Portland...	150	00
Nov.	14	Miss Olive Geroam (six years old) and her Associates, Canemah, } through William Barlow, Oregon City............................. }	13	00
		Two Gentlemen of Portland, by A. Holbrook..................	30	45
		Citizens of Oregon City...	93	00
		Do. Umatilla..	30	00
		Sanitary Aid Society, Albany, by J. Barrows..................	333	42
		Do. Do. Milwaukie, by H. Miller.......	259	84
		Ladies' Sanitary Aid Society, Portland, by A. Holbrook..............	353	22
		Citizens of Umatilla..	86	27
		Citizens of Benton County and Maple Grove, contributed at the June } Election and 4th July Celebration, thro' J. Quinn Thorton, Albany }	240	00
		Citizens of Sandy Precinct, Maltnomah County................	156	36
		Citizens of Jackson County, through C. C. Beekman............	292	00
		Do. Josephine County Do.	297	00
		Eola Sanitary Society, through Lot Livermore..................	36	03
		Citizens of Oregon City, proceeds of Lecture, through J. L. Barlow.....	32	00
		Sanitary Aid Society of Ames Chapel, raised in Camp Ground............	43	60
		Premium on Gold...	44	90
		Sanitary Aid Society, Portland.....................................	120	20
		Citizens of Portland, by A. Holbrook.......	2,120	00
		Oregon City Lecture Fund...................................	192	89
		Ladies' Sanitary Aid Society, Portland..........................	624	15
		Citizens of Portland...	62	00
		Do. Albany, Linn County..............................	264	81
		Do. Harrisburg......................................	136	93
		Do. Eugene City.....................................	293	46
	2	Oregon Branch, by Henry Failing, Treasurer..................	1,388	82
	28	Citizens of Oregon, by Do. Do.	10,119	40
	29	Proceeds of Party, by Ladies of Canemah......................	70	00
Dec.	22	Citizens of Oregon, through the Washington Office..............	115	00
	29	Do. Do. by Henry Failing, Treasurer.......	354	14
	6	Do. Do. Do. Do.	1,959	60
	8	Oregon Branch, by Do. Do. Do.	2,063	05
	21	Citizens of Astoria, Clitsop County, by Mrs. Mary Ross..................	77	10
1865.		Do. Marion County, by J. H. Moores..................	742	64
Jan.	7	Proceeds of Supper, Ladies' Sewing Society Presbyterian Church, } Corvallis, by Mrs. E. M. Clark, Secretary............................ } 150 00		
		Mrs. Margaret Gray, Corvallis, by Mrs. E. M. Clark, Secretary........... 5 00		
		Master Johnson Porter (aged five years) by Do. Do. 5 00	160	00
	30	Oregon Branch, by Henry Failing, Treasurer.....................	1,053	82
Feb.	16	Eugene City, by Mrs. C. E. Pengrie, President..................	504	15
March	9	Sanitary Aid Society, Astoria.....................................	2,110	32
		Oregon Branch, by Henry Failing, Treasurer....................	456	86
		Oakgrove Sanitary Aid Society, Eola, Polk County.............	47	00
April	13	Citizens of Oregon, by Henry Failing, Treasurer................	1,152	86
May	1	Do. Do. through Wells, Fargo & Co..............	525	67
		Do. Do. Do.	274	00
	26	Do. Do. Salem, by John H. Moores..............	675	00
June	6	Do. Do. Do.	400	00
July	27	Do. Do. Oregon, by Henry Failing, Treasurer..............	1,010	03
	8	Do. Salem, by John H. Moores..................	400	00
	28	Oregon Branch, by Henry Failing, Treasurer...................	350	88
Aug.	28	Do. Do. Do. Do.	138	05
Nov.	6	Ladies' Sanitary Committee, Portland, by Mrs. Mary E. Frazer...........	35	75

Total Amount............... $79,406|94

CONTRIBUTIONS RECEIVED FROM WASHINGTON TERRITORY.

FROM DECEMBER 4, 1862, to JANUARY 1, 1866.

1862.					Dolls.	Cts.
Dec.	4	Mr. Francis, Keeper of Light House, Shoal Water Bay......................	15	00		
1863.		Mr. Thompson, Assistant..............................Do....................................	5	00	20	00
Jan.	8	Citizens of Washington Territory, by W. W. Miller................................			1,600	00
	6	Employes of Pope and Talbot's Mills, Teehalet....................................			3,142	35
		Citizens of Washington Territory, by B. F. Kendall..............................			2,639	60
Feb.	19	Do. Do. Do. by W. W. Miller, Treasurer............			4,520	77
March	10	Do. Walla Walla, by A. Holbrook...			427	00
April	16	Do. San Juan Islands, by A. Francis, U. S. Consul....................			357	07
May	7	Do. Lewiston, by A. L. Downer, Treasurer.............................			660	70
Aug.	31	Ladies' Sanitary Aid Society, Vancouver, by Mrs. G. W. Durgin, }				
		through A. Holbrook..			470	00
Sept.	12	Collection at Thanksgiving Service, Olympia, by Geo. F. Whitworth...			90	50
	17	Port Anglos Library Association, through A. Holbrook........................			40	00
Nov.	23	Citizens of Walla Walla, by E. E. Kelly...			1,000	00
1864.						
Jan.	7	Ladies of Vancouver, through A. Holbrook...			530	00
March	3	Ladies of Olympia, proceeds of Sanitary Party, by Joseph Coushman...			500	00
	14	Thanksgiving Collection, Olympia, by George F. Whitworth..............			45	00
	31	Ladies' Association, Vancouver, by A. Holbrook............................			400	00
May	9	Sanitary Party at Clagnats, Lewis County, by J. T. Browning, Treas...			210	00
July	20	Collected at the Polls, Olympia Precinct, June 6...............................	83	00		
		Collected at Clamy and Pray's Saloon on Election Day, Olympia, by }				
		James Cushman..	54	00	137	00
	30	Citizens of Bruceport Pacific County, through A. Holbrook...............	203	00		
		Ladies' Aid Society, Vancouver...	484	00	687	00
Aug.	29	Citizens of Auburn, Baker County, through A. Holbrook...................			518	06
		Do. Eagle Precinct, Baker County, through A. Holbrook.........			284	44
		Do. Bruce and Pacific Counties, by A. Holbrook....................			50	00
		Ladies' Sanitary Aid Society, Vancouver, through W. A. Troup..........			800	00
		Citizens of Olympia, proceeds of 4th July Celebration, through S. }				
		W. Percival..			658	50
Nov.	14	Citizens of Oak Point, through Dr. Bellows.......................................	10	00		
		Children at Fort Simcoe, Do.	9	20	19	20
		Ladies' Sanitary Aid Society, Vancouver...			129	97
		Mr. and Mrs. A. Hall, Fort Simcoe, through R. H. Hewell, Olympia.....			50	00
		Ladies' Sanitary Aid Society, through Dr. Bellows.............................			10	00
		Citizens of Walla Walla...			452	76
Dec.	22	Do. Washington Territory, through the Washington Office.......			50	00
1865.						
Jan.	19	Do. Olympia...			40	00
March	9	Ladies' Sanitary Aid Society, Vancouver...			214	00
May	8	Citizens of Olympia..			165	00

Total amount.........$20.918 92

CONTRIBUTIONS RECEIVED FROM THE SANDWICH ISLANDS.

FROM JULY 9, 1862, TO JANUARY 1, 1866.

1862.							Dolls.	Cts.
July	9	Mrs. Henry Dimond, Honolulu...					25	00
1863.								
Jan.	17	Citizens of Honolulu...					1,200	00
Feb.	2	American Citizens of Honolulu, by Messrs. Alexander J. Cartwright, Charles }						
		R. Bishop, B. F. Snow, E. O. Hall, and Sherman Peck, Committee.............. }					1,180	00
	4	American Citizens of Honlulu, by ditto..					1,180	00
Sept.	8	Do. Do. Do. by Alexander J. Cartwright............................					500	00
1864.								
Feb.	6	Do. Do. Do. Do.					270	00
March	1	Do. Do. Do. Do.					250	00
Aug.	6	Do. Do. Do. Do. through H. W. B.............					1,200	00
	29	J. P. Judd, Honolulu		Do.				50	00
Oct.	7	Citizens of Sandwich Islands	Do. through H. W. B.............				1,330	00

Amount carried forward.........$7,185 | 00

Contributions received from Sandwich Islands—Continued.

				Dolls.	C.
1864.		Amount brought forward.........		7,185	00
Nov.	14	Proceeds of Sale 100 Barrels of Molasses from Capt. Makee, through } Alexander J. Cartwright, sold at Auction in San Francisco......... }	1,080 72		
		Premium on Gold..	1,113 14		
		Proceeds of Sale, Second 100 Barrels....................................	869 48		
		Premium on Gold..	895 56		
		Proceeds of Sale, one Barrel...	122 00		
		Premium on Gold..	123 22	4,204	1?
		Citizens of Honolulu, through Dr. Bellows. (Draft.)...................		660	87
Dec.	15	Proceeds of Sale of Keg Tamarinds from Sandwich Islands, through } McRuer and Merrill, San Francisco...................................... }		9	00
1865.					
Jan.	30	American Citizens, Honolulu, by Alexander J. Cartwright.................		450	00
March	8	Do. Do. Do. Do.		230	00
May	16	Dr. J. R. Wood, Honolulu, through McRuer and Merrill, San Francisco.		723	50
June	24	Proceeds of Sale 100 Kegs of Sugar from Capt. James Makee, Rose } Ranch, East Main Sandwich Islands, through Alex. J. Cartwright. }	1,304 73		
		Premium on Gold..	518 63	1,823	3?
		Proceeds of Sale 25 Kegs Sugar from Henry Cornwell Wikaper Maui, } Sandwich Islands, through Alexander J. Cartwright................... }		492	3?
		American Citizens, Honolulu, by Alexander J. Cartwright.................		100	00
July	1	Do. Do. Do. Do.		88	6?
Sept.	26	Miss Doratha Isenberg (three years old) through James B. Williams, } (in silver.)... }	1 00		
		Premium...	40	1	4?
Dec.	9	John Boardman, Honolulu..		145	2?
	21	Proceeds of Sale 100 Kegs of Sugar contributed by Captain James } Makee, sold in San Francisco by Messrs. Chas. W. Brooks & Co., } Expenses and charges amounting to $500 in Gold, not charged, } but contributed by Messrs. Brooks & Co.................................. }		1,842	0?
		Total amount.........$17,955			5?

CONTRIBUTIONS RECEIVED FROM IDAHO TERRITORY, COLO RADO TERRITORY AND VANCOUVER'S ISLAND.

		IDAHO TERRITORY.	Dolls.	Ct.
1863.				
Sept.	23	Citizens of Florence, by Samuel Wells, G. L. Story, J. H. Alvord, and J. B. } James, Committee.. }	2,110	4?
1864.				
Feb.	18	Contributions at the Polls on Election Day, October 31, 1863, at Lewiston, } by D. S. Kenyon, Treasurer... }	220	03
		Contributions at the Polls on Election Day, October 31, 1863, at Pierce City, } by A. L. Downer.. }	172	55
Nov.	14	Citizens of Warren's Diggings, through Dr. Bellows, Silver, Assayer's chip- } ping of corners... }	2,798	27
			$5,301	31
1864.		COLORADO TERRITORY.		
March	22	Contributions of Citizens of Denver, Feb. 22, 1864, by Hon. Simon Whiteley	1,025	00
1862.		VANCOUVER'S ISLAND.		
Feb.	21	American Citizens, Victoria, proceeds of six months' interest on Treasury } Note for $1,000.. }	36	5?
1863.	24	American Citizens, proceeds of Sale of $1,000 Treasury Note................	988	7?
April	16	Citizens of Victoria, by A. Francis, United States Consul...................	870	4?
			1,895	6?
1862.				
April.	22	American Citizens, Victoria, by Rev. T. Starr King.......................	300	00
		Total amount.........	$2,195	6?

No. 6.

RECEIPTS OF THE UNITED STATES SANITARY COMMISSION.
From June 27, 1861, to January 1, 1866.

	Dolls.	Cts
Maine	24,938	43
New Hampshire	1,926	84
Vermont	3,521	17
Massachusetts	15,532	00
Massachusetts, through Boston Branch	106,396	60
Rhode Island	11,823	96
Connecticut	8,418	55
New England, (States not designated)	6,683	75
New York	229,328	71
New Jersey	20,741	25
Pennsylvania	12,736	77
Delaware	775	00
Maryland	5,913	95
District of Columbia	12,124	53
Virginia	703	60
Ohio	16,049	50
Indiana	1,264	15
Illinois	4,342	50
Michigan	691	30
Wisconsin	916	00
Iowa	13	50
Minnesota	67	85
Kentucky	6,608	05
Louisiana	3,177	25
North Carolina	8	00
California	1,233,977	81
Nevada	107,642	96
Oregon	79,406	94
Washington Territory	20,918	92
Idaho "	5,301	31
Colorado "	1,025	00
Nebraska "	10	50
Vancouver's Island	2,195	61
Sandwich Islands	17,955	51
Chili	5,376	79
Peru	2,002	00
Buenos Ayres	18,412	85
Cuba	23	00
Costa Rica	84	00
Canada	441	48
New Foundland	150	00
England	11,145	33
Scotland	74	75
France	3,550	00
European Branch, (Paris)	13,372	72
London Branch	36,790	42
Belgium	100	00
Germany	843	22
Italy	50	00
Turkey	50	00
Amount carried forward	$2,055,604	33

DISBURSEMENTS OF THE U. S. SANITARY COMMISSION.

From June 27, 1861 to January 1, 1866.

EXPENSES.			Dolls.	Cts.
Rent	14,558	25		
Advertising	15,072	06		
Stationery and Office Printing	41,426	78		
Postage	15,823	59		
Telegrams	3,488	55		
Office Freight	40,226	83		
Office Expenses	59,343	80		
Travelling Expenses of Office Employes	6,517	44		
Office Salaries	136,690	21		
Stable	20,396	48		
Travelling Expenses of Members of the Commission.	8,609	30		
			362,153	29
PUBLICATIONS.				
Documents, Monographs, &c	55,830	57		
Sanitary Bulletin	30,534	07		
Sanitary Reporter	9,781	01		
			96,145	65
Statistical Bureau			45,326	17
General Inspection			129,509	97
Special Inspection			20,146	85
Hospital Directory			54,797	95
RELIEF DEPARTMENT.				
Special Relief	147,630	28		
Relief Corps	212,734	65		
Homes and Lodges	237,116	57		
Pension Bureau and Claim Agencies	115,736	87		
Hospital Transports	44,419	28		
" Cars	9,373	79		
" Visitors	4,762	52		
			771,773	96
SUPPLY DEPARTMENT.				
Purchase of Supplies	1,939,310	41		
Distribution of Supplies	252,188	33		
Transportation of Supplies	272,223	23		
Receiving Store House	23,863	48		
Distributing Store House	14,681	12		
Canvassing	65,719	98		
Canvassing in Pacific States	22,467	76		
Women's Central Association of Relief, N. Y	79,500	67		
Cincinnati Branch	15,000	00		
Cleveland "	10,000	00		
Columbus "	5,000	00		
Chicago "	10,000	00		
Lousville "	10,000	00		
Philadelphia "	314,316	08		
			3,034,271	06
Amount carried forward			4,514,124	90

Receipts of the U. S. Sanitary Commission—Continued.

	Dolls.	Cts.
Amount brought forward............	2,055,883	83
China...	2,989	90
Japan	5,000	00
U. S. Army..	1,738	30
U. S. Navy..	199	00
Boston and New England Fair............................. 50,000 00		
Yonkers, N. Y. " 12,000 00		
Flushing, Long Island " 3,934 32		
Brooklyn and Long Island " 305,513 83		
Schuyler County, N. Y. " 1,287 43		
Albany, N. Y. " 80,000 00		
Metropolitan, N. Y. " 1,184,487 72		
Warwick, Orange Co. N. Y. " 1,432 73		
Poughkeepsie, N. Y. " 16,192 27		
Hornellsville, N. Y. " 800 00		
South Adams, Mass. " 3,087 04		
Maryland State " (Baltimore.)............ 40,234 54		
Wheeling, Va. " 2,500 00		
Great Central Fair, Philadelphia............................. 1,035,398 96		
	2,736,868	84
Unknown Sources.....................................	3,952	26
Interest on U. S. Certificates............................... 37,771 71		
" " Deposits in Nassau Bank, Brooklyn...... 1,923 63		
" " " " 4th National Bank, N. Y..... 3,154 15		
	42,849	49
Receipts from Advertisements in Sanitary Bulletin... 2,160 00		
" " Subscriptions for " " ... 191 80		
	2,351	80
Contributions to Medical Fund................................	197	00
Proceeds of Sales of Furniture, Surplus Stores, &c...	72,298	07
Total amount.........$4,924,048	99	

"NEW YORK, *April* 26, 1866.

" We hereby certify that we employed Mr. James M. Halsey to examine the accounts of the Sanitary Commission, and that the letter on the other side is a true copy of his report to us of his completing his examination.

Signed,   J. J. ASTOR.
          A. A. LOW.   } Committee.
          JONA. STURGES.

Disbursements of the U. S. Sanitary Commission—Continued.

			Dolls.	Cts
SUPPLY DEPARTMENT—Continued.				
Amount brought forward............			4,514,124	90
N. E. Women's Auxiliary Association of Boston......	16,927	84		
Contributions to Aid Societies............	20,500	00		
New Jersey Branch............	500	00		
			37,927	84
HISTORICAL BUREAU.				
Expenses, (including purchase of House and Lot 21 West 12th Street N. Y)............ ....·	38,677	41		
Expenses in Washington............	3,670	23		
			42,347	64
MISCELLANEOUS.				
Western Sanitary Commission, (St. Louis)..............	50,000	00		
Metropolitan Fair, N. Y............	23,086	02		
Northwestern Fair, Chicago............	3,470	92		
European Branches, (London and Paris).................	12,344	58		
			88,901	52
CASH.				
Geo. T. Strong, Treasurer...	224,845	76		
New York Office............	2,248	14		
Washington "	2,877	99		
Louisville "	5,818	47		
Newberne " (N. C.)	2,300	00		
New Orleans "	686	99		
Canvassing and Supply Office, Philadelphia..............	6	75		
Dr. M. M. Marsh, Supt. "Lincoln Home," N. Y..........	438	99		
J. L. Alcooke, Supt. "Friends' Home," Penn Yan, N.Y.	1,524	00		
			240,747	09
Total amount.........$4,924,048				99

"NEW YORK, *March* , 1866.

J. J. ASTOR, Esq. ⎫
Jona. STURGES, Esq. ⎬ Committee.
A. A. LOW, Esq. ⎭

"DEAR SIRS:—Herewith I hand you my report of the accounts of U. S Sanitary Commission from its organization to January 1st, 1866.

"I have examined the Books and Vouchers, also securities and Cash Balanc from the Bank books, and find the same correct in every particular.

"The item of Transportation of Supplies includes the cost of Freight on sundries given to the Commission, the estimated value of which was about fifteen millions of dollars, (say $15,000,000.)   Respectfully,

(Signed) JAS. M. HALSEY.

No. 6. *Continued.*

STATEMENT OF MONTHLY RECEIPTS AND BALANCES SHOWING CONTRIBUTIONS FROM THE PACIFIC STATES, SANITARY FAIRS AND ALL OTHER SOURCES.

From October 1, 1862 to May 1, 1865.

Dates.		Receipts.	Balances.		Pacific States.	Sanitary Fairs.	Other Sources.
October,	1862.	213,964 23	Nov. 1st.	186,811 21	206,837 65		7,126 58
November,	"	103,406 18	Dec. 1st.	225,442 40	102,558 88		847 30
December,	"	168,154 14	Jan. 1st.	307,333 81	104,630 52		63,523 63
January,	1863.	49,981 66	Feb. 1st.	321,581 78	47,790 44		2,191 23
February,	"	21,091 50	March 1st.	271,822 17	15,069 15		6,022 33
March,	"	65,676 63	April 1st.	294,475 96	61,194 51		4,482 13
April,	"	2,630 38	May 1st.	267,963 77	1,451 98		1,178 40
May,	"	15,491 60	June 1st.	247,140 28	11,109 95		4,381 68
June,	"	29,172 31	July 1st.	221,669 38	11,800 00		17,372 31
July,	"	28,628 54	Aug. 1st.	158,277 06			28,628 54
August,	"	8,811 28	Sept. 1st.	126,581 27	1,973 75		6,837 53
September,	"	31,019 31	Oct. 1st.	129,130 23	26,344 68		4,674 63
October,	"	27,934 91	Nov. 1st.	126,873 33	24,235 51		3,699 40
November,	"	12,423 34	Dec. 1st.	89,450 80	1,117 60		11,305 74
December,	"	16,908 76	Jan. 1st.	41,725 28	1,060 00		15,848 76
January,	1864.	121,361 38	Feb. 1st.	122,171 52	52,753 00	50,000 00	18,608 38
February,	"	65,690 85	March 1st.	148,278 19	53,650 88		12,039 97
March,	"	351,201 64	April 1st.	419,362 53	3,722 65	316,810 23	30,668 76
April,	"	94,966 02	May 1st.	393,961 54	500 00	80,411 52	14,054 50
May,	"	1,091,606 56	June 1st.	1,222,669 33	58,234 81	1,017,625 00	15,746 75
June,	"	35,003 22	July 1st.	1,005,396 68	25,286 00	800 00	8,917 22
July,	"	210,434 31	Aug. 1st.	886,402 10	165,448 74	4,096 09	40,889 48
August,	"	126,931 99	Sept. 1st.	752,592 50	63,604 28	40,000 00	23,327 71
September,	"	67,634 03	Oct. 1st.	614,946 18	59,518 90	2,530 19	5,584 94
October,	"	27,905 81	Nov. 1st.	370,320 91	17,562 00		10,343 81
November,	"	105,553 50	Dec. 1st.	351,920 79	92,152 66	146 54	13,254 30
December,	"	237,715 41	Jan. 1st.	417,297 68	37 314 91	178,151 68	22,248 82
January,	1865.	48,443 29	Feb. 1st.	329,162 23	41,003 51	88 00	7,351 78
February,	"	1,088,025 57	March 1st.	794,341 19	36,429 65	1,035,998 96	15,596 96
March,	"	39,339 88	April 1st.	602,902 48	31,911 72	3,335 76	4,092 40
April,	"	45,571 42	May 1st.	553,922 88	37,592 26	289 50	7,689 66

No. 7.

LIST OF THE SPECIAL INSPECTORS OF THE GENERAL HOSPITALS OF THE ARMY.

FROM SEPTEMBER 1, 1862, to MAY 1, 1863.

HENRY G. CLARK, M.D., Surgeon of Mass. Gen. Hospital, *Boston,* Inspector-in-Chief.

ABBOTT, SAMUEL L., M.D., Mass. General Hospital.........................*Boston.*
ARMOR, S. G.   "   Prof. Univ. Michigan.....................*Ann Arbor.*
AYER, JAMES,   "   .... *Boston*
BELL, JOHN,   "   .... *Philadelphia.*
BELL, THEOD. S.,   "   Prof. Theor. and Pract. Univ...............*Louisville.*
BEMISS, CHARLES V.,   "   .... *Medford, Mass.*
BOWDITCH, HENRY I.,   "   Physician Mass. Gen'l Hospital..............*Boston.*
BRINSMADE, T. C.   "   .... *Troy, N. Y.*
BUCK, GURDON,   "   Surgeon N. Y. Hospital.................*New York.*
BUCKINGHAM, C. E.,   "   Cons. Physician City of Boston.............*Boston.*
CABOT, SAMUEL, Jr.,   "   Surgeon Mass. Gen'l Hospital.............*Boston.*
COALE, WM. EDW.,   "   .... *Boston.*
COGSWELL, M. F.   "   .... *Albany.*
COMEGYS, C. G.,   "   .... *Cincinnati.*
DRAPER, JOHN W.,   "   Prof. Chemistry, Univ. N. Y..............*New York.*
ELLIS, CALVIN,   "   Pathologist, &c., Mass. Gen'l Hospital......*Boston.*
FLINT, JOSHUA B.,   "   Prof. Clin. Surgery, University...........*Louisville.*
FOSTER, S. CONANT,   "   .... *New York.*
FOWLER, EDMUND,   "   .... *Montgomery, Ala.*
GAY, GEORGE H.,   "   Surgeon Mass. Gen'l Hospital.............*Boston.*
GOULD, AUG. A.,   "   Physician Mass. Gen'l Hospital.............*Boston.*
GUNN, MOSES,   "   Prof. Surgery, Univ., Michigan............*Detroit.*
HODGES, RICH'D M.,   "   Surgeon Mass. Gen'l Hospital.............*Boston.*
HOMANS, JOHN,   "   Ex-President Mass. Medical Society.........*Boston.*
HUN, THOMAS,   "   .... *Albany.*
HUNT, WILLIAM,   "   .... *Philadelphia.*
JACKSON, J. B. S.,   "   Prof. Morbid Anat., Mass. Med. College, &c..*Boston.*
JACOBI, A.,   "   Prof. Infantile Pathology, &c. Med. Col...*New York.*
JARVIS, EDWARD,   "   Member of American Statistical Society.....*Boston.*
JOHNSON, H. A.,   "   Prof. Physiology and Histology,Univ. Lind.*Chicago.*
JUDKINS, DAVID,   "   .... *Cincinnati.*
KRACKOWIZER, E.,   "   .... *New York.*

LEE, CHARLES A.,	M.D.,	Prof. Mat. Med., Med. School of Maine..*Peeksville*.
LEONARD, F. B.,	"	....*Lansingburg*.
LEWIS, WINSLOW,	"	Consulting Surgeon Mass. Gen'l Hospital...*Boston*.
MARCH, ALDEN,	"	Prof. Surgery Medical College.................*Albany*.
MENDENHALL, G.,	"	....*Cincinnati*.
MINOT, FRANCIS,	"	Physician Mass. General Hospital............*Boston*.
MITCHELL, S. WEIR,	"	....*Philadelphia*.
MOREHOUSE, G. R.,	"	....*Philadelphia*.
MORELAND, WM. W.,	"	....*Boston*.
PITCHER, Z.,	"	Emer. Prof. University, Mich.................*Detroit*.
POLLAK, S.,	"	Surgeon Eye and Ear Infirmary............*St. Louis*.
POST, ALFRED C.,	"	Prof. Surg. Univ., N. Y., &c., &c..........*New York*.
REID, DAVID B.,	"	....*St. Paul's*.
ROCHESTER, T. F.,	"	Prof. Clin. Medicine, University.............*Buffalo*.
SAGER, ABRAM,	"	Prof. Obstetrics, Univ., Michigan.......*Ann Arbor*.
SHAW, BENJ. S.,	"	Supt. Mass. Gen'l Hospital....................*Boston*.
SHATTUCK, G. C.,	"	Prof. Theor. and Prac. Med. College, &c....*Boston*.
SLADE, DANIEL D.	"	.... *Boston*.
SMITH, STEPHEN,	"	Prof. Surg. and Surg., Bellevue Hospital.*New York*.
SNOW, EDWIN M.,	"	Health Officer, &c.....................*Providence, R. I.*
TERRY, CHARLES A.,	"	....*Cleveland*.
VANDERPOOL, S. O.	"	Late Surgeon-General, N. Y..................*Albany*.
WALKER, CLEMENT A.,	"	Supt. Lunatic Asylum...........................*Boston*.
WARE, CHARLES E.,	"	Physician Mass. Gen'l Hospital...............*Boston*.
WHITE, JAMES P.,	"	Prof. Obstet., University of....................*Buffalo*.
WILLIAMS, H. W.,	"	.... *Boston*.
WYMAN, MORRILL,	"	....*Cambridge*.

No. 8.

LIST OF MONOGRAPHS,

OR

MILITARY, MEDICAL, AND SURGICAL ESSAYS PREPARED FOR THE UNITED STATES SANITARY COMMISSION.

Military Hygiene and Therapeutics.
By ALFRED POST, M.D., and WM. H. VAN BUREN, M.D.

Control and Prevention of Infectious Diseases.
By ELISHA HARRIS, M.D.

Quinine as a Prophylactic against Malarious Diseases.
By WM. H. VAN BUREN, M.D.

Vaccination in Armies.
By F. G. SMITH, M.D., and ALFRED STILLÉ, M.D.

Rules for Preserving the Health of the Soldier.
By WM. H. VAN BUREN, M.D.

Scurvy.
By WM. A. HAMMOND, M.D.

Miasmatic Fevers.
By JOHN T. METCALF, M.D.

Continued Fevers.
By J. BAXTER UPHAM, M.D.

Yellow Fever.
By JOHN T. METCALF, M.D.

Pneumonia.
By AUSTIN FLINT, M.D.

Dysentery.
By ALFRED STILLÉ, M.D.

Pain and Anæsthetics.
By VALENTINE MOTT, M.D.

Hemorrhage from Wounds, and the Best Means of Arresting it.
By VALENTINE MOTT, M.D.

Treatment of Fractures in Military Surgery.
By JOHN H. PACKARD, M.D.

Amputations.
By STEPHEN SMITH, M.D.

The Excision of Joints for Traumatic Cause.
By R. M. HODGES, M.D.

Venereal Diseases.
By FREEMAN J. BUMSTEAD, M.D.

70

ImTheStory.com

Personalized Classic Books in many genre's

Unique gift for kids, partners, friends, colleagues

Customize:

- Character Names
- Upload your own front/back cover images (optional)
- Inscribe a personal message/dedication on the inside page (optional)

Customize many titles Including
- Alice in Wonderland
- Romeo and Juliet
- The Wizard of Oz
- A Christmas Carol
- Dracula
- Dr. Jekyll & Mr. Hyde
- And more...

CPSIA information can be obtained at www.ICGtesting.com
Printed in the USA
BVOW08s1737280115

385395BV00016B/594/P